MANUFACTURING
A BETTER FUTURE
FOR AMERICA

EDITED BY RICHARD McCORMACK

Clyde Prestowitz and Kate Heidinger, *U.S. Trade Policy*

John Russo and Sherry Lee Linkon, *Deindustrialization*

Ron Hira, *Offshore Outsourcing*

Irene Petrick, *Global Supply Chain*

Peter Navarro, *Foreign Incentives*

James Jacobs, *Workforce Training*

Michael Webber, *Defense Industrial Base*

David Bourne, *Manufacturing Technology*

Alliance for American Manufacturing

The Alliance for American Manufacturing (AAM) is a unique non-partisan, non-profit partnership forged to strengthen manufacturing in the United States. AAM brings together a select group of America's leading manufacturers and the United Steelworkers. Our mission is to promote creative policy solutions on priorities such as international trade, energy security, health care, retirement security, currency manipulation, and other issues of mutual concern.

The Alliance for American Manufacturing
727 15th Street NW
Suite 700
Washington, DC 20005
(202) 393-3430
www.americanmanufacturing.org

Contents

Authors

David Bourne is senior systems scientist at the Robotics Institute at Carnegie Mellon University's Center for Integrated Manufacturing Decision Systems. He is director of the institute's Rapid Manufacturing Laboratory and is adjunct professor at CMU's Graduate School of Industrial Administration. Bourne is also president of Design One Software Inc., a manufacturing process planning software company. Bourne's research focuses on building intelligent systems for automated manufacturing. His expertise is in the areas of rapid, agile and flexible manufacturing, artificial intelligence, intelligent sensing, process planning and control design for manufacturing. Bourne is coauthor of *Manufacturing Intelligence* and he produced, directed and moderated the PBS production entitled "Back to the Cutting Edge," which highlights the problems and solutions in modern manufacturing. He has a B.S. in mathematics from the University of Vermont and M.S. and Ph.D. degrees in computer and information sciences from the University of Pennsylvania.

Kate Heidinger is research assistant at the Economic Strategy Institute where she specializes in economic and social policy, economic development, poverty and inequality. Prior to joining ESI, Heidinger worked at the Illinois State Attorney's Office and for the Minnesota House of Representatives' Public Health Policies Research Department. She is a graduate of Macalester College in St. Paul, Minn.

Ron Hira is assistant professor of public policy at Rochester Institute of Technology. Hira specializes in engineering workforce issues, high-skill immigration and innovation policy. He is also a research associate with the Economic Policy Institute in Washington, D.C. Hira is coauthor of the book *Outsourcing America*, which was a finalist for best business book in the Book Publishers Association's Benjamin Franklin Awards. In 2007, Hira served as a consultant to the U.S. House of Representatives' Committee on Science and Technology, helping organize a series of hearings on the globalization of innovation, research and development. Hira worked as a control systems engineer and program manager with Sensytech. He has worked at the National Institute of Standards and Technology and George Mason University. He has been a consultant to the U.S. Department of Treasury, RAND Corp., the Commission on

Professionals in Science & Technology, the National Research Council, Enterprise Integration Inc., and Deloitte & Touche. Hira completed his postdoctoral fellowship at Columbia University's Center for Science, Policy and Outcomes. He holds a Ph.D. in public policy from George Mason University, an M.S. in electrical engineering from GMU, and a B.S. in electrical engineering from Carnegie Mellon University. He was vice president for career activities of IEEE-USA, the largest engineering professional society in America. Hira was chairman of IEEE-USA's R&D Policy Committee.

James Jacobs is president of the Macomb Community College in Warren, Mich. He became the college's fifth president in March 2009, having previously served as director of Macomb's Workforce Development and Policy Center while also holding the post of associate director for community college operations at the Community College Research Center. He was the president of the National Council for Workforce Development. Currently, he is vice president for partnerships and collaborations for the National Council for Workforce Education, a national postsecondary organization of occupational education and workforce development specialists.

Jacobs is a national expert on workforce development and community colleges with more than two decades of experience working through community colleges to meet the training needs of manufacturers in multiple industries. At Macomb Community College, Jacobs initiated the Machinist Training Institute, a college program that trained entry-level machinists for small- and medium-sized manufacturing firms. He was also responsible for the establishment of community college training programs between the Industrial Technology Institute and Michigan community colleges.

He coordinated the Mid-American Training Group, a coalition of 15 major community colleges in the Midwest that performed education and training activities with auto and steel manufacturers. He has conducted major studies on the impact of new manufacturing technologies on skill requirements at firms, both for the U.S. Department of Education and the U.S. Department of Labor. He is on the National Advisory Board for the Manufacturing Extension Partnership program of the United States Department of Commerce. Jacobs earned a B.A. from Harpur College, Binghamton University, part of the State University of New York system, and a master's degree and Ph.D. in politics from Princeton University.

Sherry Lee Linkon is a professor of English and American studies and co-director of the Center for Working-Class Studies at Youngstown State University. She hosts a weekly radio program on WYSU and serves as book and arts editor for the journal *New Labor Forum*. Her books include *Teaching Working Class*, and two books with John Russo, *Steeltown USA: Work and Memory in Youngstown*, and *New Working-Class Studies*. Linkon was named a Carnegie Scholar in 1999. In 2003, she was named the Ohio Professor of the Year. Linkon holds a Ph.D. in American studies from the University of Minnesota.

Richard McCormack is editor and publisher of *Manufacturing & Technology News*, a publication he created in 1994. He was founding editor of *High Performance Computing and Communication Week* in 1991 and was founding editor of *New Technology Week* in 1987. Prior to that he was a reporter and became editor of *The Energy Daily*. As a Washington, D.C.-based journalist, he has covered science, technology, industry and government for 26 years, specializing in economic competitiveness and globalization. He is author of the book *Lean Machines: Learning from the Leaders of the Next Industrial Revolution*. His work has appeared in hundreds of publications and has been cited and read throughout the world.

Peter Navarro is business professor at the Merage School of Business at the University of California, Irvine. He is the author of the best-selling book *The Coming China Wars*. He wrote the path-breaking management book, *The Well-Timed Strategy*, and the bestselling investment book *If It Rains in Brazil, Buy Starbucks*. Having received his Ph.D. in economics from Harvard, Navarro is an internationally recognized expert in applications of a sophisticated macroeconomic analysis of the business environment and financial markets for investors and corporate executives. He has been featured on *60 Minutes* and his articles have appeared in a wide range of publications, including *Business Week*, the *Los Angeles Times*, *New York Times*, *The Wall Street Journal*, *Harvard Business Review* and the *MIT Sloan Management Review*, among others. He is a regular contributor on CNBC. He publishes a free weekly investment newsletter at www.peternavarro.com. His latest book is *Always a Winner!: Managing for Competitive Advantage in an Up and Down Economy*.

Irene Petrick is professor of practice and director of the Enterprise Informatics and Integration Center at Pennsylvania State University. In addition to teaching, Petrick is actively engaged in research and consulting for U.S. and international companies. Her research emphasizes supply network effectiveness and collaborative innovation. Her most recent work focuses on innovation and global teams with an emphasis on India and the migration of innovation from East to West. Petrick has more than 25 years of experience in project management, product development and R&D in both industrial and academic settings. She received a Ph.D. in engineering science and technology management from the Colleges of Engineering and Business Administration at Penn State. She holds an M.A. in economics and a B.S. in business also from Penn State.

Clyde Prestowitz is founder and president of the Economic Strategy Institute in Washington, D.C. Prior to founding ESI, Prestowitz served as counselor to the Secretary of Commerce in the Reagan administration. There, he led U.S. trade and investment negotiations with Japan, China, Latin America and Europe. Before joining the Commerce Department, he was a businessman in the United States, Europe, Japan and throughout Asia and Latin America. He has served as vice chairman of the President's Committee on Trade and Investment in the Pacific and sits on the Intel Policy Advisory Board and the U.S. Export-Import Bank Advisory Board. He is the author of the best-selling book on U.S.-Japan relations, *Trading Places*, and is coauthor and editor of several other books on international trade and business strategy including *Asia After the Miracle*, *Powernomics*, *Bit by Bit*, *The New North American Trade Order* and *Rogue Nation*. His latest book is *Three Billion New Capitalists: The Great Shift of Wealth and Power to the East*. It covers the economic rise of Asia and the upcoming rebalancing of the world economic order and its impact on the United States. Prestowitz has a B.A. from Swarthmore College, an M.A. in East-West policies and economics from the East-West Center of the University of Hawaii and an M.B.A. from the Wharton Graduate School of Business. He studied at Keio University in Tokyo and is fluent in Japanese, Dutch, German and French.

John Russo is the coordinator of the Labor Studies Program in the Williamson College of Business Administration at Youngstown State University. Russo is also a founder and is the co-director of the Center for Working-Class Studies at Youngstown State University. Since its inception, the center has provided a regional and national forum for scholarly activities. For its work, the center has been the recent recipient of two major Ford Foundation grants. Russo has written widely on labor and social issues and is recognized as a national expert on labor unions and working class issues. His current research interests involve two book-length projects: *Who Will Protect Worker Rights?: Unions and the Use of Codes/CSR, Capital Strategies, Framework Agreements and Strategic Campaigns* and a historical study of the famous GM Lordstown Assembly plant. His most recent publications are two books coauthored with Sherry Lee Linkon, *Steeltown, USA: Work and Memory in Youngstown* and a book entitled *New Working-Class Studies*.

Michael Webber is assistant professor of mechanical engineering at the University of Texas at Austin. He is also associate director of UT-Austin's Center for International Energy and Environmental Policy in the Jackson School of Geosciences, and is a fellow of the Strauss Center for International Security and Law at the LBJ School of Public Affairs. Prior to joining UT-Austin, Webber was an analyst at the RAND Corp., where he studied issues related to national security, innovation, energy and manufacturing. Prior to that, he was senior scientist at Pranalytica, where he worked on inventing sensors for use in homeland security and industrial and environmental monitoring applications. Webber received a Ph.D. in mechanical engineering from Stanford University, an M.S. in mechanical engineering also from Stanford and a B.S. in aerospace engineering from UT-Austin. His written commentary on issues relating to energy policy and international affairs has been published regularly in the *Austin American-Statesman*, *Dallas Morning News*, *San Antonio Express-News*, *Fort Worth Star Telegram* and the *Houston Chronicle*.

Introduction

Something has gone wrong with the U.S. economy.

Executives and workers in American manufacturing industries have been warning for years that it was unwise for the country to have such a cavalier attitude about the loss of U.S. industrial capability. Manufacturers argued that massive trade imbalances were dangerously sapping the wealth of the country. Unfortunately, they were proven to be right.

In the American economy, a once robust system of "traditional" engineering — the invention, design and manufacture of products — has been replaced by financial engineering. Without a robust manufacturing base, without wealth being produced in the United States, Wall Street created money it did not have and Americans spent money they did not have. Americans stopped making products they continued to buy: clothing, computers, consumer electronics, flat-screen TVs, household items and millions of automobiles. None of these were "buggywhip" industries made obsolete with time.

Economists and the financial community have rationalized the loss of U.S. production by saying that Americans are saving money "with low prices." They argue that a manufacturing sector is no longer needed; that the United States can prosper with a "service" economy.

What they didn't say was that the economic system was a giant Ponzi scheme on a scale that dwarfed the one run by Bernie Madoff. Americans have borrowed money from the same countries that make the products they buy.

Manufacturing a Better Future for America is a book written by academic and industry experts that can help set the foundation for a new economic era based on the necessity of creating millions of good-paying jobs in the private sector.

Only with a revitalized manufacturing base can America assure itself a prosperous and hopeful future.

1. The Plight of American Manufacturing

Richard McCormack
Manufacturing & Technology News

"As London is the market of England, to which the best of all things find their way, so Rome was the market of the Mediterranean world; but there was this difference between the two, that in Rome the articles were not paid for. Money, indeed, might be given, but it was money which had not been earned, and which therefore would come to its end at last.

"Rome lived upon its principal till ruin stared it in the face.

"Industry is the only true source of wealth, and there was no industry in Rome.

"By day the Ostia road was crowded with carts and mule-teers, carrying to the great city the silks and spices of the East, the marble of Asia Minor, the timber of the Atlas, the grain of Africa and Egypt; and the carts brought nothing out but loads of dung. That was their return cargo.

"London turns dirt into gold. Rome turned gold into dirt.

"And how, it may be asked, was the money spent? The answer is not difficult to give. Rome kept open house. It gave a dinner party every day; the emperor and his favorites dined upon nightingales and flamingo tongues, on oysters from Britain, and on fishes from the Black Sea; the guards received their rations; and bacon, wine, oil and loaves were served out gratis to the people.

"Sometimes entertainment was given in which a collection of animals as costly as that in Regent's Park was killed for the amusement of the people. Constantine transferred the capital to Constantinople; and now two dinners were given every day. Egypt found the bread for one, and Africa found it for the other. The governors became satraps, the peasantry became serfs, the merchants and land owners were robbed and ruined, the empire stopped payment, the legions of the frontier marched on the metropolis, the dikes were deserted, and then came the deluge."

— *"The Martyrdom of Man," by Winwood Reade, 1872*

Long before the collapse of the U.S. investment banking system in late 2008, once-dominant and important U.S. industries like semiconductors, machine tools, printed circuit boards, consumer electronics, auto parts, appliances, furniture, clothing, telecommunications equipment, home furnishing and many others suffered their own economic collapse, sputtering anemically in a global economic system that continues to be stacked against U.S.-based producers.

Many of the executives in these industries along with their workers have raised alarms, issued reports, testified before Congress and held press conferences about the plight of their U.S. manufacturing assets and the potential for widespread economic adversity. They warned repeatedly that without industry generating good jobs, wealth and the funding needed for research and development, that the United States risked an economic collapse. The federal government ignored them at every turn, and it did so at its peril. With a severely weakened industrial base — one of the only sectors of the economy that creates wealth — the U.S. financial system suffered a historic meltdown.

With the U.S. government plunging deeper into debt by trillions of dollars, it now becomes imperative for the United States to ensure that the industrial sector regains its strength and that the nation becomes an exporting juggernaut. In order to avert a slide into economic depression, the United States will have to stop going deeper into debt to pay off its bad debts. The country must restart its industrial engine and produce products that Americans need to buy and the world demands. If this does not happen, a federal government bankruptcy could dwarf the financial industry collapse of 2008. The solution to the problem no longer entails Americans to "go shopping more."[1]

Free trade economists, retailers, Wall Street mavericks who relentlessly pressured companies to move their production offshore to make a few more pennies per share, shipping companies, foreign producers, foreign countries, newspapers dependent on retailers for their ad revenue, multinational companies and all of their lawyers, lobbyists and think tanks in Washington, and most members of Congress supported by all of these interests have been in control of the economic agenda for the past 30 years. They have successfully argued that it is not necessary for the United States to maintain a strong, vibrant industrial base, because it is cheaper to buy goods from developing countries that have distinct economic advantages.

The mindset among America's economic elite — that the country does not need an industrial base — has put the country and the world economy in a ditch.

The chief economist at the National Institute of Standards and Technology, Greg Tassey, has labeled these people "Apostles of Denial."[2] They are the "single largest barrier" to the adoption of policy changes needed to provide for long-term economic stability and growth, he writes in a courageous book, *The Technology Imperative*. "Apostles of Denial will point to coincident indicators as evidence that the U.S. economy is, in fact, quite healthy," when in fact it is not.

The Apostles of Denial are "befuddling" the debate over the need for the federal government to actively defend the industrial interests of the country, nurture an environment that encourages investment in plant, equipment and workers, and fund the development of the next generation of technologies that create entirely new industries, wealth and jobs. These interests have successfully fought against any type of industrially oriented policy initiatives by citing the old stooges of "corporate welfare," "picking winners and losers" and "protectionism."

Yet they have put the United States government in the position of having to bail out the free market losers: mortgage companies and investment banking firms that issued bad debt, versus making investments in technology and pro-growth economic policies that result in the domestic manufacture of products that create high-paying jobs.

It wasn't long ago that the Soviet Empire collapsed, not because it couldn't produce nuclear warheads, but because it couldn't produce a loaf of bread. Today, the United States can produce a stealth bomber, but it can't produce a pair of shoes. The United States government and its military strategic thinkers have forgotten a basic ancient military principle: Without industry a country cannot maintain an army.

Manufacturers warned of the financial collapse that occurred in 2008 starting in 2002 after more than two years of sustained job losses and outsourcing of important production capabilities. But their voices have been outnumbered by the Apostles of Denial, who downplayed key economic facts such as the growing and massive asymmetrical U.S. trade imbalance in the important advanced technology sector. "To the degree that the decline in competitiveness is recognized, refusal to act is rampant" — blocked by interests that promote the movement of jobs and factories overseas, Tassey writes.

Two years before the crash of the U.S. financial system, President Bush's top economic team held a weekend of meetings in Camp David. Afterwards, Office of Management and Budget Director Rob Portman appeared before the media, saying there were no real problems with the U.S. economy. Instead, the problem was that the Bush administration was doing a poor job of "communicating the strength of the economy and its pro-growth economic policies" to the American public. Edward Lazear, chairman of President Bush's Council of Economic Advisors, told reporters that there were plenty of positive economic indicators that were not being appreciated by the American public. Americans were spending a lot of money and investment in real estate was strong. But neither of the men mentioned anything about ballooning consumer debt, mortgage debt, massive trade deficits and federal budget deficits. "If we look at consumer behavior rather than the response to polls, the behavior is consistent with a strong economy," said Lazear.

Former Commerce Secretary Carlos Gutierrez often claimed that the real economic problem facing the United States was the "popular coverage of media in its use of spreading anxiety for political gain." In November 2005, he told the Woodrow Wilson Center that "if you follow popular coverage, you would think that, as a country, America has peaked, but I would suggest that policy choices should not be dictated by fear." But fear is exactly what "dictated" the policy choices that were made during the great American government takeover of the U.S. financial system in 2008. "Without immediate action by Congress, America could slip into a financial panic and a distressing scenario would unfold," President Bush told the nation in a televised speech on September 24, 2008. "More banks could fail. The stock market would drop more. The value of your home could plummet. Foreclosures would rise dramatically. Millions of Americans could lose their jobs. Fellow citizens, we must not let this happen."

It happened.

The collective denial by America's economic elite of the need for an industrial base has led the country to a precipice. Domestic manufacturers and producers have grown increasingly frustrated with economists who for decades have rationalized manufacturing job losses as being good for the economy. Manufacturers argue that the federal agencies, the administration and Congress — Republicans and Democrats alike — have been negligent in their stewardship of the economy. The United States is not generating enough wealth to pay its mounting and massive debts. Cheap imports made in unsafe, low-wage factories overseas are not improving the fortunes of America's least fortunate, much less its middle class. The U.S. trade deficit in 2008 stood at $700 billion — or about $2,000 for every American. That is $8,000 for a family of four, far greater than the $2,000 in savings importers and retailers claim a family saves from the lower costs of imported products. And the $8,000 per year debt does not include the interest that must be paid over the long run.

Without a healthy industrial base, workers are no longer making a livable wage needed to maintain payments on assets like homes and they cannot afford basic necessities like energy, food, education and health care. In 2008, only 6.5 million people out of a population of 305 million Americans purchased a new vehicle from a U.S. automobile company. Total auto sales in 2008 dropped by 18 percent to 13.2 million units. In 2009, sales are projected to be 9 million, down from 17 million in 2006.

Even more alarming is the fact that without an industrial base, an increase in consumer demand, which historically pulled the country out of recession, will not put Americans back to work. Any additional consumer spending will only help workers making products overseas. This represents a fundamental break from previous recessions and has led many in the manufacturing sector to fear the growing likelihood of a sustained downturn.

Without an industrial base, the country ran out of money to fix an infrastructure that was rapidly deteriorating, with bridges and levies falling to the mighty Mississippi River. Without an industrial base, major American cities like Detroit and New Orleans lay in ruins. Without an industrial base, California's economy has gone bust. Literally thousands of other American communities have lost their local factories and are decrepit. In 2008, the largest public works project on the entire East Coast of the United States was a bridge over the Potomac River between Virginia and Maryland on Interstate 95. Even the federal Highway Trust Fund is insolvent.

Alexander Hamilton, America's first treasury secretary, understood that the United States would become a world power by focusing government resources on creating a robust and dynamic manufacturing enterprise. His "Plan for American Manufactures," written in 1791, argued for the development of an industrial economy over an agrarian economy favored by Thomas Jefferson, and it remains valid to this day.

Without an industrial base, it was only a matter of time before the contagion in manufacturing hit the financial, construction, housing and retail sectors. At some point, the contagion will reach the country's largest employers: state, local and federal governments.

Those who work in the U.S. manufacturing sector — those who own companies that produce goods — know that without Americans making products, there will not be enough wealth to support the retirement and staggering health costs of the largest generation in the history of the nation.

The United States is broke. It is broke because it has stopped producing what it consumes. The Apostles of Denial would have Americans believing otherwise, arguing that the colossal trade deficit — which in 2006 rose above 6 percent of U.S. GDP — is not an indicator of U.S. economic weakness, but of its economic strength.[3]

The financial collapse that was shocking the country in the latter part of 2008 was long ago predicted by manufacturers. Ernest Preeg, senior fellow at the Manufacturers Alliance/MAPI in Washington, D.C., wrote in 2006 that the trade imbalance was "like a gallows" hanging over the American economy and that "sooner rather than later the markets will trigger the inevitable adjustment, with what will almost certainly be more grim financial reaping."

Millions of people who are no longer working in industries that are disappearing from America's shores have already faced the "gallows." The furniture industry lost at least 60 percent of its production capacity in the United States from 2000 to 2008 with the closure of 270 major factories during that period. Imports of wood furniture accounted for almost 70 percent of the U.S. market in 2008, up from 38 percent in 2000.[4]

The printed circuit board industry shrunk from $11 billion in 2000 to $4 billion in 2007, a period during which the industry was growing globally.[5] U.S. printed circuit board manufacturers accounted for less than 8 percent of global production in 2007, down from 26 percent in 2000, yet printed circuit boards are used in tens of thousands of different products. Without a printed circuit board industry, a country cannot expect to have an industrial foundation for high-tech innovation.

The U.S. steel industry produced 91.5 million tons of steel in 2008, down from the 97.4 million tons it produced in 1999. By comparison, China's steel industry produced 500 million tons in 2008, more than five times the amount of U.S. producers and up from the 124 million tons it produce in 1999.[6]

What about the promise of the solar industry? There was only one American company (First Solar) among the top 10 worldwide in photovoltaic cell production in 2007. Among the top 20 global photovoltaic manufacturers, there were only two American-owned companies, and they account for less than 10 percent of global output.[7]

The wind energy industry? There is only one U.S. company (General Electric) ranked among the 10 largest in the world. GE's worldwide market share in 2007 was 16 percent.[8]

In the total global production of automobiles, General Motors, Chrysler and Ford accounted for 18.6 million of the 72 million autos produced worldwide in 2007, and their market share continues to decline.

The U.S. machine tool industry — the backbone of an industrial economy — produced $3.6 billion in equipment in 2007, less than 5 percent of global output of $71 billion.[9] Worse, U.S. machine tool consumption in 2007 was $6 billion, or only 40 percent of the consumption in China. Since 1998, U.S. machine tool consumption has fallen by 30 percent. Chinese consumption has increased by 700 percent, from $2.2 billion to $15.4 billion in 2007.

Dozens of other industries are nearly gone from U.S. shores. U.S. producers of luggage account for 1 percent of the American market, but virtually every American owns luggage. "There is no commercially viable domestic production of travel goods," according to the International Trade Commission.[10]

U.S.-based production of high-performance outerwear used by skiers, hikers, mountain climbers, bikers, policemen and military personnel accounts for less than 1.6 percent of all of the outerwear sold to the 306 million Americans. "There is no commercially viable domestic production of performance outerwear jackets or pants," according to another ITC study.[11]

Do you need ceramic tile for a new kitchen floor? There is one major American manufacturer that remains: Summitville Tile of Summitville, Ohio. Company president David Johnson says the industry has been "virtually wiped out" by international competitors and adds: "The industry is just about finished."[12]

Worldwide in 2008, there were 80 major chemical plants costing more than $1 billion either on the drawing boards or being constructed. None of them were being built in the United States.[13]

In 2007, only 2 percent of all new semiconductor fabrication plants (fabs) under construction in the world were located in the United States. Thirty percent of new fabs were being built in China, 25 percent in Taiwan and 22 percent in South Korea, according to Semiconductor Equipment Materials International (SEMI). In 2007, the United States produced 17 percent of the world output of semiconductors, a number that has been declining since 1995, when the U.S. accounted for 25 percent of global output.[14]

There were 1.2 billion cell phones sold throughout the world in 2008, none of which were manufactured in the United States.[15] American companies held only 9.5 percent of the global market for cell phones. Motorola held 8.4 percent of the global market in 2008, but that figure sunk to only 6 percent in the first quarter of 2009 (a 46 percent decline from the same quarter in 2008). Apple held 1.1 percent of the global market for cell phones in 2008.

The same story is true for high-definition televisions, toys, sporting goods, apparel and shoes — industries that have shed hundreds of thousands of American workers. Even the hard candy industry has moved most of its production outside the United States.[16]

The United States lost world dominance in high tech exports in 2004, when China exported $180-billion worth of information and communications technology products compared to U.S. exports of $149 billion, according to the Organization for Economic Cooperation and Development (OECD). Total U.S. imports of goods in 2007 was $1.8 trillion, or 18 percent of U.S. GDP. Total U.S. industrial production was $1.3 trillion, or 12 percent of U.S. GDP. The United States imports far more goods than it produces. Said Brian Halla, CEO of National Semiconductor: "There is a gold rush taking place in China. It's a major opportunity, and it's a major threat if we blow it. And we are blowing it — big time. The great American dream appears to be moving to Shanghai."[17]

The United States still makes products, but mostly in areas subject to strict government regulations and that receive heavy federal R&D investment like pharmaceuticals, medical equipment and military weaponry; or they are consumables, like diapers and processed foods; or they are large pieces of capital equipment. The United States even imports 83 percent of the fish it consumes, most of which is farm-raised in China. In 2007, the United States ran a trade deficit in seafood of $9.1 billion.[18]

America's domestic manufacturers know that the financial crisis gripping Wall Street in 2008 was the result of the loss of U.S. industry as much as it was the meltdown of the residential real estate market. For those who were once engaged in the production of thousands of consumer goods like blenders, coffee makers, air conditioners, golf clubs, laptops and desktops the notion that the financial crisis was caused by bad mortgages is laughable. In a few short years, the United States stopped producing what it was consuming, sending trillions of its hard-earned dollars to foreign countries. In its quest for greater corporate profits, Wall Street helped fuel the growth of outsourcing, which in turn led to its own demise. All of America's money went to oil producers and to countries that targeted America's most robust industrial sectors and whose economies were built upon exports.

An economic crisis was gripping American manufacturers long before it took hold of Wall Street. Need proof? Drive around Michigan, Ohio, upstate New York, Indiana or through portions of the Carolinas. Manufacturing is the engine of economic growth, not financial wizardry, a fact repeated every day by manufacturing company executives desperate to get their story told.

Dan DiMicco, president and CEO of Nucor, one of the most respected companies in the United States, says that the current system of globalization is "unsustainable," and that the United States is "giving its future away. The damage that we are doing to our future cannot be reversed by the present thrust of opening markets." DiMicco cannot believe what he is seeing among U.S. policymakers: an unwillingness to accept the fact that the U.S. economy is on life support, a blind trust in "free trade" principles and a government that refuses to listen to its own major employers.

"Time is not on our side and by allowing the continuing erosion of this country's manufacturing sector they are selling our future," DiMicco says. America's infatuation with "every-day low prices is costing the country more than $2 billion a day. It is time to stop this madness. We kowtow to special interests. We play geopolitics. We are a slave to a discredited free-trade theory in the face of reality. We lack the will to change. In short, we have lost our minds."[19]

We really haven't, counters the United States-China Business Council, a trade group of U.S. companies that have opened shop in China. Trade with China is boosting American wealth, the U.S.-China Business Council argues repeatedly in Washington, D.C. In 2006, the council predicted the loss of an additional 500,000 U.S. manufacturing jobs by 2010 due to additional production in China. No problem, the council said, because this "structural shift" will result in the gain of 500,000 service-sector jobs. "While this structural shift displaces some workers in manufacturing sectors and thus represents a real cost to workers in those sectors, the economy as a whole will benefit from permanent output and price effects of increased trade with China," according to the pro-China business group. "The overall impact should be a continuing and increasing positive boost to U.S. output, productivity, employment and real wages."[20]

9

The "Apostles of Denial" are in some unexpected places. The Council on Competitiveness issued a report in November 2006 arguing that the United States was the world's most innovative nation and that there was little reason to believe otherwise. Harvard economist Michael Porter led the council's charge by stating: "We have to stop this notion of believing that manufacturing is essential." Such thinking is a "real problem," he said upon the release of the council's "Innovation Index." Porter then argued that the trade deficit is not an accurate reflection of the competitiveness of the American economy. An $800-billion trade deficit "is not that big by international standards," he said. "It's not epic." When addressing growing wage inequality in the United States, Porter rationalized it by saying: "What you misunderstand is that it has gone up pretty much everywhere. This is not a unique American phenomena."

A few years prior to the Council on Competitiveness's "Innovation Index," its president, Deborah Wince-Smith, said that the United States did not have a competitiveness problem, even though many of America's most important industrial sectors were shedding hundreds of thousands of jobs every month. Competitiveness cannot be measured by "economic growth, but by productivity," she said. "Productivity is the real long-term measure of competitiveness and we are doing very well." When asked, "Is there as much alarm today as there was when [Hewlett Packard CEO] John Young started the council in 1986?" Wince-Smith replied: "Absolutely not."

As the manufacturing sector was spiraling down from 2001 through 2008, there was no bailout for U.S. manufacturers — as there had been for the financiers who killed America's manufacturing sector — nor were manufacturers asking for one. U.S. domestic producers were not advocating "protectionism." They were not interested in class warfare. They want the big multinational companies to be headquartered in the United States, produce in the United States and export from the United States. What domestic manufacturers want is for the United States government to craft economic policies that favor investment in the United States. They want the United States to abandon the economic policies that favor geopolitical global interests that have no regard for the economic health of the United States and its millions of taxpayers and retirees.

"We need a modern-day Paul Revere," says Brian O'Shaughnessy, chairman of Revere Copper Products, the oldest industrial company in the United States. "When Paul Revere tried to rouse the countryside with his wake-up call, what did the people do?" O'Shaughnessy asks.

"They certainly didn't go back to sleep. We all need to wake up and understand the forces of foreign economic mercantilism that are waging an economic war against us."

It is a war that many American manufacturing executives and their workers say the United States has lost. One only needed to watch the opening ceremony at the 2008 Summer Olympic Games in Beijing to know the destination of hundreds of billions of U.S. dollars. By late 2008, the U.S. trade deficit with China was running at close to $1 billion per day, amounting to more than $90 per month (or more than $1,100 a year) for every American.

The flood of cheap goods from China is not even helping the U.S. retail industry. Long before the September 2008 financial market crash, hundreds of retail stores announced closures, according to William Engdahl, contributing editor at the Centre for Research on Globalization.[21] By mid-2008, Ann Taylor announced plans to close 177 stores; Eddie Bauer closed at least 27 stores; Mattress Discounters announced it was bankrupt; women's retailer Cache closed up to 23 stores; Talbots closed all 78 of its kids' and men's stores and another 22 stores; Gap closed 85 stores; Foot Locker closed 140 stores; Levitz closed all 76 of it stores and went out of business; Disney announced plans to close up to 98 stores. Home Depot closed 15 stores; CompUSA closed for good; Macy's closed nine stores. Pep Boys closed 33 stores; Sprint shut down 125 retail locations; Ethan Allen Interiors said it planned to close up to 300 stores; and Bombay Company closed all 384 of its U.S. stores. "For anyone familiar with American shopping malls and retailing, this represents a staggering part of the daily economic life of the nation," noted Engdahl.

That's a big list, but not nearly as big as the list of approximately 40,000 U.S. manufacturing plants that have closed during the seven years ending in 2008. From 2001 to 2007, the U.S. economy was sustained by the housing and finance sector bubbles, not on real wealth. But starting in 2008, a new bubble began to inflate: federal spending, which in 2008 — in one year alone — increased by 25 percent or by $731 billion to $3.6 trillion.[22] Federal spending is accelerating even faster with President Obama's push for a massive economic stimulus.

But without a robust revival of the U.S. manufacturing sector, it is virtually guaranteed that the country will not sustain an economic recovery. Combined with lower tax revenues, the Congressional Budget Office is projecting a 2010 federal deficit of $1.825 trillion in 2009. That after the federal budget deficit almost tripled in 2008 to $459 billion, up from "only" $161 billion in 2007. The evidence is now irrefutable: the United States cannot sustain itself with a finance- or service-based economy. Manufacturing is the only way of assuring a better future for America.

The United States is not losing old, inefficient industries that produce obsolete products for which there is no more demand, such as "buggy-whips" — many economists' favorite line. There is still demand for televisions, consumer electronics, computers, furniture, socks and bicycles. The industries that are leaving the United States are still producing products that are in demand. Perhaps worse, however, is that as industries leave the United States, the research they support goes with them, as well as the R&D knowledge that is funded by the federal government.

The solar industry is a good example. U.S. taxpayers have poured hundreds of millions of dollars into the development of photovoltaic power systems, yet there is only one U.S. company among the world's leading producers. The same is true with nanotechnology. Without much of an industry left, the benefits of the $1-billion-a-year federal National Nanotechnology Initiative will not benefit American workers and taxpayers because the real money will be made by companies and countries that manufacture products containing nanotechnologies. Any revitalization of the U.S. manufacturing base through nanotechnology will be limited to "low-volume, pilot-scale manufacturing," according to Matthew Nordan, president of Lux Research Inc.[23] Low-volume manufacturing will not generate the millions of jobs needed in the United States.

The companies that survived the 1990s adopted best practices like lean, Six Sigma, ISO 9000 and the Baldrige Quality Award and Shingo Prize criteria. They re-engineered, right-sized and used total quality management to become agile enterprises. If they did not adopt efficient production techniques, then they didn't survive past the year 2001. These companies did not lose their competitiveness. They could compete with each other. But they could not compete against other countries — foreign governments that not only targeted specific industries but also specific companies. There is no way for U.S. industry to compete with offshore producers that are owned and subsidized by foreign governments.

The American steel industry produces one ton of steel using 15 man-hours. A comparable ton of steel in China is produced with 110 man-hours, and Chinese companies produce three times the amount of carbon emissions per ton of steel. The U.S. steel industry has not lost its competitiveness. It is an industry that has to compete against government-funded companies whose production is subsidized, and that are allowed to pollute and operate unsafe factories.

The least of American companies' worries is competing with low-wage labor. The labor cost in a coil of steel produced in the United States is less than the freight cost of a steel coil imported from China, according to Nucor CEO Dan DiMicco. Foreign producers receive subsidies, tax abatements, free buildings, free energy. They do not pay taxes. They don't have to pay Social Security, workman's comp, disability or health care. They don't have to match a 401(k) contribution. They are able to avoid more than 100 years of government regulations put on American businesses. OSHA does not exist in most developing nations. They use electricity that would never be allowed to be generated in the United States due to lack of pollution controls. The U.S. Environmental Protection Agency employs 17,000 workers. China's State Environmental Protection Administration employs only 300.[24]

The day after the Virginia Tech massacre occurred on April 16, 2007, a news item ran in *Asia Times* with the headline: "Molten Steel Kills 32 Chinese Workers." The Virginia Tech massacre also took the lives of 32 individuals. Yet had the molten steel accident occurred in the United States, Americans would have been horrified by the working conditions at a U.S. steel factory.

On April 17, at the Qinghe Special Steel Corp. in Liaoning province in China, a 30-ton ladle of steel sheared off from the blast furnace, spilling 2,732 degree F. white-hot liquid metal onto the factory floor. The molten steel spread into a nearby room where workers were gathering for a shift change, engulfing them. "They are going to have to identify the bodies through DNA testing because the victims were burnt beyond recognition," according to a report in the *Asia Times*. In an account of the accident in *Asia News*, it noted that the previous day a plant producing "triple super phosphate" in Xiaozhaiba, Guizhou, "leaked a huge amount of sulfur dioxide." The colorless gas drifted into the nearby village, "but no one warned the population" and 300 people had to be hospitalized. "Also on Monday, 47 coal miners were trapped in three mines. Two other men were trapped when the illegal mine in which they were working collapsed in the city of Jixi, Heilongjiang. In the first three months of 2007, 661 miners died in industrial accidents, according to official sources."

The United States government has been trying to revive the economy since 2001, using two rounds of trillion-dollar tax cuts, reduced interest rates and tax rebate checks sent directly to millions of taxpayers.

But without incentives for the manufacturing sector, those economic revival efforts have failed.

In 2004, Congress allowed U.S. companies to repatriate the profits they earned overseas. It was called the American Jobs Creation Act of 2004. As the Bureau of Labor Statistics describes, during the period in which the major provisions of the bill were implemented, the Jobs Act did not create a single new production job in the United States. From 2006 through 2007, manufacturers shed 433,000 U.S. jobs, according to the BLS.

Jobs should have been proliferating in the U.S. economy, due to a surge of government and consumer spending underwritten by the housing bubble. From 2001 until 2007, the United States government and households added $10.5 trillion to their debt burden, notes Charles McMillion, chief economist at MBG Information Services. Over that same period, U.S. GDP increased by a mere $4 trillion.

Total combined debt of households ($14.4 trillion) and the federal government ($9.2 trillion) was 168 percent of GDP at the end of 2007. "Yet, this record-shattering explosion of debt stimulus created the weakest seven-year job growth (4.4 percent) and one of the weakest periods of real GDP growth (18.1 percent) since the Depression," according to McMillion. There were less than 6 million new jobs created between 2001 and 2007 — at $1.8 million of debt per job.

Also over that period, the government put a massive stimulus into the economy through federal spending on the wars in Iraq and Afghanistan ($900 billion between 2002 and 2008). Those conflicts are keeping a substantial portion of the basic manufacturing sector in the United States afloat. A desert war is not easy on equipment. Sand reduces the life span of military equipment, power generators, diesel engines and mechanical drives by a factor of 10. Equipment operating in a desert must be rebuilt by companies in the United States. When the Iraq war ends "you're going to see a repeat of the 2001 downturn all over again," says David Frengel of Penn United Technology in Cabot, Penn. The wars in Iraq and Afghanistan are keeping hundreds of industrial shops busy rebuilding and replacing equipment and producing new ordinance, weapons, shells and ammo. Companies making armor are busier than ever.

Despite the surge of war spending, the U.S. manufacturing sector continues to shed hundreds of thousands of jobs and when the wars end "and we go back to maintaining a peace-time Army, you're going to see another one-million to 1.5-million manufacturing jobs disappear on top of the five million jobs lost since 2001, because we're not really producing other items," Frengel says.

In early 2008, the U.S. government decided that a direct stimulus of $152 billion would help revive the economy. The windfall may have helped the makers of flat panel televisions and iPhones in China or Middle Eastern petroleum producers selling oil for $147 a barrel, but the stimulus did not revive American manufacturing or create jobs. During the three-month peak of the disbursement of stimulus rebate checks between May and July 2008, the economy shed 162,000 jobs, including 52,000 in the retail sector, 94,000 in manufacturing and 99,000 in construction.

Most American business owners know that the 2008 stimulus rebate checks did not work. Seventy-eight percent of small-business owners said the economic stimulus checks were "useless," according to a July 2008 poll of 400 small company owners taken by Suffolk University for American Management Services. Seventy-two percent of these small business owners said the government was "bailing out Wall Street and big business," while 86 percent said the U.S. government is doing either "nothing" or "little" to help other businesses.

The federal executive branch along with the U.S. Congress has ignored the collapse of American manufacturing. During the early years of the Bush administration, Grant Aldonas, head of the Commerce Department's International Trade Administration, traveled the country listening to manufacturers and their ideas of how federal policies should be amended to make the United States an attractive place to invest and make products. At every stop around the country, manufacturing company owners blistered Aldonas, pleading with him and his subordinates to defend them against foreign governments targeting their operations. Manufacturers were neither acting as "protectionist," nor were they left-wing liberals. As conservative business owners, they were asking that the federal government uphold the trade laws that were already on the books.

The Aldonas manufacturing road show came to Washington, D.C., in late 2002. But Aldonas didn't show up for the event. Undersecretary of Commerce Sam Bodman, the department's second-highest ranking official, was scheduled to spend the day with manufacturing leaders at the meeting titled "Made in America 2020: The Future Face of Manufacturing." But Bodman didn't arrive until late in the afternoon, while Bush's lower-level political appointees kept making excuses, and speaking for how Bodman considered manufacturing to be one of the government's top priorities. When Bodman finally arrived, he listened to manufacturers discuss how the federal government needed to change its approach to industry, lest more manufacturing disappear from American soil. Tim Timken, chairman of the Timken Co. of Canton, Ohio, told Bodman that "government at all levels affects what happens in business in total and manufacturing in particular. Basically, the issue for government is to decide what it is doing that hurts U.S. manufacturing and what it could do to help U.S. manufacturing."

At the very end of the event late in the afternoon, it was time for Bodman to hold forth.

He told the manufacturers that the government wasn't going to do anything.

"A lot of what I hear you all asking — we need a leader, we need somebody to take a position and do things — that runs counter to the way the town works and you need to know that," Bodman told the executives, according to a transcript of the meeting. "There was a comment concerning a vision for manufacturing within the government. I will tell you it is very hard for this government to have a vision on anything. We are totally stove-piped and we live within these compartments. This is not by way of a complaint. This is not by way of an excuse. It is by way of a fact."

Bodman told the manufacturers that the Bush administration was "hopeful and optimistic" that there would be a turnaround in the manufacturing sector due to the huge infusion of money into the economy from the Bush tax cuts. "One way or another, before we get anything profound done at our end, we are going to see what happens and to the extent that the economy recovers, employment recovers," Bodman told the invited group of executives at the event that excluded the press. "It will be quite interesting to see what happens in the manufacturing sector and get some measure of that."

The final "measure" was that the manufacturing sector never recovered. The tax cuts did not turn the manufacturing employment situation around. They did not stop companies from shifting large portions of their production offshore. They did not stop Wall Street and the American economy from suffering a massive collapse in late 2008.

Bodman also had some disparaging words to say about the Commerce Department as a place that would represent the interest of those involved in American commerce. "The measure of one's manhood or womanhood in this town is one's budget size," he said. "We [employ] a lot of people here but we have a $5-billion budget. That sounds like a lot. It's peanuts in this town. I will tell you the inherent authority of this department within government is modest. That's not a complaint. That's not an excuse. It is a fact."

Believing that his comments were confined to the room and would never be exposed or broadcast, Bodman further confided, according to the government transcript provided through a Freedom of Information Act request: "Everybody in this town tries and works very hard at being nice to everybody else at all times almost at all cost and the reason for it is nobody knows who they will end up working for next month. That's just a fact. It's not a complaint. It's not an excuse. It's a fact."

Bodman must have been working "very hard at being nice" to somebody, because it wasn't long after his statement that he left the "peanut" agency called the Commerce Department for a deputy secretary post in the far more important Department of Treasury, during a time in which the agency did not provide any oversight of the rampageous financial sector. It was another year before his "being nice to everybody else" helped him secure an even nicer job as Secretary of Energy, a position that made him a member of the president's Cabinet. During his tenure at the Energy Department, starting in February 2005 when the price of oil was $41 per barrel, Bodman served during history's largest run-up of oil prices, further undermining the U.S. economy.

Unfortunately for many domestic manufacturers, the rules of modern capitalism are created by governments. As Bruce Scott of Harvard Business School explains: "Legislative markets create the framework within which firms operate and underpin economic markets that can be tilted to favor capital versus labor or the reverse; producers versus consumers, or lenders versus creditors." The idea that capitalism has evolved through a "benign set of circumstances where parties voluntarily come together to achieve mutually beneficial transactions may be an adequate description of commerce at a roadside fruit and vegetable stand or a flea market, but not for much of the transactional activity of a modern economy."[25]

Countries, not private companies, determine the basis for competitive advantage, notes Gregory Tassey of NIST. "Because this principle is not yet accepted in the United States, studying, understanding and formulating strategies and policies to address long-term needs of a large, technology-based economy are being shortchanged."

If anyone knows this best, it's the people who work in the economic development offices of state governments. In the global battle to attract industry and jobs, the states are at a big disadvantage against nations that are investing substantial resources to attract and nourish strategic industries that create thousands of good jobs. The traditional model of economic development has states competing with each other for companies to locate in their jurisdictions. That model has changed. Now it is states versus foreign governments, and the American states are losing. The U.S. federal government has opted out of the international competition to attract industry and jobs, leaving that task up to the states, which do not have the resources to compete with foreign governments.

A key facet of economic development is the creation of science and technology research parks that foster the development of industrial clusters of competing and complimentary firms. China and other countries in Asia are rapidly increasing their investment in these parks. "New entrants into the research park market such as China are developing research parks on such a huge scale that they are changing the market dramatically," says Rick Weddle, president and CEO of the Research Triangle Foundation of North Carolina, which operates the world-famous Research Triangle Park.[26]

"China has taken our model to the nth degree and has expanded dramatically on it, leapfrogging" the United States with massive investments in high-tech research and production zones, Weddle says. "Research Triangle Park and U.S. research parks have much to learn from the Chinese and what it will take to compete in the future: scale, nimbleness, speed-to-market and flexibility to attract talent and recruit expatriates to return."

Weddle notes that the university research system in the United States may no longer win the battle for technological superiority and future prosperity. "It would be advantageous if we had more tools in our toolbox to be able to compete," Weddle says. "All of us at the local and regional and state level need all the help we can get from the federal government."

As described in Chapter 3, China's economic development officials employ a variety of incentives to entice industry to locate their R&D and production in their country. Data compiled by IBM's Global Investment Location Database show that these incentives are working, with China and India far surpassing every country in the world for inward investment for major R&D projects and factories.[27]

According to Weddle, who runs the revered 2,500-acre Research Triangle Park for its 157 tenants, the United States has not even yet joined the debate over national economic development policies aimed at creating jobs and industries. Policymakers at the national level can't get beyond the vapid "industrial policy" debate. But at the regional and local level, there is a hearty embrace of industrial policy. Research Triangle Park was created in the 1950s based on the state of North Carolina's decision to pick chemistry as an industrial technology worth pursuing for long-term economic growth. In 1984, it added biotechnology, and continued making strategic investments in local universities.

Huge economic benefits have been generated from those investments in "picking winners and losers" — in this case winners, and Research Triangle Park has the fifth-largest concentration of life science economic activity in the United States.

"What we've done in 50 years at Research Triangle Park, China is doing in 15 years and is replicating that now and even shortening these time horizons to five to seven to eight years in some of their smaller" economic development parks, says Weddle. "We toured a research park in Suzhou that is a joint venture between the Chinese government and Singapore. We wouldn't even think about that. They partner up in ways that we wouldn't even think about or we might have issues or get all caught up in our knickers worrying about how it works out."

As a result of these investments, China surpassed the United States as the world's largest export nation in 2004.[28] Only five years earlier, the United States exported double the amount China did. "This dramatic reversal together with the increasingly high-tech orientation of Chinese exports poses a serious challenge to U.S. export competitiveness and long-standing leadership in technology innovation," says Ernest Preeg of the Manufacturers Alliance/MAPI.[29]

The Voice of Manufacturing

Among the most important economic voices in American society are those belonging to thousands of domestic manufacturing company owners and managers. These people employ millions of workers. They pay them livable wages and provide benefits. These manufacturing companies support local communities throughout the country — particularly in rural areas — and sell their products, parts and components to large industrial companies throughout the country.

They are struggling to stay alive, not because their processes are old, or because their products are no longer in demand. These companies are struggling mainly because their large customers have left the United States for cheap and protected markets overseas. The owners and managers of these once-vibrant companies are voiceless in the mainstream press, which has been usurped by the power of the retailers and multinational companies that provide the bulk of advertising dollars for almost all of America's newspapers and television outlets. These domestic manufacturing business owners and executives are among the most anxious people on the planet.

U.S. demand for manufactured goods has increased by 400 percent since 1980, says Revere Copper CEO Brian O'Shaughnessy.[30] But U.S. production of those goods increased by 40 percent. "Without foreign government trade cheating, U.S. production would have been far greater. Revere Copper's exports and domestic sales would have grown very large indeed," he says. Like thousands of other U.S. manufacturers, Revere lost 30 percent of its U.S. customers from 2000 to 2007, due to large companies shutting down or moving their production offshore. Former customers that have closed their U.S. production include Carrier, Oneida, General Electric, Smith Corona, Ethan Allen and Chicago Pneumatic.

America's oldest industry is also on the verge of extinction. The glassware industry is down to one remaining large American producer of glassware: Libbey Glass Inc. of Toledo, Ohio. The reason: "foreign companies are supported by their governments," says Libbey CEO John Meier.

During his 37-year career with Libbey, Meier has seen every single major U.S. competitor either go out of business, end up in Chapter 11 or go up for sale.[31] Corning Consumer Products, called World Kitchen, has gone through Chapter 11; Oneida is in Chapter 11; Anchor Hocking is in Chapter 11; Wheaton Glass has gone through Chapter 7 "shut down and gone," says Meier. Federal Glass is in Chapter 7 "shut down and gone." And Indiana Glass is up for sale. "Talk about an industry facing a challenge," he says.

The problem facing the industry is simple: unfair trade — "not the ideology of free trade but the reality of trade," Meier says. "The reality of trade today is far different than that described by the theorists. Comparative advantage may exist for basic commodities, but in today's world where transportation speeds products to marketplaces all over the globe, where capital flows freely to the place where it can gain the highest return, where technology can be applied in virtually any environment, competition is not governed by theories in textbooks, but by profits and national interests."

Libbey is determined to compete. The company invested $183 million in capital upgrades between 2002 and 2006, or 7.7 percent of total sales. But those investments may be for naught, given that the United States government is allowing foreign governments "to get away with subsidizing their producers and not enforcing the laws while turning to the remaining producers in the United States and saying: 'We need to make it easier for more imports to flood our markets,' " Meier says. "Effectively, many of us would tell you we have an eight-lane highway coming into Peoria, only to face a dirt road back to Rio, Jakarta or Istanbul."

This group of American businessmen believes the U.S. government has stopped representing the interests of American-owned and American-based companies and the workers they employ. Dozens of manufacturing company owners have marched to Washington, D.C., over the past seven years, angrily telling their story of toil and tragedy that has come as a result of the U.S. federal government's drive against the manufacturers. They have been derided as being "protectionists" and "whiners" and not winners — as people who represent industries that are no longer needed in America. More than anything else, they have been ignored.

"The U.S. government's policy is creating millions of jobs all right, but it is creating them in the People's Republic of China and Vietnam at the expense of hardworking Americans here at home," says James Copland, chairman of Copland Industries/Copland Fabrics of Burlington, N.C.[32] Copland believes the U.S. government's policy toward manufacturing has led to an economic crisis "unprecedented since the Great Depression." Deeply flawed U.S. trade policy toward domestic manufacturing "is the single-most important root cause of the illness."

In repeating a theme common among U.S. manufacturing company CEOs, Copland says the U.S. government bears responsibility for destroying the American dream. "Our constitutional preamble says 'a government of the people, by the people and for the people.' We have forgotten about the words 'for the people.' " Copland is no lefty heretic or revolutionary, but a corporate CEO who employs hundreds of American workers.

The unwillingness of the U.S. government to defend manufacturers from unfair currency manipulation, from foreign value-added tax rebates, from companies that are manufacturing products that would be illegally produced in the United States and selling them for below the cost of raw materials has put millions of American lives into economic turmoil. "Their jobs are being moved overseas and they can't get other jobs," Copland says. "Don't think there are high-tech jobs available for those folks, because there aren't. They are being shipped to China and India, too. People are angry now and when they connect the dots — and they are going to connect them — they are going to know where to focus their anger."

Manufacturing company owners and employers have to deal with the harrowing loss of people's livelihoods. When Moosehead Furniture closed its factory in Maine in 2007, the largest privately owned furniture company in New England had to lay off 126 employees. The company made cane chairs, but it could not compete against imports from China. Closing the company's plant "was a blow to the heart," according to a report in the *Bangor Daily News* in a story that has been repeated thousands of times throughout the country.

The 60-year-old company was producing chairs with labor that cost $11 per hour, versus its Chinese competitors who were paying workers 20 cents per hour. Moosehead Furniture's monthly health care bill was half the price of the cost of its wood, and amounted to an extra payroll per month. A fully-loaded container of chairs from China carried $7,000 worth of product. Shipping costs from China total about $4,000 per container. A similar container filled with Moosehead chairs held $55,000 worth of product produced in the United States. There was no way for the company to compete.

"I grew up in this community," says company President John Wentworth. "The people I laid off are the people I went to school with and their parents. We had two plants in this town of 600 people. You have to look at those people in the face. They've been here for 20, 30 years. Rural America is slipping away and it won't come back."

It is a common refrain: that employees have nothing do with the circumstance leading to a company's demise. "We regret the hardship this will cause the affected employees and we appreciate the dedicated and energetic service these employees have shown the company," said Furniture Brands CEO Mickey Holliman when the company announced in 2007 that it would close plants in Missouri and North Carolina and eliminate 450 jobs. When Radford Co. closed its plant that manufactured doors and windows in Oshkosh, Wis., company President Michael Walsh said it was "the worst day of my life. We have the greatest employees and so many of them have been here for so long that it made the announcement even more difficult." Radford Co. had been in business since 1871. Walsh thought 1982 was the worst year he would ever have to experience, but 2008 proved to be far worse. "I will take '82 over this anytime," he said.

O'Shaughnessy of Revere Copper says the game is stacked against American producers. The evidence is abundantly clear and it is stunning: American companies are paying for the health care costs of foreign rivals. Foreign countries use value added taxes (VAT) as their primary source of government revenue. These taxes are rebated to exporters in overseas countries and are a "legal form of tariffs approved by the World Trade Organization," according to O'Shaughnessy. Such taxes "discriminate in favor of domestic production of goods and services" compared to the U.S. system, which "taxes domestic jobs out of existence through payroll and other taxes on any entity that provides a job."

Value-added taxes are in place in 139 countries. There is only one industrialized country in the world that does not have a value-added tax: the United States. Foreign governments rebate the tax to companies when they export products, or to tourists when they travel back to their home country. Value-added taxes are being used as an enticement to U.S. manufacturers to shift production offshore. "One province in India boasts of a VAT that is over 50 percent in promoting itself as a prime location," writes O'Shaughnessy in a PowerPoint presentation on his company's Web site.[33]

When a product made in the United States is exported, the foreign country collects a value-added tax on that product. That money is then used to fund that country's nationalized health care system. U.S. companies are subsidizing foreign health care systems. With socialized health care systems, foreign companies don't have to pay the health care costs of their workers, unlike American companies. "We pay for their health care costs!" O'Shaughnessy says.

Germany raised its VAT rate to 19 percent effective January 1, 2007, which means that when a product worth $100 is shipped from the United States to Germany, it sells for $119 in Germany, whereas a $100 product shipped from Germany to the United States is sold for $81. It is virtually impossible for American companies to overcome such a differential.

Implementing a border-adjustable tax (a VAT) in the United States would increase skilled jobs, wages, the balance of trade, the standard of living and national security, O'Shaughnessy argues. But there is opposition to its adoption from foreign producers, importers, multinational corporations and their trade associations, foreign governments, U.S. politicians who are supported by those organizations and "naked free traders," O'Shaughnessy writes.

A New Debate Over Global Corporate Interests

The unprecedented power and changing motivations of multinational corporations is worrying a lot of people, including Ralph Gomory, president-officio of the Alfred P. Sloan Foundation and the 15-year director of research at IBM Corp. Gomory states bluntly: "What is good for America's global corporations is no longer necessarily good for the

American economy. Globalization leaves most Americans as losers not winners. We must change this situation."[34]

Gomory, a brilliant mathematician and soft-spoken sage, describes the current economic situation in a grand historical context: A fundamental societal change has taken place. Most economists have not yet recognized it. Over the past century and a half, Americans moved from being virtually self-sufficient (by working on family farms and in craft shops) to working for large companies that mass-produce the nation's food supply and complex products (such as automobiles) that cannot be made by small groups or individuals. Americans became dependent on large-scale organizations for their livelihoods.

"The fundamental social role of corporations is to enable people to participate in the production of the goods and services that are consumed in the modern world; the corporation enables them to earn a share of the value produced for themselves and their family," says Gomory. But over the past two decades, there has been a shift in corporate motivation away from social responsibility "towards emphasizing profits above everything else, which has had a deleterious effect on millions of people that is now being accelerated through globalization," he says. "What is good for America's global corporations is no longer necessarily good for the American economy." The economic system of individuals depending on the corporation for their livelihoods is collapsing, and the implications are profound.

America's largest global corporations are no longer responsible to employees, the communities in which they operate and to the nation. They abandoned these attributes in the 1980s when their focus on profits meant that "all other values are being sacrificed," Gomory says. "People in our government still are treating companies as if they represent the country, and they do not. The country and the companies are going off in two different directions. That is something that most people feel intuitively."

Transferring production offshore is not free trade, Gomory notes. "But if you want to do anything about the transfer of capabilities, you're labeled as interfering with free trade. Americans have been told that the shift in production is inevitable and that it will only impact those workers involved in non-competitive industries. We are assured that it is bound to make us richer in the long run after the pain of change has been absorbed. There is no basis for these claims. The people of this country should not count on some long-range outcome that must inevitably make up for the present pain. That day may never come."

Even Lawrence Summers, President Obama's chief economic adviser and an architect of the current international trading system as President Bill Clinton's Treasury Secretary, seems to agree with this growing sentiment. "The growth in the global economy encourages the development of stateless elites whose allegiance is to global economic success and their own prosperity rather than the interests of the nation where they are headquartered," he wrote in 2008.[35]

The true "protectionists," domestic manufacturers argue, are those companies that have set up operations in the "protectionist" havens of developing countries and then lobby policymakers in the United States to "protect" their investments made in those countries. The real "protectionists" are the those who claim to be "free traders."

The multinational companies and their Washington lobbying representatives say they are misunderstood, that the American populace is listening to the wrong people with regard to the impacts of globalization. These companies have failed to articulate "a win-win situation" associated with the current trade regime, said John Engler, president of the National Association of Manufacturers at a May 2008 conference in Chicago sponsored by then Commerce Secretary Carlos Gutierrez.[36] This has led to the "conundrum we find ourselves in — that the data is good but consensus behind trade has evaporated. How do we get the story told?" Engler asked Caterpillar CEO James Owens, who replied: "That's a mystifying thing to me. Trade has been demagogued in the political arena to a very disconcerting extent of late." Owens then labeled those who have been active in the "fair" or "smart" trade camp as being "protectionist," and said that if the United States becomes protectionist "it will be one of the most tragic political mistakes in our history, at least since the 1930s."

Both sides of the trade divide blame the politicians. For managers and workers who are on the losing end of the trade game, the politicians — both Democrats and Republicans — are in the pockets of the wealthy interests. They will do anything for campaign contributions. Those campaign contributions come from the big companies that, until 2008, were more profitable than ever in history.

The multinational companies see it in reverse. Politicians know how important free trade is to the economic prosperity of the country, but they "are essentially playing for votes," says Caterpillar CEO Owens. "As a business leader who spends a fair bit of time talking to people in Washington and trying to encourage [politicians] to support global competitiveness and international engagement, I can tell you a lot of congressmen and senators say, 'I understand but the people back home, the people voting for me, are vehemently opposed to trade. It's a hard sell back home.' "

Proponents of the current "free trade" policy say that the average American family is benefiting from cheap goods produced overseas. "It's more choice in consumer variety. It's good jobs at good wages," says Matthew Slaughter, a member of President Bush's Council on Economic Advisors from 2005 to 2007 and now a professor of international economics at Dartmouth University's Tuck School of Business. "For families supported by those companies, they have higher paychecks."

The U.S. Government Sides With Foreign Firms

The U.S. government trade operation presents its own challenges for American manufacturers and their workers. When Vaughn-Bassett Furniture Co. joined with 31 U.S. bedroom furniture manufacturers and five labor unions to take legal action against Chinese furniture producers and exporters, the group hired the Washington law firm of King & Spalding. The law firm filed a case with the International Trade Commission (ITC) on its clients' behalf arguing that China was unfairly dumping furniture into the U.S. market. China's share of U.S. imports of bedroom furniture had increased from 26 percent in 2001 to more than 50 percent in 2003. The U.S. industry was forced to close dozens of factories and lay off more than 35,000 craftsmen, according to Vaughn-Basset Furniture CEO John Bassett.[37]

Little did the domestic furniture manufacturing companies expect what happened next. American importers of Chinese furniture along with Chinese producers hired 21 different law firms to oppose their petition. "There was one on our side and 21 on their side," Bassett says.

The U.S. furniture manufacturers created a "Committee for Legal Trade." Its first task was to determine how they could protect themselves from the Chinese imports. It did not know anything about U.S. antidumping laws. "I've read that the government spent millions of dollars to promote the new $20 bill," says Bassett. "I know how to use a $20 bill, but I wish the government had done more to make me and other manufacturers aware of our rights under our trade laws. We did not learn about this potential remedy until it was almost too late."

The Commerce Department had too few people to investigate the thousands of Chinese producers and hundreds of Chinese exporters of bedroom furniture, according to Bassett. The Commerce Department only selected seven Chinese companies to prosecute. "It did not even select the companies that we thought were the worst dumpers." The ITC ruled in favor of the American petitioners in January 2005, but by then it was too late for most American producers and tens of thousands of workers.

One of the most egregious examples of how the United States government refused to represent the interests of U.S. manufacturers and workers is the case of McWane Inc. of Birmingham, Ala. McWane is the country's largest provider of waterworks fittings with 7,000 employees. Thousands of residential subdivisions have installed McWane water piping systems. The company brought a case before the ITC under a special provision that was created to deal with Chinese dumping of imports into the United States — the so-called "Section 421" special China Safeguard Investigation provision from the Trade Act of 1974, which was included in the WTO charter. McWane spent $1.5 million presenting its case to the ITC, which concurred with a 5-0 ruling in favor of McWane, determining that China was dumping products into the U.S. market. As is required by the legislation creating the "421" provision, the decision had to be approved by President Bush.

President Bush sided with the Chinese. "I find that the import relief would have an adverse impact on the United States economy clearly greater than the benefits of such action," Bush wrote in his memorandum denying relief, to the amazement of the U.S. trade enforcement legal community and McWane. Bush vetoed every affirmative 421 case that reached his desk on similar grounds. Knowing they would be vetoed by the president even if approved by the ITC, companies stopped filing 421 petitions.

So what did McWane do as a result of Bush's decision to side with China? "We have been forced to build facilities in China and import that product back into the United States because of governmental inaction here and the lack of any kind of protection for the investments we have made here to comply with U.S. environmental and safety laws and regulations," says David Green, executive vice president of McWane. "There has been an absolute surge of imports from China and it's gotten worse."

After the Bush decision, the company started reducing production at its ductile iron water works fittings plants in Alabama, Texas and Ohio. But it's not clear that consumers benefited from Bush's decision, as he said they would.

"You have one of our products per house in a subdivision — one fitting — and the consumer pays the same price because the only thing that happens is the contractor puts the savings in his back pocket," says Green. In fact, foreign imports might cost consumers money, given problems with quality, regulatory compliance and products being made overseas without there being any environmental controls.

A week after Bush decided against the ITC's recommendation in the McWane case, Green and his boss left for a tour of foundries in India and China. They found the conditions to be "atrocious," Green says. "It's common knowledge but nobody wants to pay attention to it: environmentally, it's putrid."

In India, foundry workers don't wear shoes, socks, headgear, ear plugs or eye protection. They wear nothing other than flimsy boxer shorts, squatting on the floor next to burning-hot furnaces.

The next stop was China. "There are no U.S. environmental regulations in China," Green says. If there are any regulations, there is no enforcement whatsoever. "If you took a U.S.-regulated, compliant facility and put it in China, there is no way you could be competitive with all the other Chinese manufacturers," he says. If McWane has to invest hundreds of millions dollars in technology to meet EPA guidelines for new foundries in the United States "then there ought to be some support" for having to do so, says Green, because there is not a single foundry in China that has to comply.

There are thousands of foundries in China that use 40-foot-tall cupolas to light industrial-grade coke, none of which have pollution collection devices at the top of the stack. Black smoke belches out, creating a plume that stretches across the Pacific Ocean.

The Chinese aren't as efficient, either. At McWane's U.S. plants, it takes 15 man-hours-per-ton to produce ductile fittings, whereas in China, it takes 150-man-hours-per-ton. Moreover, there are no standards regulating arsenic in the coking coal used to make pipes and components that carry fresh water, nor do the Chinese have certifiable radiation testing systems. The Chinese have also been found to be using asbestos to coat pipes and fittings in an attempt to minimize leakage.

Like thousands of other U.S. producers, Green says the U.S. government's unwillingness to enforce trade laws has resulted in a potentially catastrophic loss of U.S. industrial capability and wealth. He points to BLS data that show that only 400,000 new jobs between 1998 and 2007 were created for men that paid more than the median wage.

"There is such a thing as cutting your arm," says Green. "You can cut into the skin. You can cut into the fat. You can cut into the muscle and then you can cut through the bone. At this time, we're cutting into the bone. It's not that we're inefficient. That has nothing to do with it. It's because you're competing against a currency that is 40 percent undervalued, an unlimited amount of labor and lax regulatory control."

In the ductile fittings 421 case, President Bush's decision was "totally at odds with the facts," notes Paul Rosenthal, an attorney who is with the firm of Collier Shannon & Scott which represents the industry. "There has to be the political will to enforce these laws and I can say that there has been a bipartisan reluctance to enforce them. The biggest failure is the failure of the [U.S. government] to use our 421 statute to protect American manufacturing industries. That is not a failure of the law, but a failure of the political will to apply the law and stand up to the Chinese."

Other companies had a similar experience with the 421 provision. M&B Metal Products Co. took a case against China to the ITC claiming that China was dumping metal dry-cleaning hangers onto the U.S. market. The ITC voted 5-0 in favor of the U.S. industry and its unanimous injury determination was sent to the USTR. The Bush administration "caved in to unremitting pressure from the Chinese government," says M&B Metal Products Co. President Milton Magnus. The Chinese representative from China's Ministry of Commerce, Liu Danyang, repeatedly threatened that the imposition of a remedy in the hanger case would damage U.S.- China relations. "Danyang insisted that if President Bush granted relief to an injured U.S. industry it would result in 'unavoidable negative effects on the broader bilateral relationship,'" Magnus says. "I underscore that the decision in this case will not and cannot be viewed in isolation. This message was heard loud and clear because the president announced that no relief would be provided. The administration let China off the hook. It allowed them to continue operating with complete disregard for the normal functioning of open markets and contrary to U.S. law. The administration sent a clear message that the president's speeches about the importance of American business and jobs creation were nothing more than political rhetoric and that Chinese — not American — interests are uppermost to those who are advising the president on the provisions of the law."

Ward Manufacturing, a company that makes malleable and non-malleable iron pipe fittings was involved in two ITC cases involving China. It wasn't pretty. The Commerce Department "just plain allowed Chinese founders to lie to them about their factory input quantities," says company vice president Thomas Gleason. The largest foundry in China, JMC, told the Commerce Department that it did not keep track of the actual weight of the charges fed into the cupola each day. "I have been in the foundry business for over 30 years and I know of no foundry in the world that can make this claim with a straight face," says Gleason. "It is, simply put, a bold-faced lie. Even the ancient Egyptians who first started foundry production kept track of the inputs."

WTO Rulings

Beyond the 421 issue, the United States has not fared well in the World Trade Organization, either. The United States has lost the vast majority of trade cases brought against it by other nations, even though the United States is running the largest trade deficits in history. Through 2007, the WTO ruled against the United States in 40 of 47 cases. The United States lost an additional 30 of 33 WTO cases brought against it in the trade remedies area. That number is "astounding," says Robert Lighthizer, a partner in charge of the international trade group at the law firm of Skadden Arps Slate Meagher & Flom.[38] The United States "has suffered disproportionately from the problems with the WTO dispute settlement system, having been named as defendant in far more cases than any other WTO members."

Some of the cases lost by the United States required major changes of U.S. laws and administrative rules. "Rogue WTO panel and Appellate Body decisions have consistently exceeded their mandate by inventing new legal obligations that were never agreed to by the United States," says Lighthizer. "As a result of this judicial activism, our trading partners have been able to achieve through litigation what they could never achieve through negotiation. The consequent loss of sovereignty for the United States in its ability to enact and enforce laws for the benefit of the American people has been staggering. The WTO has increasingly seen fit to sit in judgment of sovereign acts running the gamut from U.S. tax policy to environmental measures to public morals."

In the trade remedies area, in which the U.S. government proposes duties provided to industries materially hurt by unfairly dumped imports, the U.S. has lost almost every case brought against it. The United States has been shut down on the Commerce Department's use of "zeroing" to calculate a company's dumping margin. The Bush administration called that WTO ruling "devoid of legal merit." The WTO has ruled against the United States in its use of the "Byrd Amendment" to distribute duties directly to the American companies impacted by dumping.

"I am not alone in this stark assessment of the WTO dispute settlement system," says Lighthizer, a former USTR deputy with the rank of ambassador during the Reagan administration. "Even ardent supporters of the WTO and legal experts hostile to the trade remedy laws have expressed amazement at the level to which WTO panels and the Appellate Body are creating new WTO obligations out of whole cloth. The threat that this poses to the trade remedy laws and, in fact, the entire world trading system, is immeasurable."

The U.S. federal government has not helped U.S. industry much in its fight against illegal trade, either. The Import Administration at the Commerce Department has seen its budget cut by appropriators in Congress. The agency, which pursues trade remedies for adversely impacted U.S. industries, had a budget in 2007 of $60 million, down from $68 million in 2004, a decline of 12 percent. The number of employees at the Import Administration fell from 388 in 2005 to 319 in 2007, a decline of 18 percent, according to Lighthizer. "In my view, cutting funding for trade enforcement is exactly the wrong policy at a time when we are facing increasing challenges from unfair trade."

China's Entry Into the WTO

Domestic manufacturers marvel at how the U.S. government and backers of China's entry into the WTO sold the country on the idea. The conclusion: Americans were duped.

The United States public has been told repeatedly that unfettered free trade with China would lead to a new era of Chinese political freedom. But this has not occurred, and the argument has led to the creation of policies based upon a "wrong paradigm," says James Mann of the Johns Hopkins School of Advanced International Studies.[39]

American policy toward China requires public support, and the way to maintain that public support "is to claim that this will serve the purpose of changing China's political system," Mann says. "Since 1989, virtually every change in U.S. policy toward China has been justified to the American public on the basis that it would help to open up China's political system."

The argument was used by President Clinton to convince Congress to pass trade liberalization with China and by President George W. Bush to support China's entry into the WTO. Congressional leaders used it to justify their vote in favor of those initiatives.

Liberalization of trade has not changed the way China's Communist Party rules the country. There are no political opposition parties in China. Censorship of the press and the Internet endure. There are no free elections. "The argument that the Chinese system is changing seeks to divert attention to smaller realities and away from larger ones," says Mann. "This paradigm of a China that is destined for political change has deep roots in American policy over the past 35 years."

When pushing the permanent normal trade relations (PNTR) legislation, President Clinton said that economic changes in China will "increase the spirit of liberty over time. I just think it's inevitable, just as inevitably the Berlin Wall fell."

In the 2000 congressional debate over PNTR with China, dozens of members of Congress argued that China would reform its human rights and trade practices.

The legislation (HR-4444) passed the House by a vote of 237 to 197 and the Senate by 83 to 15, and set the stage for China's entry into the World Trade Organization on December 11, 2001. President Clinton signed the legislation on October 10, 2000, claiming that "this is a great day for the United States." At the signing ceremony, he said that PNTR with China "is a good economic deal for America. It will increase our exports and, over the long run, will strengthen our economic position in the world."

He further stated that open markets would accelerate the information revolution in China, "giving more people more access to more sources of knowledge, which will strengthen those in China who fight for decent labor standards, a cleaner environment, human rights and the rule of law." Ten years later, there are 50,000 Chinese censors scrubbing the Internet every day for open debate or information flow. The Chinese government did not even allow the broadcast of President Barack Obama's inauguration speech.

Dozens of lawmakers echoed Clinton's claims of American economic growth and Chinese political reform.

Rep. David Dreier (R-Calif.) said the China PNTR vote would be a "win-win for America's workers, America's first-class businesses and the very important goal of promoting American values. They are opening their markets to American exporters, which means good jobs across the United States. It is good for national security and it is good for American values. This bill is key to spreading the Internet across China. That is all great."

Rep. Thomas Ewing (D-Ill.) said a "vote for PNTR is a vote for development of the Internet."

Rep. Deborah Pryce (R-Ohio) said a vote for PNTR "will assist the pro-reform elements in Chinese society. We must take the battle of freedom versus tyranny to the Chinese people."

Sen. Patty Murray (D-Wash.) said that if Congress did not grant PNTR "it will make it harder for us to promote change there and damage America's workers and industries."

Sen. Frank Lautenberg (D-N.J.) said that through China's WTO accession "we will be able to hold China accountable for its trade commitments through the WTO's transparent, rules-based dispute settlement mechanisms."

Sen. Joe Biden (D-Del.), now the vice president, voted in favor of PNTR, claiming that China would no longer "support Communist insurgents in half a dozen African and East Asian countries."

Sen. John McCain (R-Ariz.) said PNTR would "ensure that the conflict between economic growth and political repression is resolved in the direction of liberalization."

Sen. Herbert Kohl (D-Wis.) claimed that members of the WTO "will not let themselves be taken advantage of in trade matters."

Kenneth Lieberthal, special adviser to President Clinton and senior director for Asia affairs at the National Security Council, said at the time of China's entry into the World Trade Organization: "Let's be clear as to why a [U.S.] trade deficit might decrease in the short term. China exports far more to the U.S. than it imports [from] the U.S....It will not grow as much as it would have grown without this agreement and, over time, clearly it will shrink with this agreement."[40]

Since the passage of PNTR, the U.S. trade deficit with China has increased from $83 billion in 2000 to $266 billion in 2008.

The chief U.S. trade negotiator who paved the way for China's entry into the World Trade Organization now says the deal has not worked as originally intended. Robert Cassidy, former assistant United States Trade Representative for China, was the lead negotiator for the U.S.- China Market Access Agreement in 1999. Cassidy assumed that China's entry into the WTO would subject it to international laws governing trade. There were predictions that trade with China would increase U.S. exports and American jobs; that the trade deficit with China would improve; and that the industry-specific "421" safeguard mechanism would be administered by the next president. Those safeguards were intended to hold China's government accountable for unfair advantages and subsidies it provided Chinese producers.

But Cassidy never predicted that China would manipulate its currency in a manner that has radically distorted trade between the two na tions, nor did he envision that the Bush administration would not enforce the "421" China safeguard. In the meantime, China's unfair trade practices and U.S. multinational corporations' support of them have inflicted heavy damage on the U.S. economy. The trade deficit with China has doubled every five years. "I have looked at the statistics and I just question: What is happening and why did this occur?" Cassidy asks. "This is a huge problem. I don't think anybody expected what happened to happen."

American Workers Are Expendable

Traditional economic theorists argue that the current system of trade is good for American workers. "Economic theory tells us that when trade liberalization occurs, the gains of the gainers exceed the losses of the losers and the country as a whole ends up better off," says Robert Thompson, a visiting scholar at the Federal Reserve Bank of Chicago and a professor of economics at the University of Illinois at Champaign-Urbana. Like many other economists, Thompson says Americans are under a false assumption that millions of jobs are moving offshore. Some jobs have shifted, but not millions. "The problem is not nearly as large as it appears in the media," Thompson says.[41] By providing compensation to the "relatively few" people who have lost their jobs to production shifts offshore, the United States will "still end up with a net gain."

Free trade proponents often promote the federal Trade Adjustment Assistance (TAA) program that was created to help manufacturing workers displaced by foreign imports. But the Labor Department has routinely denied benefits to workers who have been laid off, and the entire TAA system "is fundamentally broken," according to a 2007 ruling by the United States Court of International Trade. The court found that "there is something fundamentally wrong with the administration of the nation's trade adjustment assistance programs." The Labor Department does not represent the interests of labor, but of employers, according to the judgment in the case, "Former Employees of BMC Software v. the United States Secretary of Labor."[42]

"Trade adjustment assistance programs historically have been — and today continue to be — touted as the *quid pro quo* for U.S. national policies of free trade," according to the first sentence in the ruling in the case. But the Labor Department's "reprehensible" mishandling of the program "has put that *quid pro quo* in jeopardy."

In dozens of cases, the Department of Labor was cited as being negligent in all aspects of its administration of the TAA program. The way in which the agency is ignoring information provided to it from workers "as well as its pattern of turning a blind eye to obvious inconsistencies and discrepancies in the record before it — is beginning to verge on contempt for administrative and judicial process and does a grave disservice to the hardworking men and women of this country," writes Judge Delissa Ridgway in her 85-page ruling.

Attorney Frank Morgan of White & Case LLP has represented workers in TAA cases before the U.S. Court of International Trade. He says that from 2002 to 2005 approximately 45 TAA cases were litigated and in all but four the Department of Labor was required to certify workers that it had previously denied benefits. "That is shocking and it shows that Labor is not fulfilling the responsibilities that Congress entrusted to it."[43]

The Department of Labor rarely considered information associated with job losses provided to it from newly unemployed workers, instead relying almost exclusively on claims from employers that workers' jobs were not shifted overseas or that the workers themselves were not producing "products" that would enable them to be covered by the statute.

Ridgway's ruling is a condemnation of a program that free trade advocates have used to justify the past 20 years of trade policies promoted by corporations, think tanks, presidents and Congress. "The very purpose of the TAA program is to provide retraining and other employment assistance to U.S. workers whose jobs have been sacrificed — in the national interest and for the greater good of the country — on the altar of free trade," she writes. "As one scholar [professor Robert LaLonde of the University of Chicago] recently put it, 'Trade is a little bit like war....Fighting World War II [was] a good thing. It [was] good for the world, and...good for the United States. But for the people who got killed, it was clearly bad. That's what trade is like.' "

The analogy "is an apt one," according to the ruling against the Labor Department. "Much as Congress has charged the U.S. Department of Veterans Affairs with caring for those who have risked life and limb for our freedom, so too Congress has entrusted the Labor Department the responsibility for providing training and other re-employment assistance to those who have paid for our place in the global economy with their jobs."

In reviewing the case brought against the government by former workers of BMC Software of Houston, Judge Ridgway cited dozens of cases — like the one she was hearing — in which the Department of Labor denied benefits after having done little investigation of the circumstances surrounding the layoffs. "This case is troubling enough viewed in isolation," she writes on page 55 of her decision. "But it is even more disturbing when it is viewed in the context of other TAA cases appealed to the court in recent years."

Others note that the lack of effective programs aimed at ameliorating the economic burdens of trade on workers, companies and communities could easily derail the free trade movement. The costs of globalization are being exacerbated by the "lack of a national comprehensive strategy to deal with economic disruptions," according to Howard Rosen, a visiting fellow at the Peterson Institute for International Economics and executive director of the Trade Adjustment Assistance Coalition. "In place of a national strategy, there is a collection of ad hoc, out-of-date and inadequate programs that provide too little assistance too late to those in need." The result has been a "significant" political backlash that may result in lower economic growth.[44]

Millions of Americans have been impacted by the loss of jobs due to trade. The TAA program alone has provided assistance to 25 million workers since it was first established in 1962, yet the program helps only a minority of workers displaced by foreign production. "Only 10 percent of the estimated group of potentially eligible workers receive assistance," notes Rosen.

China and the U.S. Treasury Department

The Treasury Department for years has favored Chinese economic interests over those of American manufacturers. In the report it prepares for Congress every six months on exchange rates, it has refused to designate China as purposefully manipulating its currency.[45] To help buttress its finding, Treasury used trade data from China, and not from the U.S. Department of Commerce.

One of the key attributes of a country that manipulates its currency is its current account surplus. A country that has undervalued its currency so its products are cheaper in world markets increases its own trade surpluses.

The China Currency Coalition in Washington conducted an analysis of the currency report and was "absolutely bewildered" by Treasury's exclusive use of Chinese government trade data, calling the practice "demonstrably wrong." By looking at trade figures from 40 of China's largest trading partners, the China Currency Coalition found that China's global trade surplus was $376 billion in 2005. China's government reported a surplus of $149 billion. The U.S. Treasury Department used the $149-billion figure.

"The frustrating thing about this is that both Treasury and the International Monetary Fund appear to making very important policy decisions based upon the wrong numbers," said China Currency Coalition director David Hartquist. "We would never stand for that within the United States government."

Even Fed Chairman Ben Bernanke noted in the written version of a prepared speech he gave in China in late 2006 that China's manipulation of its currency was an "effective subsidy," an expression he used twice in his written speech but failed to mention in the spoken version to the Chinese leadership.[46] He said: "Reducing the implicit subsidy to exports could increase long-term financial stability as well." He meant the financial stability of China, not of the United States, which shortly thereafter suffered a financial system collapse. Bernanke also said that "substantial experience has shown that modern economies, including those in early stages of development, are too complex to be managed effectively on a centralized basis." Again, that was before the U.S. government took control of Freddie Mac and Fannie Mae and "centralized" virtually the entire U.S. investment banking sector.

Also at that event, Bernanke felt compelled to criticize China's investment strategy: "China's economic growth owes much to the extraordinary share of GDP that is devoted to investment in new capital, such as factories, equipment and office buildings, which is partly financed by a very large amount of business saving. However, the rapid pace of investment growth raises concerns about whether new capital is being deployed in the most productive ways" — unlike in the United States, where capital was being deployed in a housing bubble and in what later would become known as "toxic paper."

Does the United States Still Lead in Technology?

China's meteoric rise has sparked little reaction from U.S. economic policymakers. But evidence of China's growing economic prowess based upon the success of a clearly articulated industrial policy is becoming overwhelming. The Georgia Institute of Technology's biannual "High-Tech Indicators" study found that China improved its technological standing by 9 points over the period of 2005 to 2007, thrusting that nation above the United States in technological capability for the first time since Georgia Tech started keeping score two decades ago.[47]

In Georgia Tech's scale of one to 100, China's technological standing rose to 82.8 in 2007, compared to the United States at 76.1. The United States peaked at 95.4 in 1999. China has increased from 22.5 in 1996 to 82.8 in 2007. "The message speaks out pretty loudly," says Alan Porter, co-director of Georgia Tech's Technology Policy and Assessment Center, which produces the benchmark. "I think the prospects are pretty scary."

The survey indicates that the United States does not even hold the number two position in global technology capability. "If the increasingly integrated European Union were considered one entity instead of 27 separate countries, it would surpass the United States," says the Georgia Tech indicator report. South Korea, Singapore, Taiwan, Brazil, India and Chile are all increasing their technological capabilities, while the U.S. position degrades.

The surge of China past the United States as the global technology powerhouse should have been a "Sputnik" moment, says Georgia Tech's Porter. But federal officials and politicians were silent.

When the survey was produced in early 2008, the economy was headed into a downturn and both political parties were "jumping all over each other for the instant fix — the tax rebate," Porter observed. " 'Problem is all solved. Congratulations!' Wow. Long term, there are things that are not amenable to that solution."

Dozens of countries outside of the United States are pumping resources into leading-edge research and development. They are providing companies with rich incentives to locate there. "So what is our big advantage?" Porter asks. "What scares me is China is getting better at marrying research to their low-cost production processes. When you put those together with our buzzword of innovation, China is big, they're tough and cheap. Again, where is our edge?"

In a study released in the summer of 2008, KPMG predicted that China will overtake the United States as the world's largest recipient of corporate investment within five years "and should become the most influential country in IT and telecom, industrial products and mining." It based this finding on a survey of corporate investment executives working for 311 of the largest multinational companies and in 10 private equity and sovereign wealth funds. The United States was in last place among countries in the measurement of change in percentage of corporate plans for investment between 2008 and 2014, with a 4.5-percent drop, as compared to China leading the world with a 7 percent gain.[48]

A Look at American Imports and Exports

Exports are an important indicator of America's industrial decline. In its annual analysis of trade, the Port Import Export Reporting Service (PIERS), published by the *Journal of Commerce*, noted in May 2008 that more than two-thirds of the top U.S. exporting companies via ocean container were selling junk — scrap paper and scrap metal — and bulk agricultural and chemical commodities.[49] Of the top 100 U.S. exporters via container, about 20 exported scrap paper; 20 exported bulk food or feedstock, 15 shipped bulk chemicals and seven exported scrap metals. These are products more typically exported by Third World nations.

The largest U.S. exporter via ocean container was not even an American company, but Chinese: American Chung Nam, which exported 211,300 containers of waste paper to its Chinese sister company, Nine Dragons Paper Industries.

Weyerhaeuser was America's second largest exporting company via ocean container in 2007, shipping 165,800 containers filled with paper. Most all of this paper is remanufactured into cardboard to pack valuable manufactured goods for shipment back to the United States. Like the millions of products headed to American shores, it is cheaper to manufacture cardboard in China than it is in the United States.

Only one of the top 20 U.S. exporters via ocean container — Procter & Gamble — could be considered a U.S.-based product manufacturer.

Few of America's top corporate giants were shipping manufactured goods via containers to overseas markets. General Electric was ranked only in the 23rd position in 2007 among American exporters, shipping 41,200 containers. But GE imported three times that amount — 112,900 containers — and was ranked in 11th place among importers.

Caterpillar, which is one of America's most successful international companies, was in 27th place among exporters (shipping 37,300 containers), behind 12 wastepaper exporters, according to PIERS. General Motors ranked in 68th place, selling little overseas from its U.S. factories; and Deere & Co. ranked in 77th place. The only other U.S. manufacturing company on the container-exporting list was Whirlpool, which was ranked 83rd.

Imports into the United States via container ships are another matter. The largest importer in 2007 was Wal-Mart. The world's largest company (with sales in 2007 of $374.5 billion), imported 720,000 containers of products from overseas markets, followed by Target (435,000 containers), Home Depot (365,300 containers) and Sears, which owns K-Mart (at 248,600 containers). The combined imports of these four retail companies (1,768,900 containers) equaled the exports of containers for the top 21 U.S. exporting companies, again, the majority of which sold paper.

At least 35 of the top 100 importers of containers into the United States in 2007 were retail companies selling manufactured consumer goods. The majority of other importers were high-tech manufacturing companies selling their goods to U.S. distributors and retailers. These well-known companies include, LG Group (130,000 containers), Philips (127,200 containers), Canon (66,400 containers), Nike (62,700 containers), Toyota (58,800 containers), Samsung (50,800 containers), Sony (46,900 containers), Panasonic (43,300 containers), Michelin (38,700 containers), Hewlett Packard (29,700 containers), Sharp (24,100 containers), Toshiba (17,900 containers), and many more brand name companies.

Dell Computer, which does not show up on the PIERS data, says that it imported $18 billion in parts and components from China in 2007. The company, with revenues of $61 billion in 2007, expected its Chinese import bill to reach $23 billion in 2008. Those purchases will add more than $50 billion to China's gross domestic product "and support more than two million jobs," said the company in a press release issued in Hong Kong in March 2008.

Cisco Systems, another important United States technology company, manufactures the majority of its products overseas. In 2004, Cisco CEO John Chambers said: "What we're trying to do is outline an entire strategy of becoming a Chinese company."

Other corporate chieftains believe that their futures reside overseas. General Electric Chairman Jeffrey Immelt claimed in late 2007 that a downturn in the U.S. economy would not hurt General Electric because GE's business outside the United States is "very robust and very strong."[50] General Electric had positioned itself to become less dependent on U.S. consumers. "What I'm about to say might be good news or it might be bad news: The world has never been more independent from the U.S. economy," he told Charlie Rose and a national PBS audience. "If the U.S. economy goes into recession, the rest of the world is going to feel it, but in my business life, I've never seen as much sense that there are other economies around the world that can absorb the growth."

Immelt made that statement on the Charlie Rose Show, November 7, 2007, when his company's stock was trading at $39 per share. By March 2009, after the U.S. financial system collapse and a year into the U.S. recession, his company's stock sunk to $7 per share. Little did Immelt realize that his fortunes were tied directly to the U.S. economy.

The "Gathering Storm" Has Arrived

Important scientific groups in the United States have warned repeatedly over the past five years that if the country loses its production capability, then research, development, engineering and design will quickly follow. "The proximity of research, development and manufacturing is very important to leading-edge manufacturers," according to a report from President Bush's Council of Advisors on Science and Technology (PCAST).[51] "The continuing shift of manufacturing to lower-cost regions and especially to China is beginning to pull high-end design and R&D capabilities out of the United States."

That study, chaired by George Scalise, president of the Semiconductor Industry Association, included the participation of Gordon Moore, former chairman of Intel and creator of the famous "Moore's Law." It was never publicized by the White House Office of Science and Technology Policy, which did not issue a press release about the report's completion, nor did it post the report immediately to the PCAST Web site.

Like similar reports outlining the trends of deindustrialization of the country's most important and strategic industries, it was ignored. It called for swift and decisive action on behalf of the government to counter the advantages provided to industry by Asian countries. PCAST recommended that the U.S. federal government create a new "Bell Labs" type of organization to pursue industrial research and development and be able to quickly transfer technology and people into a corporate type of environment. It never materialized.

PCAST recommended that the R&D tax credit be made permanent. It hasn't been. It recommended that President Bush form a task force to assess foreign tax programs "and their impact on investment practices, and report back on how the United States should appropriately respond." No such task force was created, although the Treasury Department did produce a report in late 2007 that recommended lower corporate tax rates and a new type of "business activity tax." That proposal, "Approaches to Improve the Competitiveness of the U.S. Business Tax System for the 21st Century," failed to generate any legislative response.[52]

PCAST's thesis — that if manufacturing leaves the country, research and development and design will follow — is playing out in the automotive industry. Former assistant secretary of the Treasury Department in the Reagan administration, Paul Craig Roberts, notes that the August 2008 issue of *Automobile* magazine reports that Chrysler closed its Pacific Advanced Product Design Center in California. Other automotive design studios in Southern California have been closed by Italdesign, ASC, Porsche, Nissan and Volvo. General Motors has only three of its original 11 design studios remaining in the United States.

Advanced automotive design studios "are popping up like rabbits in China," notes Eric Noble, president of The Car Lab, an automotive consultancy. Writes Paul Craig Roberts: "The idea is nonsensical that the United States can remain the font of research, innovation, design and engineering while the country ceases to make things. Research and product development invariably follow manufacturing."

One other important U.S. report that should have mobilized the government was released in 2006 by the National Academies of Sciences entitled "Rising Above The Gathering Storm." The storm arrived, but Congress did not rise above it.

The academies proposed that federal funding for basic research in the physical sciences and engineering, which had dropped in real terms over the previous 20 years, be doubled. Five senators hosted an overflowing press conference and promised fresh funds for the National Science Foundation, the Department of Energy and the National Institute of Standards and Technology. "Gathering Storm" author Norm Augustine, former CEO of Lockheed Martin, told the assembled press corps: "The stars are aligned to do something now and so far we have far exceeded what I expected in terms of a [political] reaction."

The senators introduced the "Protecting America's Competitive Edge Act." President Bush submitted the American Competitiveness Initiative (ACI). Congress eventually passed an "authorization" bill called the Creating Opportunities to Meaningfully Promote Excellence in Technology, Education and Sciences — the COMPETES Act. President Bush signed the bill on August 7, 2007.

Then it was time to fund the program through an appropriations bill. And that's when everything fell apart. Congress could not get its budget act together for fiscal year 2008, so just before heading off for Christmas recess in December 2007, it rushed through one of its colossal "omnibus" appropriations bills called the Consolidated Appropriations Act (HR-2764) for fiscal year 2008. Within the $515.7-billion spending bill, the physical sciences received a monumental shaft. All of the political talk about competitiveness meant nothing.

NIST's laboratories received a budget of $440 million, an increase of 1.4 percent, far less than the 11 percent increase authorized in the COMPETES Act. DOE's budget for research received a 2.6 percent boost to $4 billion, $500 million below the authorization. The National Science Foundation's budget went up by 2.5 percent, to $5.9 billion — about the amount spent by the Pentagon in two days and equal to about two-and-a-half days of the U.S. trade deficit. The increase was far below the level of inflation and the final figure was substantially less than the $6.6 billion "authorized" for NSF in the COMPETES Act.

Congress couldn't find a few extra dollars to fund basic research, but it fully funded the $191-million "abstinence" sexual education program, along with 11,900 pork barrel projects. NIST received $51 million of earmarks tucked into its budget for construction projects in Alabama and Mississippi that had nothing to do with industrial measurement technology. Alabama and Mississippi are the home states of two Senate members — Richard Shelby (R-Ala.) and Thad Cochran (R-Miss.) — who sit on the NIST appropriations committee.

The importance of basic research to the future prosperity of a nation is well understood, but the United States seems to have forgotten what made it great. In the 1990s, there was plenty of technology and research waiting to be commercialized, leading to a revolution in the deployment of digital technology. Now, there is nothing left in the cupboard: the United States has eaten its seed corn.

When the Defense Advanced Research Projects Agency (DARPA) teamed up with industry to create the National Electronics Manufacturing Initiative in the early 1990s, "the thought was that there was a lot of research but we didn't have the investment and the focus to turn this into volume [production]," explains Jim McElroy, executive director and CEO of the Herndon, Va.-based research group. "Now we've come full circle. Now people are beginning to say, 'We don't have enough research results on the shelf to pull from to create the next big wave of growth for the industry.' Where does the next wave of investment have to occur so that we can continue to come up with great new products?"

Since the commercial breakthrough of the Internet in the 1990s, there haven't been any other major technologies that have led to the creation of multibillion-dollar industries.

Even the National Science Board, which oversees the operation of the National Science Foundation, took the unusual step of publishing its own public letter of concern in the 2008 "Science and Technology Indicators" report.[53] It noted that federal support for academic R&D began falling in 2005 for the first time in a quarter of a century. That decline, along with the rapid rise of foreign investment in science, technology and engineering, has "severe implications for the future of U.S. competitiveness in international markets and the future existence of highly skilled jobs at home," wrote the board. Negative trends in U.S. support for research along with the shift of high-tech manufacturing and research overseas requires "serious national attention," wrote the National Science Board. A decline in research publications by industry authors in peer-reviewed journals "suggest a de-emphasis by U.S. industry on expanding the foundations of basic scientific knowledge. The potential impacts of persistent negative trends in R&D support on the U.S. economy and jobs are indeed troubling."

Numerous industries are beginning to suffer the consequences of paltry investment in innovation. The National Academies of Sciences found that the U.S. lead in telecommunications technology "is now at risk because of the recent decline in domestic support for long-term fundamental telecommunications research." The National Academies said the United States can no longer afford research because it has lost its ability to compete in commodity products. U.S. telecommunications equipment vendors are doing most of their research outside of the country. The academies called for the creation of a new federal research organization called the Advanced Telecommunications Research Activity, but it was never considered in a Congress that failed to address the long-term viability of the United States economy.

In the area of energy research, the Government Accountability Office has found that federal spending declined by 85 percent between 1978 and 2005, despite repeated calls for energy independence. In real terms, funding for energy R&D dropped from $5.5 billion in 1978 to $793 million in 2005. The energy R&D budget has been "subject to growing congressional earmarks in recent years," said the GAO.[54]

In the area of aeronautics research, investment has been dropping for decades. In 2008, NASA's aeronautics budget stood at $512 million, down from $594 million in 2007. The Bush administration request for 2009: $446 million. That would be less than half of what the U.S. spent on aeronautics research in 2004, when NASA had $1.057 billion. The budget cuts in aeronautics R&D are "a travesty," says Clayton Jones, chairman, president and CEO of Rockwell Collins. The lack of funding puts the United States aircraft manufacturing industry "on a glide path to irrelevance," according to the National Academies of Sciences.[55]

The United States has virtually stopped funding the development of "applied" technologies that could have substantial economic and commercial impact, due to the debate over "industrial policy." The debate is driven by economic ideologues who consistently and successfully argue that the government should not be in the business of picking winners and losers.

The "picking winners and losers" argument used successfully against government funding is a "profoundly misleading metaphor," says Michael Borrus, general partner of the venture capital firm X/Seed Capital in Menlo Park, Calif. Using the expression substitutes "sloganeering for a thorough understanding of how risky early-stage technology innovation actually works," he says.[56] "No investor, neither public nor private, picks winners and losers. Ultimately, it's the market that picks winners and losers."

Decades ago, the U.S. government played an essential role in creating massive new industries that currently generate most of the country's wealth. Federal investment has been responsible for the creation of the Internet, semiconductors, atomic energy, genetic engineering, aviation, global positioning, advanced and lightweight alloys, computer graphics, CAD software programs and many other breakthroughs. "The history of today's economy demonstrates that...government activism has been indispensable to the growth of many of our most prosperous industries and well-paying jobs in the United States," says Borrus.

For two decades, there was only one program within the federal government aimed at assuring the widespread development and commercialization of industrial technology. NIST's Advanced Technology Program (ATP) limped along for two decades after being created in the late 1980s. It was finally killed by the Bush administration and Congress in 2007. This despite the fact that the contracts awarded by the program were not decided by politicians and that the government only provided a portion of the funding. There was not a single pork barrel ATP award.

ATP more than paid for itself. Just one $5.5-million grant awarded in 1992 to a consortium that included Seagate Corp. led to the creation of the small disk drive industry which, in turn, led to the explosion of hand-held consumer electronic devices that can hold 40 gigabytes or more of music, TV shows, movies and photos.

"This program was highly successful, no question about it," says Mark Kryder, chief technology officer of Seagate, the world's largest manufacturer of disk drives. NIST and the disk drive industry both provided funding to the National Storage Industry Consortium, which included university scientists. The results made possible the iPod, iPhone, TiVo and the Xbox; all from a $5.5-million U.S. government investment.

Seagate is the only American company making these drives. "The real question is, does the United States want to continue to be a player in the disk drive industry or rely on Asia?" Kryder asks. The federal government answered his question. It killed ATP.

Other U.S. high-tech industries are on the ropes. The optoelectronics industry produces light-emitting diodes, optical switches, a new generation of flat-screen televisions, solar photovoltaics and optical sensors that are being deployed to monitor thousands of mechanical and industrial systems. The technology will radically reduce energy use. An organic light-emitting diode television set, for instance, uses about 60 watts of electricity, as compared to current plasma and LCD screens, which use 650 watts.

The markets for these optical electronic systems are "large and underpin the world economy and sustainability," says Michael Lebby, president and CEO of the Optoelectronics Industry Development Association (OIDA) in Washington, D.C. But the bullish economic prospects for the industry will not accrue to the United States because almost all of the manufacturing capacity for optoelectronics products is being installed overseas.

"Right now, whatever is coming out of research in the photonics industry is ending up outside of the country because of the trend among all the major players in photonics to ship everything offshore," says Lebby. "It's a negative trend."

The optoelectronics R&D infrastructure in the United States "has been decimated," adds Lebby. "I'm really scared because the government has not invested in the future and, without being political, it's the hope that they are going to realize that unless they do something soon, the country will lose a lot of this technology. The federal government puts some money into various aspects of photonics R&D, but I would say that is at least 1/10th if not 1/20th or 1/30th of the scale it should be."

The traditional mechanisms by which technology has been commercialized in the United States are no longer working. Given the surge of foreign investment in new technologies and the funding of commercialization efforts overseas, "the current model featuring small companies and venture capital investors is now under stress," according to Todd Hylton, director of the Center for Advanced Materials and Nanotechnology at Science Applications International Corp. (SAIC).[57]

In the traditional commercialization model, small or startup companies invest in promising technologies emerging from research labs. Larger companies then step in and provide late-stage product development funding and market access. But over the past two decades, there has been an "inexorable displacement" of the technology industry from the United States, says Hylton. Virtually all of the newest semiconductor and display manufacturing capacity is located offshore, and that will hold true with nanotechnology, which will require long-term, patient financing before new products begin to transform virtually every industry.

U.S. companies don't invest in technologies that are more than two years on the horizon. Venture capitalists don't fund products that are more than five years out. Companies wanting to invest see that most of the infrastructure to manufacture prototypes is located offshore.

A new generation of public/private partnerships dedicated to technology transition and involving large groups of research institutions, consortia of small and large technology companies and public economic development organizations nationwide need to start working together to avert the wholesale loss of technology and industrial leadership. Hylton says technology transition organizations need to be created in virtually every industrial sector: energy conversion, solar, energy storage (batteries, hydrogen), agriculture, medical diagnostics and devices, high-speed electronics, flexible electronics and high-strength materials.

Other essential industrial infrastructure maintained by the U.S. government is under stress. In an assessment of the United States measurement system, a team of 700 experts from the National Institute of Standards and Technology found that there were more than 700 "measurement-related barriers to technological innovation" in the United States that needed to be addressed in order for the country to "maintain its position as a global leader."[58] The U.S. measurement system is at a "defining moment," according to the group's 2008 "Assessment of the United States Measurement System."

It noted that Japan made the improvement of its measurement system "a strategic priority" in its science and technology plan for the years 2006 to 2010. China is proposing that its state-sponsored nanotechnology standards be adopted worldwide. The European Union is instituting "demanding requirements for assuring the accuracy of measurements used to manufacture certain types of medical equipment and other high-technology products."

As this is occurring, the United States measurement system is being starved of funds, even though a vast array of industries depend on a new generation of highly precise measuring equipment, from quantum computing, to advanced energy systems like hydrogen fuel cells, biotechnology, nanotechnology, medical devices, drug delivery systems, environmental protection, information technology, automotive and the blossoming field of "additive" manufacturing.

Individual companies in the United States cannot afford to invest in the development of advanced, highly accurate and expensive molecular measurement devices.

Stanley Williams, senior fellow at Hewlett-Packard and founding director of the company's Quantum Science Research Group in Palo Alto, Calif., says the United States is on the cusp of losing its ability to innovate.[59] In the last century, U.S. inventions of the telephone, light bulb, radio, vacuum tube, and the integrated circuit, among others, led to the creation of massive industries that employed millions of Americans, improved lives and provided tax revenue for the federal government. But toward the end of the last century, "we started to become complacent and neglectful," Williams says. "Our wonderful goose was slowly being starved, and the consequences of that were alarming indeed."

If investment is not restored in the physical sciences and engineering infrastructure of the country "the cost of failure is too grim to contemplate," Williams says. "We must do this before we lose an entire generation of American scientists and engineers and become completely reliant on other countries for our technology."

U.S. Industry Has Given Up on the Government

U.S. industry has gotten tired of dealing with the federal government's R&D programs. Evidence of industry's lack of interest became clear during the August 18-19, 2008, "National Science and Technology Summit" sponsored by the White House Office of Science and Technology Policy. The event, held in Oak Ridge, Tenn., was intended to examine the health and direction of the U.S. science and technology enterprise. Excluding the speakers who were invited from the private sector and the two who worked for government contractors, of the 250 people attending the conference, only two people came from U.S.-based industrial companies. There were more people attending the event from the Chinese embassy (three) than there were from major American companies. The vast majority of attendees worked for the federal government. Yet the whole idea of the conference was to provide a "direction forward for American competitiveness."

Hewlett-Packard, one of the world's largest electronics companies, sent a speaker to the White House-sponsored event. Wayne Johnson, director of worldwide strategic university customer relations at HP, gave the feds a tongue-lashing. He said it is senseless for the government to be funding R&D if the benefits of that research leak offshore to foreign corporations. "This is further complicated by the fact that we in the U.S. find ourselves in competition not only with individuals, companies and private institutions, but also with governments and mixed government-private collaborations," he said.

Susan Butts, senior director of external science and technology programs at Dow Chemical, said the federal government can fund all the R&D it wants, but if the United States innovation system discourages an invention from being manufactured in the United States, then American industry will not generate the taxes "that fund the federal investment in the research."

It is obvious that the United States no longer values robust investments in research. Congress allowed the R&D tax credit to expire at the end of 2007, taking until late 2008 to extend it. Congress has never made the R&D tax credit permanent. This might have been fine during an era when the United States dominated virtually every field of research, but globalization has changed the equation.

The U.S. R&D tax credit was once the world's most generous. Now it's worse than those offered by 17 other nations. The U.S. credit applies only to the increase in R&D investment a company makes year-over-year. Most other countries offer a credit for a company's entire R&D investment. U.S. companies can simply leave the United States to conduct research where there are better tax benefits.[60]

It is difficult to name one high-tech company that has been created in the United States over the past 10 years. The last batch of innovative American firms came to prominence in the mid-1990s: Amazon.com, e-Bay, Yahoo and Google. The only new companies that Americans might have heard about in the past eight years are foreign firms: Lenovo and Tata. China's Lenovo became famous when it purchased the personal computer assets of IBM and tried unsuccessfully to sell thousands of Chinese-made computers to the State Department. Tata bought Jaguar and Land Rover from Ford, and it runs a big IT outsourcing operation in India. These two companies have risen by buying the assets of American companies.

Thirty-five Chinese companies were on the Fortune Global 500 list of 2008, up from 24 in 2007, and "the best-ever showing by Chinese companies in the ranking," according to *China Daily*. U.S. companies are headed in the opposite direction. There were 153 American companies on the list in 2008, nine fewer than in 2007, "the worst showing in 10 years," added Reuters. Nike, Gap and Bear Stearns, which was acquired by JP Morgan, all disappeared from the list. The *Financial Times'* list of the world's top 500 companies included 50 companies from China, Russia and India "against hardly any presence a decade ago," the publication said in its June 27, 2008, edition.

Competing With China's Labor Costs

It will not be easy for American manufacturers to compete with Chinese labor, even as labor costs in China continue to increase. Chinese workers remain among the lowest paid in the world, according to Judith Banister in a study conducted for the Bureau of Labor Statistics.[61]

The average total compensation for 104.6 million Chinese manufacturing workers was 72 cents per hour in 2004, or $134 per month ($1,608 per year). That means the average Chinese worker's total compensation is 3.15 percent of the average U.S. manufacturing worker's hourly compensation of $22.87.

There were 56.67 million Chinese manufacturing employees working for large enterprises in 2004. Their average annual compensation was $2,179, or about 98 cents per hour.

You don't want to be one of the 24.1 million Chinese working for a small manufacturing company. Their total average hourly compensation was only 49 cents per hour — or a lowly $91 per month ($1,097 a year). Self-employed manufacturing workers had total compensation of only 34 cents per hour — or a measly $766 a year.

These hourly figures, compiled from China's First Economic Census of 2004 and analyzed by Banister, who later became director of global demographics at The Conference Board, include all of the costs of an employee including income, benefits and cash in kind. Total compensation also includes wages for piece work, bonuses, allowances, overtime pay and pay for dangerous or challenging duties. "It includes subsidies of all kinds: housing and transport provided workers, meals given to them, the value of income tax and social insurance payments deducted from wages and remitted to the government on behalf of all the employees," according to Banister.

Health care is picked up by the government, and other forms of compensation including workman's comp, disability insurance, retirement accounts and pensions — if they exist at all — are also not carried by Chinese employers, as they are in the United States. "Pensions and medical insurance systems paid into by employers and employees essentially do not exist in China outside of cities today," according to an earlier BLS report on the subject.[62]

On a purchasing power parity basis, the average take-home pay for a Chinese manufacturing employee is enough to purchase goods and services "that give the worker and family a living standard equivalent to annual take-home pay of about $5,369 in the United States," according to Banister.

For years, as the U.S. economy shed tens of thousands of manufacturing jobs per month, U.S. economists were rationalizing the loss by stating that China was losing manufacturing jobs as well. This was not true. In a paper that became widely quoted by free trade rationalists,

The Conference Board in 2004 stated that there were 83 million manufacturing workers in China in 2002, down from 98 million in 1995. The authors equated job loss in China with job loss in America.[63]

"A lot of Chinese companies are introducing the same technology and methodologies that are being used in the United States so their demand for labor is falling really fast," said Conference Board economist Matthew Spiegelman. The report stated that "China is losing many more manufacturing jobs than the developed world (including the United States) — and in many of the same industries where the developed world has seen the greatest declines."

But research funded by the Bureau of Labor Statistics in 2004 found the 83 million number to be way off the mark — by 18 million workers — a figure that is far higher than the total number of manufacturing employees in the United States. Yet the 83 million number was used throughout the policy community in Washington as an argument against the need for policies aimed at stemming outsourcing of jobs in the U.S. industrial sector.

If job loss in manufacturing was occurring in China, which was increasing production by staggering amounts at the time, then it was inevitable that hundreds of thousands of Americans would be losing their manufacturing jobs, too, argued dozens of Washington economists using data from The Conference Board's report.

Unlike in the United States, the number of people working in the manufacturing sector in China was increasing through 2007. Manufacturing employment in China peaked in 1996 at 126 million but then dropped to 101 million in 2002, due to the privatization of Chinese enterprises and increases in labor productivity. But starting in 2002, it began to steadily increase, as more foreign companies invested in new production, as exports increased and as China's GDP continued its surge above 10 percent per year.

"By 2004, China's average manufacturing employment had increased once again to 104.5 million, and by year-end 2005, the total had reached 110.6 million," according to Banister.

The number of manufacturing employees in China might be even higher than that. There are millions of Chinese who work in agriculture during the planting and harvest seasons and work in regional factories the remainder of the year. "The population census tends to over-classify people in agriculture and under-classify them in the other sectors of the economy," Banister says. This is a worldwide problem with data in developing nations, but "I don't think it really means a whole lot because you've already got massively the highest manufacturing numbers on the planet by orders of magnitude than any other country. There is no point in getting hung up over whether it's a slight under estimate or over estimate, no point."

China's manufacturing employment is far greater than all of the manufacturing workers in the G-8 combined.

Many of the manufacturing jobs gained in China came at the expense of those in the United States, according to the Economic Policy Institute in a July 2008 report "The China Trade Toll."[64] EPI estimates that 2.3 million U.S. jobs were lost due to the U.S. trade deficit with China between 2001 and 2007, including 366,000 jobs in 2007. Most of the displaced U.S. manufacturing workers who did manage to find new jobs lost an average of $8,146 in wages in 2007, worth $19.4 billion. Thirty-one percent of American manufacturing workers losing jobs due to China's surge had college degrees. "Growing China trade deficits have contributed to the loss of 200,000 scientist and engineering jobs within the manufacturing sector," the study says. "Growth in the China trade deficit has eliminated 561,000 jobs in computer and electronic products alone since 2001."

Manufacturing jobs remain among the most coveted among Americans. When Toyota announced it was going to open a new manufacturing plant in San Antonio, Texas, and hire 2,000 new workers, it was inundated: 63,000 people applied for jobs. It was easier to get into Harvard University (20,000 applicants for a freshman class of 1,600), than it was to get a job with Toyota. Toyota was expecting 100,000 applicants for its San Antonio plant and received 15,000 applicants the first day it opened the process, which it had to shut down after two weeks. Had it continued accepting job applications, Toyota projected that it would have received 200,000 applications.

The Department of Defense's Response To Globalization of Manufacturing Supply Chains

The Pentagon is growing increasingly worried about the shift of production capacity offshore, the rise of global supply chains and the movement of research and development to countries that are considered to be potential adversaries.

Those working deep in the military complex — the contracting officers having to deal with companies using counterfeit components or who can't find American companies to manufacture worn-out parts — are especially worried about the health of the U.S. industrial base.

These defense contracting officials view the Pentagon's response to global economic challenges as being inadequate to the crisis at hand. Even more alarming is the demise of the American automobile industry and its impact on the defense industrial base, let alone the loss of a huge tax revenue stream that is necessary to maintain a strong military with more than 700 bases worldwide.

As a stop-gap measure, the Pentagon and the National Security Agency (NSA) have created a little-known "trusted sources" program.[65] The idea is to certify U.S. suppliers as "trusted sources" of high-tech devices and components that are used throughout the military and in national security applications. DOD and NSA want to make sure they are buying parts that will not go haywire because they have been infected by overseas governments' use of "Trojan horses" — an expression used throughout the trusted sources program.

DOD and the National Security Agency started the "trusted" program in 2003, when it signed a 10-year, $650-million contract with IBM for safe chips produced at IBM's wafer fabrication plant in Essex Junction, Vt. That program, which was never publicized, was in response to former Defense Deputy Secretary Paul Wolfowitz's request in October 2003 that the military "ensure the economic viability of domestic integrated circuit sources. The health of the defense IC supplier community depends on the health of the larger commercial IC base."

Those who run the trusted program in the Pentagon are becoming increasingly alarmed by the loss of U.S. high-tech capability, and especially by the 2008 announcement by IBM that it was transferring its state-of-the-art 45-nanometer bulk process integrated circuit technology to Semiconductor Manufacturing International Corp. (SMIC), which is headquartered in Shanghai, China. SMIC shortly thereafter announced that it would be partnering with the Shenzhen municipal government in China to build a fab that will produce 45-nanometer chips based on its IBM license. IBM provided SMIC with a shot in the arm — allowing it to move beyond its present 90-nanometer capabilities, and leapfrog its Chinese competitors that are producing 65-nanometer chips.

The IBM "trusted" foundry contract is due to expire in 2011. But the Pentagon is worried that IBM will exit the semiconductor fabrication production business. "Where is this going to lead us?" asks the person who runs the trusted program at the Defense Microelectronics Activity (DMEA) in Sacramento, Calif. "Urgent action is needed to stem this tide."

On the DMEA Internet home page, the agency notes that rapid technology development and the "commercial microelectronics technology business climate make it difficult, if not impossible, to provide reliable, long-term support for the military's fielded systems."

But urgent action isn't on the immediate horizon. The trusted sources program "is like putting a Band-Aid on a bullet hole," said the DMEA program manager.

Within the Pentagon, the concern has risen to the top ranks. On July 16, 2008, Undersecretary of Defense for Intelligence James Clapper issued a sweeping new regulation to virtually every military office, service and contractor.[66] Called the "Critical Program Information Protection" program, its intent is to make sure the thousands of electronic components, network switches and software code embedded in weapon systems and national security devices are not infected with bugs from foreign adversaries. The directive states that DOD must protect itself against a "compromise of military and intelligence systems by components being integrated into them by foreign intelligence, foreign terrorists or other hostile elements through the supply chain or system design."

The directive will affect every DOD contracting officer and contractor working for the military, including those engaged in research and development. It calls on DOD's inspector general to start investigating contractors' use of foreign suppliers.

The problems associated with globalization of supply chains are beginning to mount. The U.S. military and national security agencies are facing an unprecedented infiltration of counterfeit electronic chips, chipsets and components. In a first-ever, government-mandated survey of the avionics electronics supply chain, the Commerce Department's Bureau of Industry and Security (BIS) in late 2008 found 7,383 electronics counterfeit incidents in military avionics systems. This is up from 5,747 such incidents reported in 2007.

The survey was comprehensive: 482 companies and organizations — virtually the entire U.S. avionics supply chain — were required to participate. Conducting the study on behalf of the U.S. Naval Air Systems Command, BIS found that the majority of counterfeit electronics products originated in China and other Asian nations, and the majority of them were discovered only after they were "returned as defective."

The proliferation of counterfeit electronics components "is a broad issue and it is prevalent in the commercial and government supply chains," said study director Kevin Kurland, director of BIS's Office of Technology Evaluation. "One of the things that brought it to light was the Navy and their field operations had systems go down that affected their operational readiness. We're trying to get a handle on this, [but] we are comfortable in saying the issue is prevalent."

The military has been aptly warned about the loss of America's technological superiority and its potential negative national security implications. In 2003, the Pentagon's Advisory Group on Electron Devices (AGED) said that the offshore movement of intellectual capital and industrial capability in microelectronics had forced the DOD "to rely on perceived system integration advantages to maintain superiority."[67]

The Defense Department did not like what it heard from its electronics advisory group. DOD never authorized release of the AGED report, which was obtained only through a Freedom of Information Act request. Ronald Sega, the director of defense research and engineering (DDR&E) at the time, refused to endorse the report. Its findings did not "factually represent" the views of the DDR&E, said Pentagon spokesman Donald Sewell.

AGED's charter states that its job is to "assume a key role in identifying when major shifts in strategy for the DOD electronics program are needed." Such a shift had occurred, said AGED, whose members included officials from each of the military services, DARPA, the Ballistic Missile Defense Office, NASA, other federal agencies and industry and academic consultants. "We recommend that immediate corrective actions must be taken in order to sustain our technology leadership," said the

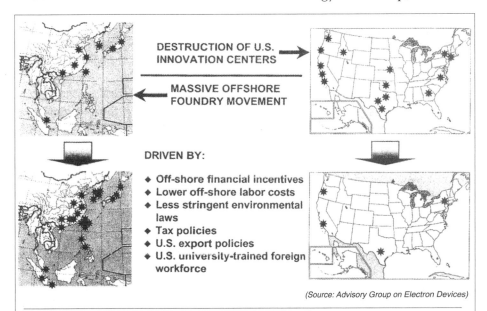

DESTRUCTION OF U.S.
INNOVATION CENTERS

MASSIVE OFFSHORE
FOUNDRY MOVEMENT

DRIVEN BY:

♦ Off-shore financial incentives
♦ Lower off-shore labor costs
♦ Less stringent environmental laws
♦ Tax policies
♦ U.S. export policies
♦ U.S. university-trained foreign workforce

(Source: Advisory Group on Electron Devices)

In 2003, the Pentagon's Advisory Group on Electron Devices described the "Destruction of U.S. Innovation Centers." The Pentagon did not authorize the findings and shortly thereafter temporarily closed the advisory group down.

AGED panel, chaired by Thomas Hartwick, a former TRW research executive. Others on the board included Jack Kilby, the inventor of the integrated circuit and Nobel Laureate; Bill Howard, director of R&D at Motorola; Andrew Yang, inventor of the infrared camera; and George Heilmeier, former president and CEO of Bellcore. AGED told DOD that it needed to put together an "analysis team to formulate actions for trend reversal." It said the U.S. government needed to counter "massive financial and tax investments" being made by foreign governments to lure U.S. companies by "increasing U.S. incentives and implementing favorable tax policies."

Shortly after the report became public, DOD closed AGED down.

But the panel's work struck a nerve. Well before offshore outsourcing became a political issue, it warned that the offshore movement of intellectual capital and microelectronics industrial capability had negatively "impacted the ability of the U.S. to research and produce the best technologies and products for the nation and the warfighter." It warned that without government leadership and "a prominent goal or mission" such as "putting a man on the moon," that the U.S. economy's "engine for growth" would be compromised, along with DOD's "continuous superiority." DOD "faces shrinking advantages across ALL technology areas," said AGED. As the United States shifts its production offshore, it "assigns those nations political and military leverage over the United States."

AGED said that U.S. technology leadership "is in decline," and that the offshore migration of semiconductor chip foundries "must be addressed." So far through 2009, the U.S. government had ignored the advice of its own advisory groups, refusing to address the root causes of offshore migration of high-technology production, which "will potentially slow the engine for economic growth," AGED said.

By 2008, that forecast came to fruition with the country experiencing its most profound economic contraction in 70 years. AGED warned in 2003 that a quick recovery would not be possible due to the "hollowing out of U.S. productive capability."

The Defense Science Board (DSB) issued its own analysis of the U.S. semiconductor industry. "Urgent action is recommended, as the industry is likely to continue moving in a deleterious direction, resulting in significant exposure if not remedied," said William Howard, chairman of the DSB Task Force on High Performance Microchip Supply, upon release of its 2005 study on the subject.[68] The U.S. semiconductor industry cannot change the competitive dynamics that have emerged globally to shift the balance of production and markets away from the United States. The task force said that addressing the problem "is a uniquely government function. The task force considers DOD the logical steward to lead, cajole and encourage a national solution to this critical problem regardless of which arm of government must act."

The study called for a broad reexamination of U.S. government policies regarding trade, its approach to the WTO, export controls, foreign investment into U.S. suppliers, protection of intellectual property, direct federal funding of trusted foundries dedicated solely for defense production, economic development incentives with the states, research and development support and acquisition policies. Again, nothing of the sort ever occurred.

Another DOD program aimed at making sure there are supplies of manufactured parts for weapons systems like tanks and trucks has also been ignored. The DOD's Diminishing Manufacturing Sources and Materials Shortage (DMSMS) program has found "escalating shortages of basic parts and processes, especially in the metal foundry and castings industries," it says.

The Defense Department has been slow to recognize the problem because the military is a relatively small buyer in the overall market, accounting for an estimated 10 percent of all castings and materials. "Because we're not buying every day, when we go back and look for these parts we're finding that the manufacturers are gone and the tooling is gone," says George Crandell, vice president of operations at the Castings Emissions Reduction Program (CERP) in McLellan, Calif. "For a pretty simple industry, it's down below the radar screen and nobody pays much attention until they can't get a long lead-time item like a transmission case."

Brian Suma, who runs the DMSMS Information Systems project at the Army's Tank-Automotive and Armaments Command, said the problem finding manufacturers for parts and suppliers of materials and chemicals is serious. "We're out here stomping on the grass to put out a grass fire, but we haven't looked behind us to see that the barn has gone up," said Suma. "I'm supposed to be the guy who is saying that not only do we have a grass fire going up, but I need to be telling you that we have a barn fire, too. How do we get that information out to people so there is visibility so that somebody does something about it?"

Numerous other areas of defense industrial and technological "vulnerabilities" are becoming apparent. Advanced manufacturing battery capability has largely left the United States, making the military almost completely dependent on foreign sources of batteries for virtually every weapon system and portable computer and electronic device that uses them. In 2008, Congress told DOD to develop a "specific" roadmap that included time-lines and estimates of funding necessary to assure the United States had "assured" access to battery technology.[69]

Measuring — Or Not Measuring — the Economic Impact of Globalization

The United States government's economic data gathering and analysis capability has not kept up with globalization. There is not an agency in the government that monitors plant closures and offshore outsourcing of jobs. Serious questions have been raised about the quality of basic government data series such as industrial production, productivity, international trade, foreign direct investment and employment.

Almost all of the economic data series run by the government were created during a time when the United States economy led the world, and there was no reason to measure the global activities of the country's largest multinational companies. Without knowing what is occurring, it is impossible for the U.S. government to initiate a response. With the closure of the Office of Technology Assessment and the Technology Administration within the Commerce Department, there is no place within the federal government today that conducts qualitative analysis of globalization and technology trends.

Productivity

Susan Houseman of the Upjohn Institute for Employment Research has found that productivity growth rates of the manufacturing sector during the past 15 years may be overstated due to the reduction of labor hours associated with offshore outsourcing.

As companies move factories overseas or start contracting with foreign firms for the production of goods they were previously making in the United States, they can reduce their American workforce. Statistically, it looks like they have substantially increased labor productivity when, in fact, they may have greatly increased the number of workers in an overseas location who are working at a fraction of the cost.

The current productivity measures are "misleading," says Houseman.[70] "Productivity growth is the basis for improvements in workers' standard of living. Yet, widespread improvement in American workers' wages has not accompanied the rapid growth in measured U.S. productivity."

Globalization has made it "exceedingly difficult" for government statistical agencies to measure changes in the flows of inputs into the production process "and hence to accurately measure productivity growth," Houseman says. "The growth of outsourcing and offshoring raises conceptual issues about what productivity statistics do and should measure, with implications for how they should be interpreted and who will benefit from measured productivity gains."

Houseman calculated that outsourcing of manufacturing jobs accounted for about half of a percent point of the growth in manufacturing productivity between 1990 and 2000, dropping the growth rate from 3.71 percent to 3.17 percent. It's more difficult to factor in offshoring of production overseas in the manufacturing sector because the government does not track the shift of production offshore. It's also difficult to ascertain productivity growth in the overall manufacturing sector because most of the gains in productivity during the 1990s were driven by rapid improvement of computer capability.

"Foreign labor is counted as a separate input, weighted by its cost share, and hence, in as much as lower hourly foreign labor costs are not commensurately matched by lower productivity, cost savings from offshoring will be counted as productivity gains," Houseman writes. "To the extent that offshoring is an important source of measured productivity growth in the economy, productivity statistics will, in part, be capturing cost savings or gains to trade but not improvements in the output of American labor and should be interpreted with caution."

Industrial Output

Offshore outsourcing might also inflate the measure of U.S. industrial output. Output is defined as value added or sales, minus the cost of purchased inputs. But if the costs of inputs are cheaper from overseas, then the value added associated with the savings increases. A study by the Upjohn Institute estimates that U.S. manufacturing output was probably growing 0.2 percent to 0.5 percent less per year than the statistics indicate.[71] That means the Federal Reserve Board's index of U.S. industrial production could be substantially higher than it is.

As measured by the Fed, industrial production increased by 13.4 percent from 2002 to July 2008, an annual increase of 2.5 percent. But if that number is really 2.2 percent, "then production in 2007 is up just 11.5 percent from 2002 and less than 6 percent from 2000," notes Dan Luria, research director at the Michigan Manufacturing Technology Center. "In other words, over a period in which U.S. GDP rose by nearly 25 percent, more than three-quarters of the increase in demand for manufactured goods would have had to have been satisfied by a rise in net imports."

Even without the statistical problems associated with offshoring, the Fed's production numbers tell a troubling story. Due to the steep economic downturn caused by the dot-com bust in 2001, the industrial production index increased by only 7.83 percent from December 2000 through June 2008 (from 103.5 to 111.6) or an annual rate of 0.95 percent. By comparison, in the previous seven-and-one-half year period (June 1993 through December 2000), the index rose from 72.5 to 103.5, an increase of almost 43 percent, or 5 percent per year. That rate was more than five times faster than the most recent period.

Industrial production from 2001 to 2008 is lagging far behind the real growth of GDP. From December 2000 to June 2008, GDP increased by 18.3 percent, 2.3 times as fast as industrial production, meaning industrial production grew at less than half the rate of the overall economy, notes Luria. Had industrial production grown at the same rate as GDP, the U.S. manufacturing sector would be generating $155 billion more in production and would not have lost 1.3 million manufacturing jobs.

There might be other problems with the industrial production numbers, however. As companies shift their manufacturing offshore or contract with foreign manufacturers for production that was formerly done in the United States, the government statistical agencies should reclassify these former manufacturers as "wholesalers." But they are slow in doing so. "There is concern that the statistics are getting thrown way off because of that," says Houseman. "This is a real issue." If former manufacturing companies are not being classified as importers/wholesalers, then the industrial production numbers that indicate growth in manufacturing might be wrong.

Employment

There are perennial questions about the federal government's unemployment numbers. The Department of Labor publishes six different versions of its unemployment statistics. The one most people know is the so-called "U-3" number, which, in June 2008, stood at 5.5 percent, growing to 7.2 percent by December 2008 and 9.4 percent by May 2009. But this number does not include many people who should be considered unemployed, and there are dozens of analysts who believe the number is a fraud because it does not include the many millions of people who want jobs but have given up looking for them. These despondent job seekers, along with those who hold part-time work and want a full-time job, are included in the so-called "U-6" unemployment number. According to John Williams, editor of "Shadow Government Statistics," the U-2 unemployment rate was 9.7 percent in August 2008. But he believes that the real figure of those who wanted to work during that month was 13.7 percent.[72]

Foreign Direct Investment

In the area of foreign direct investment (FDI) into the United States, the Bureau of Economic Analysis (BEA) quietly announced in June 2008 that it will no longer differentiate between foreign purchases of U.S. companies and investments made in new production facilities. "Free traders" constantly point to "insourcing" of foreign investment in new plants from companies like Honda, Toyota and BMW, but such "insourcing" accounts for only a small portion of total FDI. In 2007, only $22 billion — or 8.6 percent of the $255 billion in total foreign direct investment — went toward creating new businesses or building new factories in the United States.

The BEA said Congress did not provide it with the $600,000 it needs to keep track of the different forms of foreign investment.

This comes at a time when the United States is in such debt that it is selling off assets at an astounding rate. About 30 pro-U.S. manufacturing organizations led by the American Manufacturing Trade Action Coalition tried to get the data series reinstated. They told congressional leaders that "special interests, including those that receive large fees from facilitating acquisitions, have launched well-financed campaigns to obscure vital distinctions between the roughly 10 percent of FDI that goes into new businesses and 90 percent of FDI that brings existing U.S. businesses and their worldwide assets under the control of foreign interests." Among those signing the letter were the American Mold Builders Association, the American Foundry Society, the American Iron and Steel Institute, the Coalition for a Prosperous America, the North American Die Casting Association, the National Farmers Union and the Pennsylvania Manufacturers Association.

Trade Data

The trade figures for the past 20 years as reported by the Bureau of Economic Analysis might also be wrong. The U.S. trade deficit could be 10 to 15 percent higher than has been reported for the past 20 years. In 1988, the federal government was forced through litigation to allow importers to declare the value of their imported merchandize based on the price when it first leaves a manufacturing plant in a foreign country. The so-called "first-sale" rule enables importers to substantially reduce the amount they pay in duties, but it also means that the value of many imported products does not include the costs of middlemen, contract manufacturers, transportation or logistics prior to a product being loaded onto a vessel for export to the United States. Importers are allowed to declare on their forms the price of a product as it leaves a factory in a developing nation.

They can also misstate the real price of the product, which enables them to further reduce the duties they pay, or they lie about the type of merchandise they are importing. For instance, an importer can mis-classify a shipment and pay a lower duty rate by claiming a product is made out of polyester rather than cotton. Customs and Border Protection import specialists would have to physically open the imported container at the port and do a test to determine the type of textiles in any given shipment.

All of this data is provided by importers to Customs and Bureau Protection, which then feeds it to the Bureau of Economic Analysis to prepare the monthly import/export data.[73]

Offshore Outsourcing

The United States government does not track companies shifting production offshore. The only substantial study of actual job loss due to offshore outsourcing of manufacturing production was done by Cornell University professor Kate Bronfenbrenner for the U.S.-China Economic and Security Review Commission.[74] To understand the scope of the trend, Bronfenbrenner and her staff of graduate students monitored national and international newspapers, Internet sites, Lexis Nexis, trade journals, investor conference call transcripts and SEC filings. They analyzed government data from Trade Adjustment Assistance filings and the Workers Adjustment Retraining Notification notices.

What Bronfenbrenner found was that the United States was losing far more manufacturing jobs to low-cost countries than official government statistics ever indicated. She estimated that her tally of 48,417 lost jobs in one quarter of 2004 represented only about 25 percent of the total number of jobs lost to outsourcing and represented an "incredible escalation" of production shifts from her previous study conducted in 2001.

"Part of what we captured in our research is the fact that the imperfection of our [research] methods have increased even more because more and more companies are hiding what they are doing," said Bronfenbrenner. "If the government isn't going to make people report it, soon it's going to be impossible to track."

Researchers found that the "overwhelming majority" of the job shifts during the first quarter of 2004 were from large publicly held multinational companies such as IBM, Texas Instruments, Accenture, Robert Bosch, Electrolux, Earthlink and Whirlpool. Almost 75 percent of the companies shifting production from the U.S. to China and Mexico were publicly held, U.S.-based multinationals.

Bronfenbrenner found that many of the multinational companies moving their production out of the United States intended to sell their products back into the country. Amerock closed its Rockford, Ill., cabinet and window manufacturing plant after 75 years in operation and laid off 450 workers. The company's new facilities in China and Mexico will ship products to U.S. customers. "This is true for a wide variety of products that will be produced in China to sell back to the U.S. market by companies such as Carrier Corp. (air conditioners), Werner Co. (ladders for Home Depot), Union Tools (lawn and garden tools) and Remington Products Co. (electric shavers)," says Bronfenbrenner's report. The production of thousands of other products has already left the United States, to be shipped back to American consumers: Etch-A-Sketch, Converse shoes, Radio Flier wagons, John Deere cotton pickers, K2 snow shoes, Levi Strauss jeans and Bic pens.

"These data remind us that it is not a story of good jobs being stolen from U.S. workers by low-wage workers in Latin America and Asia, especially China, with whom U.S. workers can never hope to compete," the report concludes. "Instead, it is a story of the world's largest multinational corporations buying and selling companies and pieces of companies, opening and closing plants, downsizing and expanding operations and shifting employment from one community to another, all around the world. With no particular loyalty to country, industry, community or product, what our data suggest is that this global race to the bottom is driven by several unifying factors: the search for ever cheaper production costs, accessibility to expanding global markets and the flexibility that comes from diverse supply chains in an ever more volatile global economic and political climate."

Other analysts have looked at offshore outsourcing of manufacturing capability and concluded that the practice is leading to the strategic destruction of American industry. David Pritchard and Alan MacPherson of the Canada-United States Trade Center at the State University of New York in Buffalo say that Boeing is an example of a company that is "trading away" its intellectual property capabilities to supply chain partners overseas for short-term gain and long-term loss.[75] This knowledge took decades to develop through internal R&D and public support from government laboratories and research agencies. Boeing has outsourced more than 90 percent of its new 787 "Dreamliner" aircraft "even after the U.S. government provided Boeing with $1.8 billion in NASA money for the High Speed Civil Transport program, which was earmarked to develop the U.S. industrial base," according to the two researchers.

The state of Washington gave Boeing a $3.2-billion subsidy (or $3.2 million per production employee) to keep its production in Washington, yet Boeing has reduced its headcount in the commercial division from 90,000 before September 11, 2001, to about 40,000, as it continues to outsource the most important components of its new aircraft. Japanese suppliers will build the entire composite wing for the 787, which will put that country "in a position to build its own commercial aircraft as a direct result of decades of industrial offset arrangements" between Boeing and the big Japanese aerospace firms, according to Pritchard and MacPherson. "For the first time in U.S. commercial aviation history, foreign risk-sharing partners will have full control over the selection of second- and third-tier suppliers."

Services Outsourcing

The federal government does not track the outsourcing of white collar or service sector jobs, either. The only known government report on the topic was conducted by the Commerce Department. It was required by the House Appropriations Committee, which provided the Commerce Department's Technology Administration with $335,000 to conduct the analysis. After it was sent to the White House for approval, the report went from being 336 pages to 12 pages in length — at $28,000 per page — and was never published. The Technology Administration was subsequently shut down.

Congress requested the study be done by July 2004. But it was never released due to fears within the Bush administration that the controversial subject would hurt the president's re-election campaign. Gregory Mankiw, chairman of the White House Council on Economic Advisors, had embarrassed the Bush administration when he made a statement on February 10, 2004, that "outsourcing is a growing phenomenon, but it's something that we should realize is probably a plus for the economy in the long run. We don't have a comparative advantage in producing clothing, textiles and that's one of the reasons we've tended to lose textile jobs. Maybe we've learned that we don't have a comparative advantage in radiologists."

A week later, after a great deal of brouhaha, Mankiw made his way back to a podium, claiming his comments "were misinterpreted to suggest that I was praising U.S. job losses." He said that he "learned an important lesson from that experience. Economists and non-economists speak very different languages. The two languages share many words in common, but they are often interpreted in different ways."

The unreleased Commerce Department study on white collar job loss, which was finally provided via the Freedom of Information Act, provides a comparison of the average annual pay for global software workers: United States, $63,000; Japan, $44,000; Canada, $28,174; Indonesia, $12,200; Thailand, $11,124; Russia, $7,500; Philippines, $6,550; Poland, $6,400; Hungary, $6,400; Pakistan, $4,860; and China, $4,750.

Fundamental questions about the offshore outsourcing of engineering and technology jobs were raised by Intel CEO Andrew Grove in November 2003, when he spoke before the Business Software Alliance. He said he was attending the event "to be the skunk at your garden party. A large number of well-trained, diligent people are out of work. One cannot help but ask the question: Does this represent some fundamental long-term change in the industry? The job recovery of various previous cycles and the absence of recovery in the current cycle suggest that something is basically different here."

Grove, one of the country's most successful entrepreneurs and author of one of the best business books ever written (*Only the Paranoid Survive*), said that he looked everywhere in the public policy realm for a government response to offshoring of high-tech jobs. "I am hard-put to find a documented statement or public policy series on this global shift," he said. "I can't find a statement..." Six years later, no such "public policy series" has been created by the U.S. government.

---

1. "I encourage you all to go shopping more," was a quote from President George W. Bush at a press conference discussing the economy in December 2006. Bush did not use such language after the terrorist attack of September 11, 2001: http://thinkprogress.org/2006/ 12/20/bush-shopping/.
2. Tassey, Gregory, *The Technology Imperative*, Edward Elgar Publishing Ltd., 2007 (ISBN 9781845429126).
3. Cato Institute, "Are Trade Deficits A Drag on U.S. Economic Growth?" April 2007, http://www.freetrade.org/pubs/FTBs/FTB-027.html.
4. Epperson, Jerry, C.F.A., Mann Armistead & Epperson, Richmond, Va., before the June 18, 2008, American Home Furnishings Association's Manufacturing Summit in Greensboro, N.C.

5. IPC - Association Connecting Electronics Industries, Market Research Department, PCB Production Data.

6. American Iron and Steel Institute, Global Steel Industry Letter to the Chinese Ministry, March 7, 2009, http://www.steel.org/AM/Template.cfm?Section=20096&CONTENTID=31225&TEMPLATE=/CM/ContentDisplay.cfm; World Steel Association, Crude Steel Statistics, http://www.worldsteel.org/.

7. Jager-Waldau, Arnulf, European Commission Directorate General, Joint Research Center's Renewable Energy Unit in "PV Status Report 2008, Research, Solar Cell Production and Market Implementation of Photovoltaics," (EUR 23604 EN) September 2008, located at http://re.jrc.ec.europa.eu/refsys/pdf/PV%20Report%202008.pdf.

8. Krogsgaard, Per; Madsen, Birger T., BTM Consult ApS, "International Wind Energy Development World Market Update 2009 Forecast 2009-2013," March 25, 2009, http://www.btm.dk.

9. "World Machine Tool Output and Consumption Survey" from the Metalworking Insiders' Report, http://www.gardnerweb.com/consump/survey.html.

10. U.S. International Trade Commission, "Certain Textile Articles: Travel Goods of Textile Materials" (Investigation No. 332-480, USITC Publication 3957), October 2007, 26 pages, located at http://hotdocs.usitc.gov/docs/pubs/332/pub3957.pdf.

11. Certain Textile Articles: Performance Outerwear, Investigation Number 332-479, USITC Publication 3937, July 2007, http://www.usitc.gov/publications/pub3937.pdf.

12. Johnson, David, President and CEO, Summitville Tile, in testimony before the United States-China Economic and Security Review Commission hearing "The Impact of U.S.-China Trade and Investment on Key Manufacturing Sectors," September 23, 2004.

13. "The Hidden Backbone of U.S. Manufacturing: Weakening Under Chemical Cost and Supply Pressures," by the National Association of Manufacturers' Manufacturing Institute and AMR Research, 2007, http://www.nam.org/~/media/Files/s_nam/docs /238700/ 238607.PDF.ashx. The 80 chemical plant figure was from a press statement accompanying the report by NAM President John Engler dated May 8, 2007: http://www.nam.org/AboutUs/TheManufacturingInstitute /CenterforManufacturing ResearchandInnovation/TheCostsStudies.aspx?DID=%7BD66FBFF7-25C2-4901-9B27-439E8EEE3915%7.

14. World Fab Forecast is published by the Semiconductor Equipment and Materials International and Strategic Marketing Associates, http://www.scfab.com/index.php. See also remarks by Thomas Howell, partner, Dewey Ballantine, before the House Small Business Committee, October 16, 2003, "Is America Losing its Lead in High-Tech: Implications for the U.S. Defense Base," http://republicans.smbiz.house.gov/hearings/108th/2003/ 031016 /howell.asp.

15. Shirer, Michael, public relations director, IDC; first-quarter 2009 data is avaliable at http://www.idc.com/getdoc.jsp?containerId=prUS21821309.

16. U.S. Department of Commerce, "Employment Changes in U.S. Food Manufacturing: The Impact of Sugar Prices," http://ita.doc.gov/media/Publications/pdf/sugar06.pdf.

17. Halla, Brian, speaking before the "Innovation Leadership Forum," sponsored in September 2005 by the International Electronics Manufacturing Initiative (iNEMI) in Herndon, Va.

18. U.S.-China Economic and Security Review Commission hearing April 24-25, 2008, "Chinese Seafood: Safety and Trade Issues," http://www.uscc.gov.

19. DiMicco, Dan, speaking before the Westside Industrial Retention and Expansion Network (WIRE-Net) in Cleveland, Ohio, and its Northeast Ohio Campaign for American Manufacturing Conference, November 2006.

20. "The China Effect, Assessing the Impact on the U.S. Economy of Trade and Investment With China," U.S.-China Business Council, 2006, http://www.uschina.org.

21. Engdahl, William, August 2, 2008, "The Real State of the U.S. Economy," http://www.globalresearch.ca/index.php?context=va&aid=9728.

22. 2008 Financial Report of the U.S. Government, from the Department of Treasury and the Office of Management & Budget, December 2008, www.fms.treas.gov/fr/index.html.

23. Nordan, Matthew, president of Lux Research Inc., New York, N.Y., before the House

Science Committee's subcommittee on research hearing "Nanotechnology: Where Does the U.S. Stand?" June 29, 2005.

24. Economy, Elizabeth, director of Asia Studies, Council on Foreign Relations, at a hearing of the United States- China Economic and Security Review Commission, February 2-3, 2006, on "Major Internal Challenges Facing the Chinese Leadership."

25. Scott, Bruce, professor of business administration, School of Business, Harvard University before the House Committee on Science and Technology's subcommittee on investigations and oversight, May 22, 2008, hearing on "American Decline or Renewal?"

26. U.S.-China Economic and Security Review Commission hearing on "China's Impact on the North Carolina Economy: Winners and Losers," September 6, 2007, http://www.uscc.gov/hearings/2007hearings/transcripts/sept_6/sept_06_07_trans.pdf.

27. *Global Location Trends Report* is produced annually by IBM Global Business Services division using the company's Global Investment Locations Database which tracks 70,000 investment projects since 2003. The database is maintained by IBM-Plant Location International. The 2008 report is located at http://www-935.ibm.com/services/us/gbs/bus/pdf/gbl03005-usen-00hr.pdf.

28. "China Overtakes U.S. As World's Leading Exporter of Information Technology Goods," OECD, December 12, 2005: http://www.oecd.org/document/8/0,3343, en_2649_33757_35833096_1_1_1_1,00.html.

29. Preeg, Ernest, *China's Surging Trade Surplus Being Driven By High-Tech Manufactured Exports; Policy Consequences of the Growing Imbalance* (Publication ER-615), 2006, Manufacturers Alliance/MAPI.

30. O'Shaughnessy, Brian, chairman, Revere Copper Products Inc., http://www.reverecopper. com/pdf/MyCompanyCountry.pdf.

31. Meier, John, CEO of Libbey Glass, Inc., Toledo, Ohio, in testimony on January 30, 2007, before a hearing of the House Committee on Ways and Means on "Trade and Globalization."

32. James Copland before the House Committee on Science and Technology hearing on "American Decline or Renewal?" May 22, 2008, in testimony titled "U.S. Government's Uncompetitive Manufacturing Policy Hinders Economic Growth in North Carolina."

33. O'Shaughnessy, Brian, chairman, Revere Copper Products Inc., "Why the USA Is Getting Its Ass Kicked in International Trade," http://www.reverecopper.com.

34. Gomory, Ralph, president, Alfred P. Sloan Foundation, in testimony before the House Committee on Science and Technology's subcommittee on investigations and oversight in a hearing held May 22, 2008.

35. Summers, Lawrence, professor, Harvard University, "America Needs to Make a New Case for Trade," *Financial Times*, April 27, 2008.

36. Engler, John, president, National Association of Manufacturers, speaking at the 2008 National Summit on American Competitiveness in Chicago, Ill., sponsored by the U.S. Department of Commerce.

37. International Trade Commission's Investigation No. 731-TA-1058, "Wooden Bedroom Furniture From China," http://www.usitc.gov/trade_remedy/731_ad_701_cvd/ investigations/2003/wooden_bedroom_furniture/finalphase.htm.

38. Lighthizer, Robert, in testimony at the House Ways and Means subcommittee on trade, August 2, 2007, hearing on "Legislation Related to Trade with China," http://waysandmeans.house.gov/hearings.asp?formmode=view&id=6307.

39. Mann, James, School of Advanced International Studies, Johns Hopkins University, Washington, D.C., at a hearing of the U.S.-China Economic and Security Review Commission, "U.S.-China Relationship: Economics and Security in Perspective," February 1-2, 2007, http://www.uscc.gov/hearings/2007hearings/hr07_02_1_2.php.

40. Lieberthal, Kenneth, senior director for Asia Affairs at the National Security Council, as quoted in the Economic Policy Institute report, "Costly Trade With China," June 2007, http://www.edp.org/content.cfm/bp188.

41. Thompson, Robert L., Gardner Chair in Agricultural Policy, University of Illinois, Urbana-Champaign and visiting scholar at Federal Reserve Bank of Chicago in the

Chicago Fed Letter, March, 2007, "Globalization and The Benefits of Trade," http://www.chicagofed.org/ publications/fedletter/cflmarch2007_236.pdf.

42. Former Employees of BMC Software Inc. v. the United States Secretary of Labor, (Slip Op. 06-132), U.S. Court of International Trade.

43. Morgan, Frank, attorney for White & Case, LLP, in testimony before the House Science and Technology subcommittee on investigations and oversight, U.S. House of Representatives, June 24, 2008.

44. Rosen, Howard, visiting fellow, Peterson Institute for International Economic and executive director of the Trade Adjustment Assistance Coalition, before the House Science and Technology subcommittee on investigation and oversight, June 24, 2008, "Designing a National Strategy for Responding to Economic Dislocation."

45. U.S. Department of Treasury's *Semiannual Report on International Economic and Exchange Rate Policies*, May 2008, http://www.treasury.gov/offices/international-affairs/economic-exchange-rates/.

46. Bernanke, Ben, at the Chinese Academy of Social Sciences, Beijing, China, December 15, 2006, in a speech entitled "The Chinese Economy: Progress and Challenges," www.federalreserve.gov/newsevents/speech/Bernanke20061215a.htm.

47. Georgia Institute of Technology's bi-annual "High-Tech Indicators," January 2008, http://tpac.gatech.edu/.

48. "Global Corporate Capital Flows, 2008/09 to 2013/14, A Study of the Investment Intentions of Companies in 15 Countries Around the World," KPMG, 28 pages, http://www.kpmg.com/SiteCollectionDocuments/Global_Corporate_Capital_Flows.pdf.

49. Port Import Export Reporting Service (PIERS), the *Journal of Commerce*, "Special Report: Top 100 Importers and Exporters," May 26, 2008, Vol. 9 Issue 21.

50. The Charlie Rose Show, November 8, 2007, http://www.charlierose.com.

51. *Information Technology Manufacturing and Competitiveness, Sustaining the Nation's Innovation Ecosystems*, 2004, from the President's Council of Advisors on Science and Technology, http://www.ostp.gov/pdf/finalpcastitmanuf_reportpackage.pdf.

52. *Approaches to Improve the Competitiveness of the U.S. Business Tax System for the 21st Century*, Office of Tax Policy, U.S. Department of Treasury, December 20, 2007, http://www.treas.gov/press/releases/reports/hp749_approachesstudy.pdf.

53. National Science Board letter accompanying the *Science and Engineering Indicators* report: http://www.nsf.gov/statistics/siend08/.

54. Government Accountability Office, *Department of Energy: Key Challenges Remain for Developing and Deploying Advanced Energy Technologies To Meet Future Needs* (GAO-07-106), http://www.gao.gov/new.items/d07106.pdf.

55. National Research Council's Board on Science, Technology and Economic Policy, *Aeronautics Innovation: NASA's Challenges and Opportunities*, Stephen A. Merrill, editor, 2006, http://fermat.nap.edu/books/0309101883/html/.

56. Borrus, Michael, general partner, XSeed Capital, before a hearing of the House Science and Technology Committee's technology and innovation subcommittee, February 15, 2007, "The National Institute of Standards and Technology's Role in Supporting Economic Competitiveness in the 21st Century." http://science.house.gov/publications/hearings_markups_details.aspx? NewsID=1271.

57. Hylton, Todd, director of the Center for Advanced Materials and Nanotechnology, SAIC, before the Senate Commerce Committee hearing on "Developments in Nanotechnology," February 15, 2006.

58. *An Assessment of the United States Measurement System: Addressing Measurement Barriers to Accelerate Innovation*, (NIST Special Publication 1048), http://usms.nist.gov.

59. Williams, Stanley, testifying at a hearing of the House Science and Technology subcommittee on technology and innovation on "NIST's Role in Supporting Economic Competitiveness in the 21st Century," February 15, 2007.

60. Information Technology & Innovation Foundation, *Expanding the Research and Development Tax Credit To Drive Innovation, Competitiveness and Prosperity*," April 2, 2007, www.itif.org.

61. Banister, Judith, Beijing Javelin Investment Consulting Company, *Manufacturing & Employment Compensation in China*, for the U.S. Department of Labor, Bureau of Labor Statistics, November 2005, http://www.bls.gov/fls/chinareport.pdf.

62. Banister, Judith, director of global demographics, The Conference Board, "Manufacturing In China Today: Employment and Compensation," September 2007, EPWP #07-01, http://www.conference-barod.org/economics.

63. Jiang, Yuan; Liu, Yaodong; McGuckin, Robert; Spiegelman, Matthew; and Xu, Jianyi, in The Conference Board report *China's Experience with Productivity and Jobs* (Report Number R-1352-04-RR), June 2004.

64. Economic Policy Institute, *The China Trade Toll*, July 30, 2008, http://www.epi.org/content.cfm/bp219.

65. The Trusted IC Accreditation Program has 17 suppliers accredited to provide "trusted" components to DOD, as of April 2009. The supplier list is located at http://www.dmea.osd.mil/docs/AccreditedSuppliers.pdf. The Defense Trusted Integrated Circuits Strategy is run by the Defense Microelectronics Activity, http://www.dmea.osd.mil/trustedic.html.

66. *Critical Program Information Protection Instruction* (DODI 5200.39), July 16, 2008, http://www.dtic.mil/whs/directives/corres/pdf/520039p.pdf.

67. Hartwick, Thomas, chairman, Advisory Group on Electron Devices, at a hearing of the House Committee on Small Business, "Is America Losing its Lead in High-Tech? Implications for the U.S. Defense Industrial Base," October 16, 2003.

68. Department of Defense's Defense Science Board Task Force on High Performance Microchip Supply, February 2005, http://www.acq.osd.mil/dsb/reports/2005-02-HPMS_Report_Final.pdf.

69. 2009 Defense Authorization Bill (S-3001), Section 218.

70. Houseman, Susan, Upjohn Institute, *Outsourcing, Offshoring and Productivity Measurement in U.S. Manufacturing*, http://www.upjohninst.org/publications/wp/06-130.pdf.

71. Houseman, Susan, Upjohn Institute for Employment Research, *Outsourcing, Offshoring and Productivity Measurement in U.S. Manufacturing*, Revised Edition, February 2007.

72. Williams, John, "Shadow Government Statistics," http://www.shadowstats.com/.

73. In the Food, Conservation and Energy Act of 2008 (HR-2419), commonly referred to as the "Farm Bill" that passed the House and Senate on May 22, 2008, Customs and Border Protection was told in a special "Sense of Congress" provision (Sec. 15422) to look into the issue regarding importers' use of the first-sale rule. CBP started collecting information in September 2008, on whether importers were claiming value based on the first-sale or last-sale price prior to exportation of merchandize to the United States. Customs will provide this information to the International Trade Commission, which will produce a report after a year.

74. *The Changing Nature of Corporate Global Restructuring: The Impact of Production Shifts on Jobs in the U.S., China, and Around the Globe*, prepared for the United States-China Economic and Security Review Commission by Dr. Kate Bronfenbrenner of Cornell University and Dr. Stephanie Luce of the University of Massachusetts, Amherst, October 2004, http://www.uscc.gov/researchpapers/2004/cornell_u_mass_report.pdf.

75. Pritchard, David; MacPherson, Alan, Canada-United States Trade Center, State University of New York in Buffalo, *Strategic Destruction of the North American and European Commercial Aircraft Industry: Implications of a System Integration Business Model*, http://www.custac.buffalo.edu /content/documents/OccPaper35.pdf.

2. The Evolution of U.S. Trade Policy

Clyde Prestowitz
Kate Heidinger
Economic Policy Institute

From a fragile and uncertain start at the dawn of the 19th century, when many key leaders like Thomas Jefferson opposed industrialization, American manufacturing rose to global dominance by the end of World War II. As the post-war world was being created in 1948, U.S. manufacturers dominated virtually every industry and were at the leading edge of most technologies. This did not occur by chance. Rather, it was the result of specific industrial policies aimed for nearly 150 years at developing a strong manufacturing base as the main engine of America's rise to wealth and power.

These policies included a variety of industry promotion subsidies, extensive public investment in industrial infrastructure, and high tariffs that protected infant U.S. manufacturing industries from foreign competition. Partly as a result of these polices and especially as a result of the destruction of much of the rest of the world's industry during the war, not only did American manufacturing reach a commanding position, but the entire American economy became the overwhelmingly dominant economy. Indeed, by 1948, it alone accounted for over 50 percent of global GDP.

At this critical moment in history, with the Cold War just beginning and economic leadership assured, the focus of American leaders shifted from economic development to containing Communism and spreading capitalism and democracy around the world. The captains of newly dominant industries also shifted from demanding protection to calling for more open world markets. Finally, the mainstream of economic thinking reacted strongly against the protectionism of the Great Depression period.

The result was a dramatic shift in U.S. economic policies. Washington turned from protectionism to free trade while promoting domestic consumption-led growth that would turn America into the world's consumer of last resort. Not only did this mean throwing America's markets open to imports, it also entailed promoting the transfer of U.S. manufacturing abroad. These policies included many elements that put American manufacturing at a long-term disadvantage and eventually led to its relative decline from 27 percent of U.S. GDP in 1968 to 11 percent today. This decline, in turn, has contributed substantially to the chronic, large deficits that have come to characterize the current U.S. and global economies, to large declines in high-wage employment, to stagnation of R&D spending and investment and to the financial crisis that broke out in September 2008.

This chapter will review the historical development of U.S. manufacturing and will especially examine the shifts in U.S. economic and trade policies after World War II and how they led to this relative decline of U.S. manufacturing and to its collateral consequences.

The First 150 Years

After independence, debate raged in the new United States over whether or not to promote development of manufacturing. Alexander Hamilton's 1791 *Report on Manufactures* argued in favor, emphasizing manufacturing's potential for increasing national productivity and for assuring security. At this early stage of America's history, agriculture was considered by many to be the country's most promising industry, because of the vast tracts of land and natural resources with which the nation had been endowed.

Hamilton, however, argued that though manufacturing had not yet reached agriculture's level of productivity, over the long run productivity growth through mechanization would yield far greater wealth than commodity agriculture. But for that growth to take place, he insisted, some public support was necessary. Within the shelter of protective tariffs, the infant industries of the United States could develop and gain the skills and know-how necessary to compete with their more advanced European counterparts. Hamilton was joined in his thinking by George Washington who famously wore only domestically made suits and ate and drank only food and wine produced in America. Jefferson and Franklin, however, favored the virtues of agriculture and the benefits of free trade that had been emphasized by Adam Smith whose revolutionary book, *The Wealth of Nations*, had coincidentally been published in that revolutionary year of 1776.

The outcome of the debate was determined by the War of 1812, which the United States almost lost for lack of ability to make weapons and to provide for most of its necessities in the face of British embargoes.

Determined to reduce dependence on British trade in the wake of the war, Congress levied the first protective tariff in 1816, placing a 30 percent duty on iron and a 25 percent duty on cotton and woolen textiles.[1] American leaders then developed what became known as the "American System," a concerted program to establish the United States as a self-sufficient power and as a manufacturing giant in the world market. Over the course of the 19th century, U.S. policymakers supported massive investments in railroads, ports, national telegraph lines and other infrastructure and imposed high tariffs on certain targeted imports as part of their drive to build a strong and truly national economy. The Tariff Act of 1828 raised the average rate on dutiable goods to 61.7 percent.[2] From 1833 to 1842, Henry Clay engineered the gradual shift in import valuation from foreign to domestic prices, which provided domestic producers in many sectors with an even greater advantage. Those protective measures had a definite effect on manufactured imports. While U.S. exports of tobacco and cotton shot up almost 1,300 percent, manufactured goods as a percentage of imports fell from 56.3 percent in 1821 to 48.6 percent in 1860 and 29.5 percent by 1880.[3]

After the Civil War and the Morrill Tariff of 1868, the U.S. government began to subsidize and otherwise support the growth of a national rail system. The impact of efficient and expansive railway systems on the development of U.S. industry cannot be overestimated. By connecting state and local markets more closely than ever before they created a truly national market with unprecedented potential for the achievement of economies of scale in manufacturing industries. High tariffs encouraged domestic producers to realize this potential. Successive presidents supported an import tariff not just for its ability to bolster U.S. industries but for the benefits it brought to workers. Lincoln, who could as easily be called the "Great Protector" as the "Great Emancipator," wrote that, "the abandonment of the protective policy by the American government must result in the increase of both useless labor, and idleness; and so, in proportion, must produce want and ruin among our people."[4] Theodore Roosevelt proclaimed at greater length:

> "These 40-odd years have been the most prosperous years this Nation has ever seen; more prosperous years than any other nation has ever seen. Beyond question this prosperity could not have come if the American people had not possessed the necessary thrift, energy and business intelligence to turn their vast material resources to account. But it is no less true that it is our eco-

nomic policy as regards the tariff and finance which has enabled us as a nation to make such good use of the individual capacities of our citizens, and the natural resources of our country. Every class of our people is benefited by the protective tariff."[5]

Between 1871 and 1913, U.S. tariffs never fell below 38 percent.[6] During this period, manufacturers expanded from relatively small organizations to much larger national companies. Indeed, between 1880 and 1900, the United States surpassed Great Britain in percentage of total world manufacturing output.[7] And from 1890 until the Great Depression, the U.S. achieved heretofore unseen GDP growth of 3.6 percent per year.[8]

The early years of the 20th century saw the beginning of a historic shift in trade. While cotton had long been America's leading export, machinery, iron and steel industries began to challenge with exports of hundreds of millions of dollars of goods. The automobile also began to play a significant role. This era saw the introduction by Ford Motor Company of the assembly line that revolutionized production and made America the world's leading auto maker. The United States was also moving up the value-added ladder to increasingly advanced products. Airplanes were the next big step. As World War I began to rage across the Atlantic in 1915, President Wilson formed the National Advisory Committee on Aeronautics (NACA). Despite the fact that the airplane had been invented in the United States, the country was beginning to fall behind its European counterparts in aeronautics. The NACA was designed to undertake and promote aeronautical research in conjunction with private and academic entities and was based on models already in existence in the UK, France, Germany and Russia. After the war, NACA stopped researching strictly on a military basis and began cooperating more closely with commercial air interests, setting the stage for commercial airline production and service industries.

The period from 1918 to 1929 saw more pro-manufacturing action from the U.S. government. In 1919, the U.S. Navy joined with General Electric to found the Radio Corporation of America (RCA), while in 1922 Congress reestablished pre-war tariffs at 38.5 percent with the Fordney-McCumber Act. This domestic protectionism did not seem to hinder a boom in U.S. exports of manufactured goods. By 1929, U.S. exports of machinery had reached $606.8 million per year; automobiles and parts were at $541.4 million; while iron and steel exports were worth $200 million. Together, these three categories comprised more than a quarter of total exports.[9] The Great Depression, of course, took a terrible toll, but with the outbreak of war in 1939, America became the "Arsenal of Democracy" and over the next five years built the manufacturing and industrial base that won the war and made America the world's leading economy and the dominant world power.

1948: A New World Structure

The end of World War II brought with it a revolution in U.S. domestic and international economic policy. While the rest of the industrialized world had been flattened by war, America stood alone as an island of prosperity. American industry and the American economy had become more dominant than those of Great Britain or any other country had ever been. As a result of the use of advanced technology and manufacturing techniques and the realization of unprecedented economies of scale, American labor was the world's most productive. As a result, U.S. manufacturers could be the low-cost producer while paying the highest wages. Beyond economic dominance, America had also, of course, become the sole possessor of the atomic bomb and the leading military power.

This radical change in geopolitical and economic position led to an equally radical change in foreign and national economic policies. Three key factors led to an about-face in the industrial and mercantilist policies that had long powered the drive of U.S. manufacturing to global primacy. First was the combination of the outbreak of the Cold War and the need to fight it in part by preventing the further impoverishment of the war-ravaged regions of the world by fostering the rebuilding of their productive capacity and the sale of their goods in the only existing healthy market — the United States. Second was the shift of economic thinking toward more liberal open market views in reaction to the competitive protectionism that was thought to have exacerbated the Great Depression.

Finally, as the dominant player in nearly every industry, U.S. corporate leaders felt no need for protection. Instead they, along with U.S. labor unions, pressed for more open world markets that they could exploit. Indeed, the belief that U.S. manufacturing industries were invulnerable became the ruling policy assumption. The upshot of all this was an about-face to new policies that embraced free trade and global integration. Thus, the United States orchestrated the creation of the International Monetary Fund, the World Bank and the General Agreement on Tariffs and Trade (GATT), which would later become the World Trade Organization. The objective was to remove barriers to trade, create stable international monetary institutions and stimulate growth in war-torn and underdeveloped countries.

This shift had actually been foreshadowed by the New Deal. When President Roosevelt came into office in 1933, he appointed Cordell Hull as Secretary of State. Hull's belief that free trade could not only stimulate greater economic growth but also lead to democratization and peace among nations was a powerful vision that came to inspire many post-war leaders. Hull's experience during the First World War cemented his views in favor of free trade. Many years later, in his memoirs, he wrote that, "When the war came in 1914, I was very soon impressed with two points. …I saw that you could not separate the idea of commerce from the idea of war and peace." If a free-trade regime could be implemented globally, Hull continued, "one country would not be deadly jealous of another and the living standards of all countries might rise, thereby eliminating the economic dissatisfaction that breeds war, [and] we might have a reasonable chance for peace."[10] Hull envisioned a future peaceful and prosperous world in which international trade took place free from any barriers and drove the global economy out of its deep recession by expanding markets. This in turn would create a solid foundation for world peace.

From 1934 to 1947, Hull led the completion of 32 bilateral and multilateral trade agreements.[11] This represented a dramatic turnaround from the preceding 150 years, during which essentially no new trade agreements had been signed. With the end of World War II, this tentative counter movement became the driver of U.S. policy.

The International Monetary Fund and the Dollar

The first order of business in building the new global order was the reestablishment of a post-war financial system centered on the International Monetary Fund. In the 1920s, most countries adhered to the gold standard. During the Great Depression, that peg was abandoned in favor of floating currencies and competitive devaluations. During the war, the dollar emerged as the de facto dominant international reserve currency and unit of account. With the creation of the IMF, a world dollar-gold standard was established under which the dollar was to be convertible to gold (only by other governments) at $35 per ounce and all other currencies were pegged at a fixed rate to the dollar. The initial rates were set to create a strong dollar in order to favor war ravaged non-U.S. producers. The fact that the dollar was the world's key currency meant that for world trade to recover there had to be an adequate supply of dollars. The best way to get dollars to the rest of the world was for America to buy lots of stuff which, of course, was paid for in dollars. Thus, along with the Marshall Plan, there was a strong U.S. government emphasis on buying abroad and opening the U.S. market in order to increase the supply of dollars circulating in the world. There were provisions for adjusting the exchange rate along with shifts in various nations' relative national productivity, but they were never used.

The Beginnings of the GATT Trade Regime

To oversee international trade, U.S. and British leaders initially envisioned a comprehensive International Trade Organization (ITO) that would oversee trade, investment and other aspects of international commerce. This ITO never came to fruition, however, because the U.S. Congress failed to ratify its charter, citing concerns over loss of sovereignty. But part of the ITO was its General Agreement on Tariffs and Trade (GATT). This was approved and became the de facto main institution for governing world trade. Nine countries — Australia, Belgium, Canada, Cuba, France, Luxembourg, the Netherlands, the United Kingdom and the United States, representing 80 percent of world trade — signed on to the original treaties.

The objective of GATT was to reduce tariffs, which were considered the main barrier to free trade. The two pillars of GATT negotiations were most favored nation (MFN) status and the concept of "national treatment." When a country joined GATT and achieved MFN status, it enjoyed concessions made by any other member regardless of with whom the original agreement had been made. For example, when U.S. trade negotiators made a specific tariff reduction for British goods and then signed on to GATT, the U.S. had actually reduced tariffs on goods from eight different countries without those countries necessarily reciprocating. National Treatment afforded a country all the rights and privileges of a national. While this seemed fair, we will see that problems arise when one country provides a much higher level of protection and rights to its nationals than another. These two concepts, fair-minded in theory, would be, in practice, the source a major free-rider problem within GATT over the next 60 years.

The GATT's project to reduce global tariffs proceeded in a series of negotiating rounds. In the first round (Geneva Round), the major U.S. goal was to bargain away what remained of the Smoot-Hawley tariff of 1930 in exchange for the end of the British colonial preference system. Congress had authorized the president and the U.S. trade negotiators to reduce tariffs up to 50 percent in negotiations. But while U.S. negotiators offered the approved tariff deductions, the UK demurred on dismantling its preference for its colonies and former colonies. In the immediate post-war era, a "trade not aid" attitude pervaded U.S. policymakers.

The asymmetric agreement with the UK in 1948 reflected this mindset, generously offering concessions without reciprocity because such an agreement would help the British rebuild industries damaged in the war. President Truman and President Eisenhower after him, as well as most economists, assumed that U.S. industrial and technological dominance would continue unfettered for many years into the future. The "aid packages" that comprised trade agreements were not seen as giving Europe (and later Japan) any unfair advantage. Instead, they were considered strategic consolidations of a post-war coalition that could stand up to the Communist bloc and help rebuild the war-ravaged economies of Europe and Asia.

No one seemed to understand that by making the economies of scale of the U.S. market available to overseas producers while obtaining no reciprocal market access, U.S. negotiators were creating a structure that would increasingly put U.S. manufacturers at a disadvantage. In the wake of the Geneva Round, the United States saw a rapid increase in imports, although trade still comprised only a small portion of total U.S. GDP. This increase troubled policymakers because of the adverse effect of cheap foreign imports on domestic industries. As a result, the subsequent Dillon and Annecy Rounds saw little reduction of U.S. tariffs because Congress reined in the State Department's ability to negotiate by not granting the executive branch authority to negotiate reduced tariffs.

When John F. Kennedy came into office in 1961, he placed huge emphasis on freer trade and implemented policies that led to renewed trade negotiation in the 1960s. The Kennedy Round, from 1964 to 1967, produced a slightly more equitable outcome for most GATT participants. Most of the involved industrialized countries agreed to reduce tariffs by 36 percent to 39 percent.[12] This negotiating round also brought more developing nations to the GATT negotiating table. To the participating developing nations, the United States made $700 million in concessions, most of which came in the form of 50 percent tariff reductions. In return, the developing nations only conceded $200 million altogether, most of which came in tariff freezes and not actual tariff reductions.

In the end, the Kennedy Round did practically nothing to open emerging markets to American exports while exposing the U.S. to a flood of inexpensive imported goods. Average ad valorem on imports fell from 12.2 percent to 8.6 percent.[13] The first 25 years of GATT saw continued asymmetry in terms of reciprocal trade access, with European and Japanese companies capturing the economies of scale that for many years belonged solely to American producers. It is important to note here a fundamental difference of opinion among economists. For many years after 1948, the majority of economists believed that free trade, even if is unilateral, was win-win. These asymmetries of market access didn't matter, nor did the composition of trade. Other economists argued that because of economies of scale and imperfect competition, trade is not always win-win, and that nonreciprocal access does matter. This view, now gaining strength, was suppressed during most of the Golden Era between 1945 and 1972.

Japan and GATT

With the outbreak of the Korean War, rebuilding the Japanese economy became a preeminent strategic goal of American foreign policy. A democratic, capitalist Japan could serve as an "unsinkable aircraft carrier" for U.S. military forces and an engine of growth that could keep East Asian countries from falling into the hands of the communists. Japan and the United States began negotiating in 1955 to bring Japan into GATT against the wishes of the UK and other GATT members. President Eisenhower and his advisers considered the inclusion of Japan in GATT as essential to promoting democracy and growth in the country, though they never imagined Japan would become a major economic player. For example, the head of the U.S. team, C. Thayer White, told the Japanese negotiators outright not to invest in an auto industry because they would have no chance of competing with the already well-established U.S. companies. Japan refused to oblige with most of the concessions requested by the United States, saying that the sectors involved were considered strategic and under GATT could receive protection to evolve past the infant industry stage. In the end, Japan gave away very little and the U.S. conceded much.

Japan's strategy proved very successful. In just five years, Japan's

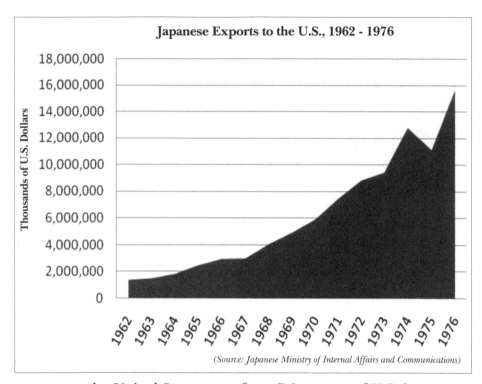

Japanese Exports to the U.S., 1962 - 1976

(Source: Japanese Ministry of Internal Affairs and Communications)

exports to the United States grew from 7.6 percent of U.S. imports to 15.4 percent. During the Kennedy Round, headway was made in reducing industrialized countries' tariffs. Japan, however, conceded essentially nothing and was able to simply sit back and reap the benefits of most favored nation status. By giving nothing away and taking advantage of the other negotiating parties' lowered tariffs, Japan made significant headway in the U.S. market. Prior to enactment of the new tariff reductions, Japanese exports to America exceeded U.S. exports to Japan by 17 percent. By 1975, that number was 50 percent.

The Golden Era

Despite the creation of an increasingly unbalanced trade situation, the period from the end of World War II until 1972 has come to be known as the Golden Era of economic growth and stability. Sparked by the Marshall Plan and the investment of U.S. companies in continental markets as they tried to get behind European trade barriers, Europe recovered and achieved extraordinary growth for a number of years. These were the years of the German Wirtschaftswunder and the Japanese economic miracle. Americans also never had it so good, as GDP and

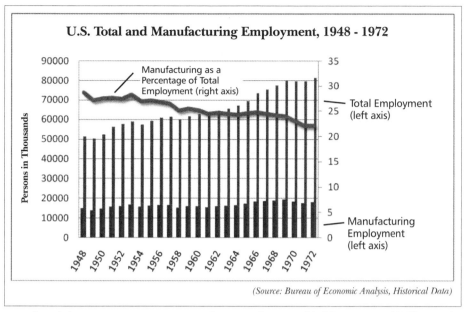

U.S. Total and Manufacturing Employment, 1948 - 1972

(Source: Bureau of Economic Analysis, Historical Data)

productivity grew at a compound annual rate of 3.67 percent.[14] The U.S. manufacturing sector remained the world leader in almost every respect. Europe and Japan did not yet produce goods that could compete seriously with U.S. manufactured products within the country's domestic market. From 1945 until 1960, manufacturing employment grew to its

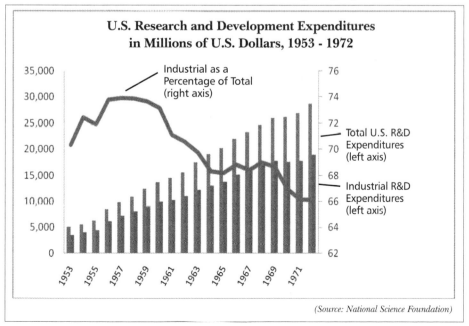

U.S. Research and Development Expenditures in Millions of U.S. Dollars, 1953 - 1972

(Source: National Science Foundation)

81

peak of 26 percent of total U.S. employment and 27 percent of total GDP.[15] Both the U.S. government and corporations themselves maintained high levels of R&D funding throughout the period. Riding high on new technologies and production techniques, manufacturing was becoming more and more efficient. Increased productivity translated into rising real wages, which doubled.

Labor unions were powerful. Total U.S. union participation hovered in the 27 percent to 30 percent range and, as a result, the Golden Era was notable not just for high growth rates, but also for the equitable returns to that growth. Strong unions meant that stakeholders — employees and communities associated with a company — had a greater influence on corporate structure and function and helped ensure that returns were more evenly distributed throughout the company. The 25-year period from 1950 to 1975 saw an unprecedented degree of income equality that has deteriorated in the 30 years since.

The hallmark of this period was the drive by American policymakers to increase domestic consumption. This entailed expanding available consumer credit, making mortgages cheaper for returning GIs in order to stimulate construction, as well as providing those same GIs with college educations. College educations ensured a growth in personal income afforded by higher-skill jobs, and higher incomes insured more consumer spending. While this proved a success in the short term, what became a consumption-led growth strategy sowed the seeds of later trouble for the U.S. economy, as we will see.

U.S. Manufacturing Wages, 1939 - 1972

Wages Per Hour, U.S. Dollars

(Source: Bureau of Labor Statistics)

U.S. Union Density As a Percentage of Total Population 1964 - 2007

(Source: Uniondata.com)

Shadows

While the average American saw a lot of sunshine during the post-war economic boom, a few shadows were already beginning to creep up on the U.S. economy. Europe and Japan had rapidly rebuilt their manufacturing industries into global competitors. Developing countries were also beginning to join the fray as low-cost producers of labor-intensive products. From 1950 to 1972, certain sectors — particularly textiles, steel and consumer electronics — began to face increasing pressure from foreign competition. The United States began negotiating voluntary restraint agreements (VRAs) in which another country (often Japan or Germany) would voluntarily limit its exports of certain goods to the United States. Another disturbing trend emerged from the GATT rounds: geopolitical considerations on the part of U.S. trade and State Department officials were taking precedence over the interests of key U.S. industries. A Cold War mentality permeated the U.S. government, and every effort was made to placate allies and encourage good relations. This appeasement included not just the negotiation of unequal trade agreements but a decided reluctance to enforce existing trade laws when faced with unfair trading practices by other countries.

These issues were compounded by the free-rider problem seen repeatedly in the GATT Rounds brought on by adherence to the ideas of most favored nation status and national treatment. Both developing and industrialized countries often conceded very little in formal negotiations, knowing that having already achieved MFN from the United States, they would benefit from whatever concessions were made. The national treatment standard also proved troublesome because one country often provided a much higher level of protection and rights to its nationals than another country. Every country wanted to be treated like an American in the U.S. market, but not every country treated its citizens and companies as well as the United States. This inevitably put U.S. companies at a disadvantage versus foreign competitors. The combination of a foreign policy-oriented executive branch and the free-rider problem exacerbated inequitable trade relations between countries and produced loud disapproval from Congress at the end of the Kennedy Round. The Senate Finance Committee, as quoted by Alfred Eckes, blamed not just foreign officials but also the U.S. executive branch:

> "Throughout most of the postwar era, U.S. trade policy has been the orphan of U.S. foreign policy. Too often the Executive has granted trade concessions to ac-

complish political objectives. Rather than conducting U.S. international economic relations on sound economic and commercial principles, the Executive has set trade and monetary policy in a foreign aid context. An example has been the Executive's unwillingness to enforce U.S. trade statutes in response to foreign unfair trade practices. By pursuing a soft trade policy, by refusing to strike swiftly and surely at foreign unfair trade practices, the Executive has actually fostered the proliferation of barriers to international commerce. The result of this misguided policy has been to permit and even to encourage discriminatory trading arrangements among trading nations....The existence of many significant tariff and nontariff barriers in foreign countries and the very small reductions in tariffs of some industrialized countries in the Kennedy Round may be attributed to the realization by certain countries that they could automatically receive all the benefits of the trade agreement without paying any of the costs."[16]

The Steel Example

From 1929 to 1958, the steel industry was the manufacturing sector that generated the largest portion of U.S. GNP. The industry was by nature very capital-intensive and concentrated in a relatively small number of large corporations. At the end of World War II, eight U.S. steel corporations represented 66 percent of all U.S. steel shipments, a statistic that increased to 75 percent by 1950.[17] During the war, U.S. steel production had reached record levels, reflecting the national and Allied need for planes, tanks and ships. By 1945, the United States maintained huge steel production capacities, much too large in proportion to postwar demand.

At the same time, the U.S. government was actively encouraging increased steel production in Germany as a matter of international security. France, associating increased manufacturing and steel production with possible rearmament, was deeply concerned with the situation and sought to closely integrate the French and German steel industries. The arrangement that evolved, the European Coal and Steel Community, closely linked French and German production under the auspices of European cooperation and joint funding and set the stage for the evolution of the European Union.[18] On the other side of the world, Japan was also taking steps to secure a place in the global steel trade. From a mid-war high of 7.5 million tons, Japanese steel production had dropped to 0.5 million tons by 1946. The newly reformed government made it a matter of national strategy to quickly revive the steel industry, beginning with loans and preferential tax treatment. In 1953, an export subsidy was enacted equal to 3 percent of export revenues. This subsidy increased to 4.5 percent over the next 12 years before being phased out in 1965.[19] During that time period, the steel industry expanded four-fold, more than meeting domestic demand. Steel exports grew at over 20 percent annually during the same period, making Japan the largest steel exporter in the world by 1969.[20] At the same time, Japan maintained a 15 percent import tariff on steel until 1967 when they conceded a 3 percent decrease in the Kennedy Round.[21]

In 1959, U.S. steel imports exceeded exports for the first time in over 100 years as foreign producers captured increasingly larger segments of the U.S. market. The American steel industry saw profits drop from 11.4 percent in 1957 to 6.2 percent in 1961. The U.S. government attempted several times to inject capital into the steel industry by rewriting industrial tax law and also negotiated voluntary export restraint agreements with Japan and West Germany. Nevertheless, by 1971, steel imports captured 17.9 percent of U.S. market share.[22] In the 1980s, the Reagan administration began implementing trigger price mechanisms in an effort to prevent Japanese and European producers from selling below cost in the U.S. market. This was just another instance of the pattern that repeated itself over and over again in the 1970s and 1980s.

The Dollar Float

The establishment of the dollar as the world's reserve currency allowed the United States to purchase imports in its own currency. In return, other countries could use those dollars to purchase U.S.-made goods. However, the transformation of the United States into the world's consumer of last resort combined with asymmetric market access pushed the country into a serious trade deficit by the early 1970s. This imbalance led to an accumulation of dollars in central banks around the world. This dollar accumulation drove up inflation rates worldwide and led foreign central banks to try and curb that inflation converting the dollars into the gold held at Fort Knox. As the U.S. gold supply steadily dropped, the dollar's peg to gold under the IMF currency regime came increasingly into question. Finally in 1972, President Nixon unilaterally cut the dollar's tie to gold. Henceforth, the United States would not redeem dollars for gold and the dollar would float in world currency markets as the first fiat currency.

The president's move eviscerated the currency system that had been in place since 1948. Foreign central banks were unable to continue converting dollars into gold, limiting their ability to control inflation or deal with the United States' balance-of-payments deficit. Faced with dismayed central bankers from around the world, Nixon's Secretary of Treasury John Connelly famously said, "The dollar is our currency, but it's your problem." Unable to sustain the current monetary system, the British Pound, German Deutschmark, Swiss Franc and the Japanese Yen also made the switch to fiat currencies in the next few years.

The Tokyo Round

In addition to floating the dollar, American policymakers saw the need for a new round of trade negotiations. The Tokyo Round began in 1973 with 99 participating countries, and finally ended in 1979. Developed countries agreed to a 33 percent tariff reduction on dutiable manufactured goods. For the United States, this meant reducing tariffs from 8.1 percent to 5.6 percent.[23] The major issue of the Tokyo Round, however, was the attempt finally to address non-tariff barriers. These non-tariff barriers included subsidies, product standards, government procurement and customs valuation among other things. The goal was to create a code that, despite the various national trade philosophies represented, would smooth over trade distortions not approached in previous tariff-centric negotiating rounds. Ultimately, developing nations failed to sign on to the code — only the European Community, the United States and Japan agreed. Even then, non-tariff barriers remained prevalent in the signing countries. Government procurement proved particularly disappointing, as the U.S. opened four times the amount of national procurement opportunities as the other participating nations.

The Tokyo Round focus on non-tariff barriers was primarily aimed at Japan. Despite having lowered tariffs, American and other nations' exporters were having great difficulty accessing the Japanese market while Japanese exporters were expanding rapidly in the global scene, particularly in the U.S. market. Going into the Tokyo Round negotiations with an $8.9-billion trade surplus and a current account surplus of $18.1 billion, the U.S. economic situation turned around completely. By the end of negotiations in 1980, the United States had a $35-billion trade deficit and a $15-billion current account deficit. During those seven years, much of the deficit accrued to OPEC as energy costs spiked. However, the trade deficit with Japan would grow by leaps and bounds during the 1980s.[24]

Japan and the 1980s

During the 1960s and 70s, the Japanese utilized high levels of government research funding, subsidized credit and provided tax credits for exporting companies to dominate the export market in consumer electronics. In contrast to the United States, the Japanese government played a key role in crafting Japan's post-war economic recovery. Japan's Ministry of International Trade and Industry (MITI) was given broad authority to work in conjunction with the private sector to develop new industries and capabilities and manage Japan's international economic policies.

To take just one example, MITI was instrumental in the development of the Japanese semiconductor industry. The effort began in earnest in the early 1960s, when American firms like IBM, Fairchild Semiconductor and Texas Instruments were the leaders in this emerging new high-tech sector. Instead of simply importing semiconductors from American companies, Japanese bureaucrats decided that the semiconductor industry represented the wave of the future — and hence Japan should develop its own capabilities in order both to avoid relying on foreign suppliers and to build up domestic expertise that would come with innovative new technologies. Japan wanted to capture the 'spillover effects' of leading-edge new technologies, and thus identified semiconductors as a strategic priority for the Japanese economy.

MITI launched its efforts to promote Japanese semiconductors by raising import tariffs against imported semiconductors and computers. When American companies like IBM sought to get around these tariffs by applying for permission to manufacture in Japan, MITI responded by insisting that IBM license its basic patents to 15 Japanese companies, and insisted that MITI be given authority over the IBM products that would be allowed to be manufactured and sold in the Japanese market. IBM could not introduce new models without the prior approval of MITI. Other American companies faced similar obstacles, and MITI often informally limited the market share of U.S. companies in Japanese markets in order to leave room for emerging Japanese producers.

Japanese firms like Fujitsu, Toshiba, Hitachi and others were granted preferential access to capital, tax breaks and other benefits to ease their entry into the new information technology sectors. MITI also organized industry-wide efforts to collaborate on research and development. With this combination of government support, subsidized capital and protection from foreign competition, within a few short years Japanese firms became major players in the global semiconductor industry. As they gained new skills and expertise, and their products became more competitive, Japanese producers expanded internationally, spreading out from the protected Japanese market to conquer new market share abroad.

By the 1980s, Japanese companies had a virtual monopoly on black and white TVs and VCRs. With the support of MITI, Japanese producers also moved into the computer and semiconductor industry. By 1980, Japanese semiconductor manufacturers had caught up to the leading American firms — not just in terms of the cost and quality of their products, but also in terms of their technological advancement. Nippon Telephone and Telegraph (NTT) was the first in the world to develop a 256K RAM processor, and by 1981, Japanese firms had captured 33 percent of the global market for semiconductors.[25] At the end of the 1980s, Japan held the largest export-to-import ratio in consumer electronics of any country in the world, exporting $58.3 billion and importing just $7.7 billion in 1987. In comparison, the United States exported $35.6 billion in consumer electronics compared to $53.5 billion in imports.[26] By 1985,

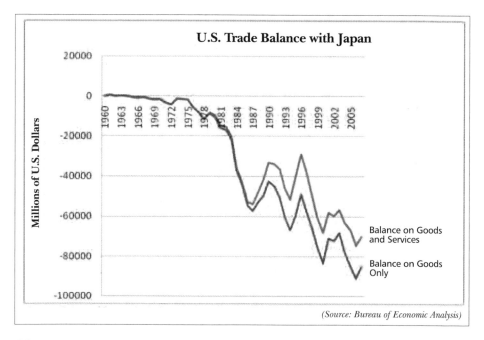

(Source: Bureau of Economic Analysis)

the United States was coping with a serious recession, a huge trade deficit of $121.8 billion and unemployment around 11 percent.[27] There was a popular call for action by the Reagan administration.

Leading up to 1985, President Reagan had negotiated some trade arrangements meant to correct the U.S. trade imbalance including a voluntary import restraint on automobiles with Japan in 1981. But even after three major (and three minor) trade negotiating rounds under GATT, asymmetrical access to markets still existed. By the end of the Reagan administration, U.S. imports had still risen 99 percent (a high proportion being Japanese goods) while exports had only grown by 43 percent. The administration continued to make the Cold War a much higher priority than achieving balanced trade — the free world coalition was maintained at the expense of taking action against unfair trade policies.

The Asian Tigers

The U.S. trade deficit at this time largely had to do with Japanese trade. However, the developing nations of the world, particularly the East Asian countries that pursued Japanese-style, export-led growth strategies, were beginning to play a larger role in the global economy and take up a growing proportion of the U.S. import market. In the wake of the Kennedy Round, several East Asian countries with low labor costs began recruiting global corporate investment. Countries like Singapore, Taiwan and Malaysia — following in the footsteps of Japan — developed export-led growth programs and enticed many U.S. corporations to invest and produce in their territory. They did this by offering free production facilities, lower costs, fewer regulations, capital grants and tax abatements. Labor-intensive industries like textiles, consumer electronics and computer parts began to move to the tax havens and special export zones cropping up in East Asia. Latin American countries like Mexico and Brazil were also attractive production locations, due to their closer proximity to the United States.

A series of oil shocks had driven up the price of production which, combined with high labor costs in the United States, made lower-wage countries extremely attractive. The East Asian countries like Taiwan and Singapore not only offered cheap labor but also actively worked to attract foreign investment and production facilities in advanced high-tech industries. This was in sharp contrast to the attitude of American officials as expressed by one leading government economist who quipped,

"Computer chips, potato chips; they're all chips!" There was no consideration within U.S. presidential administrations as to the strategic difference between producing high-tech, high value-added products and any other type of product. The movement of all types of high-tech production began to slowly move to less developed countries and widened the U.S. trade deficit even further. American manufacturing employment took serious hits in several key industries, with 100,000 jobs being lost in Silicon Valley alone.

Taiwan provides a great example of the strategic industrial policy embraced by the Asian Tigers. In the 1980s, the Taiwanese government, following in Japan's footsteps, targeted semiconductor production as key to the future of the Taiwanese economy. Government officials offered Morris Chang — an engineer born in China, educated and naturalized in the United States, and retired after a career at Texas Instruments — subsidized government funding to find a way to build a Taiwanese semiconductor industry. Chang came up with a brilliant idea — the semiconductor foundry.

Building production facilities was expensive for the manufacturers involved, a problem compounded by the cyclical nature of the semiconductor business. With funding from the Taiwanese government, Chang established the Taiwanese Semiconductor Manufacturing Corporation

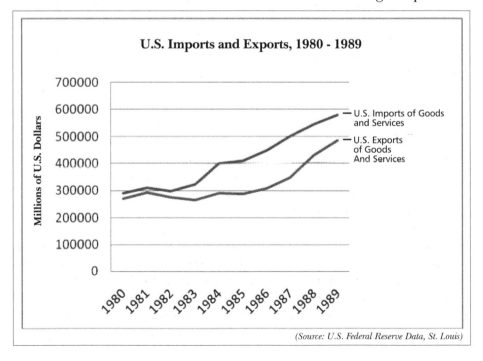

(Source: U.S. Federal Reserve Data, St. Louis)

(TSMC). When business was hot, companies like Intel and Texas Instruments could farm out production to TSMC instead of building a new production facility. Eventually, however, TSMC's business model became so popular that many foreign companies began designing semiconductors but not producing them; all the production had been moved to Taiwan.

The Plaza Accord and the Uruguay Round

With the U.S. trade deficit exploding and a recession threatening, in 1985, U.S. Treasury Secretary James Baker orchestrated a complex series of negotiations at the Plaza Hotel in New York that concluded on Sept. 22, 1985, in a deal very similar to the one President Nixon and Treasury Secretary Connelly had done at the Smithsonian Institute in August 1971. The United States, Japan, West Germany, France and the U.K. undertook to have their central banks intervene in international currency markets to engineer a gradual devaluation of the dollar. Adjusting the yen/dollar exchange rate was of particular importance to the negotiators. The Japanese Central Bank, in an effort to promote sustained Japanese exports, prevented the yen from appreciating as quickly as might be expected, considering Japan's strong trade position in relation to the United States. After the Plaza meeting, the yen had dropped from 238 to 128 yen to the dollar within three years.[28] The Plaza Accord engineered a short-lived boost in competitiveness in U.S. exports, but many countries continued to manage their currencies against the dollar and the U.S. trade deficit continued to grow.

As developing countries became more visible players in the global market, the Uruguay Round was aimed at integrating lower-income countries into the GATT. The round concluded in 1994 with the ratification of the World Trade Organization. The WTO was meant to replace the GATT and provide a permanent forum for trade negotiation and dispute settlement. Indeed, it was at long last the realization of the original ITO. The final treaty included agreements on previously unaddressed issues like anti-dumping measures, trade in services and intellectual property rights.

With the formation of the WTO came an unprecedented level of cooperation between developing and developed countries; developed nations agreed to phase out protection for industries that developing countries were most competitive in (textiles, agriculture) in exchange for recognition of intellectual property rights and other issues. The deals made essentially showed developed countries' willingness to allow labor-intensive, low value-added industries to move to lower-income countries in favor of developing their high-tech industries.

U.S. trade negotiators estimated that joining the WTO would open export markets and bring in nearly a $1 trillion in income over the coming decade. This guess was 525 percent higher than OECD's prediction, which was the next closest.[29] While those guesses were considerably off, the WTO did provide one important improvement which GATT lacked: a dispute settlement mechanism. Since 1994, the U.S. Trade Representative has been increasingly unwilling to address unfair trade practices. The table below shows the number of cases brought by the U.S. against other countries and other countries' suits against the U.S. Only four of the suits brought by the United States have been lost, with the other 55 cases being won or resolved to U.S. satisfaction. However, the Uruguay Round and the establishment of the WTO did nothing to solve the problem of free-riding, caused by abuses of most favored nation and national treatment status. Further, the export-led strategies adopted by the East Asian countries remained unaddressed despite the fact that such economies exacerbated the already asymmetric trading system.

WTO DISPUTES, 1994-Present	U.S. as Complaining Party	U.S. as Responding Party
Resolved without Litigation	26	19
Win for U.S.	29	15
Loss for U.S.	4	34
Source: USTR		

NAFTA

The North American Free Trade Agreement represented another part of U.S. policymakers' attempts to correct the trade imbalances that became so prevalent in the 1980s. NAFTA represented an opportunity to encourage investment in North America, particularly Mexico, in order to stem immigration from Mexico to the United States by creating job growth in Mexico as well as to prevent the movement of jobs and production to Asia. The agreement involved very little tariff negotiation, since by 1992 U.S. tariffs on Mexican products averaged 2 percent while Mexican tariffs averaged 10 percent.[30] The real center of negotiations was Mexico's stringent foreign investment code. Foreign ownership in Mexico was limited to 49 percent while other types of foreign investment were strictly prohibited. NAFTA sought to liberalize the Mexican economy and open up investment opportunities for American and Canadian businesses and individuals. It was hoped that the end result would raise Mexican income and provide all three countries with larger, freer export markets. U.S. Treasury Secretary Lloyd Bentsen and Trade Representative Mickey Kantor predicted that the deal would create roughly 200,000 new U.S. export jobs, paying 12 percent to 17 percent higher wages than the average U.S. job.[31]

Bilateral trade between Mexico and the U.S. immediately increased with the signing and congressional approval of NAFTA. U.S. agriculture, in particular, saw major gains of 9.5 percent per year in exports to NAFTA partners.[32] However, the Peso Crisis of 1994 made already inexpensive Mexican imports appear even less expensive.

From 1993 to 2003, the U.S.-Mexico trade balance went from a U.S. net positive of $4.9 billion to a U.S. net negative of $40.6 billion.[33] America's merchandise deficit with both Mexico and Canada reached $95 billion in the same time period. At the same time, U.S. investment in Mexico soared from $13.7 billion to $52.2 billion in 2001 and U.S. companies employed 729,000 Mexican workers, mostly in low-skilled, labor-intensive production.

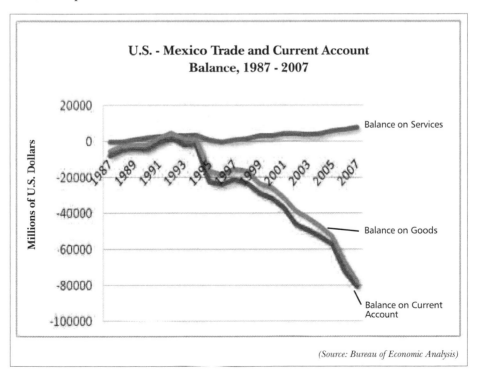

(Source: Bureau of Economic Analysis)

93

During the same period, the U.S. textile and apparel industry saw a loss of 740,000 jobs.[34] The auto industry saw a more balanced outcome. While imports of cars and auto parts from Mexico more than doubled in value from 1993 until 1998, the U.S. auto industry saw car exports increase 14-fold and auto part exports rise 30 percent.[35] It is still difficult to tell the full implications of NAFTA, in part because China has attracted many of the factories that originally went to Mexico and has become the major exporter of manufactured goods to the U.S. market.

The Asian Century

As noted earlier, East Asia has followed an export-led growth formula and achieved incredible economic growth rates over the last 60 years. The models vary slightly; Japan and Korea chose to build up domestic firms to a competitive place in the global market while countries like Singapore grew by attracting foreign firms to set up shop there. Over a very short period of time, the East Asians moved up the value-added ladder, strategically attracting high-tech industry and production.

China has combined the East Asian methods and created an export juggernaut. The Chinese are subcontractors for foreign firms, build their own companies up from scratch and play a major role in global financial markets. Perhaps history will prove otherwise, but no other trade relationship in U.S. history seems to have altered the American economy as

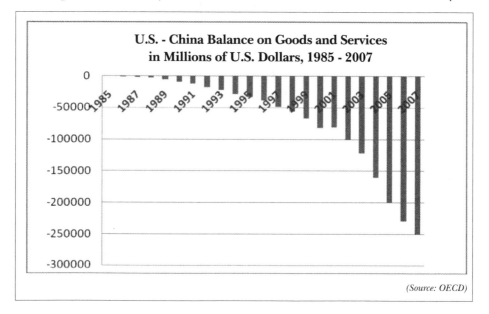

(Source: OECD)

much as its ties to China. In January 1979, China and the United States established formal diplomatic relations and signed a bilateral trade agreement by July. Most favored nation status was mutually adopted in 1980. Establishing positive economic and diplomatic ties with a country — and political ally against the USSR — that exported primarily low-value, labor-intensive products was a step that must have seemed innocuous. At the time, trade between China and the United States was $1 billion per year, making China America's 32nd largest export market and the 57th largest source of U.S. imports. The annual Chinese GDP per capita in 1980 just barely exceeded $400, roughly 3 percent of U.S. per capita income.[36]

Just as U.S. economists approached Japan with a sense of over-confidence and condescension in the immediate post-war years, negotiators with China severely underestimated the Chinese ability to embrace economies of scale and strategically move up the value-added ladder. The U.S. merchandise trade balance with China went from a positive $2.7 billion in 1980 to negative $83.1 billion in 2001. From 2001 to 2007 the U.S. deficit with China grew to -$256 billion, a much higher rate of growth than the previous 20 years.[37]

These numbers are quite impressive considering that total U.S. merchandise imports from the entire world were valued at only $257 billion

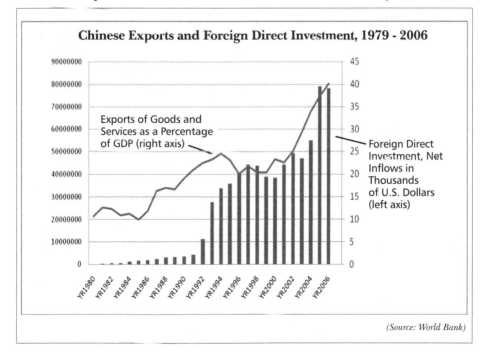

(Source: World Bank)

95

in 1980.[38] In 2007, total trade between the two countries reached $387 billion; China became the third largest export market for U.S. goods and surpassed Canada as the number-one supplier of imports to the American market.[39] China no longer specializes solely in low-value products, with computer, communications as well as audio and video equipment joining apparel and miscellaneous manufactured products as the top five exports to the United States

Much of this is produced in China by American and other global companies. China is an extremely attractive export platform, with cheap labor, large financial incentives, an undervalued currency and lax environmental or quality control regulations. Multinational corporations have responded with an unprecedented wave of investment in and outsourcing to China. Today, 60 percent of Chinese exports are shipped by foreign firms operating in China, equal to over $730 billion. However, statistics show that today a 10 percent increase in the level of U.S. investment in China is associated with a 7.3 percent increase in U.S. imports from China and a 2.1 percent decrease in exports to China.[40]

The Decline of U.S. Manufacturing

For the past 60 years, the needs and interests of American manufacturers have taken a back seat to the country's geopolitical interests and the interests of the U.S. financial sector. In the wake of World War II, U.S. manufacturers helped rebuild the world. But other countries' manufacturing sectors soon retooled and began exporting to the United States. The American domestic market was the "consumer of last resort" and the engine of the global economy.

The unbalanced trade agreements the United States entered into over the past 60 years and a continued emphasis on a strong U.S. dollar put U.S. manufacturers at a disadvantage. It became more and more difficult for them to export, even as they faced more and more competition in the domestic market. And because the United States lacked any overarching economic strategy, public policies designed to support U.S. industry were random in their application, ill-conceived and usually ineffective at helping domestic manufacturing become more competitive in the global market.

Instead, policies designed to promote consumption-based growth combined with asymmetric trade relations led to massive imbalances in global trade. Since the 1970s, the United States has accumulated a colossal trade deficit with nearly every major trade partner. And while output

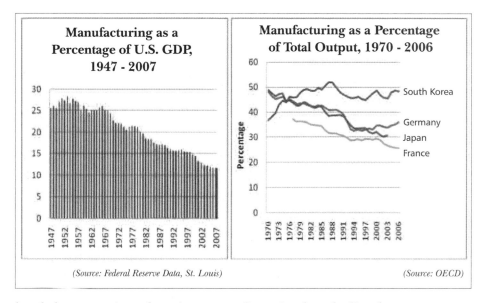

(Source: Federal Reserve Data, St. Louis)   (Source: OECD)

levels have continued to rise, manufacturing has declined as a percentage of total GDP since its peak in the 1960s. U.S. manufacturing as a percentage of GDP has declined to a much lower level than other industrialized countries. More and more formerly-U.S. based production is being shifted overseas, even in the high-tech industries in which the U.S. has maintained a historical advantage.

The FormFactor Story — A Case in Point

In 1978, a Ukrainian refugee, Igor Khandros, arrived in New York City and worked his way to a Ph.D. at Stevens Institute of Technology. He went on to work at IBM's semiconductor works in Fishkill, N.Y., where he conceived a brilliant idea for testing semiconductor wafers with probe cards. After obtaining venture capital, Khandros established FormFactor in Livermore, Calif., to produce these devices. The company quickly became a major force in the wafer test market. Today the company does about $500 million in sales, exports 80 percent of its production to Asia and employs about 1,000 people who, on average, have less than a high school degree but who start at $40,000 a year in salary with stock options and full benefits. When American leaders talk about the future of the U.S. economy, this is the kind of company they describe, entrepreneurial, high-tech, high-value added and globally oriented.

Unfortunately, FormFactor may play less and less of a role in America's future. A few years ago, the giant Korean semiconductor firm Hynix, with the support of Korea's Ministry of Industry, instigated the creation of Phicom, a new company dedicated to producing the same kind of probe cards as FormFactor. Indeed, Phicom essentially cloned the FormFactor product. The Koreans believed they could make this kind of product competitively once they got past the infant industry stage, and that this was precisely the kind of industry that would be the future of their economy. Korea's economy is market-based and capitalist, but Korean leaders believe the market needs government help from time to time in getting to the main objective — a dominant position in a number of high technology, high value-added industries. Of course, Phicom's cloned product infringed a number of FormFactor's Korean patents. But when FormFactor filed injunctions with the Korean courts, requesting Phicom to at least pay a license fee for use of proprietary technology, the judges annulled the FormFactor patents even as the Korean Patent Office affirmed the validity of the original patent grants. FormFactor was threatened with the loss of its proprietary technology even as the Korean government provided Phicom with financial incentives for production in Korea.

As this situation developed, the Economic Development Board of Singapore became aware of the tightening squeeze on FormFactor and began to visit Livermore offering tax holidays, free land and capital grants if the company would relocate all or part of its production to Singapore. Khandros faced a dilemma. Without adequate intellectual property protection, he would need to increase R&D spending in order to innovate faster and stay ahead of Phicom's cloning operations. But such expenditure would reduce his profitability and share price, thus increasing his cost of capital. This was unless, of course, he could find a way dramatically to cut costs. The Singapore proposal offered him exactly this opportunity by essentially providing a government subsidy in exchange for the move to Singapore.

But Khandros felt an obligation to the United States and hoped to keep production in America. He therefore went to Washington in search of help. The officials with whom he met essentially brushed him off, saying that the U.S. government could not offer FormFactor any assistance in allaying the costs of expanded research needs or protecting its intellectual property rights. The most telling response came from a high-ranking Commerce Department official who, completely unaware of the Singaporean visits to FormFactor, suggested that Khandros might do well to move the company offshore to a place like Singapore.

In fact, that is now what Khandros is considering, but only after appealing to California's two senators and learning that they could not find the time to meet with him and that the state had no development office and no incentives to offer as an offset to the Singapore tax breaks and capital grants. As a result, several hundred highly desirable jobs that should have been created in Livermore will be created in Singapore. The most significant effect may be the transfer of enormous technical knowledge and skills to non-U.S. workers. Successful global companies bring their business management style and technology with them when they relocate. This valuable knowledge spreads to the native population and other home-grown companies searching for the tools to become global competitors. Research and products that could add to the U.S. economy in a positive way are instead bolstering the economies of other countries and adding to their productivity with an influx of human capital.

The FormFactor story poses a number of questions. The position in which manufacturers find themselves is complex, resulting not just from international trade relations but a host of other issues. Khandros' story points to the disconnect between U.S. policymaking and the issues facing manufacturers. It is troubling indeed to hear of a U.S. government official who suggests moving productive capabilities to a different country.

Equally troubling are what the specifics of the FormFactor story say about American technological advancement. Since the 1960s, American industry has shouldered an increasingly larger portion of R&D, today

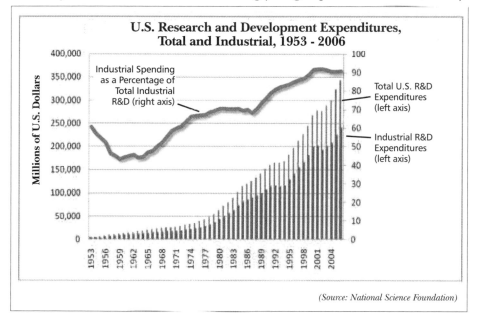

(*Source: National Science Foundation*)

paying for over 90 percent of all industrial R&D that takes place. As industries become increasingly mechanized and take advantage of higher levels of technology, it should be no surprise that the costs of related R&D are on the rise. Faced with rising costs and downward pressure on prices from foreign competitors as more countries move up the value-added ladder into high technology products, American manufacturing leaders like Dr. Khandros are in a fix. The types of things America produces affect its technological capabilities. The computer, semiconductor and aviation industries are the high value-added industries in which advanced countries like the United States must remain competitive if they expect to prosper in the high-tech, globalized economy of this new century. Yet their ability to maintain high levels of R&D spending is declining while government support for R&D has virtually collapsed in key areas. This can only bode ill for the future both of American manufacturing and of America itself.

What the U.S. produces and how much also affects its trade status with other countries. As of 2007, exports of manufactured goods reached $911.3 billion and comprised 55.4 percent of U.S. exports. Services exports brought in $497.3 billion or 30.2 percent. The top export goods were electronic circuits/semiconductors and aerospace goods, export totals valued at $46.3 billion and $45.6 billion respectively.[41] Including both goods and services, the United States claimed $1.65 trillion in exports during 2007. The number seems impressive enough, but was not even

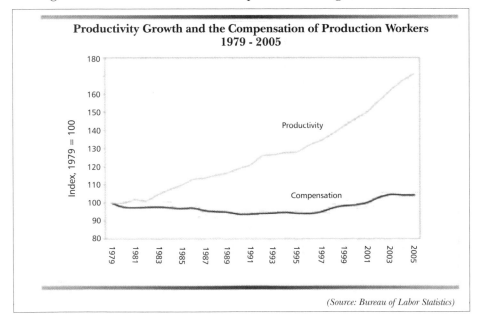

(Source: Bureau of Labor Statistics)

close to compensating for U.S. imports. In the same year, there were $1.97 trillion in goods imports to the United States — over 83 percent of total U.S. imports.[42] If manufactured goods comprise the bulk of American exports, and the country suffers from an extreme trade deficit, it is clear that an increase in manufacturing is essential to solve the problem. Yet, manufacturing continues to drop as a percentage of U.S. GDP. Moreover, U.S. manufacturing capacity is not being fully utilized.

From World War II until the 1980s, manufacturing saw a steady increase in wages. That wage increase came through increased productivity. From the 1980s until today, however, wages have not come close to matching productivity gains. Generally speaking, manufacturing productivity is higher than the U.S. average — if total U.S. productivity increases, manufacturing productivity should be growing at a faster rate. However, that productivity has not been reflected in rising wages. A number of leading trade experts and economists attribute part of the wage stagnation to downward pressure as the result of imports. This does not explain the phenomenon entirely, but a reduction in manufacturing jobs as a percentage of total employment will have the effect of lowering average wages. Laid off manufacturing employees are much more likely to be reemployed for lower wages at a job lacking health insurance benefits. Manufacturing employs a higher proportion of workers lacking college educations and pays around 9 percent more than non-manufacturing jobs per hour. In some states, the manufacturing wage premium for workers without college degrees reaches as high as 20 percent.

Conclusion

Over the past 60 years, America has seen a shift in its strategic foreign policy goals and its economic doctrines that has dictated a dramatic shift in economic policy and priorities. Up until World War II, U.S. foreign policy took a back seat to issues of economic development. U.S. economic policymakers focused on creating a domestic market that stretched from the Atlantic to the Pacific, and on building up the manufacturing capacity to supply the national economy with the machines and materials necessary to power growth. America adopted a mercantilist stance for most of the century, in part because it did not yet possess the economic and military might to play a decisive role in world affairs. Its focus was on "catching up" to Great Britain, Germany and France. To that end, policymakers adopted trade and industrial policies that promoted the development of domestic manufacturing and protected U.S. firms from foreign competition.

With the end of World War II, America assumed the position of the leading economic and military power in the free world. As the Cold War competition with communism mounted, strategic foreign policy trumped domestic business interests in the formulation of America's international economic policies. America dropped the protectionist policies of its past and embarked on a mission to promote capitalism and democracy worldwide. In conjunction with its allies, the United States built new post-war institutions to promote free trade and investment, and to manage the international monetary system. These institutions (the GATT, WTO and IMF) largely succeeded in their goals of containing communism and spreading capitalism throughout the world. But they also positioned the United States as the world's consumer of last resort, and created a tilted world in which production capacity left the United States even as its consumption rose to unprecedented levels.

The domestic U.S. market became the engine of growth for export-led economies around the world — first in Europe and later in East Asia. Trade agreements enacted during this era were the result of American initiatives: the U.S. opened its domestic market to foreign goods and promoted the growth of manufacturing production abroad. But American concessions were often not matched by its trading partners. Many countries maintained high import tariffs or other barriers to trade, managed their currencies against the dollar to keep them undervalued (and hence their exports are more competitive in U.S. markets), and wooed multinational companies to set up shop by offering substantial packages of benefits — from capital grants and infrastructure improvements to tax holidays and lax regulations. Meanwhile in the United States, a culture of consumption, the lack of industrial policies, a focus on maintaining a strong dollar and the lack of access to foreign markets combined to weaken domestic manufacturing. Eventually, the asymmetry of U.S. international trade relations created unsustainable imbalances in the international trading and financial systems. The U.S. ran large trade and current account deficits that could only be funded through increasingly large sales of debts to foreign investors. On the domestic front, U.S. manufacturing shed millions of jobs and its share of total U.S. GDP declined.

Today, the world is witnessing the end of the post war system in which the United States served as the world's consumer of last resort. The global economy is in the midst of a severe financial crisis that promises to radically alter the trading and investment relationships of the world's great economic powers. The United States is no longer the world's preeminent economic power, but is merely one of several developed economies in a multipolar world. The current state of the U.S. economy is fundamentally unsound. While much foreign capital has been invested in the United States in recent years, most of it has not been invested in productive assets in manufacturing and infrastructure that could provide the basis for future generations' wealth and income. Instead, it has been wasted on a series of asset bubbles and conspicuous consumption. Much as in 1945, the U.S. stands at a crossroads of policy change. America can rebuild its productive engine of economic growth — the manufacturing sector — but only with the help of sustained and decisive public policies that promote innovation and encourage investments to flow into new productive capacities. Both America's domestic economy and the international economic system can and must be reshaped. But it will take wise and determined leadership to get us there.

---

1. Eckes, Alfred, E. Jr., *Opening America's Market: U.S. Foreign Trade Policy Since 1776*, page 22.

2. Ibid, page 23.

3. Ibid, page 24.

4. Nicolay, John George, *Abraham Lincoln: Complete Works, Comprising His Speeches, Letters, State Papers, and Miscellaneous Writings By Abraham Lincoln*, John Hay, published by The Century Co., 1907.

5. *The Roosevelt Policy: Speeches, Letters and State Papers Relating to Corporate Wealth and Closely Allied Topics*, by Theodore Roosevelt, Theodore Roosevelt, IV, contributor William Griffith, published by Kessinger Publishing, 2004.

6. Eckes, page 28.

7. Whaples, Robert, *Historical Perspectives on the American Economy: Selected Readings*, "The Origins of American Industrial Success, 1879-1940," by Gavin Wright, page 456.

8. Lovett, William, et al, *U.S. Trade Policy: History, Theory and the WTO*, "U.S. Trade History," by Alfred Eckes, page 130.

9. Eckes, page 130.

10. Irwin, Douglas, "Trade Liberalization: Cordell Hull and the Case for Optimism," Council on Foreign Relations Working Paper, July 31, 2008, pages 5-6, available at: http://www.cfr.org/publication/16873/.

11. Lovett, page 57.

12. Lovett, page 66.

13. Lovett, page 67.

14. Bureau of Economic Analysis, (percent change in GDP from previous period data), http://www.bea.gov/national/nipaweb/TableView.asp?SelectedTable=1&ViewSeries=NO&Java=no&Request3Place=N&3Place=N&FromView=YES&Freq=Year&FirstYear=1931&LastYear=2008&3Place=N&Update=Update&JavaBox=no#Mid.

15. Bureau of Labor Statistics, "Manufacturing Employment Data," http://data.bls.gov/cgi-bin/dsrv, and Federal Reserve of St. Louis, GDP by Industry Accounts.

16. Lovett, page 70.

17. Prechel, Harlan, 1990, "Steel and the State: Industry Politics and Business Policy Formation, 1940-1989," *American Sociological Review*, page 7.

18. Verdier, Daniel, et al, "European Integration as a Solution to War," *European Journal of International Relations*, Vol. 11, No. 1, 99-135 (2005), page 105.

19. Ohashi, Hiroshi, "Learning By Doing, Export Subsidies and Industry Growth: Japanese Steel in the 1950s and 1960s," *Journal of International Economics*, Elsevier, Vol. 66(2), pages 297-323, July, page 299.

20. Ibid, page 300.

21. Ibid, page 302.

22. Prechel, page 15.

23. Lovett, page 75.

24. Ibid, page 77.

25. Prestowitz, Clyde, *Trading Places: How We Allowed Japan to Take the Lead*, page 135.

26. Dahlman, Carl, "Electronics Development Strategy, The Role of Government," The World Bank Industry and Energy Department, 1990, page 5.

27. St. Louis Federal Reserve, Balance on International Trade Data: http://research.stlouisfed.org/fred2/series/BOPBGS?cid=125.

28. Ibid.

29. Lovett, page 84.

30. Lovett, page 81.

31. Lovett, page 82.

32. Burfisher, Mary, et al, "The Impact of NAFTA on the United States," *Journal of Economic Perspectives*, Volume 15, Winter 2001, pages 125–144, page 135.

33. Lovett, page 82.

34. Lovett, page 83.

35. Burfisher, page 135.

36. Morrison, W. M., "China-U.S. Trade Issues" (RS33536), Washington, D.C., Congressional Research Service., page 1: http://digitalcommons.ilr.cornell.edu/key_workplace/498/37 USITC DataWeb, 2008.

38. Lovett, page 14.

39. Lovett.

40. Blonigen, Bruce, et al, "Please Pass the Catch-Up: The Relative Performance of Chinese and Foreign Firms In Chinese Exports," NBER working paper, August 2007, page 2.

41. U.S. Census Bureau Foreign Trade, Bureau of Economic Analysis.

42. Bureau of Economic Analysis.

3. Benchmarking the Advantages Foreign Nations Provide Their Manufacturers

Peter Navarro
University of California, Irvine

Over the last decade, under the banner of free trade, the United States has lost millions of high-paying manufacturing jobs. This transfer of American jobs overseas to low-wage hubs in Latin America and Asia has depressed wages and materially reduced the standard of living of millions of Americans. This "hollowing out" of the manufacturing base has helped induce recessionary conditions throughout the United States.

Under the banner of free trade, the United States has also run chronic and historically large trade deficits. In fact, one country alone — China — accounts for more than half of the entire U.S. trade deficit once expenditures for oil imports are excluded.

As a long-term strategic threat, America's chronic trade deficits have led to a dangerous buildup of U.S. dollar reserves in the sovereign wealth funds of several of those countries where the lion's share of American jobs have been lost, again most notably in China. A clear and present danger is that these sovereign wealth funds will use their dollar reserves to purchase or gain controlling interests in American companies and then strip these companies of either their technologies or jobs, or both, further weakening the U.S. economy and manufacturing base.

Given these severe negative impacts, it is hardly surprising that America's commitment to free trade has come under intense fire. This chapter seeks to shed light on whether the loss of American manufacturing jobs, depressed wages and the presence of chronic American trade deficits are the inevitable results of a free trade system that, on balance, will be both "good for America" and "good for the world" over time. Alternatively, are the negative effects of free trade the pernicious results of America's trading partners adopting "beggar thy U.S. neighbor" mercantilist and protectionist trade policies that run contrary to free trade principles? If so, does the "end game" of free trade in a world of protectionism and mercantilism involve a permanent weakening of, and second-tier nation status for, the United States?

There is a difference between protectionist and mercantilist. In this analysis, a protectionist is defined as any country that adopts strategic trade policies to exclude or restrict access to its domestic markets. As described in this chapter, common protectionist tools include tariffs and quotas as well as a wide variety of "nontariff barriers" — from local content rules, restrictive import licensing, and port-of-entry restrictions to anti-competitive standards, a nontransparent regulatory environment and corruption and bribery.

In similar fashion, a mercantilist is defined as any country that adopts strategic trade policies that violate free trade principles to promote export growth at the expense of its free trading partners. Common mercantilist tools range from currency manipulation and illegal export subsidies to counterfeiting and piracy, lax environmental and health and safety standards, export restrictions on raw materials and the use of slave labor and repression of workers' rights.

As a practical matter, most countries that engage in protectionism also engage in mercantilism. In fact, the two sets of policies often work hand-in-hand in the international trading arena to convey an unfair competitive advantage to those countries that adopt such policies. Nonetheless, it is useful to conceptually separate protectionism from mercantilism as a means of understanding the full scope of these powerful threats to a global system of free trade that benefits all nations.

Only one of America's five major trading partners in manufactured goods systematically engages in a highly sophisticated and comprehensive set of protectionist and mercantilist trade policies that clearly violate the principles of free trade established by the World Trade Organization. That country is China. Because China is the world's biggest protectionist and mercantilist nation, much of the focus of this analysis will be on China's strategic trade policies. However, the trade policies of the Eurozone, Japan, Mexico and Canada — America's four other major trade partners — will also be briefly examined.

The Promise — and Perils — of Free Trade

Free trade advocates typically argue that free trade is a "positive sum" game in which all countries win. In particular, these advocates argue that both economic growth and job growth will be higher for all trading partners under free trade than they would be in a state of "autarky," which is the absence of trade. This free trade argument dates back to the writings of 18th century classical economists like Adam Smith and

David Ricardo and is based on two of the most important concepts in all of economics — the "gains from trade" and the "principle of comparative advantage."

To understand the gains from trade, consider a world in which there are only two countries, and neither country trades with the other. If these two autarkic countries enter into free trade, each country won't have to produce everything each needs. Instead, each country can specialize according to its own "comparative advantage," where comparative advantage is simply a way of saying that each country will specialize in that which it does best. Through this process of specialization, each country will then benefit from a greater division of labor and greater economies of scale, and, in doing so, use its resources more efficiently. The result will be a higher level of total production and job growth in the two countries combined than would exist in a state of autarky.

Free trade advocates also argue that chronic trade imbalances cannot persist in a free trade environment. As with the concept of the gains from trade and the principle of comparative advantage, this faith in the balance of trade rests on economic concepts that again date back several centuries to the writings of classical economists, particularly David Hume.

The modern version of Hume's balanced trade argument rests on the crucial assumption that all free trading countries operate in a system of floating exchange rates without managed interventions. In a freely floating exchange rate system, if one country runs a trade deficit, the value of its currency will fall through the forces of supply and demand: surplus dollars abroad exert downward pressure on the dollar. Of course, once this exchange rate adjustment takes place and the deficit country's currency cheapens, the exports of the deficit country will become relatively cheaper and imports from the rest of the world will become relatively more expensive. As exports rise from the deficit country and imports fall, trade comes back into balance — or so the classical argument goes.

How Free Trade in the Real World Becomes A Zero-Sum Game

While 18th century classical economic theory portrays free trade as a mutually beneficial positive-sum game for all participants, free trade in the 21st century may turn into a zero-sum game with big winners and big losers *if* the critical assumptions underlying the free trade argument are violated.

The first critical assumption is that all free trading countries will refrain from the practices of either mercantilism or protectionism. The second critical assumption is that all free trading countries will participate in an exchange rate system that allows for currency adjustments to take place in a timely way so as to prevent chronic trade balances, with a floating exchange rate system the most effective. If these assumptions are violated, free trade will very likely not be mutually beneficial at all. Instead, any free-trading country that trades with a protectionist country will see a net loss of jobs to the protectionist country relative to a free trade environment while economic growth will be slower than it would otherwise be. Secondly, any free trading country that trades with a mercantilist country will not only lose jobs and experience slower growth but will also likely run chronic trade deficits with the mercantilist country.

It is for these two reasons that it is critical to understand the strategic trade policies that clearly violate free trade principles and result in a global market environment more akin to a mercantilist and protectionist zero-sum game than a mutually beneficial, positive-sum, free trade system.

Protectionism in the 21st Century

Just as individual companies regularly adopt strategies to improve their competitive advantage in world markets so, too, do governments adopt strategic trade policies to enhance competitive advantage in the global marketplace. Table 1 on the next page describes each of the major protectionist policies used in the 21st century trade of manufactured goods. The primary goal of these protectionist policies is to shield a country's domestic manufacturers from foreign competition. In this way, a protectionist country increases its domestic output and job growth at the expense of would-be exporters to that domestic market.

The most visible protectionist policies are those involving quotas or tariffs. A quota is simply a numerical restriction on the level of imports allowed into a domestic market. By restricting supply, market forces raise the price of the good. A tariff, on the other hand, represents a tax on imports. By effectively raising the price of the imported good, the tariff provides a price shield to higher-cost domestic producers. Note that for any given quota level, there is a corresponding equivalent tariff that will produce the same level of import restriction.[1]

TABLE 1: PROTECTIONIST TRADE POLICIES IN THE 21ST CENTURY

POLICY	DESCRIPTION
Quotas and Tariffs	• Quotas set numerical limits on imports to directly restrict imports. • Tariffs tax imports and indirectly restrict imports through pricing.
Port-of-Entry Restrictions	• Block, slow down or otherwise impede the flow of imports into the domestic market at ports of entry.
Inflated Customs Valuations	• Inflate the price of an import using spurious customs valuations methods and thereby raise the associated import duties. They are often used to offset tariff reductions.
Local Content Rules	• Require domestic industries to use domestic content, thereby effectively locking out foreign competitors.
Import Licensing Restrictions	• Require and restrict the number of import licenses. Often used as a "bargaining chip" to impose local content rules (or force technology transfer).
Technical Barriers to Trade	• The use of discriminatory regulations, standards and certification and testing procedures to benefit domestic industries at the expense of foreign exporters.
Discriminatory Tax Policies	• Consumption, income and other tax policies that favor domestic industries, such as income tax refunds for the purchase of local content.
Corruption and Bribery	• Rigged bidding and other corrupt practices that often favor domestic industries.

Beyond the imposition of tariffs and quotas, there are many other kinds of protectionist barriers that have been very loosely classified under the heading of "nontariff barriers." As with tariffs and quotas, virtually all are prohibited under the rules and norms of the General

Agreement on Tariffs and Trade (GATT) and the World Trade Organization (WTO).

One common form of an illegal nontariff barrier involves any one of a number of port-of-entry restrictions. The goal of port-of-entry restrictions is to block, slow down or otherwise impede the flow of imports into the domestic market at ports of entry — a de facto form of protectionism.

Closely related to that problem is the hurdle of inflated customs valuations. Inflating customs valuation is a common strategy used by protectionist governments. The game is to offset any tariff reductions these governments have promised as part of free trade agreements. If customs officials use spurious methods that significantly overvalue imported goods, any lowered tariffs can be offset by higher customs valuations and attendant higher customs duties.

A third type of nontariff barrier involves the specification of domestic preference or local content rules that require a certain percentage of the components of a particular good be produced locally. Local content rules not only prop up the prices and profits that domestic producers can receive, but they also increase the market share of the domestic industries that benefit from the rules, while reducing sales and jobs in the countries where the foreign competitors are affected.

Local content rules are often strategically forced on foreign investors via another nontariff barrier, that of import licensing restrictions. Requiring importers to have a license to import and then placing significant restrictions on the number of licenses granted is, in itself, a very effective form of protectionism. So, too, is a more subtle method to restrict import licenses, making it very difficult, costly or time-consuming to obtain an import license. However, as in the case of China, import licensing restrictions also provide protectionist countries with a valuable "bargaining chip" to force both technology transfer and the adoption of domestic content rules otherwise prohibited by the WTO.

Yet another form of nontariff barrier involves various technical barriers to trade, such as discriminatory regulations, standards or certification and testing procedures. For example, a complex regulatory system that is not transparent can be impossible for foreign companies to navigate and penetrate. In such systems, foreign companies often encounter contradictory decisions, overlapping jurisdictions and long delays in regulatory decisions. The practical effect is a subtle but effective form of protectionism.

Similarly, a government may impose a national standard that runs contrary to well-established international standards to protect a domestic industry. A well-known example involves China's specification of its home-grown cell phone standard of TD-SCDMA, despite well-accepted and more advanced standards in the United States and Europe.

Discriminatory tax policies likewise can be used both for protectionist and mercantilist purposes. In the case of protectionism, a government may adopt consumption and income tax policies that favor domestic industries through the use of income tax refunds for the purchase of local content.

Finally, there is the protectionist problem of corruption and bribery. Endemic corruption and bribery in a country may result in a de facto type of protectionism for several reasons. Bribes raise the cost of penetrating a market and thereby help protect domestic industries. At the same time, navigating a corrupt system can be very difficult for foreign companies unfamiliar with that system. Again, the result can be a de facto barrier to market entry.

Mercantilism in the 21st Century

While the doctrine of mercantilism has been variously defined, the modern meaning of the term has come to be most closely associated with the failed trade policies of 17th century Spain. During that period, Spanish leaders believed that national wealth was measured by the amount of gold and silver a country possessed and that the road to prosperity therefore lay in selling exports to the world and accumulating as much gold and silver as possible. Of course, what Spain got out of its pursuit of mercantilism was hardly prosperity but rather a very nasty case of "demand pull" inflation, with too much money in its coffers chasing too few goods. It would take Adam Smith to figure out the flaw in mercantilism: that a nation's wealth is measured not by its money supply or foreign reserves but rather by its real, inflation-adjusted gross domestic product.

Today, the modern version of the 17th century mercantilist state involves any country that adopts any one of a number of the unfair "beggar thy neighbor" policies listed in Table 2 on page 113. These strategic trade policies are explicitly designed to boost exports at the expense of the mercantilist's trading partners. By artificially boosting exports, the mercantilist country thereby is able to accumulate large foreign reserves — the 21st century equivalent of the accumulated gold and silver of an earlier era.

At the top of the list in Table 2 on page 113, there is the broad category of export subsidies. While any form of export subsidy is generally prohibited under the World Trade Organization rules, many countries that are members of the WTO nonetheless choose to violate these rules for the simple reason that export subsidies represent a very effective strategy to lower a country's export prices and thereby gain competitive advantage. One common way to convey an export subsidy is through discriminatory tax policies. For example, an exporter may be given some type of tax credit or tax rebate. In China and throughout most of the world, value-added tax (VAT) rebates are commonly used.

Export subsidies that are far more difficult to detect are those that indirectly lower production costs through subsidizing inputs that go into the manufacturing process — anything from capital, energy and freight to land, water and other utilities. Any one of these indirect subsidies can contribute to lowering production costs, while the application of all of them can provide considerable competitive advantage. (Imagine you are opening a business in the United States and the government gives you free land, access to zero-interest loans that you do not have to pay back, and reduces by half your energy and utility bills? Don't you think that you could make a profit?)

In addition to export subsidies, a very effective way for a mercantilist to boost competitive advantage is through currency manipulation by undervaluing the domestic currency. This not only reduces the home country's export prices in world markets, thereby boosting exports, but also serves a protectionist function by discouraging imports. In this way, the mercantilist "makes exports cheap and imports dear," improving the country's trade balance on both sides of the ledger — a classic form of "beggar thy neighbor."

Counterfeiting and piracy likewise function as a means of enhancing strategic global advantage in a mercantilist country. Piracy refers to the unauthorized production, distribution or use of a good or service. The goal of a pirate is to create a look-alike "knockoff" that can be sold to a customer as such. Counterfeiting involves trying to pass off the pirated products as that of the real, branding corporation. Thus, a golf club that looks like a Callaway driver but has a name like "Hallaway" is a pirated knockoff, whereas a knockoff sold as a "Callaway" club is counterfeit.

Counterfeiting and piracy convey competitive advantage in several important ways. Intellectual property theft reduces the expenditures necessary on research and development to produce a product. In industries like autos and pharmaceuticals, the cost savings can be quite large along with an attendant large gain in competitive advantage. At the same time, counterfeiting eliminates the need for marketing expenditures as the counterfeiter "free rides" on the advertising, brand name and good

TABLE 2: MERCANTALIST TRADE POLICIES IN THE 21ST CENTURY

POLICY	DESCRIPTION
Export Subsidies	• Direct export subsidies such as discriminatory tax rates on exported goods. • Indirect export subsidies through the subsidization of inputs such as capital, energy, freight, land, water and other utilities.
Currency Manipulation	• Undervaluing the domestic currency through currency manipulation to make "exports cheap" and "imports dear."
Counterfeiting And Piracy	• Counterfeiting reduces marketing and production costs to hone competitive advantage. Piracy reduces R&D and information technology costs.
Forced Technology Transfer	• Require technology transfer and/or the export of a country's R&D facilities as a condition of market entry. Steal or reverse-engineer technology through industrial espionage in violation of patent law.
Lax Environmental And Health and Safety Regulations	• Maintain regulations below international norms to reduce compliance and production costs. Encourages a "race to the bottom."
Unfair Labor Standards And Practices	• Establish labor standards below international norms to suppress wage costs. Lack of a livable wage. Deny the right to organize. Tacitly allow sweat shops and the use of slave labor.
Entrustment Or Direction	• The use of companies under the direction of the government to boost the export trade. For example, a financially healthy company will be required to bail out a financially distressed company.
Export Restrictions	• Restrict the export of energy or raw materials to suppress factor input prices in the mercantilist country and raise world market prices for competitors.
Mercantilist-Driven Foreign Direct Investment	• Attract levels of FDI above what would otherwise exist through the lures of an undervalued currency, lax environmental and health and safety regulations, and unfair labor practices and standards.

will of the authentic product. A pirate company can also enjoy huge savings on information technology expenditures by stealing both software and hardware.

Still another way for a mercantilist country to gain unfair advantage is through forced technology transfer. By forcing (or stealing) technology from a trading partner, the mercantilist is able to increase its rate of productivity to a level higher than it would otherwise be. Higher levels of productivity translate into lower costs and lower export prices. On top of this advantage, forced technology transfer also saves the mercantilist country on research and development expenditures in much the same way that piracy does.

As a practical matter, there are several methods mercantilist countries commonly use in the 21st century to force technology transfer — all of which are prohibited under the WTO. One method is to explicitly require the transfer of technology as a condition of market entry. This method is often used in conjunction with protectionist import licensing restrictions.

A second, more indirect method is to require the transfer of research and development activities from the exporting country to the mercantilist country as a condition of market entry. This type of mercantilist strategy — practiced, for example, with great success by China against the U.S. auto and pharmaceutical industries — has a much longer-term impact as intellectual capital is forced to migrate to the mercantilist country.

A third method to force technology transfer is through industrial espionage. This need not involve clandestine penetration of secure facilities. One common practice is to send large cadres of agents to various trade shows and fairs. By doing this, China keeps abreast of the latest product developments. Its agents obtain samples of products that can then be reverse engineered. These products are often manufactured in the mercantilist nation even before the original vendor has put the product on shelves.

Turning to yet another mercantilist practice, a country that maintains environmental or health and safety standards below world norms can gain a significant, unfair competitive advantage. This is because the country's domestic industries are able to forego the expenditures otherwise borne by industries in competing countries. For example, complying with EPA and OSHA regulations in the United States significantly increases costs for industries ranging from autos and chemicals to steel and textiles.

As a practical matter, this mercantilist problem can manifest itself in one of two ways: a country may simply have lax standards, or it may have strict standards that are not enforced. Either way, the result is an unfair competitive advantage — one that can help trigger a "race to the bottom" in the areas of both environmental protection and worker health and safety.

In a related vein, countries that engage in unfair labor practices effectively suppress wage costs and thereby gain competitive advantage. Unfair labor practices include both the lack of a living wage and the suppression of the right to organize and unionize. In extreme cases, countries may also condone the use of slave labor. Not only is this extremely inhumane, but slave labor acts as a further depressant on wage levels and likewise conveys a substantial cost advantage.

Another common mercantilist practice is a government policy known as entrustment or direction. In effect, a mercantilist government will direct either state- or privately-owned companies to engage in practices that advance the country's overall export mission. A common practice in China is to require a financially healthy company to bail out or cross-subsidize a financially struggling company that is successful in the export market.

The use of various export restrictions on energy and raw materials constitutes yet another practice used by mercantilist countries. If a country imposes an export quota on domestic supplies of iron ore to help the domestic steel industry, for instance, the effect is to ensure the domestic industry preferential access to the raw material. But a secondary impact is an increase in the world price for the raw materials that are affected, thereby raising costs in competing countries. The mercantilist country is provided with further and considerable cost advantages for its industries that are heavily dependent on those raw materials.

One of the most important indirect effects of mercantilism is how these various practices can lead to an unfair distribution of foreign direct investment (FDI) across free trading countries. FDI is a very important driver of strategic trade advantage because it accelerates the transfer of the most technologically advanced production and process technologies. FDI also brings managerial best practices and skills to the host country because many of the financed enterprises are managed by foreign talent. FDI is often tied to the improvement of both the marketing and distribution skills of domestic enterprises.

These observations are important because the mercantilist practices of export subsidies, currency manipulation and lax environmental and health and safety standards all conspire to raise levels of FDI in the mercantilist country to levels higher than they otherwise would be in a regime of free and fair trade. FDI is higher in the presence of export subsidies because foreign investors are attracted by higher profits. Foreign companies can produce more cheaply in the mercantilist country because of laxer environmental and health and safety regulations. Japan, South Korea and the United States export their pollution by offshoring to China. Additionally, an undervalued currency is a very powerful magnet for FDI: It allows foreign money to buy into the mercantilist country at a much lower rate.

America's "Big Five" Trade Deficit Partners

This analysis began by examining the arguments in support of free trade and illustrating how the introduction of protectionist and mercantilist practices effectively eliminate the global benefits of free trade. This analysis then systematically catalogued each of the major 18th century protectionist and mercantilist practices used in today's 21st century global trading environment.

The next task is to determine the extent to which America's chronic trade deficits and associated economic problems may be attributed to the application of various protectionist and mercantilism strategies by America's five major trading partners. These major trading partners are listed in Table 3. Together, China, the Eurozone, Japan, Mexico and Canada account for almost 75 percent of the U.S. trade deficit.

What is perhaps most interesting about Mexico and Canada is that they are America's two treaty partners in the North America Free Trade Agreement. The interesting question raised by their being on this list is whether NAFTA is a misnomer, given that this "free trade agreement" has resulted in such large trade imbalances. Upon closer inspection, however, it turns out that roughly half of the trade deficits with both Canada and Mexico may be attributable to large quantities of imported oil from these countries. It is Canada, not Saudi Arabia, that is America's largest source of imported oil. Mexico ranks a very close third behind Saudi Arabia.

As for the third largest entry on the list, there is Japan, with a trade imbalance of $83 billion with the United States. In a review of Japan's trade policies, the single biggest mercantilist culprit driving this trade imbalance is Japan's own particular version of currency manipulation. In addition, Japan continues to heavily protect key markets such as its automobile industry.

TABLE 3: AMERICA'S 'BIG FIVE' TRADE DEFICIT PARTNERS		
(BY SIZE OF TRADE DEFICIT)		
Country or Trading Zone	**U.S. 2007 Trade Deficit**	**Percent of Total**
China	$256 billion	32%
Eurozone	$107 billion	14%
Japan	$83 billion	10%
Mexico	$74 billion	9%
Canada	$64 billion	8%
Total	**$584 billion**	**74%**

(Source: 2008 National Trade Estimate Report on Foreign Trade Barriers, Office of the United States Trade Representative, March 2008, Appendix.)

As for the second largest entry on the list, the Eurozone countries generate a trade imbalance of $107 billion, with $44 billion of this deficit accounted for by Germany alone. While there is considerable free and fair trade between the United States and Europe, there are notable instances of protectionism, particularly in Europe's aircraft industry.

Finally, China stands head and shoulders above all other trading partners as a source of America's chronic trade deficits. In 2007, America's trade deficit with China reached a historic high of $256 billion. This sum represents almost one-third of America's overall trade deficit of $700 billion (32 percent) and fully 55 percent of America's trade deficit excluding purchases of imported oil.[2] Moreover, the China-U.S. trade imbalance dwarfs all others. In fact, China turns out to be the poster child for world mercantilism and protectionism and arguably the greatest impediment to free and fair trade in manufacturing goods in the international arena.

18th Century Protectionism in 21st Century China

Each year, the United States Trade Representative publishes its National Trade Estimate Report on various protectionist and mercantilist practices practiced around the world. This report provides scant — or no — coverage of the many mercantilist and protectionist policies catalogued in this chapter. This problem is particular evident for the policies of China, to which we now turn.[3]

Chinese Tariffs and Quotas

While China has reduced tariffs in many industries since joining the WTO, it has often sought to offset any tariff reductions through the application of numerous nontariff barriers. In addition, there remain very troublesome aspects of China's tariff policy. China continues to maintain "high duties on some products that compete with sensitive domestic industries."[4] These industries range from motorcycles and audio recorders to video and digital video. Tariff rate quotas remain a common fixture of China's protectionist landscape. While they are mostly reserved for the restriction of agricultural rather than manufacturing imports, one important exception is fertilizer. At least partly as a result, U.S. fertilizer exports to China have declined sharply.

Port of Entry Restrictions

China sends container ships all over the world filled to the brim with its exports. From Long Beach to Europe, these container ships are efficiently processed, and Chinese goods find their way quickly into the marketplace. This is not always the case in China, however. As noted by the United States Trade Representative, "massive delays are not uncommon, and the fees charged appear to be excessive and are rising rapidly."[5]

Inflated Customs Valuations

According to WTO rules, imported goods should be valued on the basis of their "transaction price," that is, the price the importer actually pays. In China, however, customs officials frequently use "reference pricing," which typically results in much higher duties.

Local Content Rules

Perhaps the most visible form of local content rules exists in the importation of copyright-intensive products such as movies, DVDs, music and books. Despite intense pressure from Washington, "China has not yet given foreign entities trading rights for the importation of these goods."[6]

In addition, all layers of China's government have adopted varying forms and practices of "buy domestic." While China is not a signatory to the WTO Agreement on Government Procurement, it did commit in its protocol of accession to the WTO to abide by that agreement as soon as possible. To date, little progress has been made. China continues to follow internal rules that "direct central and sub-central government entities to give priority to 'local' goods and services, with limited exceptions."[7]

Most broadly, China's complex matrix of local content rules loom as a key protectionist measure to breed its "national champions" and to protect its "pillar industries." One Chinese industry where local content rules have played a key role is telecommunications equipment. Since 1998, the Ministry of Information Industry has had in place an internal circular "instructing telecommunications companies to buy components and equipment from domestic sources."[8]

In addition, some of the biggest beneficiaries of China's protectionist local content rules are China's auto and auto parts manufacturers. These industries have been strategically targeted for growth as part of China's comprehensive industrial policy.

China has used a very potent combination of protectionist and mercantilist policies to create a cycle of offshoring U.S. parts production to China. On the strength of these policies, "in less than 20 years, China has gone from a country with an extremely small and undeveloped automotive (including auto parts) sector to the third largest automobile producer in the world [and] the second largest national supplier of auto parts to the United States."[9]

Import Licensing Restrictions

Import licensing restrictions play a key role in China's strategy to offset tariff reductions with nontariff barriers. Import licensing restrictions also represent an important "bargaining chip" used by China to force both technology transfer and the adoption of local content rules otherwise prohibited by the WTO.

One industry that has been particularly victimized by China's use of licensing requirements is that of scrap recycling. Scrap exports constitute one of the largest U.S. exports to China by value. Under the Chinese system, overseas exporters must apply for the right to export to the Chinese market. If the license is denied, companies must wait for three years before reapplying.[10]

Another industry that has been stymied almost completely by import restrictions is telecommunications. As the United States Trade Representative has noted, "the lack of foreign participation in the telecommunications sector... is indicative of a licensing regime that has generally, with few exceptions, not been conducive to foreign investment."[11] Protectionist national standards that deviate from well-established international standards have served as significant barriers to entry in this industry.

A third industry victimized by China's import licensing restrictions is the auto and auto parts industry. This example is particularly telling because it helps illustrate how China strategically and synergistically uses import licensing restrictions to achieve goals related to both local content and forced technology transfer that are clearly prohibited under WTO rules. Here's how this strategy works in China:

China first limits the number of licenses granted for final automobile assembly. Foreign automakers then must compete for the licenses in the dimensions of local content and technology transfer, and the winners of this competition are the companies most willing to agree to conditions that are otherwise prohibited by the WTO. As professor Eric Thun of Princeton has described this process: "The central government would announce that it was going to approve one final assembly joint venture, and foreign firms, desperate not to be locked out of one of the last great auto markets, would claw over one another to get the contract."[12]

A typical case in point involves General Motors. Not only has GM "been a major conduit of technology,"[13] but in exchange for licenses, GM "has committed to purchasing $10 billion annually in Chinese-produced auto parts by 2009." Moreover, Ford also has "made at least $3 billion in commitments to buying substantial quantities of Chinese-produced parts for export to four plants worldwide."[14]

As another example of the collusion of a protectionist Chinese government and American corporate interests, there are the events surrounding a dispute before the WTO over the doubling of tariffs on imported parts and components by China. In the ensuing negotiations, China agreed to postpone imposing the higher tariffs "but only after holding high-level meetings with the CEOs of BMW and Daimler-Chrysler Northeast Asia. These meetings produced commitments to increase local parts purchases by $274 million and $740 million respectively."[15]

In observing this behavior, it is hard to assess which is the most disturbing: the flagrant and blatant use of illegal protectionist and mercantilist policies by the Chinese government — or the eagerness of American corporations to kowtow to those protectionist measures as a condition of entry into the Chinese market.

Technical Barriers to Trade

As noted by the United States Trade Representative, in its Protocol of Accession to the WTO, "China committed to ensure that its regulatory authorities apply the same standards, technical regulations and conformity assessment procedures to both imported and domestic goods and use the same fees, processing periods and complaint procedures for both imported and domestic goods."[16] This is, however, yet another area where China has failed miserably in meeting its WTO commitments.

In fact, technical barriers to trade have actually increased as China has sought to use such technical barriers as a further means of offsetting tariff reductions. That China has been guilty of this is revealed by a strategy report that was issued in September of 2004 by a key government agency: the Standardization Administration of China. This report explicitly promoted "China's development of standards and technical regulations as a means of protecting domestic industry as tariff rates fall."[17]

National Standards

One type of technical barrier China has used to protect its pillar industries is the development of unique national standards as the basis for its technical requirements. These national standards have been promulgated despite the existence of well-established international standards. In effect, these national standards serve as a shield for domestic industries. The sectors that have been most affected include automobiles, automotive parts, telecommunications equipment, wireless local area networks, radio frequency identification technology, audio and video coding, fertilizers, food products and consumer products, such as cosmetics.[18]

The most high-profile example of China seeking to promote a national standard to exclude foreign competition is the case of China's homegrown "3G" telecommunications standard known as TD-SCDMA. A second case involves mobile telephone battery standards. China has sought to develop a national standard that diverges significantly from international standards.

Certification

China is also using certification procedures as a subtle form of protectionism. One example involves the compulsory product certification system that was put into place in August 2003. This system created a safety mark called the China Compulsory Certification (CCC) mark. This mark is now required for over 130 products, ranging from electrical machinery and information technology equipment to household appliances.

This certification requirement is posing a number of difficulties for would-be foreign importers. First, many domestic products are allowed to be sold without the mark. Second, the "certification requirements and procedures remain difficult, time-consuming, onerous and costly."[19] Third, companies must submit their applications in person at the Beijing offices of China's National Certification & Accreditation Administration (CNCA). This is difficult for many small- and medium-size companies without a presence in China.[20] Fourth, "many U.S. testing labs as well as the U.S. exporters that rely on their services, find China's foreign accreditation requirements for CCC mark certification unwarranted and overly restrictive."[21] Finally, "U.S. companies also cited problems with a lack of transparency in the certification process, burdensome requirements and long processing times for certification."[22]

China may even be using the certification process as a subtle means of forced technology transfer. The problem, as noted by the United States Trade Representative, is that companies that submit sensitive technology and intellectual property for mandatory testing are vulnerable to intellectual property theft.[23]

Regulatory Barriers

China frequently uses a complex web of nontransparent regulations to block entry into its markets. The biggest victims of these particular types of barriers are not manufacturing firms, but rather service-sector providers such as those in banking, insurance and packaging delivery.

More broadly, "laws and regulations in China tend to be more general and ambiguous than in other countries. While this approach allows the Chinese authorities to apply laws and regulations flexibly, it also results in inconsistency and confusion in application." The problem is further complicated by the fact that "regulations are also promulgated by a host of different ministries and governments at the central, provincial and local levels, and it is not unusual for the resulting regulations to be at odds with one another."[24] The United States Trade Representative has correctly concluded that "this lack of a clear and consistent framework of laws and regulations can be a barrier to the participation of foreign firms in the Chinese domestic market."

Discriminatory Taxation

Discriminatory income taxes, consumption taxes and particularly VAT taxes play an important role in China's protectionist and mercantilist trade policies. For example, "China uses a substantially different tax base to compute consumption taxes for domestic and imported products."[25] Foreign imports that have been affected by its discriminatory tax system include alcoholic beverages, automobiles and cosmetics.

Corruption and Bribery

Corruption and bribery are rampant practices in China. Indeed, in international surveys, China regularly ranks as one of the most corrupt business environments in the world of any major country.[26] Corruption and bribery raise the cost of penetrating a market and thereby help protect domestic industries. At the same time, navigating a corrupt system can be very difficult for foreign companies unfamiliar with that system. In China, the result has been a significant de facto barrier to market entry. As one important example of the problem, "U.S. suppliers complain that the widespread existence of unfair bidding practices in China puts them at a competitive disadvantage."[27]

18th Century Mercantilism in 21st Century China

While China employs a sophisticated suite of policies to protect its domestic markets and grow its pillar industries, its use of an even more sophisticated and comprehensive set of mercantilist policies means that China truly stands head and shoulders above the rest of the world.

Export Subsidies

China's complex web of export subsidies constitutes the "Mercantilist Kingdom's" most potent weapon (along with currency manipulation) as an accelerator of China's export-driven economy. This vast network for subsidies exists despite the fact that as a condition of entry into the World Trade Organization in 2001, the Chinese government promised to eliminate, or at least greatly scale back, virtually all of its export subsidies. Today, however, those industries that continue to be hardest hit by China's export subsidies include "steel, petrochemical, high technology, forestry and paper products, textiles, hardwood plywood, machinery, copper, and other nonferrous metals industries."[28]

What makes it extremely challenging for these industries to individually fight back is "a general lack of transparency [that] makes it difficult to identify and quantify possible export subsidies provided by the Chinese government."[29] Al Lubrano, president of Technical Materials, Inc., provides insight into the problem:

"The subsidization of manufacturing by the Chinese government extends beyond what might be considered normal bounds to even include the acquisition of raw materials. A fellow NAM [National Association of Manufacturers] member in the copper industry tells us that exports of copper and brass scrap to China have increased about 50 percent a year for several years, driven in large part by a special subsidy of 30 percent of the VAT tax applied by the Chinese government to imports of scrap. This subsidy is given to the scrap consumer to invest in upgrading facilities. This subsidy amounts to about seven cents a pound of the copper content in a market where the successful bidder may be determined by a margin of a quarter cent."[30]

While the exact levels of China's export subsidies remain difficult to quantify, it is relatively easy to catalogue them. First, energy and water remain heavily subsidized.[31] Many manufacturers benefit from subsidized rent, cheap or free land and preferential access to land by local and regional governments.

Second, China's state-owned banks continue to hold a large portfolio of nonperforming loans, often issued without expectation of repayment. The biggest beneficiaries of this "free money" policy have been struggling state-owned enterprises (SOEs), which are concentrated in heavy industries like steel and petroleum. Because of continued inefficiencies, many of these industries run at a loss.

However, the Chinese government is loath to allow them to go bankrupt because of the loss of jobs that this would entail. Accordingly, nonperforming loans historically have represented a major lifeline to these enterprises, with the enterprises responsible neither for interest payments on these loans nor repayment of principal. In the area of credit subsidies, it is also worth noting that government ownership of key export companies and industries plays a key role. As Andrew Szamosszegi of the Economic Strategy Institute has noted, "Government ownership is a virtual guarantee of access to capital, either in the form of loans, additional equity infusions or excess retained earnings."[32]

Third, China uses a very complicated list of tax preferences to both attract foreign direct investment and to encourage exports. The cornerstone of this discriminatory tax policy is an extensive value-added tax rebate system for its export industries.[33] China's VAT is imposed over multiple stages of the domestic production and distribution process, generally in the range of 13 percent to 17 percent. In some cases, the Chinese government first collects, and then rebates, this tax for exports. In other cases, exporting firms are simply exempted from the tax.[34]

Such VAT tax preferences are, of course, a blatant violation of the WTO rules. Not surprisingly, China has come under great pressure to eliminate these rebates; at least some small progress has been achieved in this area.

For example, China has reduced its rebates on the export of textiles, apparel, shoes, hats, paper products, goods made from plastic and rubber and furniture. China has also eliminated the rebates as a means of directing funds to clean up its environment for a number of polluting industries including leather, chlorine, dies, chemicals, some fertilizers, metal carbide and activated carbon products and lumber, to name a few. Nonetheless, VAT tax preferences continue to riddle the Chinese export economy and are particularly prevalent in pillar industries. Moreover, the shifting sands of China's VAT tax policies have created significant disruptions. Consider how China's VAT tax machinations have rippled across the Pacific to affect the U.S. steel industry:

> "In November 2006 and in April 2007, China reduced export VAT rebates that had been available on a wide range of semi-finished and finished steel products, as part of its efforts to discourage further unneeded creation of production capacity for these products in China. At the same time, these export VAT rebate reductions did not target all steel products, and the result was that Chinese steel producers shifted their production to steel products for which full export VAT rebates were still available, particularly steel pipe into products, causing a significant increase in exports of these products — many of which found their way into the U.S. market."[35]

It's not just the VAT tax that China uses as an important mercantilist tool. As part of its industrial policy to stimulate technological development, China "allows qualified high-technology companies registered in special economic zones to be exempt from income taxes for the first two years."[36]

For a graphic example of the discriminatory tax policies that the Chinese government uses to drive its export machine, look at the China-Singapore Suzhou Industrial Park, which is typical of China's Special Economic Zones. This industrial park was founded as a joint undertaking by the governments of Singapore and China. As reported by Andrew

Szamosszegi of the Economic Strategy Institute, tax incentives available to exporters are incredibly extensive. The very long list includes the following:

- A preferential corporate income tax of 15 percent (rather than 30 percent);
- A local income tax exemption of 3 percent;
- A full tax exemption in the first two years and a 50 percent tax exemption in the third year;
- A 10 percent preferential income tax rate for enterprises that export 70 percent of their output;
- A preferential 10 percent tax rate on dividends, interest, rental, royalty and other incomes;
- VAT tax exemptions for companies that export at least 50 percent of their output,
- The refund of all VAT taxes on the purchases of domestic machinery, equipment, raw materials, spare parts, components, packing materials and construction materials; and
- Refundable VAT taxes on water, power and gas purchased by firms producing for export.[37]

Here is the question that must be asked: How does a company in Michigan, Ohio, California or Pennsylvania compete against a Chinese counterpart that enjoys such a vast array of government subsidies?

Currency Manipulation

Since 1994, China has pegged its currency, the yuan, to the U.S. dollar at roughly an 8-to-1 ratio. Under pressure from the United States and the international community, China adopted a "managed float" regime in 2005 based on a market basket of currencies. For all practical purposes, however, the dollar peg remains intact, and the yuan remains, by most estimates, considerably undervalued. Table 4 provides a representative sample of some of the more credible estimates of the degree of this undervaluation, as well as the estimation methods used.[38]

As noted by the U.S.-China Economic and Security Review Commission, "China's undervalued currency encourages undervalued Chinese exports to the U.S. and discourages U.S. exports because U.S. exports are artificially overvalued. As a result, undervalued Chinese exports have been highly disruptive to the U.S. and to other countries as well, as evidenced by trade remedy statistics."[40]

In thinking about the global effects of currency manipulation, it is critical to also take into account the import content of exports. Any ben-

TABLE 4: ESTIMATES OF CHINESE CURRENCY MANIPULATION[39]		
Source	**Range**	**Method**
Coudert & Couharde (2005)	44%	Fundamental Equilibrium Exchange Rate
Preeg (2002)	40%	Fundamental Equilibrium Exchange Rate
Williamson (2003)	Over 25%	Fundamental Equilibrium Exchange Rate
Goldstein (2003)	15-25%	Fundamental Equilibrium Exchange Rate
Funke & Rahn (2005)	8-12%	Permanent Equilibrium Exchange Rate
Yang and Bajeux Besnainou (2004)	0%	Purchasing Power Parity

efits from selling exports with an undervalued currency will be at least partially offset by the need to buy from foreigners the raw materials, electronic components and other imported inputs used in the manufacturing process with that same weak currency. In fact, the import content of most Chinese manufactured goods has been estimated to be quite high, which substantially mutes the currency effect.

Lawrence Lau (2003)[41] and William Overholt (2003) suggest that this content is in the range of 75 percent.[42] This dynamic notwithstanding, there are several larger problems with China's currency manipulation that extend well beyond artificially stimulating Chinese exports and suppressing U.S. exports to China.

The Myth of the Asian Savings Glut

One problem is that China's currency manipulation has forced other Asian nations — most prominently Japan, South Korea and Taiwan — to engage in their own brands of currency manipulation to defend their own shares of the U.S. market against Chinese incursion. The result has been a huge U.S. trade deficit with Asia often mythologically portrayed in the media — and by current Federal Reserve Chairman Ben Bernanke — as the result of an "Asian glut of savings." The image this myth projects is that of the thrifty Asian citizen versus profligate Americans. In fact, the "Asian savings glut" is much more the product of forced savings behavior imposed by Asian currency manipulation.

The Japanese brand of currency manipulation is particularly interesting since currency manipulation is Japan's primary mercantilist tool to penetrate U.S. markets, particularly with automobiles. Japan does not maintain a fixed peg with the dollar. Instead, it uses a combination of a "managed float" and an ultra-easy monetary policy to suppress the value of the yen. The easy money form of currency manipulation is particularly clever: By maintaining short-term interest rates at close to zero, Japan has spawned a "carry trade" in bonds that keeps significant downward pressure on the yen.

In this carry trade, investors borrow yen at low short-term interest rates and then use the yen to purchase long-term bonds at much higher interest rates in other countries. However, in order to purchase these foreign bonds, carry-trade investors must first convert yen for the foreign currency; that depresses the value of the yen through the laws of supply and demand operating the currency markets. While Japanese exporters benefit from the cheapened yen, carry-trade investors make money on the "spread" between the short-term loans and the long-term bonds.

China's Currency Manipulation Sovereign Wealth Fund Threat

In addition to forcing other Asian nations to engage in currency manipulation as a defensive mechanism, China's currency manipulation has led to an extremely large buildup of U.S. foreign reserves in China's central bank — and the potentially very dangerous emergence of China's sovereign wealth funds. In order to maintain its fixed peg between the yuan and the dollar, China recycles its export dollars back into U.S. financial assets.

Some years ago, China's "dollar recycling" efforts were limited to purchasing U.S. government bonds. Now, however, China's reserves have grown so large that China is using some of its excess reserves to form sovereign wealth funds. A clear and present danger is that these sovereign wealth funds will use their dollar reserves to either purchase or gain controlling interests in American companies and then quietly over time strip these companies of either their technologies or jobs, or both, further weakening the U.S. economy and manufacturing base.

The Mercantilism of China's Counterfeiting and Piracy

China is not the only country engaged in counterfeiting and piracy. Other hotbeds include Russia, India, Vietnam and South Africa. However, China is considered to be the largest pirate nation; it accounts for an estimated two-thirds of the entire world's pirated and counterfeited goods and 80 percent of all counterfeit goods seized at U.S. borders. Moreover, professor Oded Shenkar at Ohio State's Fisher School of Business estimates that intellectual property theft contributes anywhere from 10 percent to an astonishing 30 percent of China's total GDP.[43]

It's critical to understand that Chinese counterfeiting and piracy extends way beyond the high-profile theft of Hollywood movies, music, publishing and expensive fashion items. As noted by Frank Vargo of the National Association of Manufacturers:

> "China is the epicenter of the counterfeits boom.... Just a few years ago, counterfeiting was all Gucci bags and fake perfume. Now it's everything. It has just exploded. It is many times larger a problem than it was only a few years ago. The counterfeit inventory ranges from cigarette lighters to automobiles to pharmaceutical fakes that can endanger a life. I would bet that there are companies in this country [the U.S.] that don't even know they're getting screwed around the world."[44]

In this regard, the United States Trade Representative notes a dizzying array of industries affected by Chinese counterfeiting and piracy. It includes "business and entertainment software, pharmaceuticals, chemicals, information technology, apparel, athletic footwear, textile fabrics and floor coverings, consumer goods, food and beverages, electrical equipment, automotive parts and industrial products, among many others."[45]

A key problem is that "legal measures in China that establish high thresholds for criminal prosecution and/or conviction preclude criminal penalties for many instances of commercial scale counterfeiting and piracy" and "create a 'safe harbor' for pirates and counterfeiters" while "other procedural burdens, such as an inability to investigate based on suspicion of criminality also weaken the criminal intellectual property rights system."[46] Despite repeated anti-piracy campaigns in China and an increasing number of civil intellectual property rights cases in Chinese courts, "overall piracy and counterfeiting levels in China remained unacceptably high in 2007."[47] The USTR said, "Levels of piracy in China across all lines of copyright business range between 80 percent and 95 percent based on data for 2007, which indicates little or no overall improvement over 2006."[48]

China's counterfeiting and piracy has a strong mercantilist element because it lowers the research and development, marketing and IT costs of those Chinese manufacturers that engage in IP theft. Consider, for example that the rate of software piracy in China is well over 90 percent. This provides substantial savings in both the operating and capital budget portions of the balance sheet for most Chinese enterprises. In addition, Chinese counterfeiters need not incur either significant research and development expenditures or substantial advertising and marketing costs to promote their "brand." As noted by A.T. Kearney, "counterfeiting allows skipping the investment necessary to create, develop and market products and go directly to profits. No R&D headaches. No brand building. No advertising."[49]

In addition, industries such as autos, biotechnology, semiconductors and pharmaceuticals are particularly R&D-intensive, with R&D expenditures as a percentage of revenues in the range of 15 percent or more. More broadly, based on sector-level data reported by *Technology Review*, the weighted average of R&D spending across all sectors of the global economy is estimated to be 8.5 percent.[50] Chinese exporters that do not have to bear these costs thereby gain a significant competitive edge.

There are also more diffuse cost savings and far more difficult-to-estimate effects of counterfeiting and piracy not accounted for in these calculations. Legitimate companies face warranty costs that often must be honored even when a counterfeit part leads to failure. Legitimate companies incur costs of protecting their own intellectual property. Companies like Nike, Louis Vuitton, Microsoft and IBM now spend considerable sums on IP protection, funds that could be spent on developing innovative products. They also suffer damage to their goodwill and reputation when counterfeit products fail — and when they fail to be recognized as counterfeits.

According to Ohio State law professor Daniel Chow, "no problem of this size and scope could exist without the direct or indirect involvement of the state."[51] Much of China's counterfeiting and piracy is state-sanctioned because counterfeiting and piracy boost the Chinese economy in at least three ways: by lowering marketing and advertising expenses; by lowering research and development expenditures; and by reducing software and other information technology expenditures. The result is the creation of millions of jobs, better control of inflation and a higher standard of living for hundreds of millions of Chinese consumers — all at the expense of shareholders and workers around the world who bear the costs of the IP theft.

Forced Technology Transfer

A key element of China's industrial policy has been to rapidly move up the value chain from low-technology, lower-wage products such as toys and cheap electronics into higher value-added and higher-wage industries such as automobiles, aircraft and pharmaceuticals. One of the most potent weapons China has used to move up the value chain is forced technology transfer. It is only through the acquisition (rather than internal development) of sophisticated technologies that Chinese companies have been able to rapidly enter and expand in sophisticated industries such as automobiles, aircraft, pharmaceuticals and other high-tech areas.

Forced technology transfer is an extremely effective mercantilist tool because China has the capability to "absorb and apply technology." As noted by GlobalSecurity.org: "China has no shortage of well-trained scientists, engineers, mathematicians or other technical experts, unlike the United States. Chinese scholars educated abroad over the last decade reportedly make up more than half of the top scientific researchers now working on key research projects and receiving priority in conducting this research."[52]

Consider the development of China's auto industry. China has very effectively used import licensing restrictions as a "bargaining chip" to effect technology transfer from companies like General Motors and Ford when they are setting up production facilities in China with the intention of selling into the Chinese market. The dynamic working here is that "China is a buyer's market. As such, the leverage of such an enormous potential market allows Chinese officials to frequently play foreign competitors against one another in their bids for joint venture contracts and large-scale, government-funded infrastructure projects in China. The typical result is usually more technology being transferred as competitors bid up the level or type of technology that they are willing to offer."[53] In fact, "most U.S. and other foreign investors in China thus far seem willing to pay the price of technology transfers — even 'state-of-the-art technologies' — in order to 'gain a foothold' or to 'establish a beachhead' in China with the expectation that the country's enormous market potential eventually will be realized."[54]

The case of pharmaceuticals in China is equally interesting. In this industry, China has used both counterfeiting and pirating of prescription drugs like Viagra and Lipitor to develop a large-scale manufacturing capability. However, an even more effective method for the longer term has been to force (or lure) American pharmaceutical companies in China to set up research and development facilities in China as a condition of market entry.

As for the aircraft industry, much of the technology that China has acquired for both its civilian and military aircraft production has been through industrial espionage. As noted by the Heritage Foundation, "China's government-sanctioned theft of advanced-technology intellectual property is another regular feature of China's industrial policy."[55]

It's not just the aircraft industry that has been subject to the theft of advanced technology. Chinese agents have been caught stealing, or attempting to steal, a wide variety of technologies from companies ranging from Cisco Systems and Sun Microsystems to NEC Electronics and Transmeta.[56]

It should be clear that forced technology transfer is an important component of Chinese industrial policy. It should be equally clear that much of the transfer that takes place occurs under conditions of coercion that clearly violate free trade principles. The bottom mercantilist line as noted by GlobalSecurity.org is this:

> "Technology transfer is both mandated in Chinese regulations or industrial policies (with which U.S. companies wishing to invest in China must comply) and used as a deal-maker or sweetener by U.S. firms seeking joint venture contracts in China. Unless significant changes are made to China's current investment regulations and import/export policies, U.S. commercial technology transfers to China are likely to continue, potentially enhancing Chinese competitiveness in high-technology industry sectors such as aerospace and electronics. The U.S.-China trade imbalance may continue to worsen in the short term as commercial offset demands and foreign-invested enterprise exports increase and in the long term as China's plans to develop indigenous capabilities in both basic and advanced technology industries are implemented."[57]

China's Environmental Pollution Competitive Edge

On the environmental front, China is rapidly becoming one of the most polluted countries in the world. It is home to 16 of the world's 20 most polluted cities. Of its almost 100 cities with over a million people each, two-thirds fail to meet World Health Organization air quality standards.

China is also the world leader in sulfur dioxide and CO_2 emissions. It releases 600 tons of mercury into the air annually, nearly one-fourth of the world's non-natural emissions,[58] and it is the world leader in the generation of substances that deplete the world's ozone layer. Acid rain, which severely damages forests, fisheries and crops, affects one-fourth of China's land and one-third of its agricultural land. As much as 50 percent of the acid rain in Japan and Korea is of Chinese origin. According to the Chinese Academy on Environmental Planning, more than 400,000 Chinese die prematurely each year from air-pollution related diseases, primarily from lung and heart disease.[59] That number is expected to reach more than 500,000 within a decade.

The statistics on water pollution are equally stark. Seventy percent of China's seven major rivers are severely polluted, and 80 percent fail to meet standards for fishing.[60] Ninety percent of China's cities and 75 percent of its lakes suffer from some degree of water pollution,[61] and 700 million Chinese "have access to drinking water of a quality below World Health Organization standards."[62] Liver and stomach cancers related to water pollution are among the leading causes of death in the countryside.[63] All of China's coastal waters are moderately to highly polluted.[64]

Not all of China's air and water pollution can be blamed on its manufacturing industries. Other major sources include pesticide and fertilizer runoff in the agricultural sector and large quantities of human and animal waste that are dumped into waterways or seep into ground water. However, China's industrial sector is the primary contributor of toxic (versus organic) pollution.

The worst polluting industries include paper and pulp, food, chemicals, textiles, tanning and mining. The most common toxic pollutants include dioxins, solvents, PCBs, various metals such as mercury, lead and copper, and highly persistent pesticides ranging from chlordane and mirex to DDT.[65]

Many of the polluting factories are small-scale and locally owned. Even when such enterprises are unprofitable, they represent important job generators in rural areas plagued by high unemployment. That makes it difficult for a local environmental protection bureau to close the polluters down, fine them or force them to comply with pollution control standards.

In addition, in many cases, large factories equipped with the latest and most sophisticated pollution control technologies simply don't use the technologies for fear of driving up production costs. Typically, this is done without any fear of sanctions by lax regulators and often complicit local officials.

China has some strict environmental laws on the books, but the fines that may be levied to enforce the regulations are so insignificant that they are seen merely as a cost of doing business rather than a true deterrent. Local authorities that collect the fines will often recycle the revenues back to the polluters as tax breaks. In addition, as with its weak health and safety regime, China's legal system makes it extremely difficult for pollution victims to properly seek any redress.

A major problem with enforcement is that China's state environmental protection agency is critically understaffed and under-budgeted. While the U.S. Environmental Protection Agency employs close to 17,000,[66] China's State Environmental Protection Administration (SEPA) has only 300 — this to oversee environmental protection in a country with well more than a billion people. Perhaps no one is more aware of the impotence of the China SEPA than its outspoken Deputy Director Pan Yue who has warned that: "China's population is so big and its resources so scarce that if we continue to ignore our environmental problems, that will bring disaster for us and the world."

From a free trade versus fair trade perspective, China's lax environmental regulations and weak enforcement provide a variety of cost advantages to its industrial sector. Enterprises save money by not providing protective equipment for workers. Many don't have to invest in pollution control technologies. Companies that do purchase such equipment save money by not operating it. Waste disposal costs are considerably reduced.

From a trade perspective, the advantages offered by China's lax environmental regulations hit hardest at precisely those manufacturing industries in the United States that face the highest compliance costs. For example, U.S. Steel reports spending roughly 3 percent of its revenues on environmental expenses. By comparison, China's Bao Steel spends only about one-tenth as much. The figures for Dow Chemical versus China's Sinopec are similar.

More broadly, John Blodgett of the Congressional Research Service provides a summary of pollution control compliance costs in the U.S.

that accounts for both capital expenditures and pollution abatement operating costs.[67] As a percent of value added, costs vary widely across industries. They range as high as 17 percent for petroleum, 9 percent for pulp mills, and 4 percent for chemicals to less than 1 percent for industries such as food, textiles and printing, with an overall average of 1.48 percent.[68]

One final observation may be useful here from a policy perspective. Whatever China's environmental cost advantages are at the individual enterprise level, they are likely being completely offset by the aggregate social costs of Chinese pollution. The World Bank estimates that pollution annually costs China between 8 percent and 12 percent of its more than $1 trillion GDP in terms of increased medical bills, lost work due to illness, damage to fish and crops and money spent on disaster relief.[69] These figures suggest that any cost-benefit analysis would favor China cleaning up its environment rather than "racing to the bottom" to gain a mercantilist edge.

China's Lax Health and Safety Regulations

While the Chinese government instituted new health and safety laws in 1995, few enterprises, either public or private, abide by them. Moreover, because the goal of economic growth has taken precedence, there is very little enforcement by either the central government or local and provincial governments. Nor is there any properly functioning legal system to protect workers and ensure fair compensation for those who are injured. The result: The legal liabilities of Chinese manufacturing enterprises are very limited.

According even to China's own under-reported statistics, China is one of the most dangerous places to work in the world. The highest-risk industries include building materials, chemicals, coal production, machinery manufacturing, metallurgy, plastics and textiles. Diseases ranging from silicosis and brown lung to a variety of cancers caused by the ingestion, inhalation or contact with toxic chemicals and waste are endemic. Workplace injuries are endemic. This passage from the *New York Times* indicates the scope of the problem:

> "Yongkang, in prosperous Zhejiang Providence just south of Shanghai, is the hardware capital of China. Its 7,000 metal-working factories — all privately owned — make hinges, hubcaps, pots and pans, power drills, tool boxes, thermoses, electric razors, headphones, fans and

just about anything else with metallic innards. Yongkang, which means "eternal health" in Chinese, is also the dismemberment capital of China. At least once a day someone... is rushed to one of the dozen clinics that specialize in treating hand, arm and finger injuries, according to local government statistics.... The reality, all over China, is that workplace casualties have become endemic. Nationally, 140,000 people died in work-related accidents last year, according to the State Administration of Work Safety. Hundreds of thousands more were injured."[70]

The cost advantages to Chinese manufacturers inherent in this lax health and safety regulatory regime range from the use of cheaper equipment for workers and fewer safety-related expenses to savings on training and safety-related large capital expenditures. For example, Chinese textile companies are unlikely to invest in anti-noise or dust control equipment. Chinese coal mining companies tend to skimp on masks, goggles and emergency rescue facilities. In other industries, adopting wet drilling systems increases costs by as much as 60 percent over dry drilling systems. Wet drilling systems significantly reduce hazardous dust emissions, but they are rarely used.

Unfair Labor Standards and Slave Labor

According to the *New York Times*, "nearly a decade after some of the most powerful companies in the world — often under considerable criticism and consumer pressure — began an effort to eliminate sweatshop labor conditions in Asia, worker abuse is still commonplace in many of the Chinese factories that supply Western companies, according to labor rights groups. The groups say some Chinese companies routinely shortchange their employees on wages, withhold health benefits and expose their workers to dangerous machinery and chemicals, like lead, cadmium and mercury."

One major problem is the severe restrictions on union organizing that exist in China. A second major problem is the lack of an enforceable minimum wage. Both of these problems are compounded by the existence of significant pockets of slave labor.

Some of China's real slaves are the children and women and occasionally men who are routinely kidnapped and forced to work in the brick kilns, coal mines and countless sweatshops of the Chinese hinterlands with no payment other than a floor to sleep on, some rice gruel to eat, and the occasional beating for objecting to their enslavement.

Others of China's real slaves are the millions of religious and political dissidents trapped in the Chinese equivalent of the old Soviet gulags. These prisoners-of-conscience are forced to work for nothing more than a crowded jail cell and meager rations. This passage from *American Legion Magazine* grimly describes the modern horror of China's primitive "laogai camps":

> "After Mao Tse-tung established the People's Republic of China in 1949, he created a network of slave labor camps to maintain control over his subjects. The camps were called laogai based on a Chinese acronym for the phrase "reform through labor." Even though Mao died decades ago, the laogai camps remain an integral part of Beijing's tyranny. …Today, an estimated four to six million people are rotting away in the laogai camps, serving out varying years and degrees of involuntary penance to the state Mao erected. Laogai prisoners produce everything from bottled water and tea to electronics and engine parts. Given the religious reasons for many laogai sentences, it is a sickening irony that some camps even produce rosaries, Christmas lights and toys — all for export to the West."[71]

In addition to China's real slaves, there are millions more contractual slaves. These are the Chinese workers that arrive at the factory door wide-eyed and naive direct from the farms expecting decent working conditions and a livable wage. In some cases, they are fed and housed, but their wages are withheld in a form of economic slavery. In other cases, these economic slaves may want to leave the job because it has not lived up to their expectations. However, the penalties for leaving are so steep that they are stuck. To see what often confronts the typical Chinese worker seeking fortune in the big city consider this excerpt from The *New York Times*:

> "Each eyelash was assembled from 464 inch long strands of human hair, delicately placed in a crisscross pattern on a thin strip of transparent glue. Completing a pair often took an hour. Even with 14-hour shifts most girls could not produce enough for a modest bonus. 'When we started to work, we realized there was no way

to make money,' said Ma Pinghui, 16. 'They were trying to cheat us.'

"She and her friend Wei Qi, also 16 and also a Chinese farm girl barely out of junior high school, had been lured here by a South Korean boss who said he was prepared to pay $120 a month, a princely sum for unskilled peasants, to make false eyelashes....Two months later, bitter that the pay turned out to be much lower, exhausted by eye-straining and wrist-wrenching work, and too poor to pay the exit fee the boss demanded of anyone who wanted out, they decided to escape. But that was not easy. The metal doors of their third-floor factory were kept locked and its windows — all but one — were enclosed in iron cages....Said Ms. Wei, 'What they called a company was really a prison.' "[72]

This systematic ill treatment of Chinese workers could not take place without the complicity of the Chinese government. The practical economic result of is that both Chinese and multinational companies enjoy a real mercantilist cost advantage — and therefore unfair competitive advantage — over countries where workers are far better protected and respected.

Entrustment

In its mercantilist quest to boost its export regime, China seemingly leaves no industrial policy stone unturned. One particular type of subsidy that is relatively rare in the international environment but common in China is the strategy identified as "entrustment" or "direction." China will use one of its financially healthy companies to bail out or subsidize a company having problems. A classic case was identified by Andrew Szamosszegi of the Economic Strategy Institute. When China's largest bearings manufacturer, Luoyang Bearing, found itself in serious financial straits in 2004, the Chinese government ordered the state-owned Yoncheng Coal to bail out the bearings manufacturer.[73]

Export Restrictions

While the USTR report has been uneven in its coverage and treatment of protectionist and mercantilist elements, it has been crystal clear on both the extent and impact of China's various export restrictions that provide China with another mercantilist advantage: "Despite China's commitment since its accession to the WTO to eliminate all taxes and charges on exports...China has continued to impose restrictions on exports of raw materials, including quotas, related licensing requirements and duties, as China's state planners have continued to guide the development of downstream industries."[71]

As further noted by the United States Trade Representative, China's export restrictions "affect U.S. and other foreign producers of a wide range of downstream products, such as steel, chemicals, ceramics, semiconductor chips, refrigerants, medical imagery, aircraft, refined petroleum products, fiberoptic cables and catalytic converters, among numerous others."[75] Moreover, the restrictions are widespread.

Consider that "China maintains export quotas and sometimes export duties on antimony, bauxite, coke, fluorspar, indium, magnesium carbonate, molybdenum, rare earths, silicone, talc, tin, tungsten and zinc, all of which are of key interest to U.S. downstream producers."[76] This enables China's domestic downstream producers to produce lower-priced products from raw materials and thereby creates significant advantages for China's domestic downstream producers when competing against foreign downstream producers both in the China market and in export markets.[77]

This problem is getting worse not better. As the United States Trade Representative noted: "Over time, China's state planners have increased the artificial advantages afforded the Chinese downstream producers by making export quotas more restrictive and by imposing or increasing export duties on many raw materials at issue."[78]

Mercantilist-Driven Foreign Direct Investment

Among developing nations, China has become the leading destination of foreign direct investment. Since 1983, FDI has grown from less than $1 billion a year to over $60 billion, 72 percent of which targets manufacturing.

Of China's FDI, 20 percent to 30 percent is estimated to be of domestic origin. It is the result of the "round tripping" of mainland Chinese capital, primarily through Hong Kong and the Virgin Islands. This "round tripping" is driven by the special preferences the Chinese government awards to FDI in the form of lower tax rates, land-use rights and subsidies, administrative support and other subsidies, most of which represent violations of WTO rules, as well as by a desire to evade foreign exchange controls.[79]

Other major FDI participants include the United States, Japan, Korea and Taiwan. While the availability of cheap labor and the allure of China's growing and largely untapped consumer market certainly play a major role in attracting these participants, lax environmental and health and safety regulatory standards synergistically factor into investment decisions. In this regard, multinational companies are increasingly being criticized within China for exporting their pollution from everywhere else in the world to mainland China. In addition, China's undervalued currency also provides considerable FDI synergy. An undervalued yuan makes Chinese assets appear relatively cheap to foreign investors.

China's catalytic FDI provides a variety of competitive benefits. It finances the transfer of the most technologically advanced production and process technologies. It has brought with it managerial best practices and skills as many FDI-financed enterprises are managed by foreign talent. FDI is also often tied to the improvement of both marketing and distribution skills.

When all of these attributes are tied to one of the least expensive labor forces in the world, FDI becomes a powerful competitive driver. As noted by *Business Week*, "as capital floods in and modern plants are built in China, efficiencies improve dramatically. The productivity of private industry in China has grown an astounding 17 percent annually for five years."[80]

Chinese FDI is driven by protectionism and its mercantilist market environment, and it thereby constitutes an unfair trade advantage. Consider China's textile industry. It has been the largest purchaser of both new shuttle-less looms and spinning equipment in recent years, much of it paid for with FDI. The result is that Chinese textile workers now achieve rates of high productivity similar to those of U.S. textile workers.[81]

Protectionist and Mercantilist Practices by America's Other Major Trading Partners

As a benchmark of comparison, what follows is an analysis of the four other major trading partners of the United States. But this analysis is rather brief because, unlike China, these four other major trading partners normally play by the rules set forth by the WTO and GATT.

The Eurozone

The Eurozone is America's second largest trading partner behind China. In 2007, Eurozone countries collectively ran a $107-billion trade surplus with the United States, more than $40 billion of which was accounted for by Germany.

Many of the problems that exist in trade relations between the United States and the Eurozone countries revolve around the agricultural and pharmaceutical sectors. However, there are several important issues that materially affect trade in manufactured goods.

One of the biggest bones of contention is the existence of ongoing "measures that subsidize the development, production and marketing of large civil aircraft."[82] In this regard, Europe makes the same kind of complaints about the subsidization of America's civilian aircraft industry that the United States makes against Airbus. The USTR report makes it clear, however, that considerable unfair trade support exists for Airbus suppliers and aircraft engine production.

For example, its government "subsidizes Belgian manufacturers that supply parts to Airbus."[83] At the same time, "France provides aid in the form of reimbursable advances to assist the development by French manufacturers of products such as planes, aircraft engines, helicopters and on-board equipment by French manufacturers."[84] For its part, United Kingdom's government provides considerable support to Rolls-Royce for the development of aircraft engines.[85]

The chemical industry is the second American manufacturing industry that has been impacted by Eurozone nontariff barriers. The problem here is that U.S. producers of chemicals and downstream users of chemicals "face the EU's comprehensive new regulatory regime known as Registration, Evaluation and Authorization of Chemicals, which adopts a particularly complex and burdensome approach that appears to be neither workable nor cost-effective."[86]

A third problem that varies considerably on a country-to-country basis involves the application of local content rules and government procurement. The countries of greatest concern include the Czech Republic, Greece, Lithuania, Portugal and Spain.

Japan

Japan is America's third largest trading partner as measured by the size of America's deficit with Japan — $83 billion in 2007. Japan is also America's second largest trading country behind only China. Japan is America's fourth-largest export market.

Perhaps the biggest problem with U.S.-Japan trade relations is the indirect manipulation of the yen by Japan's central government and central bank. Curiously, this mercantilist weapon, which has been particularly injurious to the American automobile industry, has been totally ignored in the USTR report.

The USTR report nonetheless identifies several important protectionist and mercantilist policies that contribute to the U.S.-Japanese trade imbalance. While many of these policies serve to protect and promote Japan's agricultural industries, some of these policies impact the trade balance in manufactured goods.

"Japan continues to restrict the importation of U.S.-manufactured wood products through tariff escalation [and] elimination of tariffs on wood products remains a long-standing U.S. government objective." Japan also protects its leather and footwear industry using a tariff-rate quota that "substantially limits imports into Japan's market, and establishes these quotas in a nontransparent manner."[87]

Japan also continues to fiercely protect its automobile and auto parts sectors. As noted in the USTR report, "a variety of nontariff barriers have traditionally impeded access to this market, and overall sales of North American-made vehicles and parts in Japan remain low."[88]

To a lesser extent, Japan also uses protectionist methods such as local content rules to promote its civilian aerospace products. Japan's Ministry of Defense "has a general preference for domestic production or the licensing of U.S. technology for production in Japan to support the domestic defense industry."[89]

America's NAFTA Trading Partners

It is useful to treat Canada and Mexico as a pair in this analysis because both countries are party to the North American Free Trade Agreement (NAFTA) that was put into place in 1994. Today, under NAFTA, the United States, Canada and Mexico engage in an almost textbook-like, free-trade regime.

Mexico is America's fourth largest trading partner, as measured by the size of the U.S. trade imbalance with Mexico. The American goods trade deficit with Mexico was $74 billion in 2007. Despite this trade imbalance, Mexico is the second largest export market for U.S. goods.[90]

As for Canada, it is the fifth largest trading partner of the United States as measured by the size of the trade deficit and the largest export market for U.S. goods. More broadly, the United States and Canada engage in the world's largest bilateral trade relationship, with total merchandise trade (exports and imports) exceeding $500 billion a year.[91]

Half of the U.S. trade imbalance with Canada is attributable to large quantities of imported oil. While trade relations between the United States, Canada and Mexico are relatively free of either protectionist or mercantilist influences, a few areas of concern have been raised that affect the manufacturing sectors of both countries.

Mexico

One major area of concern in U.S.-Mexican trade relations focuses on import licensing restrictions. As noted by the United States Trade Representative, to be eligible, U.S. exporters of more than 400 different items to Mexico must apply and "be listed on a special industry sector registry" while industries affected include "agricultural products, textiles, chemicals, electronics and automotive parts."[92]

American exporters have complained that "registering is bureaucratically difficult and this requirement sometimes causes costly customs clearance delays when new products are added to the list of subject items with immediate effect, thereby denying importers sufficient notice to apply. They also report that certain importers have been summarily dropped from the registry without prior notice or subsequent explanation, effectively preventing some U.S. exporters from shipping goods to Mexico."[93]

A second area of concern involves inflated customs valuations. Mexico "uses estimated prices for customs valuations of a wide range of products imported from the United States and other countries, including... chemicals, wood, paper and paperboard products, textiles, apparel, toys, tools and appliances."[94]

Yet a third problem relates to "continuing high levels of piracy and counterfeiting in Mexico."[95] However, most of this piracy and counterfeiting affects the entertainment industry and software industry. This is in sharp contrast to the kind of intellectual property theft that takes place in China, which is aimed at reducing production costs in many of China's key manufacturing industries.

Canada

As for Canada, perhaps the biggest problem is subsidies for Canada's aerospace and defense industries. These subsidies are administered under the Technology Partnership Canada program that supports research and development activities in Canada. Essentially, the

Technology Partnership Canada organization provides subsidized loans to these pillar industries.

A second problem identified by the United States Trade Representative is that of local content rules. While U.S. companies are allowed to compete on the nondiscriminatory basis for federal government contracts, "Buy Canada" programs remain in place at the provincial government level.

These issues notwithstanding, trade between the United States and its neighbors, Mexico and Canada, adheres far closer to the principles of free trade than to the problems of protectionism and mercantilism that mars the U.S.-China relationship. While there remain some problems in trade relations between the United States and the Eurozone, Japan, Mexico and Canada, these problems are minor compared to the protectionist and mercantilist practices of China. If the United States wants to make headway in reducing its chronic trade imbalances, the primary policy focus should be on addressing Chinese protectionism and mercantilism.

Summary and Conclusions

The ultimate purpose of this chapter is to provide policymakers with the facts with which to evaluate trade relations with America's five largest trading partners — China, the Eurozone, Japan, Mexico and Canada. These five major partners account for the lion's share of America's chronic trade deficits — roughly 75 percent.

As the foundation for this analysis, the narrative first noted that America's chronic trade deficits — and collateral transfer of millions of manufacturing jobs overseas — are significantly weakening the economic and political fabric of the United States. The transfer of American jobs overseas to low-wage hubs in Latin America and particularly Asia has depressed wages and materially reduced the standard of living of millions of Americans. The "hollowing out" of the U.S. manufacturing base has helped induce recessionary conditions in key regions of the United States particularly in the Midwest.

In addition, America's chronic trade deficits have put severe downward pressure on the dollar, creating inflation while reducing American purchasing power and lowering the standard of living. At the same time, America's political sovereignty and economic base is increasingly threatened by the rise of sovereign wealth funds that have the power to use their dollar reserves to purchase and gain controlling interests in American companies and then strip these companies of either their technologies or jobs, or both, further weakening the U.S. economy and manufacturing base.

In light of these negative effects, the big question raised is whether the loss of American manufacturing jobs, depressed wages and the presence of chronic American trade deficits are the inevitable results of a free-trade system that, on balance, will be both "good for America" and "good for the world" over time. Alternatively, are the negative effects of free trade the pernicious results of America's trading partners adopting "beggar thy U.S. neighbor" mercantilist and protectionist trade policies that run contrary to free trade principles?

The most important conclusion of this analysis should be unmistakable: America's largest trading partner by the size of the trade imbalance, China is engaging in the most massive campaign of mercantilism and protectionism ever witnessed. While this chapter purposefully refrains from proposing any specific policy solutions, the author's hope is the information provided along with the framework used in the analysis will assist policymakers in thinking through this critical problem.

---

1. There are many different kinds of tariff instruments. The simplest form is the "ad valorem tariff," which is levied as percentage of price. A more complex tariff is that of "tariff escalation." This involves higher import duties on semi-processed products than on raw materials and progressively higher tariffs on finished products. In this way, tariff escalation protects domestic processing and finishing industries while discouraging the development of these industries in the countries where the raw materials originate. As a hybrid form of the quota and tariff, there is also the "tariff rate quota." This protectionist tool sets a tariff on imports below a specified quantity and then raises that tariff on higher quantities.

2. According to *Petroleum Intelligence Weekly*, America's import bill for foreign oil equaled $327 billion in 2007. "U.S. Oil Import Bill to Top $400 billion This Year, Says Petroleum Intelligence Weekly," Business Wire, March 7, 2008, http://findarticles.com/p/articles/mi_m0EIN/is_2008_March_7/ai_n24380607

3. "2008 National Trade Estimate Report on Foreign Trade Barriers," United States Trade Representative, http://www.ustr.gov/Document_Library/Reports_Publications/2008/2008_NTE_Report/Section_Index.html?ht=. Given its obvious limitations, the USTR Report would be greatly enhanced if it adhered more closely to the comprehensive compendium of protectionist and mercantilist practices set forth in Tables 1 and 2 and the framework of analysis set forth in this chapter.

4. USTR Report, page 82.

5. USTR Report, page 83.

6. USTR Report, page 79.

7. USTR Report, page 134.

8. USTR Report, page 81.

9. Szamosszegi, Andrew, "How Chinese Government Subsidies and Market Intervention Have Resulted in the Offshoring of U.S. Auto Parts Production: A Case Study," page 5.

10. USTR Report, page 97.

11. USTR Report, page 123.

12. Thun, Eric, "Industrial Policy, Chinese-Style: FDI, Regulation, and Dreams of National Champions in the Auto Sector," *Journal of East Asian Studies* (September-December 2004) at n. 85.

13. Szamosszegi, page 11.

14. Szamosszegi, page 15.

15. Szamosszegi, pages 16-17.

16. USTR Report, page 91.

17. USTR Report, page 92.

18. USTR Report, page 91.

19. USTR Report, page 93.

20. USTR Report, page 93.

21. USTR Report, page 93.

22. USTR Report, page 93.

23. USTR Report, page 93.

24. USTR Report, page 139.

25. USTR Report, page 90.

26. See, for example, the annual survey results of "Transparency International, the Global Coalition Against Corruption," http://www.transparency.org/policy_research/surveys_indices/cpi/2007.

27. USTR Report, page 141.

28. USTR Report, page 104.

29. USTR Report, page 104.

30. Statement of Al Lubrano, President, Technical Materials, Inc., House Small Business subcommittee on tax, finance and exports, May 27, 2005.

31. China's policy of offering free land use to multinationals has been particularly effective in attracting foreign direct investment.

32. Szamosszegi, page17.

33. It is worth noting that the Chinese government has suspended the VAT tax rebate in a number of industries, including most prominently semiconductors. However, it did so only after threats from the U.S. of filing WTO complaints. See, for example, "China Encourages IC Research & Development," *China Daily*, September 8, 2004.

34. For details, see "China VAT & Export Rebates," Dezan Shira & Associates. http://www.dezshira.com/china_export_rebates.htm.

35. USTR Report, page 104.

36. USTR Report, pages 88-89.

37. Szamosszegi, page 20-22.

38. Purchasing power parity (PPP) is based on the "law of one price." The Fundamental Equilibrium Exchange Rate (FEER) is based on a comparison of a country's internal and external current and capital account balances. Another frequently used method is the Behavioral Equilibrium Exchange Rate (BEER), which uses the modeling of economic fundamentals like business cycles, productivity growth and interest rate differentials.

39. Coudert, V. and Couharde, C., "Real Equilibrium Exchange Rate in China: Is the Renminbi Undervalued?" working paper, Centre D'Etudes Perspectives et D'Informations Internationales (CEPII), 2005; Preeg, E., "Exchange Rate Manipulation to Gain an Unfair Competitive Advantage: The Case Against Japan and China," Manufacturers Alliance/MAPI, October 2, 2002; Williamson, J., "The Renminbi Exchange Rate and the Global Monetary System," Institute for International Economics, October 29, 2003; Goldstein, M., "China's Exchange Rate System," testimony before the Committee on Financial Services' subcommittee on domestic and international monetary policy, trade, and technology, Institute for International Economics, October 2003; Funke, M. and Rahn, J., "Just How Undervalued is the Chinese Renminbi?" *The World Economy*, 28/4, (2004), 465; Yang, J. and Bajeux-Besnainou, I., "Is the Chinese Currency Undervalued?" Occasional Paper Series, School of Business and Public Management, The George Washington University, GW Center for the Study of Globalization, CSGOP-04-26, February 10, 2004.

40. "The Importance of Trade Remedies to the U.S. Trade Relationship With China."

U.S.-China Economic and Security Review Commission, May 16, 2005.
41. Lau, Lawrence J., "Is China Playing By the Rules?" Congressional-Executive Commission on China, September 24, 2003, http://www.cecc.gov/pages/hearings/092403/index.php.
42. Overholt, William, "Exposing the Myths," *South China Morning Post*, November 17, 2003.
43. Shenkar, Oded, "The Chinese Century: The Rising Chinese Economy and Its Impact on the Global Economy, the Balance of Power, and Your Job," Wharton School Publishing, 2004.
44. Quoted in "Genuine Problem: Counterfeit Products from China Continue to Bedevil Makers of Legitimate Goods," *Journal of Commerce*, June 27, 2005.
45. USTR Report, page 111.
46. USTR Report, page 106.
47. USTR Report, page 103.
48. USTR Report, page 112.
49. A.T. Kearney, "The Counterfeiting Paradox." Undated, http://www.atkearney.com/shared_res/pdf/Counterfeiting_Paradox.pdf.
50. "R&D 2005," *Technology Review*, September 2005.
51. Statement of professor Daniel C. K. Chow, Congressional-Executive Commission on China, May 16, 2005, "Intellectual Property Protection as Economic Policy: Will China Ever Enforce Its IP Laws?" http://www.cecc.gov/pages/roundtables/051605/Chow.php, testifying before the U.S. Senate Committee on Governmental Affairs in April 2004. In Ted Fishman, *China, Inc.* (New York: Scribner, 2005), page 237.
52. GlobalSecurity.org, "Weapons of Mass Destruction (WMD), Technology Transfer to China," http://www.globalsecurity.org/wmd/library/report/1999/techtransfer2prc.htm.
53. Ibid.
54. Ibid.
55. Heritage Foundation, "The U.S. Must Face Up to China's Trade Challenges," 2003, http://www.heritage.org/research/tradeandforeignaid/bg1698.cfm.
56. Ibid.
57. GlobalSecurity.org.
58. Pottinger, Matt; Stecklow, Steve; and Fialka, John J., "Invisible Export — a Hidden Cost of China's Growth: Mercury Migration," *The Wall Street Journal*, December 20, 2004. http://yaleglobal.yale.edu/display.article?id=5058.
59. Watts, Jonathan, *The Guardian*, "Satellite Data Reveals Beijing as Air Pollution Capital of World," October 31, 2005.
60. Zhang, Guang-Xin and Wei, Deng "The Groundwater Crisis and Sustainable Agriculture In Northern China," *Water Engineering & Management* 149(4), April 13, 2002.
61. "China Says Water Pollution So Severe That Cities Could Lack Safe Supplies," *China Daily*, June 28, 2005.
62. Butler, Tina, "China's Imminent Water Crisis," Mongabay.com, May 30, 2005, http://news.mongabay.com/2005/0531-tina_butler.html.
63. Ibid.
64. Xinhua Agency Report, "The Frequency of Offing Red-Tide Increasing," http://monkey.ioz.ac.cn/bwg-cciced/english/warnings/warnings.htm.
65. "Toxic Chemicals To Be Phased Out," China.org.cn, November 11, 2004, http://www.china.org.cn/english/2004/Nov/111804.htm.
66. "Bureaucracy: A Controversial Necessity," *Democracy in America*, http://www.learner.org/channel/courses/democracyinamerica/dia_8/dia_8_video.html.
67. Blodgett, John, "Environmental Protection: How Much It Costs and Who Pays," Environment and Natural Resources Policy Division, Congressional Research Service, April 16, 1997. Note that this may be the best survey available as it is based on the last annual surveys of pollution control costs conducted by the Bureau of Census and Bureau of Economic Analysis. These surveys were discontinued after reportage of the 1994 data, http://www.ncseonline.org/nle/crsreports/risk/rsk-10.cfm.

68. For a summary of some of the early literature, see U.S. Office of Technology Assessment. 1992, "Trade and the Environment: Conflicts and Opportunities," Report No. OTA-BP-ITE-94. Washington, D.C., Government Printing Office, Appendix E: "Assessing Trade and Competitiveness Impacts of Environmental Regulations on U.S. Manufacturing," http://www.ciesin.org/docs/008-067/appendixe.html.

69. World Bank, "Clear Skies, Blue Water: China's Environment in the New Century," Washington, D.C., 1997.

70. Kahn, Joseph, "China's Workers Risk Limbs in Export Drive." *The New York Times*, April 7, 2003, http://www.asria.org/ref/library/social/lib/031208_NYTimes_sweatshops_inchina.pdf.

71. *The American Legion Magazine*, "An Interview With Harry Wu: Exposing China's Hidden Gulags," April 2006, http://www.laogai.org/news/newsdetail.php?id=2524.

72. Kahn, Joseph, "Chinese Girls' Toil Brings Pain, Not Riches," *New York Times*, October 2, 2003, http://www.international.ucla.edu/asia/rights/Chinesegirls031002.asp.

73. Szamosszegi, page 18.

74. USTR Report, page 103.

75. USTR Report, page 103.

76. USTR Report, page 103.

77. USTR Report, page 103.

78. USTR Report, page 103.

79. Numerous studies have examined this phenomenon. See, for example, World Bank 2002, "Global Development Finance 2002," Washington, D.C., page 41.

80. Engardio, Pete; Roberts, Dexter; with Bremner, Brian in Beijing and bureau reports, "The China Price," *Business Week*, December 6, 2004, http://www.businessweek.com/magazine /content/04_49/b3911401.htm.

81. Kincanon, Michelle; Gutzwiller, Charles; El-Badawi, Sharif; Jung, Kyle; Fan, Lawrence; Cook, Jr., Christopher; Ibanescu, Cosmin; and Wei, Andy, "The China Price: A Look Into the Textile Industry," March 15, 2006, unpublished manuscript available online at www.peternavarro.com/chinapriceproject.html.

82. USTR Report, page 193.

83. USTR Report, pages 217-218.

84. USTR Report, pages 217-218.

85. USTR Report, pages 217-218.

86. USTR Report, page 202.

87. USTR Report, page 301.

88. USTR Report, page 310.

89. USTR Report, page 311.

90. USTR Report, page369.

91. USTR Report, page 59.

92. USTR Report, page 372.

93. USTR Report, page 372.

94. USTR Report, page 372.

95. USTR Report, page 374.

4. The Globalization of Research, Development and Innovation

Ron Hira
Rochester Institute of Technology

The narrative that is repeated constantly by the experts and pundits promoting the current flavor of globalization, whether they are ideologically on the left or the right, is that it is inevitable that low-skill, low-wage, labor-intensive jobs will move to low-cost countries. But that is fine, because the United States will specialize in technology sectors that create highly skilled, well-paid jobs that depend on creativity and innovation.

The narrative and its prescriptions rest on a division-of-labor hypothesis: The U.S. response to increased offshoring should be to "move up" the innovation and skill ladder. Countries like the United States need to specialize more intensely in sectors and jobs where they hold a comparative advantage, and in the case of the United States, it's in innovation. The story acknowledges that low-skill, low-wage workers will face increased competition from workers abroad and some may lose their jobs, but it offers a solution for them too. They can be easily retrained for higher skill and higher wage jobs, and end up better off.

Economic theory, the story says, holds that the overall gains from offshoring will be so great that theoretically the "winners" (firms and consumers) could easily pay off the "losers" (workers and smaller firms) for the costs they incur, and still have a lot of money left over. The fact that the winners historically have never paid off the losers seems to be of little importance. A similar story is told about specific industries. If certain industrial sectors, like textiles or computer manufacturing, are lost, that's all right since they will be replaced by "better" industries. In this ideal tale, everyone goes home happy, because everyone is either the same or better off than they were before offshoring.

But what happens to the narrative if in reality, the tasks and jobs moving to low-cost countries are in the very same high-skill innovation and high-tech sectors in which the United States is supposed to hold an advantage? What if the sectors that are lost are the "better" industries?

A variety of indicators show that some high-tech jobs and sectors have already moved to low-cost countries like India and China, and there is even more evidence that this migration will increase. The growth could be substantial. Princeton economist Alan Blinder estimated the vulnerability to offshoring of all 838 Department of Labor job categories, and found absolutely no correlation with skill level. This means that many occupations requiring advanced skills are vulnerable to offshoring, including nearly all science and engineering job categories.

In response to these facts, another narrative supporting status-quo globalization has been constructed. In this muddled tale, the rise of India and China is seen as both a challenge and a boon. In response to the challenge, American workers and industries that cannot take advantage of offshoring must "run faster and jump higher" or "adjust" by moving to new functions or sectors. The experts argue that innovation is a panacea, and that more public money should be directed to increase U.S. technological capacity. They offer a simple three-ingredient cocktail: increase R&D spending (and R&D tax breaks); produce more scientists and engineers; and improve K-12 science and math education.

Of course, all of these put the onus on taxpayers to pick up the bill.

These investments are seen as providing the "infrastructure" for creating new firms and high-wage jobs. As this line of thinking goes, doubling public investments in science and technology will encourage or complement private investments in science and technology and a new wave of high-wage, high-technology jobs and companies will be created in the United States. The path to redemption is clear, so don't change the flavor of globalization just speed up innovation.

This story is boosted by the media and other institutions, like higher education. These days, every university president in the nation seems to be only able to utter one slogan out of his or her mouth: innovation. It is couched in terms of the need to be globally competitive.

But it doesn't stop there since the proponents wisely chose a multi-pronged approach. To reassure people, they again bring up the division of labor hypothesis, claiming that while some "R&D" might be going offshore, it isn't really the important stuff. The noncritical, noncore R&D might be moving offshore, but it is work that is either "last generation" or is geared toward localization — customizing products for local needs. The really high-tech, cutting-edge research is staying in the United States.

But what happens to this new narrative if private R&D spending and the highest skilled jobs move to low-cost countries? If those countries are also investing in their public technological research infrastructure, what happens when these countries start capturing more of the core R&D and leading-edge innovation?

That's where the "boon" part of the new, muddled tale comes into play. Here the story goes that any new discoveries abroad from research and development will add to overall human welfare. As some have put it, who would or could complain if a cure for cancer was discovered in China? So the promoters get to have their cake, eat it too, and stick U.S. taxpayers with the bill.

This chapter explores how much offshoring of research and development and technological innovation is taking place, some of the discussion about its implications and what the United States has chosen to do about it.

The Political, Economic and Policy Context

India and China have attained the ability to produce world-class science- and engineering-based goods and services. This is a very new and surprising phenomenon, and various American institutions are responding to it. Congress has been holding hearings; businesses are responding to new competitors and opportunities; management consultants are promoting high-end offshoring to businesses as a way to save money; site selection consultants are promoting new geographies for new R&D facilities; academics and experts are studying it; top business schools are setting up centers of excellence to teach their MBA students how to manage innovation offshoring; U.S. universities are going global, setting up outposts in low-cost countries to train the workers for the businesses that are offshoring; foreign governments and business groups are marketing their low-cost R&D capabilities; experts are offering various prognostications about it; and the business press has been reporting on it.

Simply put, this is the beginning of a fundamental shift in the global production of innovation and R&D, and it will have a profound impact on the U.S. economy, including the types of jobs available for millions of Americans, sectoral specialization, military position, and competition and opportunities for businesses.

Yet even with all of the attention it receives, the state of knowledge about the magnitude and direction of Indian and Chinese technological capability remains meager, at best. There are a variety of reasons driving this state of affairs. First, the data available is limited, stale and narrow, and is of poor quality.[1] The federal government has devoted virtually no resources to improve this data situation. Second, the businesses benefiting from sourcing high-technology products and services from China and India have strong incentives to understate, misstate or simply not disclose their activities there, making data collection and forecasting especially difficult even in ideal circumstances. But the challenge is exacerbated by the fact that science- and engineering-based production are characterized by long lag times, risk, prolonged learning curves, learning by doing, positive feedback loops, network effects, specialized and expensive human capital development and path dependencies. Today's investments will not appear in actual products and innovations until some time in the future, if they do at all. Coupled together, these factors make predicting the trajectory and nature of the globalization of R&D and innovation especially difficult.

Putting the data and forecasting issues aside, there is another important factor muddying the public discussion of the offshoring of innovation: It is difficult to precisely identify the future impact of R&D on the U.S. economy and its workers. Even in an ideal scenario, where the government could document the offshoring of high technology for the next 20 years, economic theory doesn't provide guidance on how it could impact the United States.

Technological innovation is neither measured well nor modeled formally. It is generally treated as a residual or, as Stanford University economic historian Nathan Rosenberg calls it, a black box.[2] Much of the important literature on innovation comes from the evolutionary branch of economics, which is more like storytelling than formal modeling. It describes a nation's capacity to innovate in terms of ecosystems and other such metaphors. Linkages between and behaviors of various actors are often more important than the sheer size of resource inputs. And predicting specific economic outcomes is especially difficult.

Second, the traditional neoclassical models of trade have not factored in much about offshoring, despite claims of the proponents of globalization. Offshoring isn't simply trade in the narrow sense that political economist David Ricardo or the theory of comparative advantage that is usually invoked, but instead shifts in productive capabilities across countries. Contrary to many pundits' popular beliefs, economic theory does not say this will automatically be good for the United States. In fact, rhetorical claims by prominent economists that it is guaranteed that the United States would be better off were rebuked by Nobel Laureate Paul Samuelson, who accused pro-globalization economists like Columbia University professor Jagdish Bhagwati and Dartmouth's Douglas Irwin of engaging in "polemical untruths" by misrepresenting what comparative advantage says and doesn't say.[3] Samuelson's arguments rest on the fact that offshoring results in shifts of relative productivity. So if China gets more productive at the things the United States does well, the United States may actually become a net loser.[4]

Samuelson has covered the economic implications of offshoring in general, but not specifically the offshoring of innovation. If offshoring of everyday jobs can shift relative productivity, it's likely that offshoring of science- and engineering-based production to other countries will also shift relative productivity. Ralph Gomory, renowned mathematician and former head of research at IBM, has done groundbreaking work in this area of economics pointing out the common fallacies made about how trade theory is invoked even by sophisticated economists. His testimony before Congress summed up what economic theory can and cannot offer about offshoring:

> "Conclusions about trade in the narrow sense with fixed capabilities should not be confused with conclusions about the effect of productivity shifts. There is nothing in either common sense or economic theory which says that improvement in the productivity capabilities of other countries is necessarily good for your country. This observation holds true even if these productivity shifts are brought about by the free and unfettered actions of corporations. When the U.S. trades semiconductors for Asian T-shirts, for example, that is trade in the narrow sense. And the conclusion of the most basic economic theories is that this exchange clearly benefits both countries. But when U.S. companies build semiconductor plants and R&D facilities in Asia rather than in the U.S., then that is a shift

> in productive capability, and neither economic theory nor common sense asserts that shift is automatically good for the U.S. even in the long run."

In light of these facts, some advocates draw on history to argue that even if this occurs the United States won't suffer. They argue that this movie has been shown before with the rise of the Japanese industry in the 1980s and early 1990s. Even with the Japanese rise, the United States economy boomed in the 1990s while Japan's economy stagnated. They argue that this history should be the guide.

But one of the most important and least understood differences today versus the experience with the rise of Japan is the change in business behavior. The ties of corporations to a specific country and its workers have broken down. As Craig Barrett, CEO of Intel Corp., one of the quintessential success stories of the new economy of the 1990s, put it, "Intel can succeed without ever hiring another American."[5] Companies are no longer rooted in a specific country.

In a 2006 article in *Foreign Affairs* magazine, IBM CEO Sam Palmisano gave the eulogy for the multinational corporation, and introduced in its place the globally integrated enterprise.[6] Palmisano said: "Many parties to the globalization debate mistakenly project into the future a picture of corporations that is unchanged from that of today or yesterday....But businesses are changing in fundamental ways — structurally, operationally, culturally — in response to the imperatives of globalization and new technology." The multinational corporation model in which firms replicated their organization in each country where they sold goods, is now giving way to the globally integrated enterprise model, where firms geographically separate their production from the markets in which they sell.

When discussing his firm's aggressive moves to shift its share of workers to low-cost countries, Ron Rittenmeyer, CEO of EDS, the largest U.S.-based IT services firm, said he "is agnostic specifically about where" EDS locates its workers, choosing the place that reaps the best economic efficiency. By 2008, EDS had 43 percent of its workforce in low-cost countries, up from virtually zero in 2002.[7] The public policy discussion has not included this change in the behavior of businesses.

During the 2004 election, presidential candidate John Kerry repeatedly called CEOs who offshore jobs "Benedict Arnolds." He was roundly lambasted by the press for making the statement and eventually capitulated. His comment was silly indeed, but not for the reasons given by the press. What people didn't understand, including Kerry, is that the business world had radically changed. CEOs of globally integrated enterprises are neither "patriots" nor "traitors." They are business executives with clear incentives.

Corporate boards tie CEO compensation to earnings and share prices. Many CEOs receive bonuses and outsized pay packages even while running their company into bankruptcy. One thing is clear: Their compensation is never tied to whether the United States economy grows or how many American jobs they create. The old Charlie Wilson quote of what's good for GM is good for America needs to be updated to. "What's good for IBM may not be good for the U.S., and what's good for the U.S. may not be good for IBM."

Yet the public discussion is still moored in the 1950s Charlie Wilson economy. A notable exception to this rule is Ralph Gomory, who says, "In this new era of globalization the interests of companies and countries have diverged. In contrast with the past, what is good for America's global corporations is no longer necessarily good for the American people." Whether Congress is listening or understanding this is unclear. What is clear is that Congress has acted as though this profound shift hasn't happened. It is also clear that large multinational firms have inordinate influence over the U.S. policy process and will pursue their own political interests regardless of the impacts on the nation.

This change has special ramifications for science and engineering-based jobs and innovation policy. Before the advent of the globally integrated enterprise, firms had the bulk of their science and engineering workers in their home country and would provide them with the latest scientific tools and technologies. Nowadays, it would be silly for globally integrated companies to give preferential access to tools and technologies to workers in any one country. Instead, they are providing the latest tools and technologies to the engineers in low-cost countries.

This is a critical change since one of the primary outputs of public investment in research and technological innovation is embodied in new and better tools and technologies. They are adopted by a wide range of firms and are then used to benefit the entire economy and workers. One of the traditional spillover benefits of public investment in research and development — new tools and technologies — are now much more footloose and "leaky" across borders. Coupled with improvements in communications technologies, the Internet and low-cost telecommunications, the global diffusion of tools and technologies has already been occurring much faster, even without firms stepping on the accelerator pedal by taking them to their overseas workers.

Some have argued that there are factors that will keep jobs in the United States. They argue that product development needs to be co-located with the end customer, and since the United States is the most sophisticated market, it will retain a substantial number of high-end jobs. The problem with this observation is that it is too simplistic. The largest growth markets are in India and China, so that's where significant job creation will be and, contrary to popular wisdom, many of the markets are quite sophisticated. India's wireless market is larger and more technologically sophisticated than the one in the United States. Is it any surprise that Motorola does 40 percent of its software development there?[8]

Even for technology work that must be done in the United States, firms are increasingly relying on foreign workers. The largest and most sophisticated IT services customers are in the United States, but Indian offshore outsourcing firms have been gaining market share and are the market leaders in this space. How do they do it? They don't hire Americans. Instead, they send foreign workers to the United States to do the jobs on-site by exploiting loopholes in U.S. immigration laws. It is simply a matter of time before this business model spreads to many other sectors.

Many observers, like Alan Blinder, have pointed out that America's superior higher education system is a source of strength and comparative advantage in technology. But universities have caught the globalization bug too. A transformation similar to the multinational corporation to the globally integrated enterprise is happening in elite universities, even if it is still in its infancy. Elite universities are "venturing abroad," tapping new markets of students in low-cost countries. Cornell, the largest Ivy, declares in its mission statement that it is the first "transnational university."

Never mind that it's a land grant university that gets large amounts of funding from both New York state and the federal government. Dozens of other elite universities are establishing — or are exploring the possibility of establishing — science and engineering programs in low-cost countries. Those schools include Rice, Purdue, Georgia Tech and Virginia Tech.[9] Various programs have already been initiated by major engineering colleges. Carnegie-Mellon offers its technology degrees in India in partnership with a small private college there. Students take most of the courses in India because it is less expensive, and then they spend six months in Pittsburgh to complete the Carnegie-Mellon degree.[10] Call it the globally integrated university (GIU) approach.

No one has good information about how many overseas university programs are being negotiated and the terms of their commitments. More important though, is why universities are behaving this way, and what the implications are for America. Surprisingly enough, no one within the university community even bothered to reflect on whether these actions are good for America or American workers. Cornell University President David Skorton defended his courtship of India with language straight out of IBM's globally integrated enterprise playbook, saying: "American higher education doesn't need protectionism."[11] But universities are not the same as for-profit corporations working in the free market. Most universities have tax exempt status and get a large share of their funding from governments, whether through research and other grants or through tuition subsidies and subsidized loans for students.

As a result of these significant changes to corporate and university behavior, it is unlikely that the traditional policy levers will work as expected since the U.S. innovation system itself has morphed into a fundamentally different enterprise. Yet the policy discussion has largely acted as though the U.S. innovation system is the same.

Another shortcoming of the discussion is the belief that the technological challenge is solely from China and India. Many other developed countries are betting on technological innovation as the appropriate way to respond to the increasing competitiveness of low-cost countries, leading to an increasingly crowded field. Singapore can no longer compete in low-cost manufacturing so it is targeting opto-electronics and biotechnology. It is funding the so-called "Biopolis" to attract biotechnology firms and pharmaceutical research. Ireland is trying to diversify away from its specialization in software services. Other developed countries are ratcheting up their investments in innovation and R&D.

Why Offshoring of R&D and Innovation Matters

Science- and engineering-based production receives special attention by policymakers because of its ramifications on economic growth, job creation, health care and military capability. The federal government will spend about $150 billion on R&D in fiscal year 2009. While much of this money is spent on specific missions, such as national defense, competitiveness is often a rationale for government investment. For example, the Bush administration's effort to boost R&D spending was called the American Competitiveness Initiative (ACI), and Congress recently passed the America COMPETES Act.[12]

Regardless of where one's sensibilities may lie, there is near consensus among both proponents and detractors of this flavor of globalization that innovation is an important advantage for the United States. America's capacity to stay on the edge of technological frontiers is a significant economic advantage, and there is consensus that policies should be put in place to maintain and expand those advantages. If R&D begins to be offshored some wonder if innovation will follow. Others, like Amar Bhide and Christopher Hill, argue that the location of R&D doesn't matter because wealth and jobs are really created by the downstream innovation, technology adoption and commercialization activities rather than technology creation.[13] If this is true, then states like New York are foolish to be pouring hundreds of millions of dollars into nanotechnology research in Albany because, after all, the goal is to create geographically localized spillover benefits from the research in the form of firm and job creation.

Perhaps more important is the drive by India and China to create their own innovations, so-called "indigenous innovation." In China's case, this is driven by the state, in India's case, by the private sector. Even if these efforts meet with limited success in creating breakthrough technologies, they indicate the ability to work with advanced technologies and attract advanced design, development and production work.

Data on the Offshoring of R&D and Innovation

The larger problem faced by policy makers is that policy proposals are being made and adopted with limited knowledge about how much innovation and R&D is actually being done in low-cost countries. The indicators of India's and China's innovation and research capabilities offer a decidedly mixed picture. The data is sometimes conflicting, with some showing an unmistakable rise in their technological prowess, while other data show these countries terribly lagging. For example, in 2006 China was by far the leading exporter of advanced technology products to the United States, surpassing all of the European Union combined. While it was also a significant importer, China is running a large and increasing trade surplus in these types of products with the United States.[14] Yet not a single publicly traded Chinese company is a top 100 spender on R&D.[15] And the number of triadic patents —those filed in Europe, the United States and Japan — awarded to Chinese inventors in 2002 was a mere 177 versus more than 18,000 for American and more than 13,000 for Japanese inventors.[16]

India's indigenous information technology services companies, like Infosys and Wipro, have become the market leaders in their sector, forcing U.S.-based competitors like IBM and HP to adopt their offshore outsourcing business model. But, in 2003, India only produced 779 engineering doctorates compared to the 5,265 produced in the United States.[17]

How Much Offshoring of Innovation and R&D Is Happening?

Since innovation cannot be directly measured, proxies are used to identify common elements of — and inputs to — innovation. Some of these metrics include high-technology trade, R&D spending and human capital.

Traditional leaders in science and technology are the United States, the European Union, Japan and more recently Taiwan, Israel, Ireland, Singapore and South Korea. The rise of India and China seem to be reported widely in the press, but many of the common R&D and innovation metrics provide a more nuanced picture. Some of those common indicators are examined below.

R&D Services Trade

The research, development and testing (RD&T) services sector is a relatively small and specialized industry sector comprising firms that complete contract research and other activities, such as environmental lab testing.[18] In 2003, RD&T accounted for $12.5 billion (around 6 percent) of the $204 billion of R&D performed by industry in the United States.[19] (The Bureau of Economic Analysis has only been capturing trade data for RD&T since 1999.)

The United States ran a trade surplus in RD&T of $3.4 billion, exporting $10.1 billion while importing $6.7 billion worth of these services in 2005.[20] The surplus in 2005 was the lowest recorded level in the 2001-2005 timeframe. While exports increased by 33 percent between 2001 and 2005, imports increased at almost double the rate: 64 percent.

RD&T trade data is further broken down by "affiliated" cross-border transactions within a multinational corporation, and "unaffiliated" cross-border transactions between independent firms. Most RD&T trade, 79 percent, is between affiliates — that is, within multinational corporations. In this category, the United States ran a trade surplus in 2005, but imports were rising much faster than exports. Trade between affiliates is not reported by country, so the sources of the shifts in trade are unknown.

For "unaffiliated" trade in RD&T, there was a small surplus in 2001 of $321 million that shifted to a deficit of $1 billion in 2005, most of which was attributable to trade with Europe. For unaffiliated trade with India, the balance went from a modest $15-million surplus in 2001 to a deficit of $43 million in 2005. Similarly, unaffiliated trade with China went from a $5-million surplus to a $15-million deficit. While the numbers are moving in a direction indicating a shift toward offshoring, the scale of the RD&T trade with India and China is puny. The two countries combined only account for 3 percent of unaffiliated trade in RD&T.

But RD&T trade with many other locations with high levels of research and innovation production are also quite small. For example, Japan, which is the third largest R&D spending country, accounts for only 7.6 percent of unaffiliated RD&T trade, and other countries well-known for their innovation — Taiwan, South Korea, Israel — each account for about 1 percent.[21] Even in well-established countries, RD&T may be a poor indicator of shifts in R&D across borders. If R&D and innovation is increasingly produced in, and shifted to, India and China, then RD&T may not reveal it.

It is also possible that cross-border RD&T is undercounted. In 2005, unaffiliated imports from India were reportedly worth $61 million. HCL Technologies, a major India-based engineering firm, claims to have sold $512 million worth of R&D services in 2008.[22] It is possible that significant shares of cross-border technology activities, especially in services, are simply not being picked up in the official data. As Timothy Sturgeon has pointed out, measures of the services sector, particularly with respect to trade, are woefully inadequate.[23] And the numbers that are reported by different government sources can vary quite dramatically. The U.S. Government Accountability Office found that India reported exporting 20 times more business, professional and technical services to the United States than the United States reported as imports of those services from India.[24]

Advanced (High-Technology) Trade Balance

Other trade measures provide insight into the kinds of skills and capabilities required to produce tradable products. Again, there is widespread belief that high-skill, high-technology products are made in high-cost countries, and that low-skill, low-technology products are made in low-cost countries. But that is not the case.

The United States is running large and growing trade deficits with China in the "advanced technology products" (ATP) category. The advanced technology products category, defined by the Foreign Trade Statistics division of the Census Bureau, captures trade in goods (services are excluded) that require a high amount of research and development to produce. The ATP series was created in the late 1980s to easily identify the U.S. trade position in high technology.

The United States began running a trade deficit in advanced technology products in 2002, and that deficit increased to $38 billion in 2006 as shown in Figure A. Much of the deficit can be attributed to the rapidly declining trade position with China, dating to its accession to the World Trade Organization in 2001.

Looking at exports and imports separately, China ranks number one for both exports and imports. The United States exported more ATP — $24 billion — to China than any other country in 2006, up more than two-fold from $11 billion and 8th place in 2000. But the

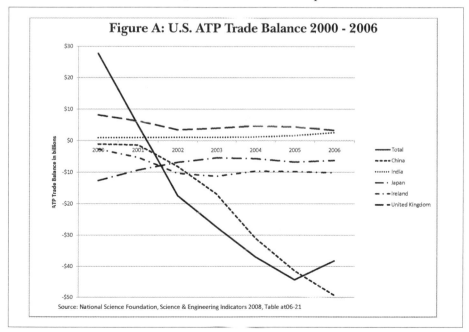

Figure A: U.S. ATP Trade Balance 2000 - 2006

Source: National Science Foundation, Science & Engineering Indicators 2008, Table at06-21

remarkable story, as shown in Figure B, is the massive five-fold increase in ATP imports from China between 2000 and 2006, going from $12 billion and 7th place to $73 billion and a dominant 1st place (Mexico is a distant second at $31 billion), accounting for one-quarter of all U.S. ATP imports.

The importance of China's rapid rise in ATP trade is in dispute. Some believe it shows rapid technological advances and, coupled with China's plan to spur indigenous innovation, poses a significant threat to U.S. competitiveness.[25] Others believe it exaggerates China's high-technology capabilities, explaining that it simply reflects global production networks, where production is increasingly fragmented across countries, and the rise in Chinese ATP exports is the result of export processing.[26] While the end product might indeed be high technology (i.e., China has content that requires R&D and high-skilled labor), the portion produced in China only required relatively low-skilled workers.

Others explain that the increase in Chinese ATP exports is due mostly to foreign multinational investments, either wholly foreign owned or joint ventures, and that indigenous Chinese firms account for less than 10 percent of ATP exports. Furthermore, those exports are mostly in two sectors, information and communications technology and optoelectronics.[27]

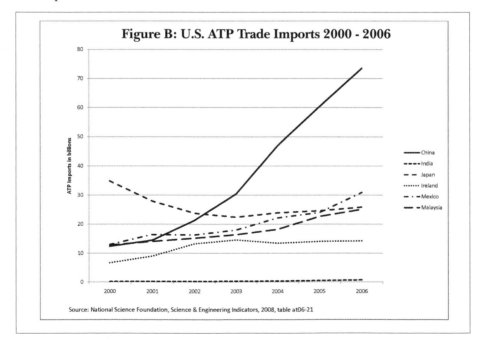

Figure B: U.S. ATP Trade Imports 2000 - 2006

Source: National Science Foundation, Science & Engineering Indicators, 2008, table at06-21

In the case of India, the United States ran a slight surplus of $2.6 billion in 2006, up from $913 million in 2000. Exports to India increased from $1 billion and a rank of 28th in 2000 to $3 billion and a rank of 20th in 2006. Many predicted that India would become a large market for U.S. ATP exports, as the offshoring of IT services and "business process outsourcing" exploded. The expectation was that Indian workers would be buying Dell computers and telecommunications equipment from Americans, but it simply hasn't materialized. Information and communications ATP exports to India increased $470 million between 2003 and 2007, from $650 million to $1.12 billion, while the Indian offshoring industry exploded.[28] Aerospace is the one sector where U.S. ATP exports have increased significantly.

R&D Spending

When the OECD released data estimating that China overtook Japan as the number two country in R&D spending, it raised a lot of eyebrows. As Figure C shows, China overtook Germany in 2002 and Japan in 2006 in R&D spending. While China remains below the United States, at $136 billion versus $338 billion in 2006, its recent (1999-2003) R&D spending growth has averaged 23 percent in comparison to 5 percent for the United States.[29]

China's spending on R&D is substantial and growing. A number of analysts have argued that, by using purchasing power parity (PPP) exchange rates, the OECD is overstating China's real R&D spending.

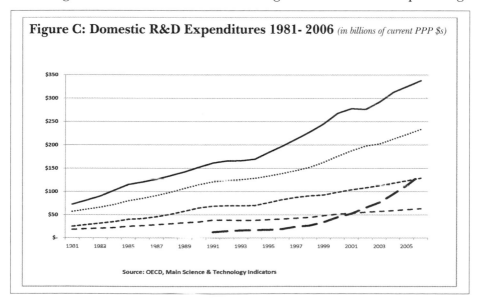

Figure C: Domestic R&D Expenditures 1981- 2006 *(in billions of current PPP $s)*

Source: OECD, Main Science & Technology Indicators

While wage rates for researchers may be lower in China compared to the United States, the market prices for lab equipment are likely equivalent. So absent an R&D-specific PPP, obtaining an apples-to-apples comparison is difficult. China's spending is heavily weighted towards the development side of R&D.[30] (India's R&D spending is not reported.)

Multinational R&D Investments and Linkages

U.S. multinational corporations performed about 85 percent of their R&D ($152 billion) at the parent company in the United States in 2004. About 15 percent ($28 billion) was performed by majority-owned foreign affiliates, most of which was in Europe. The foreign-affiliate share has risen slightly from 12 percent in 1994.[31] China's share was a modest 2 percent of the foreign affiliate R&D spending, accounting for just $622 million. India's share was even less at 0.6 percent, or $163 million.[32]

Foreign multinational corporations performed $30 billion of R&D at their affiliates in the United States. The amounts from Chinese and Indian multinational corporations are so small that they don't appear in the data. About three-quarters of the R&D performed in the United States by foreign firms comes from European companies. While foreign multinational R&D spending in the United States is higher than U.S. multinational spending abroad ($30 billion versus $28 billion), the difference is small. The United States does not appear to be a major magnet for R&D.[33]

Low-Cost Countries Attract R&D Sites

Another new phenomenon is competition by low-cost countries for R&D site selection. Defying the product life cycle pattern of technological investments proposed by Raymond Vernon, India and China have successfully attracted R&D and innovation facilities.[34,35] Vernon argued that newly invented products were initially produced in developed countries and only after they matured did production move to developing countries. Any R&D done in developing countries would be limited to customizing the product for the domestic market.[36] The criteria used for placing R&D facilities are multifaceted, including lower labor and capital costs, proximity to markets, specialized talent, as well as government subsidies and incentives. Experts have also pointed out that some governments, especially China, are requiring companies to place R&D facilities and transfer technologies as a condition of access to the Chinese market.[37,38]

Recent surveys of corporate R&D managers indicate that India and China have become much more attractive as destinations for R&D investments. A survey by the U.N. Conference on Trade and Development of the top 300 worldwide R&D spenders found that China was the top destination for future R&D expansion, followed by the United States, India, Japan, the U.K. and Russia.[39] A survey of 248 R&D managers of U.S. and European multinational companies, conducted by Thursby and Thursby for the National Academies' Government University Industry Research Roundtable, found more firms had new or planned facilities "central to overall R&D strategy" to be located in China than in the United States, and a large number are slated for India.[40] The study also found that the managers expected R&D employment growth in India and China, and that more respondents expected U.S. R&D employment to decline than those who expected it to increase. Their findings also point to a division of labor between R&D, where "new science" tended to be located in developed countries, whereas "familiar science" tended to be located in emerging economies. In 2007, *The Economist* magazine surveyed 300 executives about R&D site selection. They asked them to name the best overall location for R&D excluding their home country. India was the top choice, followed by the United States and China (Canada followed as a distant fourth).[41] Eight of the top 10 R&D spending companies have R&D facilities in China or India, (Microsoft, Pfizer, Chrysler, General Motors, Siemens, Matsushita Electric, IBM and Johnson & Johnson).[42]

It appears that the emerging economies of India and China have leap-frogged certain stages of economic development by attracting private-sector R&D production. This may result in greater competition between regions for attracting R&D investments. An important rationale for public sector investment in R&D is that it helps to attract private-sector R&D investment in the same location. Public sector investments, often accompanied by tax and other subsidies, may become less effective at attracting those private investments.

Patents

Patents are another common proxy for research and innovation output. By this measure, the inventive activity of developing countries like India and China is quite low. In 2003, inventors from China were granted only 573 (0.3 percent of the total) U.S. patents. Inventors from India received only 341 (0.2 percent of the total). That same year, U.S. inventors received 87,901 patents (52 percent of the total), and Japanese inventors were awarded 35,517 (21 percent).[43]

Some have argued that because many patents have limited economic value, analysts should use so-called triadic patents — those patents that are granted in Japan, Europe and the United States, the three major markets — to try to identify high-value patents for products with global markets. By this measure, in 2002 Chinese inventors received 177 triadic patents (0.3 percent of the total), and Indian inventors were awarded 78 (0.2 percent). U.S. inventors were granted 18,324 (35.6 percent), and Japanese inventors received 13,195 (26 percent) of the worldwide total of triadic patents.[44]

By patent measures, inventors in China and India are not inventing many products for the United States or global markets. But it may be just a matter of time before this activity increases. If we look at patent activity from South Korea and Taiwan, often referred to as the East Asian Tigers, we see that patents granted have increased markedly from 1990 to 2003. In the case of South Korea, the number of U.S. patents granted grew from 225 to 3,944, and in Taiwan's case from 732 to 5,298.[45]

Yet even the Council of Competitiveness claims that patents are not a good indicator of innovation. In its 2007 "Competitiveness Index" it notes that Apple Computer is considered to be the world's most innovative company, yet it ranked 187th in receipt of U.S. patents in 2005 with 84. "Apple actually spends less on R&D as a percentage of sales than the average for its industry," the council says. Google, which was in second place in the global innovation rankings, did not even muster 40 patents in 2005, ranking it below the top 400 companies receiving U.S. patents. Yet Google is ranked as the second most innovative company in the world. IBM, which has for years been the top recipient of U.S. patents, is ranked only in 10th place among the world's most innovative companies. The second largest recipient of U.S. patents, Canon, doesn't even make the list of top 25 global innovators. Hewlett Packard, in third place among patent recipients, isn't considered to be a top global innovator, either. The same is true of Matsushita, Hitachi, Toshiba and Fujitsu, all of which are on the top 10 list of U.S. patents but don't make the top 25 list of global innovators.

So what is true of companies might also be true of countries:

patents might not be a good indication of innovation. China and India have innovation systems that are quite immature. It may be simply a matter of time before there are increases in patenting activity. Weak intellectual property regimes, however, may continue to hinder inventive activity in those countries.

Royalties from Intellectual Property

Royalties from intellectual property are another indicator of cross border flows of technology. The size of the flows is relatively small, with the United States receiving $4.8 billion from other countries and paying them $2.2 billion in 2003. The two-way royalty flow for the United States with both India and China is very small. The U.S. receipts from China were $100 million, and from India they were $22 million. U.S. payouts were even smaller, $3 million and $1 million, respectively.[46]

While these values may begin to rise, they are unlikely to ever be very substantial. U.S. royalties from Japan were $1.3 billion, and payments to it were $524 million in 2003.[47]

Science and Engineering Articles

A significant output of research activity, especially academic research, is the publication of scientific articles. China's article output increased more than four-fold between 1995 and 2005, moving it from being ranked 14th to 5th in just a decade. The 2005 Chinese output of around 42,000 articles still significantly lags the United States and European Union, each of which accounted for over 200,000 articles, but China's scholarly article contribution is now three-fourths the size of Japan's. India's output, which was nearly equal to China's in 1995, has increased at a much slower rate, with about 15,000 articles published by its scientists and engineers in 2005. It began 1995 and ended 2005 as the 12th ranked country.

A potentially more significant figure is how China has focused its efforts on particular technical fields. The data cited above include social sciences as well as natural and physical sciences. China appears to be primarily investing in the physical sciences (engineering and mathematics). In engineering and chemistry, China became the second leading publisher of articles, supplanting Japan. And in physics and mathematics, it moved into third place (behind Japan and France, respectively).[48]

In the leading-edge field of nanotechnology, China is now ranked number two, behind the United States, in the number of nanotechnology papers published.[49] By contrast, India was only in the top 10 in chemistry (7th) and physics (10th), maintaining the same country ranking it had in 1995.

Like patents, articles vary in quality, so citation counts are often used as a proxy for quality. Chinese and Indian citation numbers still lag the United States, European Union and Japan significantly. In the case of China, the citation counts are increasing, indicating improved quality, and this increase in citations has occurred at the same time as the overall quantity of articles has increased.[50]

Human Capital Measures

Chinese and Indians are responding to the increased opportunities in science, technology and engineering occupations, from offshoring as well as overall growth. In India, the response has been mostly in the private sector through a proliferation of private colleges and training academies. In China, the state has played a bigger role in expanding the talent pool at all levels, with a dramatic difference especially at the doctorate level.

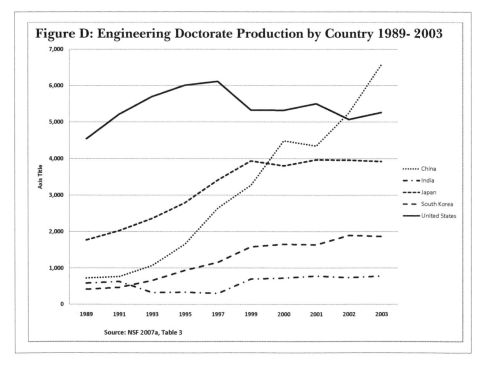

Figure D: Engineering Doctorate Production by Country 1989- 2003

Source: NSF 2007a, Table 3

As Figure D on the previous page shows, India's engineering doctorate production hardly budged from 1989 to 2003, but China's production increased nine-fold, surpassing Japan in 1999 and America in 2002, moving to first place.[51]

Explaining the Competitive Advantage of the Indian IT Services Industry

One of the most important technology stories of the past decade has been the swift rise of the Indian IT services industry. This sector includes India-based firms like Wipro, Infosys, TCS, Satyam, as well as U.S.-based firms like Cognizant and iGate that use the same business model. There is no need to speculate about whether the Indian firms will eventually take the lead in the sector sometime in the future; they already have. By introducing an innovative, disruptive, operational business model, the Indian firms have turned the whole industry upside down in the matter of four short years. It caught U.S. IT services firms like IBM, EDS, CSC and ACS flat-footed. Not a single one of those firms would have considered Infosys, Wipro or TCS as direct competitors as recently as 2003.

The U.S. firms are now moving as fast as possible to adopt the Indian business model, moving as much work to low-cost countries as possible. The speed and size of the shift is breathtaking.

IBM held a historic meeting with Wall Street analysts in Bangalore in June 2006, where the whole IBM executive team pitched their strategy to adopt the Indian offshore outsourcing business model. During the two-day event, punctuated by more than 300 PowerPoint slides, the IBM executive team explained why it believed the talent pool in India and other low-cost countries will continue to deepen, and that IBM would be investing $6 billion to expand its Indian operations.[52]

IBM's headcount in India has grown from 6,000 in 2003 to 73,000 in 2007, and it is projected to be 110,000 by 2010.[53] This compares to a headcount in the United States of about 120,000. Accenture passed a historic milestone in August 2007, when its Indian headcount of 35,000 surpassed any of its other country headcounts, including the United States, where it had 30,000 workers.[54]

In a 2008 interview with an IT trade publication, EDS chief executive Ron Rittenmeyer extolled the profitability of shifting tens-of-thousands of the company's workers from the United States to low-cost countries like India, and he outlined plans to continue the process through 2008. He said that outsourcing is "not just a passing fancy. It is a pretty major change that is going to continue. If you can find high-quality talent at a third of the price, it's not too hard to see why you'd do this."[55]

ACS recently told Wall Street analysts that it plans its largest increase in offshoring for 2009, when nearly 35 percent of its workforce will be in low-cost countries. The 2009 offshoring efforts will involve more complex and higher-wage jobs than in prior offshoring efforts, including jobs in application development and project management.[56]

So why have the American firms so aggressively increased their low-cost country headcounts? The answer is that the Indian offshore outsourcing business model is significantly more profitable. Table 1 compares financial performance of four companies, two offshore outsourcing firms (Infosys and Wipro) against two of the largest U.S.-based IT service firms (EDS and CSC). The data is from 2005 because this was when U.S.-based IT services firms began to seriously ramp up their offshore presence. As can be readily discerned, the market capitalizations of Infosys and Wipro were much higher than EDS and CSC even though their sales were a small fraction.

In other words, Wall Street was saying loud and clear that Infosys and Wipro were market leaders. The reason for the extraordinary val-

Table 1: Comparative Financial Data for Traditional IT Services Versus Offshore Outsourcing Firms

Company Name	Headquarters	Market Cap (mill)	Latest FY Sales (mill)	Profit Margin (5 yr Avg)
Infosys	India	$19,877	$1,592	27.93%
Wipro	India	$15,268	$1,627	20.59%
Electronic Data Systems	US	$12,517	$25,865	2.74%
Computer Sciences Corp	US	$10,015	$14,059	3.23%
Dollar figures in millions; Retrieved from Reuters, www.reuters.com on November 13, 2005				

uations of Infosys and Wipro was their net profit margins (based on sales) were multiple times those of EDS and CSC. Infosys averages a remarkable 28 percent profit margin in an industry where 6 percent to 8 percent is considered a good year. Infosys maintained these margins while growing its revenues and headcount by 40 percent per year, so it comes as little surprise that the CEOs of EDS and CSC began to slash U.S. and European workforces and ramped up hiring in India and other low-cost countries.

The success of the Indian software service business model is built on a company's ability to maximize the amount of work that can be done in a low-cost country with rock-bottom wages. Firms can hire fresh computer science graduates from good universities at $5,000 per year.

The Indian government grants tax holidays on software and business process outsourcing exports. This advantage translates into much lower effective tax rates for Infosys and Wipro (between 13 and 14 percent) than for their U.S. rivals, which had effective tax rates of approximately 35 percent.

The upshot is that the Indian IT firms have been wildly successful in selling high-technology services to the world's most sophisticated market — the United States — without hiring or employing Americans. This is even more remarkable since most economists long considered that most high-tech services were nontradable.

The offshore outsourcing industry is now targeting higher-end innovation and other engineering services work and jobs. Considering the pace and depth of their success in software services it may not be long before they pick off more of the highest-skilled American sectors and jobs.

The software services industry is a key example of the new era of globalization that has not been fully appreciated by millions of Americans. The industry pays high wages and hires workers with advanced degrees and training in engineering and other technology fields. Industry firms are innovators and spread advanced technical abilities to their customers. Yet the sector does hardly any formal R&D. In fact, EDS doesn't even report any R&D spending in its financial statements.

Anyone who focuses solely on R&D spending or patents is blind to this major loss of American innovation jobs. Second, and more important, is how the U.S.-based firms reacted to the competitiveness challenge from Indian offshore outsourcing. Instead of investing in their American workers with tools, technologies and training that would make them more competitive, they jettisoned them in favor of low-cost workers. The era of the globally integrated enterprise is upon us. The IBM and EDS strategy of shifting workforces to low-cost countries may well succeed, but for whom?

India's success is not lost on the Chinese government, which has created a state-owned joint venture with Microsoft for the express purpose of helping China develop a world class IT services offshoring capability. IBM is also playing its part. The company is training 100,000 IT services professionals in Jinagxi.

Rapid growth has also enabled offshore outsourcing firms to raise extraordinary sums from public offerings on stock markets. At the same time in 2003 that Google was raising $1 billion in an initial public offering (IPO) on Wall Street, Tata Consultancy Services, the largest Indian IT firm, raised a similar amount with an IPO on the Indian stock exchanges.

R&D Activities in China and India

Trends in R&D site selection are simply not tracked by the U.S. government. Recent announcements show that many are being placed in low-cost countries. For example, Applied Materials announced the opening of a major R&D complex in China in March 2007. According to *Site Selection* magazine, 22 of the 25 largest facility investments in semiconductor plants since January 2006 have occurred in Asia, including nine of the top 10. A University of Texas study recently found that of the 57 major global telecommunications R&D announcements in the past year, more than 60 percent (35 announcements) were located in Asia, whereas a meager 9 percent (five) were located in the United States.

According to the China's Ministry of Commerce, foreign multinational corporations have established 1,160 research institutions. There were 30 such institutions in 1999, approximately 200 by 2001 and 700 by 2005. These research institutions have to meet government standards to be counted.

Major corporations are using many tactics to ensure that these investments pay off. For example, the leading professional group representing R&D managers from U.S. multinational companies is the Industrial Research Institute (IRI). A major initiative of the group, and "one of IRI's fastest growing programs," is what is called the China Forum for Senior Technology Executives. IRI has a program specifically targeted at foreign multinational companies setting up shop in China and wanting to take advantage of indigenous innovation there. This is not an isolated effort. For example, Oracle Corp. underwrote a 2007 R&D meeting in China called "China and R&D Globalization: Integration and Mutual Benefits." The goals of the meeting were to explore:

- How foreign R&D can further contribute to the Chinese national innovation system.
- How China can better contribute to the global knowledge pool through further integration into the global knowledge system, outward investments, exchanges of highly skilled human resources and increasing international trade in knowledge.
- The unfulfilled potential for international cooperation between Chinese and foreign players in R&D and innovation.
- How to nurture a more fruitful interface between foreign R&D activities and Chinese domestic innovation capabilities.
- How the design of China's future National Innovation System could better integrate the role of foreign R&D activities with outgoing R&D investment by Chinese firms.

There is no comprehensive list of R&D investments by U.S. multinational corporations being made in China, and American companies are not required to disclose foreign R&D activities in financial filings. Below are some of the R&D activities from which two patterns seem to emerge: the R&D activities and investments in India and China are relatively new, and they are growing. Figures in the parentheses show the firm's R&D spending rank (for U.S.-based firms only) and its spending for fiscal year 2007.

General Motors (No. 1, $8.1 billion)

- GM in India: The India Science Lab, one of eight General Motors research labs, is located in Bangalore and was established in 2003. More than 70 percent of its researchers hold a Ph.D.[57] Also, GM has created collaborative research laboratories with two Indian universities to focus on specific R&D topics. GM has nine such labs with universities, and two of the three outside the United States are in India.[58]

- GM in China: In October 2007 General Motors announced it would build a wholly owned advanced research center in Shanghai to develop hybrid technology and other advanced designs. GM already has a 1,300-employee research center in Shanghai through a joint venture with Shanghai Automotive Industry Corporation.[59]

Pfizer (No. 2, $8.1 billion)

• Pfizer in India: Pfizer has been outsourcing significant drug development services to India. Forty-four new drugs are under clinical trials involving 143 medical institutions and at least 1,800 patients. The company is now looking to expand into drug research in India through collaborations.[60]

• Pfizer in China: Pfizer has approximately 200 employees at its Shanghai R&D center, which supports global clinical development. It also uses a number of contract research firms for R&D there. It plans significant expansion of its R&D in China.[61]

Microsoft (No. 5, $7.1 billion)

• Microsoft in India: Microsoft employs more than 4,000 workers in India. The Microsoft India Development Center was established in 1998. It has grown more than 10-fold since 2003, when it had 120 people.[62] With 1,500-plus workers, it is the company's largest development center outside the United States.[63]

• Microsoft in China: The Microsoft China R&D Group is more than 10 years old and currently employs 1,500 workers. Activities are for both localization and global markets. The Microsoft China R&D Group focuses on five areas: mobile and embedded technology; Web technology products and services; digital entertainment; server and tools; and emerging markets.[64] Microsoft broke ground on a new $280-million R&D campus in Beijing in May 2008.[65] In November 2008, Microsoft announced it is significantly expanding its R&D operations in China by investing an additional $1 billion over the next three years, thus making it the largest R&D center behind the United States.[66]

Intel (No. 6, $5.8 billion)

• Intel in India: Intel began with a sales office in 1988 and established an R&D center in 1998. It now has about 2,500 R&D workers in India, and it has invested approximately $1.7 billion in its Indian operations.[67] In 2007, Intel's Bangalore Development center contributed about half the work towards its "teraflop research chip."[68] In September 2008, Intel unveiled its first microprocessor designed entirely in India, and the first time that 45 nanometer technology was designed outside of the United States. The Xeon 7400 microprocessor is used for high-end servers.[69,70] In 2005, Intel announced a planned investment of $800 million in India to expand research operations and an additional $250 million to launch a venture capital fund targeted at Indian start-ups.[71]

• Intel in China: Intel is building a $2.5-billion, 300mm semiconductor fabrication facility in Dalian, China, its first fab in Asia.[72] In April 2008, Intel announced that its $500-million Intel Capital China Technology Fund II will be used for investments in wireless broadband, technology, media, telecommunications and "clean" technology. The first fund's size was $200 million.

Examples of Intel's first China fund company investments include Neusoft Group, Supcon Group, A8 Music, Chinacache International, Chipsbank Microelectronics, DAC, HiSoft Technology International, Kingsoft, Legend Silicon, Montage Technology and Palm Commerce. Notable liquidity events involving portfolio companies from Intel's first fund include Actions Semiconductor, Kingsoft and Neusoft Group.[73]

Figure E reproduces a slide from a May 2005 presentation by Peter Liou, former director of Intel's China Research Center, on Intel's R&D strategy in China.[74] The slide indicates that Intel's China Research operations are expected to achieve world-class status before 2010.

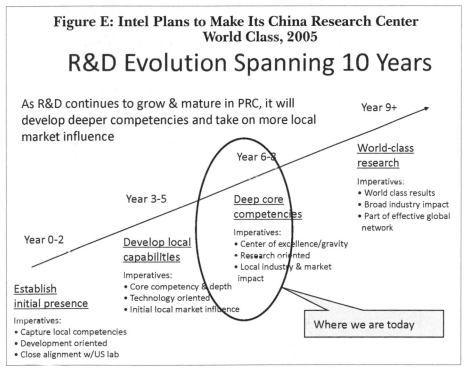

Figure E: Intel Plans to Make Its China Research Center World Class, 2005

Why the Stats Don't Match the Business Reality

If one reads only the typical science and engineering indicators, as reported by the National Science Foundation, a particular image seems to appear. China is investing large sums in building up its R&D and innovation infrastructure, but the innovation outputs have been mixed, with healthy increases in publications and production of Ph.D.s, but a very limited number of patents. The huge increases in advanced technology products trade seem almost independent of these actions. One view of China is that it's just a matter of time before it becomes home to indigenous innovation. On the other hand, India appears to be significantly backward when it comes to the traditional innovation indicators. The government isn't investing in R&D and in-novation, and its research outputs, publications and Ph.D. production have been stagnant for the past 20 years, yet it is able to attract foreign investments in R&D.

Contrast the official statistics with the buzz by management con-sultants and business school professors who promote Indian and Chi-nese research capability right now. Why does the large gap exist? For one thing, the official data is stale. Table 2 shows that much of the data

Table 2: Data Availability for Innovation Indicators

Innovation Indicators - Year Most Recent Data Available	
Category	**Most Recent Data Available**
Patents	2003
Triadic Patents	2002
MNC R&D Investments	2004
R&D Spending	2006
PhD Production	2003
Royalties from Intellectual Property	2003
RDT Services Trade	2005
Advanced Technology Products Trade	2008
Science & Engineering Articles	2005
Sources: NSF 2007a; ATP Trade data available from Foreign Trade Statistics, U.S. Census Bureau	

is three or even five years old. High-end offshoring is relatively new and growing fast. For example, IBM has increased its headcount in India more than 10-fold, from 6,000 in 2003 to 73,000 in 2007. Contrast that with the most recently available data.

Conclusions

China and India are both defying Raymond Vernon's traditional product life cycle model for international investments in technology. Businesses are making increasing investments in R&D and innovation in emerging countries like China and India. However, the scale and scope of these investments is still not clear. China and India are likely on very different technological development trajectories.

China, whose export prowess is based on manufacturing, appears to be building its innovation system through major investments in R&D spending, attracting foreign firms and advancing education. While it has major initiatives to spur indigenous innovation, it is still too early to tell how fruitful those efforts will be. India, on the other hand, has created a specialization in white-collar services exports. These sectors generally do little formal research or patenting even though they are innovative and create large numbers of high-wage, high-technology jobs. India's indigenous firms are market leaders in key sectors like IT services, but India does not appear to be investing heavily in building its innovation system, instead relying on the private sector to take the lead.

The rise of India and China in these sectors will affect how the United States benefits from its investments in innovation. There are significant structural changes including shifts in employment relations, private sector management strategies, university internationalization and a more uncertain and volatile domestic science, technology and engineering labor market. These structural changes mean that the system will react differently to policy changes.

Will government R&D investments result in the same kind of domestic production payoffs as in the past? Or do the downstream benefits of the development and production jobs leak out rapidly to countries that have lower costs, the technological capacity (human and infrastructure) to absorb those jobs, and the globally integrated enterprises that are able to transfer the technologies and knowledge more rapidly? The economic and national security outcomes of increased investments into the innovation process are going to be different than they have been in the past. The United States needs fresh thinking about policies that reflect this new reality.

Most forward-looking indicators point to a rapid increase in the offshoring of R&D and innovation, yet there is poor information on the nature of the work moving overseas. Is it advanced or mundane? Is there indigenous innovation, or is it mostly being done by U.S.-based multinationals? The private sector has strong incentives to withhold making public information on the offshoring of innovation, and the U.S. trade data on services is woeful. If, as many experts believe, leadership in innovation is key to America's future competitiveness, the government needs to immediately collect detailed information on offshoring, including new data series that capture the realities of trade, investment and job distribution in the age of globally integrated enterprises.

What is known and not known about the offshoring of research, development and innovation — and its likely long-term economic impacts — have been analyzed here. The stakes are high but little action has taken place. Limited data and the need for more analysis are no longer valid excuses to continue the current state of policy paralysis. There are clear indications that America's standing as a technological leader is threatened by the offshoring of research, development and innovation. It will take more than just additional federal funds thrown at training and education to ameliorate the trends. The time to act is now because of the significant lag before current policies manifest themselves in long-term economic decline. The U.S. has overestimated its technological lead throughout history, whether it was with the Soviet Union and Sputnik or the rise of Japanese manufacturing. It appears the country is under the same illusion now.

1. Sturgeon, Timothy J., "Why We Can't Measure The Economic Effects Of Services Offshoring: The Data Gaps And How To Fill Them," Industrial Performance Center, MIT, Cambridge, Mass., 2006.

2. Rosenberg, Nathan, *Inside the Black Box: Technology and Economics*, Cambridge University Press, Cambridge, UK,1983.

3. Lohr, Steve, "An Elder Challenges Outsourcing's Orthodoxy," *New York Times*, September 9, 2004.

4. Gomory, Ralph E., in testimony before U.S. House Science and Technology Committee, "The Globalization of Innovation and R&D: Overview," June 12, 2007.

5. Friedman, Thomas L., "Tuning in to Jon Stewart and Britney Schmidt," *New York Times*, May 6, 2005.

6, Palmisano, Samuel J., "The Globally Integrated Enterprise," *Foreign Affairs*, 85, No. 3 (May/June, 2006), 127.

7. Jackson, Brian, "EDS CEO Says No Problem," ITBusiness.ca, April 23, 2008, http://www.itbusiness.ca/it/client/en/home/DetailNewsPrint.asp?id=48091.

8. Kenney, Martin, "The Globalization of Innovation and R&D: How Do Companies Choose Where to Build R&D Facilities?" in testimony before U.S. House Committee on Science and Technology, October 4, 2007.

9. Selingo, Jeffrey, "Cornell Courts a Subcontinent," *Chronicle of Higher Education*, March 2, 2007.

10. Sengupta, Somini, "India Attracts Universities From the U.S.," *The New York Times*, March 26, 2007.

11. "Cornell, Others Support Globalization of Education," *Gannett News Service*, July 26, 2007.

12. U.S. Public Law 110-69, America Creating Opportunities to Meaningfully Promote Excellence in Technology, Education and Science (COMPETES) Act, Washington, D.C., 2007.

13. Bhide, Amar, *The Venturesome Economy: How Innovation Sustains Prosperity in a More Connected World*, Princeton, Princeton University Press, 2008; Hill, Christopher T., "The Post-Scientific Society," *Issues in Science & Technology*, Fall 2007.

14. National Science Foundation, *Science & Engineering Indicators 2008*, Arlington, Va.

15. Hira, Ron, and Ross, Phillip E., "R&D Goes Global," *IEEE Spectrum On-Line*, November 2008.

16. National Science Foundation, 2007a, *Asia's Rising Science & Technology Strength: Comparative Indicators for Asia, European Union, and the United States*, NSF 07-319, Arlington, Va.

17. Ibid.

18. RDT is NAICS industry group, 5417, and includes "establishments conducting original investigation undertaken on a systematic basis to gain new knowledge (research) and/or the application of research findings or other scientific knowledge for the creation of new or significantly improved products or processes (experimental development)," (http://www.census.gov/prod/ec02/ec0254slls.pdf, p.122)

19. National Science Foundation, 2007b, *Research and Development in Industry: 2003*, Arlington, Va.

20. National Science Foundation, 2008.

21. National Science Foundation, 2007a.

22. Hira, Ron, and Ross, Phillip E., 2008.

23. Sturgeon, Timothy J., 2006.

24. U.S. Government Accountability Office, *U.S. and India Data on Offshoring Show Significant Differences*, Washington, D.C., 2006.

25. Preeg, Ernest, "Technological Advances in Key Industries in China," testimony before the U.S.-China Economic and Security Review Commission, Washington, D.C., July 16, 2008.

27. Amiti, Mary, "Research and Development, Technological Advances in Key Industries, and Changing Trade Flows with China," testimony before U.S.-China Economic & Security Review Commission, July 16, 2008.

28. Ferrantino, Michael; Koopman, Robert; Wang, Zhi; Yinug, Falan; Chen, Ling; Qu, Fengjie; and Wang, Haifeng, "Classification and Statistical Reconciliation of Trade in Advanced Technology Products: The Case of China and the United States," Brookings-Tshingua Center for Public Policy Working Paper Series, 2007.

28. U.S. Census Bureau, *Foreign Trade Statistics, Advanced Technology Product Data*, http://www.census.gov/foreign-trade/statistics/product/atp/select-atpctry.html (accessed November 12, 2008).

29. Organization for Economic Cooperation & Development, "China Will Become World's Second Highest Investor in R&D by End of 2006, Finds OECD," 2006, OECD.org.

30. Einhorn, Bruce, "The OECD Takes a Second Look at Chinese R&D," Eye on Asia Blog, *BusinessWeek.com*, August 30, 2007. http://www.businessweek.com/globalbiz/blog/eye-onasia/ archives/2007/08/the_occd_takes.html (accessed November 10, 2008).

31. National Science Foundation, 2008.

32. Ibid.
33. Ibid.
34. Kenney, Martin, "The Globalization of Innovation and R&D: How Do Companies Choose Where to Build R&D Facilities?" testimony before U.S. House Committee on Science & Technology, October 4, 2007.
35. Vernon, Raymond, "International Investment and International Trade in the Product Cycle," *The Quarterly Journal of Economics*, (The MIT Press) 80, No. 2, May 1966, 190-207.
36. Hedge, Deepak; and Hicks, Diana, "The Maturation of Global Corporate R&D: Evidence from the Activity of U.S. Foreign Subsidiaries," *Research Policy*, 37 390-406, 2008.
37. McMillion, Charles, "China's Soaring Financial, Industrial and Technological Power," unpublished, 2007, Washington D.C., Small Business Administration.
38. Atkinson, Robert, in testimony before House Science and Technology, subcommittee on technology and innovation, "The Globalization of Innovation and R&D: How Do Companies Choose Where to Build R&D Facilities," October 4, 2007.
39. United Nations Conference on Trade and Development, 2005, World Investment Report 2005: Transnational Corporations and the Internationalization of R&D, New York, United Nations.
40. Thursby, Jerry; and Thursby, Marie, "Factors in International Location and Type of Corporate R&D," testimony before the U.S. House Committee on Science and Technology. Washington, D.C., October 4, 2007.
41. Kenney, Martin, 2007.
42. Atkinson, Robert, 2007.
43. National Science Foundation, 2007a.
44. Ibid.
45. Ibid.
46. Ibid.
47. Ibid.
48. Ibid.
49. Preeg, Ernest, 2008.
50. National Science Foundation, 2007a.
51. Ibid.
52. IBM, "IBM Global Briefing," ibm.com, June 6, 2006.
53. Lakshman, Nandini, "IBM's Big Deal in India," *BusinessWeek*, December 28, 2007.
54. Chatterjee, Sumeet, "Accenture to Raise India Staff to 35,000 by August," *Reuters*, January 29, 2007.
55. Jackson, Brian, 2008.
56. Thibodeau, Patrick, "Outsourcing Vendor ACS to Move 'Higher-Level' IT Jobs Offshore," *Computer World*, November 3, 2008.
57. General Motors, "India Science Lab," Research & Development Organization Overview, http://www.gm.com/experience/technology/research/overview/isl/isl.jsp (accessed Nov. 10, 2008).
58. General Motors, 2008a, "Global R&D Network," http://www.gm.com/experience/technology/research/global_rd_network/index.jsp.
59. Bradsher, Keith, "G.M. to Build Hybrid Research Center in China," *New York Times*, October 29, 2007.
60. Unnikrishnan, C.H., "Pfizer to Look at India, China for Collaborations," *Wall Street Journal*, December 18, 2007.
61. Wadhwa, Vivek; Rissing, Ben; Gereffi, Gary; Trumpbour, John; and Engardio, Pete, 2008, "The Globalization of Innovation: Pharmaceuticals," Duke University, Kauffman Foundation, 43.
62. "MS India Centre Plans Tie-Ups With Universities," *The Economic Times of India*, June 8, 2007.
63. Microsoft, 2008c. Microsoft India Development Center, http://www.microsoft.com/india msidc/default.aspx.
64. Microsoft, 2008b, "Microsoft China R&D Group Overview," http://www.microsoft.com

/ china/CRD/EN/overview.mspx.

65. Microsoft, 2008a, "Microsoft Breaks Ground on New R&D Campus," press release, http://www.microsoft.com/china/CRD/en/newsrelease/press20080506.mspx.

66. Chien, Kirby; and Wei, Michael, "Microsoft to Spend $1 Billion on R&D in China." *Reuters*, November 13, 2008.

67. Krishnadas, K.C., "With Assist from Intel, India Designs First Microprocessor." *EE Times*, September 16, 2008.

68. Ribiero, John, "India Plays Growing Role in Intel R&D," *Infoworld*, February 22, 2007, http://www.infoworld.com/article/07/02/22/HNindiaintelrandd_1.html.

69. Krishnadas, K.C., 2008.

70. "Intel Unveils First Made-in-India Chip," *Economic Times of India*, September 17, 2008.

71. Hesseldahl, Arik, "Intel's Eager Passage to India," *BusinessWeek*, December 6, 2005.

72. King, Ian and Janet Ong, "Intel Forms $500 Million Fund for China Investments." *Bloomberg.com*, April 8, 2008.

73. Mutschler, Ann Steffora, 2008, "Intel Puts $500M Toward 2nd China Fund," *EDN*, April 8, 2008.

74. Liou, Peter, May 28, 2005, http://www.csun.edu/~ys9503/Nanjing_meeting/Open%20Forum/Peter_Liou.ppt.

5. The Social Costs Of Deindustrialization

John Russo and Sherry Lee Linkon
Youngstown State University

During the 2008 presidential primary election season, political candidates and journalists from around the world visited Youngstown, Ohio. For the politicians, Youngstown provided dramatic visual backdrops of boarded-up businesses and decaying factories for speeches on economic development and the importance of blue collar workers and jobs. For journalists, Youngstown area residents gave faces and voices to stories about economic struggle and questions about how the working class votes.[1] This attention was not new. Every four years, reporters and candidates return to Youngstown to test conventional wisdom about economic renewal and political responses in the face of deindustrialization. Since the 1980s, when it lost 50,000 jobs in steel and steel-related industries, Youngstown has been the poster child for deindustrialization.

Over the next three decades, Youngstown and the surrounding Mahoning Valley have faced a long-term economic struggle, seen declines in population and tax base, and battled persistently-high crime rates, urban decay and questions about whether there just wasn't something wrong with the community. Local leaders have used tax abatements to entice new employers to the area, including prisons, warehouses and most recently computer software companies, all in the desperate hope of digging out of 30 years of economic hardship. While new urban planning and state funding for the development of high-tech industries help, the area has continued to hemorrhage jobs, most recently because of the downsizing of the automotive sector, such as at Delphi Automotive.

Yet Youngstown is not alone in this story. Since 2000, the state of Ohio has experienced the worst job losses since the Great Depression, and factories around the country continue to close and downsize.[2]

The changes wrought by deindustrialization do not affect only places like Youngstown, Ohio, or Gary, Ind., or only industries like steel and automaking. Today, communities with strong high-tech industries, like San Jose, Seattle, Austin and Cambridge, are experiencing significant job losses due to offshoring as globalization makes it easier for companies to hire well-trained but less expensive workers somewhere else.[3] Most American workers and their communities are vulnerable to dislocation, even when their work and economies have nothing to do with manufacturing. As the U.S. economy struggles in 2009, we see the whole country experiencing the kinds of struggles that places like Youngstown and its sister cities around the nation know all too well. Thousands of American communities are facing economic hardships that could last a generation or more.

When deindustrialization was seen as a matter of losing jobs in "dinosaur" industries, few leaders seemed to care. But as the middle class and "knowledge workers" face the economic and social struggles of major job loss, policymakers and corporate leaders began to take note. Even former treasury secretary and current chairman of President Obama's White House National Economic Council, Lawrence Summers, now acknowledges the "growing disillusionment" among Americans and the growing "anxiety about the market system that is unmatched since the fall of the Berlin Wall and probably well before."[4]

White collar and professional jobs are now being lost. Forrester Research, a consulting firm, estimates that 3.4 million white collar jobs will be sent offshore between 2003 and 2015. It is a harbinger of a new round of deindustrialization in other economic sectors. Forrester estimates that the exodus will include 542,000 computer jobs, 259,000 management jobs, 191,000 architectural jobs, 79,000 legal jobs and 1.6 million back-office jobs.[5] Alan Blinder, former vice chairman of the Board of Governors of the Federal Reserve and a member of Bill Clinton's original Council of Economic Advisors, estimated that between 30 million and 40 million high-end U.S. service sector jobs could be outsourced. "Shipping electrons is a lot easier and cheaper than shipping physical goods," said Blinder, a professor of economics at Princeton University and director of the university's Center for Economic Policy Studies. While still in its infancy, "electronic offshoring has already begun to move well beyond traditional low-end jobs such as call center operators to highly skilled jobs such as computer programmers, scientists and engineers, accountants, security analysts and some aspects of legal work — to name just a few."

Communities around the country are learning that unemployment brings reduced standards of living and a variety of social disruptions not only for displaced workers and their families but also their communities and states. Youngstown's story in the 1980s is America's story today.

In the introduction to their edited collection, *Beyond the Ruins: The Meanings of Deindustrialization*, Joseph Heathcott and Jefferson Cowie point out that, "Deindustrialization is not a story of a single emblematic place, such as Flint or Youngstown, or a specific time period, such as the 1980s; it was a much broader, more fundamental, historical transformation. What was labeled deindustrialization in the intense political heat of the late 1970s and early 1980s turned out to be a more socially complicated, historically deep, geographically diverse and politically perplexing phenomenon than previously thought."[6]

Indeed, while deindustrialization is often thought of as a trend of the 1970s and 80s and its history dates back to the early 20th century, it is not merely history. On the one hand, the social costs of deindustrialization persist over decades and generations. Jobs lost in the late 1970s continue to affect communities and individuals today. On the other hand, factories are still closing and industries are still downsizing, so deindustrialization continues to affect American workers and their communities. As scholars such as Cowie, Tami Friedman and others have noted, beginning as early as the 1910s and continuing through the 1980s, one community's plant closing often meant new jobs for another community in another region.[7] According to economist Barry Bluestone, the 1980s saw some growth in manufacturing of new products like instruments, paper products and electronic equipment. But today, even plants that opened a few decades ago are closing, and when factories remain open, new technology and increased wage competition due to globalization allow companies to downsize, displacing thousands of workers. As Bluestone suggests, "technologically driven productivity is a double-edged sword. While manufacturing is holding its own, manufacturing employment continues to shrink."[8] Between January 2000 and April 2009, manufacturing employment dropped by 5 million jobs.[9]

Conservative commentators and economists have long claimed that deindustrialization is merely a "natural" shift from a manufacturing to a service economy. Using Joseph Schumpeter's concept of "creative destruction," they argue that deindustrialization and disinvestment allow for the mutation of assets and individuals from older industries to more productive and efficient uses.[10] Seen in a national context, this concept suggests that deindustrialization frees capital for more efficient use in new industries and ultimately creates new jobs for displaced workers. But deindustrialization is not necessarily natural or creative, nor does it reliably generate good jobs to replace those that are lost. Rather, it is the result of a complicated set of factors including globalization, offshoring, deregulation, downsizing and technological change that are inherently interconnected. For example, technological change not only allows for more efficient production but also makes the movement of money and material goods, communications and management easier across great distances. Consequently, reinvestment is not confined to any particular country and so may not generate an economic or industrial transition for the nation or displaced workers. In addition, deindustrialization is largely controlled by corporations to enhance stockholder value. Put differently, the economic shifts of the past 35 years are the direct result of decisions made by corporate and government leaders to pursue economic profit rather than the good of either communities or the environment.

Yet America still makes things. While much of today's economy could be described as either a service economy or, to use a buzz phrase, a "knowledge economy," manufacturing continues to play a key role, employing 9 percent of all U.S. workers (12.3 million) and 9 percent of all scientists and engineers. Manufacturing produces 12 percent of the total gross domestic product and is responsible for 60 percent of the nation's research and development.[11] Stephen Cohen and John Zysman argue that "we are experiencing a transition not from an industrial economy to a service economy, but from one kind of industrial economy to another."[12] In other words, while manufacturing continues to be a major part of the U.S. economy, the quality of industrial jobs has changed in significant ways, and this combines with ongoing major job losses in the manufacturing sector to create a real crisis not only in the economy but in the quality of American community life.

This is not just an American phenomenon. Across the developed world and increasingly in developing countries, social, political, technological and economic changes have enhanced the ability of companies to move work to wherever labor is cheapest. So even in China, which is widely seen as the winner in the global battle for industrial jobs, workers have been displaced, first by privatization and more recently by companies moving factories to Indonesia and other countries where they can pay even less and face fewer environmental regulations. While our focus is on the American situation, we must keep in mind that deindustrialization reflects changes in the global economy.

The social costs of deindustrialization are significant, long-lasting and wide-ranging, if for no other reason than sheer numbers. The deindustrialization of the 1970s and 80s was "cataclysmic"; more than 32 million jobs were lost, according to Bluestone.[13] More recently, Howard Rosen has found that between 1995 and 2004, almost 700,000 firms closed each year, affecting 6.1 million workers, and an additional 1.7 million firms contracted annually, affecting another 11.8 million workers.[14] But job loss does not affect individuals only, although it touches many who, having dedicated their lives and sometimes their health to employers, now feel betrayed and economically expendable. As a laid-off Johnson Controls worker in Louisville, Ky., explained, "I've always been a hard worker....You go in there and give a guy a day's work for a day's pay." But, he lamented, the company didn't see it that way: "I gave them 110 percent. They paid me for 110 percent but they did everybody out there wrong."[15] Another laid-off worker suggested that U.S. companies were "letting the people of America down," and this would "eventually come back to them."[16]

Deindustrialization undermines the social fabric of communities, states and the nation. The social costs of deindustrialization include the loss of jobs, homes and health care; reductions in the tax base, which in turn lead to cuts in necessary public services like police and fire protection; increases in crime both immediately and long-term; decaying local landscapes; increases in suicide, drug and alcohol abuse, family violence and depression; declines in nonprofits and cultural resources; and loss of faith in institutions such as government, business, unions, churches and traditional political organizations.

Even when workers find new jobs or when communities succeed in bringing in new employers, these new jobs often pay less, offer fewer benefits, are less likely to provide union protections and, in many cases, are temporary, contingent or part-time. Finally, widespread job loss, especially in communities that rely on just one or two industries, undermines the community's identity and sense of competence. Deindustrialized communities too often become sites of persistent struggle, creating a cycle of failure from which it is difficult to escape.

Economic Struggle as a Social Cost

Whether caused by offshoring, outsourcing, new production methods, technological change or privatization, and regardless of industrial sector, deindustrialization creates economic struggles that affect both individuals and their communities.[17] While most measures of deindustrialization emphasize how many workers have lost jobs, the real figures both of people affected and economic costs are much larger. Many of them cannot be measured. Individual workers and their families face several specific economic challenges because of unemployment — challenges that are exacerbated when unemployment is concentrated by large-scale plant closings or industry cutbacks. But these individual struggles are just part of a large, complex economic web that shares the social costs of economic struggle with whole communities. Further, because communities in economic distress often turn to state and federal governments for assistance, the social costs of deindustrialization affect every citizen in the nation.

Job loss creates economic crises for workers and their families as they lose wages and often benefits — losses that can create long-term financial difficulties. This is especially true when unemployment lasts more than six months. Over the past three decades, as American industries have declined, long-term unemployment has become a larger portion of overall unemployment. In 1979, 8.6 percent of the unemployed had been out of work for more than six months; in 2005, 19.6 percent experienced long-term unemployment. Since 2001, this has become particularly significant as a result of "jobless recoveries" that varied from historical, cyclical patterns of unemployment. After six months, many individuals have exhausted government assistance and largely depleted their savings. Many resort to increased personal and credit card debt, reducing retirement savings, and, if necessary, incurring relocation expenses.[18]

Long-term unemployment occurs most often in communities where many people have lost jobs due to plant closings. Local economies simply cannot absorb so many displaced workers, and widespread unemployment persists, often for years. In Flint, after several years of cutbacks at GM and the closing of its Buick plant, unemployment in 1980 was over 25 percent.[19] In 1982, after a series of staffing decreases and closings at several companies in Newberry County, S.C., unemployment tripled in the course of a year to 16 percent, four times higher than normal.[20] In Gary, a few years after a major downsizing in the steel industry, one-fifth of local households lived below the poverty line.[21]

Similar patterns occurred in other Rust Belt cities like Detroit, Cleveland, St. Louis and Milwaukee. More recently, consistent unemployment associated with deindustrialization stretches from Baltimore and Philadelphia to Oakland, Fresno and Sacramento.[22] The highest unemployment rates in the nation are mostly in the Far West. Among the 14 American cities with the highest unemployment rates in the nation, 10 were in California. El Centro, Calif., had the highest unemployment rate in the nation, topping out at 24.5 percent in February 2009, followed by Merced, Calif. (19.9 percent), Yuba City, Calif. (18.9 percent), Elkhart, Ind. (18 percent), Visalia, Calif. (17 percent), Modesto, Calif. (16.9 percent), Salinas, Calif. (16.2 percent) and Stockton, Calif. (15.8 percent).

While the economic crisis associated with job loss may not hit immediately, before long even workers who were earning good hourly wages (and who therefore may have some accumulated savings) encounter difficulty securing basic needs like food, clothing, utilities and transportation. Many working-class families regularly live paycheck-to-paycheck, and the loss of a job can throw them quickly into poverty. In Flint, the local United Way reported a 25 percent increase in calls for assistance during the months after GM closed its plant there.[23]

Unable to keep up with mortgage payments, or forced to move in search of work, some families lose their homes. While this can occur with any type of unemployment when major local employers shut down, local housing markets can become glutted, making it as hard to sell a house as it is to find a new job, and for the same reasons. In Rock Island, Ill., after International Harvester, John Deere and Caterpillar all closed plants or reduced their workforces, the unemployment rate was more than 10 percent, a number of houses had been abandoned and home prices fell by about 20 percent.[24] For many working-class households, the home represents the family's largest and in some cases its only investment. Losing that home due to foreclosure or losing money on the sale of that home represents a significant reduction in the family's worth.

Of course, jobs provide more than just wages to families. Despite COBRA programs, many displaced workers and their families lose access to health care. A recent report by the Urban Institute predicts that each time the unemployment rate rises by one percentage point, another 1.1 million people become uninsured.[25] While some workers retain some form of health insurance when they are laid off, they may nonetheless find themselves unable to afford co-pays and deductibles and so avoid seeking treatment. For others, the loss of the job means losing both insurance and the ability to pay out-of-pocket health care costs. Along with exacerbating health problems, lack of access to health care creates an additional source of stress. As a laid-off worker from the KEMET factory in Shelby, N.C., explained in 1999, "We're up a creek [if] anybody gets sick or dies. There's just that little feeling in the pit of your stomach like please don't let disaster come."[26]

Industrial jobs also brought the promise of good pension programs. When factories close, the best scenario for displaced workers is that they would stop accruing pension funds and have to work for more years in another job. In their study of workers laid off from two plants near Louisville, Ky., Joy Hart and Tracey K'Meyer explain that "the reward for hard work in brutal conditions was not just high wages, which people felt they deserved, but the promise of a comfortable and early retirement. These workers felt robbed of the latter, coloring the lessons they would take from the whole experience."[27]

Bitterness and a longer worklife are only part of the problem. For many workers, companies ultimately defaulted on pension programs altogether. In some cases, pension programs have been underfunded, and some companies have used bankruptcy to escape their pension obligations. When this occurs, the Pension Benefit Guarantee Corporation (PBGC) steps in to provide payments. While workers affected by such moves may still receive pension payments, the value of those payments can decline precipitously.

For example, a typical steelworker with 30 years of service in the 1980s might receive about $1,800 a month, including a $1,000 pension payment, $600 for health care and a $200 shutdown bonus. But by declaring bankruptcy, some steel companies shifted the burden to the PBGC, which guarantees only 80 percent of the pension benefit and provided no other benefits. Thus, the PBGC would pay the same worker just $800 a month, less than half of what he had been promised. That $800 would have to cover health care costs as well as any other household expenses.[28] In some cases, displaced workers have been offered early retirement. But as pension programs falter, many older workers must find new jobs, often in the low-wage retail and service sector. This combined with the move to defined contribution pension plans, reduced access to health care and the recent declines in housing and stock values, makes "early retirement" a misnomer. Worse, this pattern not only reduces the standard of living of these workers, it also reduces opportunities for young workers to enter the labor force.[29]

Dramatic hardships for workers and their families filter directly into communities. The sources of economic challenge for cities are a bit different, but as with families, communities lose their source of income: taxes. Cities rely on local sales, property and income taxes to provide various community services. Large-scale plant closings drastically reduce cities' budgets, and this is especially true for smaller cities where a single employer or industry dominates. The closing of a major local employer often creates a ripple effect.

As other local businesses lose customers after a plant closing, they, in turn, lay off workers. In Anaconda, Mont., for example, within two months of the closing of ARCO, other local businesses had laid off about 20 percent of their workers. Over time, many local businesses simply closed.[30] That can create a cycle of fiscal problems for cities, as Camden, N.J., discovered when it began to lose jobs in the 1950s. Federal assistance helped for a while. Then the state stepped in, but ultimately, the city grew increasingly isolated. As Howard Gillette, Jr. writes, "Disinvestment is not a one-time process. It has cumulative effects."[31]

The loss of tax income for cities creates a variety of social problems. Among the most obvious cumulative effects of plant closings are cutbacks in local services. From police and fire protection to maintenance of city parks and streets to garbage collection, cities must cut their costs when they lose a significant portion of the local tax base. Those cuts create further problems. Cuts in police and fire protection make it difficult to respond to the increases in crime or waves of arson that often accompany unemployment and the threat of losing homes. Lack of maintenance or reduced garbage collection makes the local landscape look run-down and unattractive, which in turn makes it difficult to attract new businesses or residents. These changes can bring down property values, which reduce taxes even more. Deindustrialized cities often find themselves trapped, without the funds to improve their circumstances and, as Gillette points out about Camden, N.J., with "few tools available to alleviate its permanent fiscal crisis."[32]

Crime increases in deindustrialized communities for several reasons and over a long period of time. While some crime occurs as laid-off workers run out of money and options, and decreased police presence contributes to the problem, crime is a long-term problem for such communities. Criminologists have found that street crimes increase as unemployment spreads, but after a lag period, more serious criminality can develop.[33]

In the 1990s, a decade or more after Gary and Youngstown were both hit by deindustrialization, the two cities traded back and forth the embarrassment of having the highest per capita murder rates in the United States.[34] During that period, criminal justice experts determined that most of the murders in the Youngstown area were being committed by young adults who were born between 1977 and 1984, the most intense period of the deindustrialization. But for the mill closings, Youngstowners of this age might have been earning a decent living in the steel industry. Having a reputation for crime also creates a tough challenge for local boosters in bringing new jobs to the area.

In order to preserve police and fire protection, many cities cut back on maintenance. As a result, local streets may not be repaired regularly and street lighting may be cut back. Landscaping in pedestrian areas may not be maintained or cleared of trash quite so often. All of this creates a kind of "broken window syndrome" in which decay begets more decay. Such problems are often exacerbated by other economic costs.

When companies abandon factories, they often leave behind significant soil and water pollution. This can create large swaths of unusable or undesirable land. In Youngstown, for example, much of the area where the steel mills once stood remains empty 30 years after the structures were torn down. Although Environmental Protection Agency regulations push companies to clean up these areas, such rules sometimes backfire. When Anaconda, Mont., was named a Superfund site, selling homes and bringing in new industries became even harder, because no one wanted to buy a home or build a business in an area known to be polluted with dangerous toxins. While the community eventually built a golf course on the brownfields near the abandoned mines, the course has specially-trained workers to retrieve golf balls that land in areas where parts of the mine are still exposed, and other rules strive to ensure that golfers don't contribute to erosion that would release toxic chemicals into local drinking water.[35]

But a site doesn't need toxic chemicals to scare away visitors or new residents. The downtown areas of many former industrial towns fell into decay and gained a reputation for crime and ugliness when the local economies declined. Bryant Simon describes how this decline occurred in Atlantic City as that city struggled economically in the 1960s:

> "With department stores and small shops closing, taking people off the sidewalks, the few middle-class patrons who did come downtown to see a film hustled back to their cars when it was over and raced home....Without customers milling around, storeowners locked up before dark and turned their shops into fortresses. The few window shoppers had to peer through metal gates. German shepherds barked back at them as they glanced at shoes and cabana wear. The dogs and bars replaced the eyes of the street, the free-form dance of people that the influential urbanist Jane Jacobs has argued kept traditional mixed-use urban areas, like Atlantic City's Main Street, safe and alive."[36]

Deindustrialized communities across the country have witnessed similar transformations. When small shops close because of lost business, their boarded-up facades create a sense of abandonment, even though neighboring businesses may still be operating. As Simon suggests, this creates a ripple effect. Decades later, cities may still struggle to entice area residents downtown. In Youngstown, for example, neither new businesses and entertainment venues nor a crackdown on street crime has persuaded some residents of nearby suburbs that the city is a safe and attractive place to spend an evening. Yet again, disinvestment becomes cyclical. If people won't patronize downtown businesses, the area will continue to struggle long after real problems may have been solved.

Decay affects residential neighborhoods, as well. When displaced workers cannot keep up with mortgage payments or move away in search of work, their abandoned homes create problems for neighbors and the city. In some cases, drug dealers have taken over abandoned properties. Elsewhere, abandoned homes have been looted and vandalized. Any items worth selling, such as moldings, light fixtures, copper pipes, and old-fashioned door knobs, have been stolen, making the home less attractive to any potential buyer. Eventually, such properties become not only unsightly but also dangerous, and they must be demolished. This cost is often borne by cities, which can ill afford such additional expenses.

In some communities, people have turned to an alternative "solution": arson. As economic distress increases, homeowners who are threatened with foreclosure have a strong economic incentive to engage in arson, because that may be the only way to hold on to some of their investment. Similarly, neighbors in areas where many homes have been abandoned and are falling into disrepair may view arson as a way of protecting their own property values.[37] This is one of the reasons why Detroit became known as the arson capital of the world.

In some cases, the declining tax base of deindustrialization directly undermines a city's ability to redevelop. In Ohio, city governments use property taxes to repay loans for development projects, but this creates a double trap. As property values in deindustrialized areas decline, loans taken out 10 years ago for redevelopment projects are harder to repay today because the city takes in less tax money but owes the same amount. Moreover, state law requires voters to approve property tax hikes to pay those loan costs, and workers who have experienced job loss are not likely to support new taxes. Thus, Ohio cities like Cleveland face an additional challenge in creating economic development.[38]

193

In most communities, nonprofit organizations help to address the needs of families and neighborhoods that have fallen on hard times. When job loss and the associated problems are widespread, the need is even greater. Unfortunately, the economic woes that face displaced workers also lead to declines in donations to local nonprofits. Similarly, cultural institutions that provide inspiration and enrichment also struggle with funding. Not only do these declines affect local residents directly, they also make the community less attractive to new businesses. Disinvestment creates an almost inescapable cycle.[39]

As Howard Gillette illustrates in his study of Camden, N.J., when cities falter they usually turn to state and federal governments for assistance. Some of this involves direct appeals for aid, but much of it takes the form of increased demand for services. When unemployment increases and wages and hours decline, workers turn to welfare and food stamps. While the demand for public assistance has fluctuated over the years due to changing economic conditions, eligibility rules, enlistment drives and natural disasters, the dramatic increase in recent years is the result of the continued downsizing of America's industries. In 2008, 27 million Americans were receiving food stamps and the average enrollment in the food stamps program surpassed the record set in 1994.[40] This is higher now than during previous recessions and is expected to grow even higher. Not only is this occurring in areas traditionally associated with manufacturing, such as Ohio, Michigan, Illinois and Pennsylvania, but also in Arizona, Florida, Maryland, Nevada, North Dakota and Rhode Island, despite apparent economic growth.[41]

Demand may also increase for higher education, as displaced workers seek training for new jobs, and this means more requests for loans and grants as well as increases in state subsidies and funding for colleges, universities and training programs. Demand may also increase for mental health programs, many of which get at least some of their funding from government sources.

All of these demands make deindustrialization costly not only for local communities but also for states and the federal government.

At the same time, deindustrialized communities are likely to lose political clout. On the one hand, communities lose political power because of population loss, which may lead to consolidation of state and federal legislative districts, declines in local donations to state and national political parties and candidates, and the fact that legislators can no longer claim that their districts represent important industries. On the other hand, as deindustrialized communities demand more support from state and federal sources, they can come to be seen as problems rather than as assets. Where such regions once contributed significant economic strength to a state or region, they may now be seen as draining public resources. So at a time when a struggling community most needs to enlist support from state and federal governments, it may find itself with the least political influence.

Job Loss and Health Problems

Deindustrialization and job cuts often lead to long periods of unemployment, intermittent employment and increased underemployment, and the effects transcend simply the loss of pay, medical benefits and purchasing power. Financial strain creates stress, depression and family tensions, which can manifest in a variety of ways, from increased use of drugs and alcohol to suicide and domestic violence. At the same time, unemployment correlates with increased physical health problems. Reduced access to health care makes it less likely that displaced workers and their families will receive appropriate care. The mental and physical health costs of deindustrialization do not harm only patients; increased demand for health care combined with decreased economic resources leads to health care workers and systems that are overburdened and ultimately unable to meet the community's needs.

Displaced workers, especially primary breadwinners, are likely to feel significant pressure and anxiety about providing for their families. But job loss causes more than just financial distress; work plays a key role in shaping individual identity and social relations. The loss of work can disrupt an individual's sense of self and his or her value and competence. As Al Gini writes, "To work is *to be* and not to work is *not to be*."[42]

Even when clear external reasons exist for layoffs, individuals may internalize the loss, blaming and doubting themselves. Given that job loss undermines both financial and personal security, it's not surprising that many studies have shown that unemployment correlates with higher levels of anxiety and depression.[43] A 1988 study showed that workers displaced by the closing of an Indiana RCA plant reported significantly higher levels of symptoms of depression. While 5 percent of employed workers indicated on a survey that they "very often" felt "hopeless about the future," 38.2 percent of the displaced workers gave the same response.[44] More than half of physicians surveyed in the south-suburban area of Chicago indicated that they were seeing higher rates of alcoholism after a series of plant closings.[45]

While it might be expected that men struggle more than women with the loss of work — given their traditional role as breadwinners and the image of masculinity associated with some industrial jobs (such as steel making) — studies show that women, especially single mothers, display more symptoms of depression and anxiety after being laid off.[46]

Plant closings limit workers' economic opportunities, and "anxiety, depression, and other forms of anguish may be the normal result of rational calculation of these life chances," according to Hamilton.[47] Finding a new job does not entirely alleviate these fears, because the experience of being laid off can generate persistent fear about losing the next job. The security that workers once felt, especially those who worked for local companies that seemed to be dependable employers, disappears.

These problems are exacerbated by the loss of social networks that come with deindustrialization. Workplaces provide connections for most people that are built on shared experience and daily interaction. Many workers describe their co-workers as being "like family." For many, the workplace becomes a site of their most intimate relationships. When plants close, workers lose this easy day-to-day interaction. Feelings of shame, anger and sadness may make it difficult for co-workers to maintain close ties once their shared work disappears. To lose such networks during a time of personal crisis is doubly hard. Displaced workers without good social support networks show higher rates of both physical and mental illness.[48] For a significant number of individuals in a single community to lose a major support system at one time is devastating.

Job loss also correlates with increases in family violence. Perrucci found that almost one-third of displaced workers (31.7 percent) indicated that the financial strains of unemployment were undermining marital relationships. Job loss also undermines men's feelings of self-sufficiency and disrupts household structures. Such tensions related to gender roles increase the probability of domestic violence.[49] A 2002 study found that the risk of domestic violence increased 30 percent when a man's contributions to household income declined and increased 50 percent for every period of unemployment.[50] This probability is increased even further when economic distress exists throughout a community.[51] Increases in interpersonal violence may not be limited to the family. According to Steve May and Laura Morrison, "observers have begun to note the relationship between deindustrialization and workplace (and domestic) violence, workplace litigation and workplace stress and injury."[52]

Laid-off workers also experience declines in physical health. Studies consistently report that physical health problems, such as headache, high blood pressure, cardiovascular disease and digestive problems, as well as mortality rates, increase when people lose their jobs. Increased death rates result from disease as well as from suicide and accidents.[53]

As M.H. Brenner has shown, in cross-cultural studies conducted over the last 25 years, unemployment contributes to elevated mortality rates.[54] These effects can appear quite quickly: within a year after a major mine closing in Lewis County, Wash., the county public health office reported that it was already seeing increased rates of death due to heart disease as well as an increase in the death rate for people between ages 25 and 44.[55]

When unemployment is combined with other problems associated with economically-struggling communities, such as poor housing, increased levels of drug use and higher crime rates, the result is what the *Executive Intelligence Review* terms "death zones" — areas where the death rate for various age groups exceeds the national average.[56]

Health problems caused by deindustrialization also affect local clinics and hospitals, and this may reduce access to health care for everyone in the community. Public hospitals, which provide care for patients in financial need, including the poor and unemployed, feel the strain when demand from such patients increases. These hospitals already struggle to provide care as they face cuts in Medicare reimbursements and increased demand as the percentage of Americans without health insurance rises. Add increased demand from a significant number of laid-off workers and their families, and they face a serious crisis.

Hospitals have attempted to address the financial strains by cutting services and staffing, including emergency rooms, which further reduces both access and quality of care, but sometimes even these cuts are not enough. A 2005 report shows that public hospitals in cities and the surrounding suburbs, especially lower-income suburbs, are already closing at significant rates.[57] While these closings may not be traced directly to deindustrialization, they illustrate the connection between economics and public health.

A recent report by the Urban Institute suggests that the problem will only worsen, as rising unemployment could add hundreds of thousands of children and adults to state and federal health programs, requiring an increase of $3.4 billion for Medicaid and the State Children's Health Insurance Program. Of the additional money needed, $1.4 billion would come from the states.[58]

Deindustrialization Undermines the Quality Of Jobs for Everyone

Although unemployment in deindustrialized areas often remains high for a number of years after major plant closings, many workers do find new jobs. What is too often left out of this discussion is any consideration of how old and new jobs compare or how declines in large-scale manufacturing and industrial unions have affected the quality of jobs in other sectors.

When so many steelworkers in Youngstown lost their jobs in the 1980s, anyone with a pickup truck and toolbox could move into construction. The flooding of the labor market with displaced steelworkers reduced employment opportunity and wages for union contractors and their employees. Called "independent contractors," the displaced steelworkers became part of an underground economy that evaded government regulation, especially in relation to occupational safety and health and workers' compensation.[59]

Deindustrialization harms workers and communities not only by eliminating existing jobs but also by undermining the quality of the jobs that remain, and when families and communities rely on lower-quality jobs, there are social as well as economic costs.

Conservative commentators and traditional economists often argue that the job losses associated with plant closings and widespread declines within specific industries reflect larger trends that are part of a "natural" economic change. Among the most common variation of this argument has been the claim that the manufacturing economy is giving way to a service economy. But this shift has contributed to the nation's growing inequality. Between 1979 and 2005, the employment share of goods-producing industries dropped by over 11 percent while the service sector grew by almost the same amount. Many of the job losses were in high-paying sectors, including manufacturing, that have been affected by deindustrialization.[60] Employment gains were made in the low-wage and benefit service sector. This may explain why *New York Times* business writer Louis Uchitelle found that even when displaced workers find new jobs, within two years of being laid off they still earn only about 40 percent of their previous income.[61]

If service-sector wages and benefits in the United States were more closely aligned with those in manufacturing, as they are in European countries, deindustrialization wouldn't reduce household income as much, and income inequality would not continue growing so quickly.[62]

The idea that deindustrialization is part of a "natural" economic shift reinforces the argument that the solution to job loss is retraining. The assumption is that plenty of good jobs are available, but that workers are not appropriately prepared for them. This belief in the power of education runs deep in American culture, in part because it fits well with the "pull yourself up by your bootstraps" view of the American Dream. A belief in education also reflects a modernist, progressive view of history that assumes that something new and better is always coming.

In recent years there has been much talk about the growing "knowledge economy," and displaced workers are increasingly encouraged to seek training in high-tech areas. This encouragement has been widely supported by state and federal aid to both individuals and educational institutions.[63] To be effective, however, training programs must be geared to emerging labor needs in the local area. Otherwise, the implicit promises of education prove empty.

In the Youngstown area in the years after the steel mills closed, hundreds of local workers enrolled in training programs in refrigeration or computer repair. Yet there were almost no jobs in refrigeration, and computer repair jobs disappeared as simple modular replacement, which required little or no special training, became the industry standard. The training proved largely useless.

More recently, after a major textile plant closing in Kannapolis, N.C., the local community college was not given permission to develop training programs for small business skills, even though the local area needed more people with these skills to work in small businesses like real estate and cosmetology.[64]

Ironically, both cases reflect a conflict between training needs and government programs that were intended to help displaced workers. When education programs provide irrelevant training, workers' frustration increases. Some will internalize the experience, blaming themselves for failing, while others will feel more resentful and angry toward local institutions and government regulations. The result is the growing politics of resentment and the loss of faith in basic institutions and the American Dream.[65]

Even when retraining programs work, new jobs are often not as good as the jobs from which workers were displaced. In manufacturing, especially, while the work was sometimes dangerous, physically difficult and tedious, unionization ensured good wages and benefits. Working in a major local industry or for the largest local employer offered a sense of belonging as well as security. Despite irregular work patterns due to slowdowns, workers in the steel and auto industries had job security and seniority that balanced occasional economic strain with long-term certainty, until plants closed permanently. In many cases, new jobs offer less of everything, from wages to security.

In many communities, tourism and entertainment have been touted to revitalize deindustrialized communities. While bringing in visitors' dollars does help the local economy as a whole, for displaced workers, the jobs associated with the entertainment industry represent a sharp and dramatic decline. When a new Wendy's fast food store opened in downtown Gary in 1985, local officials saw it as a sign of economic growth, but S. Paul O'Hara points out that "several of the new employees of the restaurant were former steelworkers who had traded their mill wages for $3.35 an hour." As one local worker explained, they had little choice: " 'Sure we would rather have the $15-to-$20-an-hour jobs that the steel mills used to provide, but that is not reality.' "[66]

At the same time, the shift from industrial to retail and service jobs may hit workers of color especially hard. As Robert O. Self argues in writing about deindustrialization in Oakland, "The service sector was extraordinarily slow in absorbing African-American and Latino workers, except in low-paying 'back of the house' occupations."[67]

The shift to lower wages, fewer benefits and less unionization has occurred not only in the service sector but also in manufacturing, where restructuring, technology, and specialization have created a niche for smaller companies. Even within unionized industries such as the auto industry, restructuring has created lower-wage tiers for many workers, especially newer employees. Some might argue that lower wages simply reflect a correction of the "inflated" wages and benefits unionized workers once earned in the steel and auto industries — labor costs that some claim were the cause of America's industrial decline.

Starting in the 1950s, American industrial workers began to earn high enough wages to gain middle-class lifestyles, and they bargained for benefit packages that included good health insurance and pensions. The pay and benefits negotiated by unions rippled through the national economy, raising the standard of living for all workers in what economists call wage pull. But deindustrialization and associated deunionization have had the reverse effect. As unionized industries close, wages and benefits have fallen across the board, for all workers. At the same time, benefits are declining, as workers are being asked to pay for all or part of their health insurance. To put this differently, one of the social costs of deindustrialization is the declining economic security of the entire American middle and working class. Even workers who were never displaced by plant closings or industry declines have been affected.

Job security has also declined, again not only for the individual workers displaced by deindustrialization but across the board. Especially in the service sector, jobs are more likely to be temporary, part-time and contingent. Workers without unions have little or no protection against lay-offs.

For companies, these policies reflect a move toward greater flexibility, even as they allow employers to offer lower wages and fewer benefits to more workers. Those who work less than 40 hours per week and those who remain on a specific job for less than six months can more easily be denied raises and benefits.

The lack of job security no doubt helps the corporate bottom line, but for workers — and perhaps especially for workers who once enjoyed the benefits and protections of unionized jobs — the financial insecurity of the new employment patterns can be devastating. For many, replacing a single good industrial job requires working two or three service industry jobs, adding to household stress and increasing vulnerability to sickness and injury.

These patterns can be traced not only to changes in business management practices but also to the overall decline in unionization. While government and business policy play an important role in this trend, workers' own experiences of deindustrialization also play a part.

Displaced workers often lose faith in institutions of all kinds, including unions. If the union couldn't protect them from losing a factory job, how could it provide protection in a different industry? At the same time, workers have been encouraged to fear that unionization activism will drive employers away.

Tami Friedman notes that this pattern appeared in Yonkers, N.Y., as early as the 1950s. After local companies began to downsize, the local newspaper "warned unionists to consider the enormous need for caution against upsetting our bread-winning applecart." When one company sought wage concessions, even during a period of record sales and profits, "frightened union members quickly accepted the firm's proposals by a nearly three-to-one margin."[68]

More recently, a PBS Nightly Business Report story during the 1998 General Motors strike in Flint, Mich., used images of abandoned buildings and steel mills in Youngstown to illustrate a warning that the demands of workers could drive the company to move jobs to Mexico, something that had already happened in the Youngstown area. The story closed with reporter Stephen Aug's comment that autoworkers "may have jobs now, but what about next year, and the year after?"[69]

In an environment where workers are afraid of losing jobs — and in communities that have experienced wide-scale job loss such fears are endemic. Warnings like these are likely to be taken to heart. The problem is that without unionization, workers earn less, receive fewer benefits, endure poorer working conditions and have less job security.[70]

Deindustrialization and deunionization have additional effects. When displaced workers in Youngstown entered the construction industry in 1980s and 1990s, employment opportunities in construction became more episodic. This led many younger workers to reject the idea of entering apprenticeship programs in the building trades. Employers began to worry about the "graying" of the workforce.

In other industries, lower wages and benefits have led to higher turnover rates, which means that companies have fewer skilled employees. The "churning" of the workforce may undermine the quality of American manufacturing. In 2008, Ohio Policy Matters researchers found that despite the weak labor market in Ohio, employers were having difficulty hiring skilled workers. The report cites evidence of declines in apprenticeship programs and occupational shortages in both manufacturing and health care. They argued that recent employer concerns about occupational shortages and skill deficits should be taken seriously. Furthermore, government and business leaders must work together and engage in a "comprehensive long-term human resource strategies that provide meaningful career opportunities for workers."[71]

While deindustrialization may not be caused by a "natural" economic shift, it has clearly contributed to wide-ranging changes in the nature of work in America. Those changes are making economic stability and upward mobility increasingly elusive for many workers.

New employment patterns developed in what some call the "post-industrial era" are affecting workers in many industries, from manufacturing to health care, education to the media, finance to government. Job security, good benefits and long-term relationships between employers and workers are becoming relics of a fading past. The result is economic vulnerability, constant change and uncertainty that are reshaping the experience of work as well as the management of companies.

While current management theory extols the virtues of flexibility, in the long run it remains to be seen whether this shift will contribute to or continue to undermine the American economy.

Deindustrialized Communities Face Long-Term Economic and Social Challenges

Any community in which a significant portion of the population loses good jobs at the same time will face a crisis. For communities that have relied primarily on one or two key industries, the social costs of deindustrialization can be especially damaging. In both structural and social ways, communities lose the essential resources that allow them to function well. As Robert Bellah argued in his 1985 study of American community life, *Habits of the Heart*, communities thrive when they have a shared sense of history and identity, a "community of memory" that facilitates common visions of the community's strengths and weaknesses and collective faith in the community's ability to take effective action on its own behalf.[72]

A "community of memory" is not idealized or nostalgic; rather, it embraces the triumphs and difficulties of a community's past, identifying in a shared story of "who we are" the basis for moving ahead. Industrialization provided many cities with clear identities, tying Pittsburgh to steelmaking, Detroit to automaking, Lowell to textiles and so on. When this shared identity is lost, communities struggle. The loss of population, decline of the local landscape, loss of faith in both the community and its institutions, and internalization of an image of the community as a site of failure undermine the social resources that might otherwise allow communities to recover and redefine themselves. When this happens, communities can become desperate, and the economics of desperation can further undermine a city's well-being.

Deindustrialization often leads to population declines, both immediately after major job losses and in subsequent years, as some displaced workers move in search of work. While such moves may or may not provide workers and their families with more secure futures, their departures undermine the effectiveness of the communities they leave behind. As Robert Putnam and Lewis Feldstein have argued, social capital is an important resource for responding to community challenges, and social capital is created through human networks. By working together, playing in softball or bowling leagues and serving on church or neighborhood committees, people who live near each other create community. They come to know each other, build trust and develop a sense of investment in the place where they live, its culture and its people.[73] Especially in cities where many people work for the same company or industry, shared work contributes to this sense of belonging, so social networks in places like Youngstown, Flint, the Silicon Valley, or various mining towns become especially strong. When people leave these areas, the loss involves more than simply numbers.

Social capital involves not only people's relationships with each other but also their relationships with place. Lost jobs in a major industry ripple through the community, affecting other businesses, leading to home foreclosures and increases in crime and reducing the tax base that allows cities to respond to problems like abandoned houses and rising crime rates. As a result, an almost iconic marker of deindustrialization is urban decay: boarded-up businesses, abandoned buildings, once-vibrant neighborhoods that become eerily quiet and seemingly dangerous. At the same time, when industries shut down, they often leave physical markers on the landscape — crumbling factory buildings or brownfields where factories once stood. This landscape of loss also undermines social capital, in two ways.

First, as Dolores Hayden has argued, landscape is an important "storehouse" for memory, providing visual cues that represent major events and aspects of individual and community life.[74] When buildings are torn down or allowed to decay, communities lose a resource for the shared memory that is the basis for effective action. At the same time, the altered landscape creates a new sense of place. To put it simply, living in a deteriorating environment reinforces feelings of hopelessness that often accompany job loss. Further, this response affects not only displaced workers but the community as a whole. Anyone who visited the downtown area of a place like East St. Louis, Braddock, Penn., or Compton, Calif., during the years after their local industries shut down, understands this effect.

Over time, a struggling community may become divided, as those who promote a new vision of the city blame displaced workers for the area's problems. For example, civic leaders and developers in Anaconda, Mont., blamed former smelter workers for having the "wrong mentality." As one planner explained, the community's main problems were "not the economic loss or ecological impact that had torn the social fiber of the city, but a particular mentality embraced by the community."[75] Another stated that she hoped the redevelopment would, " 'inject' the community with new kinds of residents," an attitude that, as Kent Curtis suggests, reflects the "marginalization of members of the traditional working-class community, who, like the ruins of the hillside, were mere props to be trotted out when circumstances seemed to demand, but who were otherwise useless to the future of the town."[76]

The division between workers and developers in Anaconda shows that even when communities begin to revitalize, economic growth can happen at the expense of local cohesion and community memory. As Curtis explains, displaced workers saw the development of a new golf course "as only the latest stage in a long process of change that has been alienating them from their place in the community since the early 1970s."[77]

Dissolving social networks and decaying landscapes work together with unemployment and declining local tax bases to undermine deindustrialized communities' confidence. While those who study deindustrialization understand that corporations shut down plants for a variety of reasons that usually have little to do with local culture, affected communities often move from initial anger at the departing company to self-doubt. Some area residents, and too often local leaders, begin to wonder whether a plant closing could be attributed to some quality of the community and its people, and this can in turn persuade area residents that the city's failure to bounce back is its own fault. In some cases, this attitude is couched in specific terms.

In Yonkers, N.Y., for example, Friedman reports that local leaders began to worry about the city having a "bad labor name" as early as 1954. They suggested that the area couldn't attract new business due to its reputation for a strong local labor movement.[78]

In Youngstown, some local residents have come to assume that their community is almost naturally incompetent. When the public address system at Youngstown State University's football stadium ran into problems during a game a few years ago, one exasperated fan was heard to comment, "Well, what do you expect? This is Youngstown." Such attitudes both reflect and contribute to the community's loss of confidence in its ability to take effective action.

For many residents of such communities, loss of confidence in the community is part of a larger pattern of lost confidence in institutions. Area workers paid their taxes, tithed at church, devoted their work lives and sometimes their health to corporations, maintained union memberships and faithfully voted for whatever political party dominated in the local area for years, expecting that they could count on these institutions to reward their loyalty and to have the power to protect them from serious problems. For many, these institutions represented reciprocal and core community relationships.

In exchange for workers' support, cities were supposed to maintain streets, churches would provide spiritual comfort, employers would provide and unions would protect jobs, and politicians would protect the community, and all failed. When the organizations that people count on all prove unable to bring back old industries or attract new jobs, people become skeptical and resentful. In some cases, people become insular and wary of outsiders, trusting only their closest social networks. If people come to see institutions as inherently ineffective, they may view most efforts at development or addressing crime and urban decay as doomed from the outset. Lacking strong leadership or faith in the effectiveness of local institutions, some communities have become paralyzed and unable to launch effective responses to deindustrialization.[79]

Deindustrialized and economically struggling communities risk losing control of their identities as citizens lose faith in the community. Outsiders, especially the media, are left to define the area's story. Too often, deindustrialized communities are assigned negative images as places of failure and loss. Places like Gary and Youngstown know this difficulty all too well. O'Hara suggests that loss of its former identity made Gary vulnerable to being defined in entirely negative terms:

> "Without the sense of itself as a producing steel town, Gary lost the ability not only to create or control its own urban image but also to defend itself against its harshest critics. Instead, Gary became a national example of deindustrialized rustbelt decay. This dramatic change in the composition and viability of local image is one of the strongest and longest-lasting effects of deindustrialization."[80]

During the two decades after the mills closed, Youngstown was defined first as a site of struggle. Immediately after the shutdowns, local religious and labor leaders organized an effort to buy and operate the mills locally. As the city fell into decay and lost more jobs, Youngstown became one of several places (together with Gary and Flint) that took on iconic status as "symbol[s] of the failure of American industry."[81]

When the city did not recover within a decade, as the crime rate rose in the early 1990s and when a series of incidents made local patterns of political corruption visible nationally, Youngstown became known for corruption. During the same period, as the city grabbed at every possible opportunity for economic development — often coming up empty handed — the area gained a reputation for desperation. These versions of Youngstown's story told by the national media resonated in the community because local residents were themselves frustrated about the continuing problems.

When deindustrialized communities are defined in persistently negative ways, that image becomes an additional barrier to recovery. The city must fight even harder to attract new businesses, engage community members in development efforts and promote their cause in the public arena.

Combine this image problem with the competition for jobs, and we see former industrial areas going to great lengths — and often undermining their own stability — in order to attract new economic opportunities. In some cases, deindustrialized cities have pinned their hopes on tourism, hoping to attract visitors and their dollars through convention centers (Youngstown's Chevrolet Center), amusement parks (Flint's Auto World), casinos (Gary, Ind.), golf courses (Anaconda, Mont.), shopping malls (Homestead, Penn.), or historic sites built around and sometimes literally on abandoned industrial sites (Bethlehem, Penn.). Such efforts provide construction jobs initially, and the more successful efforts bring in new tax dollars, but they rarely bring high-quality jobs. City tax coffers may gain, but area workers continue to struggle.

Elsewhere, deindustrialized communities have welcomed public and private prisons. Northumberland County, Penn., a former mining community, built two prisons in the 1990s, creating jobs for about 550 people, and in 2001 they considered building another. As the chairman of the County's Board of Commissioners explained, "Anything that can bring recession-proof jobs, we want it here."[82]

Similarly, Youngstown saw prisons as a growth industry in the 1990s, supporting the development of four new prisons within a five-year period, including a state super max facility and a private prison operated by the Corrections Corporation of America (CCA). While some area workers found jobs building these facilities and later as guards, neither the pay nor the working conditions made them high-quality jobs.

When six prisoners escaped from the CCA prison, investigations suggested that they were assisted by guards whose low pay had made them susceptible to bribes. Worse, the city's reputation for crime and economic desperation was exacerbated when it became known as a prison economy, which made it more difficult for the area to attract other kinds of businesses.[83]

Among the tools that struggling communities use to attract new businesses are tax abatements. By deferring or waiving taxes, cities lower the cost of establishing a company in the hope of attracting new jobs. But the idea that such deals generate new jobs is often simply a myth.

Greg LeRoy has found that companies often take advantage of deindustrialized communities, rely on taxpayers' confusion about the relationship between subsidies and job creation, and are rarely held accountable for the promised investments and jobs.[84]

Even when tax abatement succeeds in attracting new employers, it may also bring its own problems. First, because new industrial sites often require less extensive or complex physical structures, companies easily leave communities behind once the tax abatements end. This process is facilitated by the ongoing competition among communities for jobs. As Robert Self argues, "...the frantic competition for private capital investment" creates a "savage rivalry" among cities as they fight to attract jobs and investors.[85]

This benefits the corporations but puts cities at risk as they gamble on whether the businesses they attract by waiving taxes will stay long enough to make a real contribution to the local economy. When these opportunities fail to transform the local economy, people's expectations of failure are further reinforced.

In the long term, communities face significant challenges in re-defining their identities and rebuilding their economies. In a 2007 report, MIT researchers identified some 150 cities, mostly in Northeastern, mid-Atlantic and Midwestern states, that continue to struggle long after major plant closings. Three chronic problems affect communities like Camden, Allentown and Hartford, according to the report: "a lack of civic engagement and institutions, inadequate governing capacity and a chronically negative collective mindset." They have "been left behind by the global economy, the media, major foundations and policy trends." These "forgotten cities," as MIT calls them, have difficulty creating effective coalitions and revitalization schemes.[86]

Yet while these cities may have been forgotten by some, they still matter to the people who live there. Some can't leave and others choose to stay and continue to struggle economically. Some of these "forgotten" areas are experiencing a boomerang effect, as a combination of loyalty to place, family ties and affordable housing lure former residents back home. Urban development specialist Hunter Morrison notes that such communities often have a "loyal diaspora" for whom their home towns, regardless of economic struggles, remain at the core of their individual identities. That loyalty, authenticity and a sense of a real place may serve as countervailing resources to help deindustrialized communities recover, even after long periods of economic difficulty.[87]

At the same time, deindustrialized communities continue to wrestle with some core structural problems, especially declining populations, economic development, crime and poverty. Some have come to accept economic decline and the hollowing out of neighborhoods and are trying to redefine themselves as smaller cities. As part of a planning process begun in the early 2000s, Youngstown decided that the only way to move forward was by embracing a new identity as a shrinking city. A community planning effort, forcefully directed by a local city planning agency, created the "2010 plan" for rezoning some areas for light industry, turning some largely abandoned residential areas into green spaces, and discontinuing city services in some neighborhoods.[88] In its annual "ideas" issue in 2006, the *New York Times Magazine* named Youngstown's "Creative Shrinkage" plan one of the nation's best ideas.[89]

On the one hand, the 2010 plan acknowledges and attempts to deal proactively with one of the most immutable realities of deindustrialization: declining population. On the other hand, it's unclear whether shrinking the city will in fact contribute to economic development. Turning decaying neighborhoods into green space may prove to be just another phase of the "undevelopment" story, or worse, another injury to an already wounded community.

While MIT's "Forgotten Cities" report highlights communities that continue to struggle, other areas have been held up as shining examples of recovery, including places like Cleveland, Providence and Pittsburgh. In these and other former industrial towns, one can see new office buildings, riverfront parks, gentrified neighborhoods and increased pedestrian traffic downtown. No doubt, such cities should be applauded for reinvigorating their urban cores.

Yet localized development, such as downtown projects, can provide the appearance of recovery while masking deeper continuing problems. Despite new areas of development, unemployment, crime and poverty rates remain high long after plant closings occur. In the past decade, Cleveland has revitalized its lakefront area with new museums, attracted visitors downtown with an annual film festival and revitalized old working-class neighborhoods with ethnic restaurants and loft housing, but it still has among the highest poverty and crime rates of any city its size in the United States.[90] Similar stories could be told about other supposedly recovered cities, because the wounds of large-scale job loss and major economic shifts simply do not heal quickly.

Nor is the poverty caused by deindustrialization confined to urban areas. Suburbs are also suffering. While the suburban areas around Cleveland, Cincinnati, and Columbus, Ohio, do not look like deindustrialized cities, they are among the 16 U.S. metropolitan areas with the highest poverty rates in 2008.[91]

The development we see today in Cleveland may well be the first signs of a more widespread recovery that will eventually reduce the area's poverty rates and in turn lower crime. But such a recovery cannot be built on tourism and entertainment alone. Cities and regions that have been devastated by the major economic shifts of the past three decades need secure, high-paying jobs that are not in constant danger of disappearing.

Conclusion

Hundreds of cities in America now know what Youngstown learned in the 1980s. Youngstown learned about the social costs of deindustrialization, but the community also, sadly, came to understand just how difficult it is to recover from the loss of major industry and the injuries done to thousands of workers, their families and the community itself.

Deindustrialization is not a new story. Nor does it, as some have suggested, follow the traditional historical narratives about natural economic evolution. Those who have lived in deindustrialized communities have long argued that the social costs and significance of deindustrialization are larger and more lasting than the dominant economic discourse about "creative destruction" and the fading of the old industrial economy. Deindustrialization is the direct result of corporate and governmental decisions that have not only displaced millions of American workers, but also done major harm to American communities. These injuries to our cities create social and economic costs that everyone pays.[92]

Unfortunately, many economists still don't get it. In *Outsourcing America: The True Cost of Shipping Jobs Overseas and What Can be Done About It*, Ron and Anil Hira have described the current public debate over the outsourcing component of deindustrialization as "misleading." In fact, they have been "amazed at the lengths they [proponents of outsourcing] are willing to go to throw away any semblance of objectivity in their analysis."[93]

Unfortunately, public policy toward globalization, outsourcing, technological change and unemployment has largely remained wedded to increasingly discredited neo-liberal economic concepts. The result is what *New York Times* reporter Steve Greenhouse describes as a "...glaring disconnect between the way government and business leaders talk about globalization and the way average Americans view it."[94]

The point here is not to say "we told you so." It is, rather, to suggest two things. First, because the social costs of deindustrialization affect every American, policymakers should take more seriously the long-term and widespread consequences of major industrial declines, regardless of industry. Second, addressing the social costs of deindustrialization and preventing further industrial losses in the U.S. will require a dramatic rethinking of the nature of the economy and the corporation as well as the role of government in creating a business environment that promotes investment and generates good jobs.

As William Galston argues in *The American Prospect*, "we should use public policy to spread the gains of economic growth, create equal opportunity for all and insure workers against wage and income losses against which they cannot protect themselves."[95]

We should advocate a new vision of capitalism that takes social and human capital every bit as seriously as it does materials and money. And we should advocate policies that encourage forms of economic development that build strong communities as well as strong companies.

---

1 Kaufman, Jonathan, "White Men Hold Key for Democrats: Contest May Hinge on Blue Collar Vote: Opening for McCain?" *Wall Street Journal*, February 19, 2008, 1. MacGillis, Alec, "How to Read the Buckeye Vote," *The Washington Post*, March 6, 2008, A 11. Muscat, Sabine, "Weifs, Mannlich, wichtig," *Financial Times Deutschland*, March 5, 2008, 15. Other examples include the *St. Louis Post Dispatch*, BBC America, National Holland News Service, Swedish National Radio, PBS Nightly Business Report, and *The Asahi Shimun (Japan News Service)*.

2. McMillion, Charles, "Ohio's Job Losses: 2000-2007 Worst Since the Great Depression," MBG Information Services, Washington, D.C., February 2008.

3. Greenhouse, Steven, *The Big Squeeze: Tough Times for American Workers*, New York: Knopf, 2008, page 203.

4. Ibid, page 210.

5. McCarthy, John C., "3.3 Million U.S. Services Jobs To Go Offshore," TechStrategy(tm) Research Brief, Forrester Research, November 11, 2002. Outsourcing can also have a negative effect on the workers who remain in the United States. A study by three Harvard economists estimates that for every 1 percent that employment falls in a manufacturing industry because of moving overseas, wages fall by five-tenths of 1 percent for workers who remain. As the recent concessionary bargaining at American Axle suggests, those numbers may be an underestimate.

6. Cowie, Jefferson and Heathcott, Joseph, "The Meanings of Deindustrialization," in *Beyond the Ruins: The Meanings of Deindustrialization*, Cowie & Heathcott, eds. Ithaca and London: Cornell UP, 2003, 2.

7. See Cowie, Jefferson, *Capital Moves: RCA's Seventy-Year Quest for Cheap Labor*, Ithaca

and London: Cornell UP, 1999, and Friedman, " 'A Trail of Ghost Towns across Our Land' " in Cowie & Heathcott.

8. Bluestone, Barry, foreward to Cowie & Heathcott (7).

9. "Employment in Non-Farm Payrolls by Major Industrial Sectors," Department of Labor, Bureau of Labor Statistics, 2008.

10. Schumpeter, Joseph A., *Capitalism, Socialism and Democracy*, 1942, New York: Harper, 1972, 82-85.

11. "Manufacturing, Agenda for Shared Prosperity," Economic Policy Institute. www.sharedprosperity.org/topics-manufacturing.htm.

12. Quoted in Lisa Fine, *The 'Fall' of Reo in Lansing, Michigan, 1955-1975*, in Cowie & Heathcott, 46.

13. Bluestone, (9).

14. Rosen, Howard, "Designing a National Strategy for Responding to Economic Dislocation," testimony before the House Science and Technology subcommittee on investigation and oversight, Washington, D.C., June 24, 2008.

15. Hart, Joy L. and K'Meyer, Tracy E., *Worker Memory and Narrative: Personal Stories of Deindustrialization in Louisville, Kentucky*, in Cowie & Heathcott, 293, 284.

16. May, Steve and Morrison, Laura, *Making Sense of Restructuring: Narratives of Accommodation Among Downsized Workers*, in Cowie & Heathcott, 274, 278.

17. This includes such terms as downsizing, rightsizing, delayering reengineering and/or forms of contingent labor — consultants, independent contractors, contingent staffers, special assistants, representatives, flexible staffers, hired guns, floaters, temp slaves, 1099ers, lone rangers, permalancers, e-lancers, information backpackers. The use of contingent labor has become known as the "vanguard of insecurity or America's migrant labor." Michael Jonas, "Lone Rangers," *Commonwealth Magazine*, Summer 2005, page 62.

18. Mishel, Lawrence; Bernstein, Jared; Allegretto, Sylvia, *The State of Working America 2006/ 2007*, Ithaca and London: ILR/Cornell UP, 2008, 226-230.

19. Scherer, Ron, "What a GM downturn does to Flint," *Christian Science Monitor*, August 21, 1980, 11. Online, 222.lexisnexis.com, July 21, 2008.

20. "South's Textile Mills Closings Continue From '74 Recession," *New York Times*, February 17, 1982, A-13, online wwwlexisnexis.com, July 21, 2008.

21. O'Hara, Paul S., *Envisioning the Steel City: The Legend and Legacy of Gary, Indiana*, in Cowie and Heathcott, 230.

22. "Local Area Unemployment Rates for Fifty Largest Cities, 2000-2007, City Data Tables, Local Area Unemployment Statistics," Bureau of Labor Statistics: Washington, D.C., http://www.bls.gov/lau/#tables.

23. Horak, Kathy, "Cries for Help on the Rise in Michigan," Associated Press, July 6, 1980, online, wwwlexisnexis.com, July 21, 2008.

24. Greenhouse, Steven, "Bitter Time for Quad Cities," *New York Times*, December 25, 1984, online www.lexisnexis.com, July 21, 2008.

25. Sack, Kevin, "Study Warns Job Losses Will Strain Government Health Programs," *New York Times*, April 29, 2008, online, www.nytimes.com, July 11, 2008.

26. Quoted in May and Morrison, page 272.

27. Hart and K'Meyer, page 298.

28. Discussion with Youngstown steelworkers and with Dennis Brubaker, staff representative, United Steelworkers Union, Subdistrict Office, Niles, Ohio.

29. Morrissey, Monique, "How Economic Conditions Affect Retirement," *Economic Snapshots*, Economic Policy Institute, June 25, 2008.

30. Curtis, Kent, *Greening Anaconda: EPA, ARCO, and the Politics of Space in Postindustrial Montana*, in Cowie & Heathcott, page 99.

31. Gillette, Howard, Jr., *The Wages of Disinvestment: How Money and Politics Aided the Decline of Camden, New Jersey*, in Cowie & Heathcott, page 157.

32. Ibid.

33. Linkon, Sherry Lee; and Russo, John, *Steeltown USA: Work and Memory In Youngstown*,

Lawrence, University of Kansas Press, 2002, page 196.
34. Linkon and Russo, 193.; O'Hara, page 232.
35. Curtis, pages 101, 110.
36. Simon, Bryant, *Segregated Fantasies: Race, Public Space, and the Life and Death of the Movie Business in Atlantic City, New Jersey, 1954-2000*, in Cowie & Heathcott, page 75.
37. Morrison, Hayli, "Reports of Arson Increase Alongside Foreclosures," Realestate, February 3, 2008, www.banks.com/blogs/realestate/2008/02/03/reports-of-arson-escalate-alongside-foreclosure-rates/.
38. Gomez, Henry, "City of Cleveland Faces Credit Squeeze," *The Plain Dealer*, December 11, 2007, online, www.cleveland.com/plaindealer/, July 21, 2008.
39. Morrison, Hunter, personal interview, May 2, 2008.
40. Wolf, Richard, "New Breed of American Emerges in Need for Food," *USA Today*, May 18, 2008.
41. Eckholm, Erik, "As Jobs Vanish and Prices Rise, Food Stamp Uses Nears Record," *New York Times*, March 31, 2008, online www.nytimes.com/2008/03/31/US/31foodstamps.html.
42. Gini, Al, *My Job, My Self: Work and the Creation of the Modern Individual*, New York, Routledge, 2000, ix.
43. See for example Carolyn C. Perrucci, Robert Perrucci, Dena B. Targ, and Harry R. Targ, "Plant Closings: International Context and Social Costs," New York: Aldine de Gruyter, 1988; V. Lee Hamilton, Clifford L. Broman, William S. Hoffman, and Deborah S. Renner, "Hard Times and Vulnerable People: Initial Effects of Plant Closings on Autoworkers' Mental Health," *Journal of Health and Social Behavior*, Vol. 31 (June 1990), page 123-140; Margaret W. Linn, Richard Sandifer, and Shanta Stein, "Effects of Unemployment on Mental and Physical Health," *American Journal of Public Health* 75:5 (May 1985), pages 502-506, online www.ajph.org/cgi/reprint/75/502.pdf, July 11, 2008; and Ronald C. Kessler, James S. House, and J. Blake Turner, "Unemployment and Health in a Community Sample," *Journal of Health and Social Behavior*, March 28, 1987, pages 51-59, among others.
44. Perrucci, et al, pages 91, 94.
45. Perrucci, et al, page 84.
46. Perrucci, et al, page 88; Hamilton et al, page 129.
47. Hamilton, et al, page 137.
48. Linn, Sandifer, and Stein, page 502.
49. Weissman, Deborah M., "The Personal is Political — and Economic: Rethinking Domestic Violence," *Brigham Young Law Review 2007*, online, findarticles.com, July 15, 2008.
50. Fox, Greer, Litton; Benson, Michael L.; DeMaris, Alfred A.; and Van Wyk, Judy, "Economic Distress and Intimate Violence: Testing Family Stress and Resources Theories," *Journal of Marriage and Family* 64 (August 2002), pages 793-807, 803.
51. Weissman.
52. May and Morrison, page 261.
53. See Perrucci, et al, Kessler, House, and Turner; and Linn, Sandifer, and Stein. For a useful summary of a number of international studies correlating unemployment and health, see Colin D. Mathers and Deborah J. Schofield, "The Health Consequences of Unemployment: The Evidence," *Medical Journal of Australia* 168 (1998): 178-182, online www.mja.com.au/public/issues/feb16/mathers/mathers.htm, July 11, 2008.
54. Brenner, M. H., "Estimating the Effects of Economic Change on National Health and Social Well-Being," Joint Economic Committee, U.S. Congress, Washington, D.C., 1984; Brenner, M.H., "Unemployment and Public Health in Countries of the European Union, European Commission," Director General for Employment and Industrial Relations and Social Affairs, Luxembourg, 2003.
55. Lewis County Public Health, "Health Impacts of Unemployment," January 30, 2007, online https://fortress.wa.gov/lewisco/home/Files/Departments/Public_Health/docs/ TAreport.pdf, July 11, 2008.

56. EIR Economics Staff, "The Case of Baltimore: Deindustrialization Creates 'Death Zones,' " *EIR*, 6 January 6, 2006, 5.
57. Siegel, Bruce, "The Emergency Department: Rethinking the Safety Net for the Safety Net," *Health Affairs*, March 24, 2004, online http://content.healthaffairs.org/cgi/reprint/ hlthaff.w4.146v1, July 14, 2008. See also Janice Billingsley, "Public Hospitals in Poor Suburbs Closing Doors," *PharmDaily* (2005), online, www.pharmdaily.com, July 11, 2008.
58. Sack.
59. Russo, John, "New Directions in the Construction Industry in Northeastern Ohio," Report for the Builders Association in Northeast Ohio and Western Pennsylvania and Western Reserve Building Trades Association, 1994.
60. Bernstein, Michel, and Allegretto, pages 168-171.
61. Uchitelle, Louis, *The Disposable American: Layoffs and Their Consequences*, New York, Knopf, 2006, page 46.
62. Mishel, Berstein, and Allegretto, pages 168-171.
63. Moore, Jeanie, "The Rebirth of Kannapolis," in testimony before the House Science and Technology subcommittee on investigation and oversight, Washington, D.C., June 24, 2008.
64. Ibid.
65. Russo, John, in testimony before the House Science and Technology subcommittee on investigation and oversight, Washington, D.C., June 24, 2008.
66. O'Hara, page 231.
67. Self, Robert O., *California's Industrial Garden: Oakland and the East Bay in the Age of Deindustrialization*, in Cowie and Heathcott, page 179.
68. Friedman, pages 33-35.
69. Nightly Business Report, Miami: Community Television Foundation of South Florida, July 10, 1998.
70. Shaiken, Harley, "Unions, the Economy, and Employee Free Choice," EPI Briefing Paper 181, February 22, 2007.
71. Honeck, Jon, "Occupational Shortages in Healthcare and Manufacturing: A Report from Ohio Policy Matters," July 3, 2008, online, www.policymattersohio/occupational-shortages2008.htm, July 9, 2008.
72. Bellah, Robert N., et al., *Habits of the Heart: Individualism and Commitment in American Life*, Berkeley, University of California Press, 1985, page 153.
73. Putnam, Robert D.; Feldstein, Lewis; and Cohen., Donald J., *Better Together: Restoring the American Community*, Simon & Schuster, 2003.
74. Hayden, Dolores, *The Power of Place: Urban Landscapes as Public History*, Cambridge, MIT Press, 1996, page 20.
75. Curtis, page 108.
76. Curtis, pages 107, 111.
77. Curtis, page 106.
78. Friedman, page 34.
79. See Lorlene Hoyt and Andre Leroux, "Voices from Forgotten Cities: Innovative Revitalization Coalitions in America's Older Small Cities," *PolicyLink*, CHAPA and MIT School of Architecture and Planning, 2007.
80. O'Hara, page 221.
81. Williamson, Michael, quoted in Linkon and Russo, page 160.
82. Wiggins, Ovetta, "A Rural PA Township Seeks Out a 3rd Prison," *Philadelphia Inquirer*, January 21, 2001, online, www.lexisnexus.com, July 9, 2008.
83. Linkon and Russo, pages 234-236.
84. Greg LeRoy, *The Great American Jobs Scam: Corporate Tax Dodging and the Myth of Job Creation*, Bartlett-Kohler Publishers Inc., San Francisco, 2005.
85. Self, page 161.
86. Hoyt and Leroux, page 8.
87. Morrison, Hunter, telephone interview, July 16, 2008.

88. "The Plan," Youngstown 2010, online www.Youngstown2010.com/plan/plan.htm, July 22, 2008.

89. Lanks, Belinda, "Creative Shrinking," *New York Times*, December 10, 2006, online, www.nytimes.com/2006/12/10/magazine/10sectionB.t-3.html, July 21, 2008.

90. "Cleveland is the Poorest Big City in U.S.," *Associated Press*, September 24, 2004.

91. Price, Rita; Ferenchik, Mark, "Suburbs Share in Suffering," *The Columbus Dispatch*, June 1, 2008.

92. Greenhouse, Steven, *The Big Squeeze: Tough Times for American Workers*, New York: Knopf, 2008, page 203.

93. Greenhouse, page 203.

94. Greenhouse, page 210.

95. Galston, William, "How Big Government Got Its Groove Back," *American Prospect*, June 9, 2008, online, www.prospect.org, July 21, 2008.

6. The Diminished Role of Training And Education in Manufacturing And the Imperative for Change

James Jacobs
Macomb Community College

As the American economy tumbles into a severe recession, there is, perhaps, one bright spot: Americans might soon realize that an economy cannot be based upon fictitious financial products, and that the only escape is through a rebirth of innovation and production. Both are dependent upon creating a new generation of skilled and knowledgeable workers. Within this context, there is new hope that the United States will finally create a manufacturing policy that includes education and training for the millions of American workers who rely on healthy and innovative manufacturing companies for their jobs.

A renewal of manufacturing in America will be predicated on whether the appropriate skills for the economy are still present when the nation emerges from its current economic nightmare. Currently, much of the manufacturing infrastructure and the skills associated with manufacturing have disappeared.

Yet even within an unfavorable business climate, companies have been faced with shortages of skilled workers. In the state of Michigan with over 300,000 manufacturing jobs lost in the past eight years and an official unemployment rate now above 12 percent (the highest in the nation) there are still help-wanted signs in small- and medium-sized plants for skilled CNC machine-tool operators. These manpower shortages constrain the ability of manufacturing to recover.

Creating a highly skilled workforce is an important public policy issue that is, sadly, not a new topic. Twenty years ago, training and education of manufacturing workers was considered to be a pillar of U.S. global economic power. Yet, for reasons discussed in this chapter, attention to improving the technical and management skills of workers has largely disappeared. If there is to be a revitalization of the manufacturing sector — and there has to be — there will be a need to revisit these issues and learn from previous mistakes.

The manufacturing sector accounts for 11 percent of America's gross domestic product, providing 12 million Americans with jobs that pay 20 percent higher than the national average. The importance of manufacturing jobs to the income of ordinary Americans is underappreciated. A strong manufacturing base produces a stable, broad middle class and a more equitable society. It should be made very clear that human resource issues are the key to improvements in productivity, innovation and new capacity. Training a highly skilled manufacturing workforce is one of several policies that must be implemented to revive the American economy.[1]

Workforce Development in Manufacturing

A "traditional" manufacturing company — one that has had difficulty surviving repeated economic downturns — does not care about hiring front-line workers with formal educational experience. For decades, a high school education or postsecondary degree was never a major condition for being hired or for advancement within most American manufacturing enterprises.

In 1973, half of all manufacturing workers had not completed high school. Only 8 percent of production workers had any postsecondary educational experience.[2]

Large manufacturing companies in automotive, steel and other traditional industries hired engineers and other white-collar workers with college degrees, but many small- and medium-sized companies were led by individuals with modest educational achievement. These people either inherited the company from family members or created their company based on the skills they learned from experience in other factories.[3]

Throughout most of the 20th century, workers were hired under the operating principles articulated by Frederick Taylor, who said that a fragmented manufacturing process should consist of specific patterns of repeated physical activity. For most workers, on-the-job training essentially meant watching others work.[4] The one exception was in the training of skilled workers.

Some of these individuals honed their skills in corporate "training schools" such as the Henry Ford Trade School established by Ford Motor Company in 1916. These private facilities provided selected workers with advanced skills and management training. Most skilled workers, however, learned their trade on the job in the first half of the 20th century, either through formal apprenticeship programs run by senior craft workers (a common source of training among immigrant workers from Europe), or through the informal process of "stealing a trade" by moving from machine to machine and shop to shop until one acquired the threshold skills to work in the tool room. Little of this would apply to production workers, who were taught a single set of repetitive motions as assemblers or machine tender.[5]

The opportunity for many workers to move into the skilled trades was opened up by the unions in the mid-20th century through the adaptation of the apprenticeship system similar to that in the construction industry. Trained workers were segmented by their different specific skill sets — pipe fitters, electricians, carpenters — just as they would be organized on a construction site. Each had detailed and specific information they were required to learn. Contracts negotiated with the unions often specified the number of skilled trade workers needed.

New workers were selected through competitive tests and formal training programs that combined some classroom instruction and an assignment to work with a skilled worker on the job. When individuals became classified as being "skilled," they usually received higher pay, had greater access to overtime and achieved a higher level of job security. Access to skilled trades was an important part of the upward mobility of workers within manufacturing. Organizations such as the United Steel Workers and the UAW played a major role in developing technical training for front-line workers.[6]

In the system of mass production that developed after World War II, the workplace was dirty and filled with unskilled workers who followed strict rules created by management. "Park your brain at the door" was a common understanding among production workers at traditional manufacturing plants. The exception was the small number of skilled workers who were required to maintain and repair machines and equipment.[7]

The picture of the manufacturing workforce began to change as American manufacturers were forced to adjust to the first wave of imported products in the late 1970s and early 1980s. Increased competition came from European and Japanese manufacturers that did not organize their production systems or utilize technology in the same manner as American companies. Yet these foreign competitors managed to produce high-quality products that won substantial portions of U.S. market share. Their success raised fundamental questions as to whether traditional American manufacturing processes and work structures were worth maintaining.

Many of the European countries based their industrial work systems on strong apprenticeship systems. A report from the U.S. Office of Technology Assessment in 1990 on manufacturing training noted: "In their pre-employment screening, Japanese automakers value willingness and ability to learn more highly than previous experience or specific skills. Their training programs emphasize individual and group responsibility along with job skills. U.S. automakers look for more experience and their training tends to stop with narrow technical skills for craft workers, and brief on-the-job sessions for unskilled workers."[8]

Questions about the industrial work systems in traditional American manufacturing have been raised before. While a growing number of psychologists and organizational experts called for changes in the workplace to encourage more rank-and-file participation and change, these were not taken seriously until the early 1980s as the first major wave of imports challenged manufacturers. During this period, the concern was to improve the international competitiveness of American industry, and the strategies to do so took two main courses. First, there were calls to utilize computer-based manufacturing technology to increase productivity and lower costs. Second, there was the need to develop a higher trained workforce that could deploy and utilize the new digital production technologies.[9]

As a result of international competition, significant numbers of unskilled production jobs disappeared as computer-based technologies replaced hands-on labor. Large firms from the auto, steel and electronic components industries downsized considerably. In the 1950s, a factory producing engines might have 3,000 to 4,000 workers. By the late 1980s, such a plant could be run with fewer than 1,500 workers. However, of the remaining jobs, there were more skilled positions required to maintain, repair and program the equipment.

New digital production technology fundamentally changed the structure of industry through the rise of decentralized factories making modular parts. Production processes began to be distributed to supplier companies. Whereas in the past, economies of scale were realized through centralization of production of one product, it was now possible to remain profitable by producing many variations of a basic product on the same manufacturing line. The experience of some European companies proved that small firms working in clusters could effectively bring high-quality and innovative products to market.[10]

With the adoption of digital production processes many of the most physically demanding and difficult jobs were eliminated. The use of computer-based equipment demanded a much cleaner production environment. Factory floors changed their physical appearance. The assembly line was supplemented by work cells and production workers were organized into teams. Workers learned to operate different sets of machines and rotated from task to task. In many cases, repairing and maintaining computer-based equipment cut across the traditional skilled jobs, forcing a reconsideration of how trades were developed.[11] Front-line supervision was often eliminated and workers were made responsible for operational outcomes. The manufacturing workplace became a very different physical environment that remained demanding and stressful, but no longer resembled the traditional mass production model.[12]

All of these changes elevated the need to train and educate manufacturing workers. To make the manufacturing operations productive and profitable there was a belief that front-line workers needed to possess formal skills that were necessary to utilize new technologies. Companies developed training and education as an important new part of their enterprise.

A study by the Industrial Technology Institute, a state-initiated center in the 1980s to advance the rapid adoption of computer based manufacturing technologies, found that training in all skill categories increased as a result of the introduction of new technology. Not only were technical skills important, but companies also devoted additional resources to raising the basic skills of all employees. They also encouraged them to return to school through the establishment of company-paid tuition programs.

For the first time, manufacturers began paying attention to the training and education needs of their hourly workforces. Larger companies established formal in-house training; smaller firms tended to rely on informal job training.[13] In unionized workplaces, this resulted in the development of joint company-union administered training funds that were established to provide continuous training in health, safety and such "soft" skills as problem solving and total quality management. In their 1982 contract negotiations, the United Auto Workers and the Big Three automakers established joint education and training organizations that were funded from money diverted out of the contract settlement. Because of the size of the domestic OEMs and the number of unionized workers, substantial sums of money were amassed to create some of the largest private training organizations in the United States.[14]

In addition, many states initiated customized training programs for workers as a strategy to retain existing companies and attract new ones. Most of these programs were directed at manufacturing companies and accounted for the majority of funding for training hourly workers. Many were administered through community colleges that developed and implemented custom training programs for companies deemed to be important to local and state economies. By the late 1990s, a survey of community colleges indicated that the automobile companies were the largest private-sector "customers" of contracted training programs.[15]

In late 1989, the first Bush administration introduced the Manufacturing Extension Partnership (MEP), the first federal program aimed at promoting the growth and development of manufacturing. This organization was designed to assist small- and medium-sized manufacturers in the deployment of new technologies. Its creation was justified by the need to foster the competitiveness of U.S. manufacturers against their Japanese and German rivals.[16]

Through the 1990s, both Republican and Democratic presidential administrations considered training and education of the workforce to be a national priority. Under the first Bush administration, the Department of Labor initiated the Secretary's Commission on Achieving Necessary Skills (SCANS), which defined the skills necessary for a successful workplace. Building on these endeavors, the Clinton administration supplemented existing apprenticeship programs under a new education policy entitled "School-to-Work," which was based on the experiences of the "dual system" of worker training as practiced in Germany. The Department of Labor also developed an on-the-job apprenticeship program for young people. It created the National Skill Standards Board (NSSB) to establish appropriate skills for various key sectors of the American economy. This board helped form the basic principles needed for educational institutions, community organizations, labor unions and others to provide world-class training to the American workforce.[17]

In a major shift of federal training policy, schools and educational institutions were considered essential in driving a competitiveness agenda for America. Education was seen as the critical aspect of creating high-skilled jobs with high wages.[18] Much of the new agenda called for reform of the K-12 educational system and integrated workplace learning by using the "dual system" common in Western European countries.[19]

This large-scale national education response to the global competitive challenge produced significant interest in and expansion of training and educational activities within state and local governments. Governors developed new economic development programs based on improving the skills of the local workforce combined with the age-old practice of providing companies with financial incentives and tax abatements on land. Many states initiated aggressive customized training programs that doled out state funds to companies promising to add new jobs or to protect existing ones.

As part of the plan to address international competition, there were calls by policymakers to develop "high-performance" workplaces that required greater education and worker participation in corporate operations and improvement. The growth of noncredit customized training courses among the 1,200 American community colleges was driven by new demand from manufacturers. Unions also started developing their own training programs for workers, deploying technologies that would help companies maintain their competitive edge and help retain good-paying jobs in American communities.[20]

By the late 1990s, there was even more interest in creating manufacturing jobs that paid well and demanded new skills. A new infrastructure of training providers was created to prepare people for these jobs. Although there remained differences between labor and management and the political parties on specific strategies to create a trained workforce, most plans were focused on the activities of the 1,200 American community colleges. These institutions had already developed large and influential programs with local manufacturing companies through the 1980s and 1990s.[21] They were considered to be the backbone of the national training and retraining system for most adult workers, even though they were funded by local and state governments.[22]

But the infrastructure was even broader and deeper. Community-based organizations were created in urban centers to provide inner-city residents with manufacturing skills. These programs enjoyed significant support from local businesses that turned to them as suppliers of front-line workers. Organizations like Project Quest in San Antonio were able to partner with community colleges and develop programs for manufacturers in their community. Focus Hope in Detroit created a major machinist training center that supplied skilled workers to auto suppliers in the Detroit metropolitan area. In Milwaukee, the Wisconsin Training and Education Partnership provided training programs for a collective group of manufacturers that were seeking entry-level workers.[23]

These new "intermediary" organizations were created outside of the traditional private training system. They were based on the concept that preparing a skilled manufacturing workforce was too important to be left to the private sector. A trained workforce would help foster a modern manufacturing system and was necessary for the success of local and state economic development initiatives. They also helped stabilize economically troubled local communities. This nationwide effort was based on the assumption that there was a "high road" in manufacturing that needed to be created and sustained so that workers would receive good wages and the communities in which they lived would prosper.[24]

As a result of these activities, national surveys of firms and analysis of census data indicated substantial increases in training activities within manufacturing firms. About 80 percent of all firms possessed formal training programs. Ninety-one percent of companies with unionized production workers experienced growth in training programs.[25] Education and training programs were 35 percent more likely to be found in "high-performance" manufacturing firms than other firms of equal size.[26]

Education and training gained traction deep within manufacturing companies. Much of the training went beyond technical issues or even health and safety. A good deal of what was offered to workers was in both basic skills to improve reading and writing, total quality management techniques such as Six Sigma and lean, and international quality standards such as ISO 9000 that were being adopted by companies exporting goods overseas and selling to foreign transplants in the United States.

Much of the new emphasis on training was tied to a need to involve workers in the process of work organization and decision-making. One of the most heralded new ventures was GM's creation of Saturn as "a new kind of car company." Developed as a response to lessons learned from Japanese manufacturers, GM poured billions of dollars into a separate division within the company designed by joint teams of managers and union representatives. New processes and worker participation were added to all aspects of the production process. Workers were even given responsibility for selecting employees for the new Saturn plant in Springhill, Tenn. In addition, every Saturn non-union worker was obligated to develop an individual training plan and was evaluated on whether they fulfilled their training assignment.[27]

By the late 1990s, the preparation of the workforce for a modern manufacturing enterprise had emerged as an important public policy issue. There was an understanding of the need to preserve a manufacturing base for America's economic growth and stability. There was a belief that a well-trained and educated workforce would be the decisive reason for companies to maintain production in the United States and that it would act as a magnet for foreign company investment.

In hindsight, this view failed to comprehend that the same factors contributing to the focus on training — the application of computer and communications technologies that allowed for distributed work organizations — were leading to a new global manufacturing order that would result in millions of America's highest skilled production jobs being sent overseas. The myriad of training and education programs just described were about to be altered by new corporate interest in overseas investment.

Globalization Puts an End to the Era Of Workforce Training

The renaissance of American manufacturing abruptly ended in the late 1990s. What emerged was an economy that was not based on a national renewal of U.S. production capacity, but on the globalization of production to remote parts of the world where there were no skilled workers and plenty of cheap labor. The "high road" strategies of the 1990s deftly articulated by policy wonks were jettisoned in favor of earning tons of money from easily exploitable low-wage workers. Indeed, the ability of American corporations to quickly globalize their supply chains refuted the argument by corporate executives and their political patrons that a skilled and highly educated workforce was the essence of a world-class manufacturing capability.

In many respects, the trends promoting globalization and ending U.S. support for programs aimed at improving U.S. competitiveness resided deep in the American economy from the end of World War II. Additional momentum for free trade policies promoting the shift of production offshore was generated by the collapse of the Soviet Union and the opening of China.[28]

American corporations continued to expand their investments under the banner of "free trade" all over the world. One important signal was the passage of the North America Free Trade Agreement, which revealed to the American public and workers that there was consensus among leaders in corporate America and the U.S. government that pursuing free trade was the country's primary economic strategy. The central question today is whether that sole economic pursuit has backfired on America.

The shift to investing offshore was not new, but it was justified by American manufacturers in an entirely different way. Instead of viewing national competitiveness as dependent upon an educated and trained workforce, policymakers became more focused on how they could assist American companies improve profitability through overseas investments. The economic justification for this change in strategy was the production of cheaper goods for American consumers. The goal was to allow the United States to become the technical and administrative hub of a global manufacturing enterprise. In this view, front-line manufacturing workers were expendable because of the inevitable move toward low-wage countries. They were not considered to be a value-added resource, and were viewed as an unnecessary and bothersome expense. Axing them was justified under the banner of creating much better "knowledge" jobs, which, it was further assumed, would remain in the United States.

Coupled with this was the extreme "financialization" of the economy, where short-term profitability, quick investment decisions, manipulation of stock prices and the development of esoteric financial instruments became the dominant concerns of the large companies. Manufacturing was not an industry for aggressive young entrepreneurs. Instead, the production of goods was left to non-American, low-cost contract manufacturers who could generate record profits for U.S. companies and their investors. The initial focus on sending production to Mexico soon widened to include China, Eastern Europe and Southeast Asia.

Central to this policy shift was the belief that new computer-based technologies had "leveled the playing field." The ability of rural areas in China to apply new production technologies and compete with manufacturing facilities in the Midwest was celebrated as a process that would more efficiently and effectively utilize the scarce resources of the world.[29]

As economic policymakers and commentators discussed how the American economy should concentrate on high-tech and service industries, there was a profound silence over the increasing number of industrial jobs being lost to outsourcing. These losses were not driven by technology but by decisions made by companies to remain profitable by finding cheap labor and places to exploit all over the world. As more jobs were permanently lost, the level of public unease grew, yet policymakers refused to change.

The significant loss of manufacturing jobs created a new ethic surrounding education and training. Millions of displaced manufacturing workers, who would never again work in the manufacturing sector because it was being outsourced overseas, were sent to "retraining programs" for jobs that would never provide them with the wages or benefits they previously received in manufacturing.[30] Other high-tech workers were even involved in training their own permanent foreign replacements.

Over the past eight years, there has been a significant shift in the human resource policies of many U.S. manufacturing companies. Borrowing from their Japanese competitors, American manufacturers began adopting the idea that the development of skills was no longer the responsibility of the company. Workers should be selected from pools of people with specific skill sets. Individual workers would be responsible for improving their skills or learning new ones that were in demand. The companies only needed to create new programs to assess workers who possessed the appropriate skills. They would train workers in the proprietary features of their products and processes, but they expected individuals to come to the job having paid for and mastered their own foundation and technical skills.

What is important to emphasize here is the abrupt shift taken by companies to provide less training to incumbent workers, and to stress more hiring of "necessary skills" through elaborate processes of assessing potential workers. In some ways, this approach attempted to emulate the Japanese practice of carefully selecting all front-line manufacturing workers. Public training dollars intended to be used by companies were diverted to develop assessment criteria that would hone down the applicant pool. Training a workforce was no longer necessary. In some instances, the costs of assessing the skills of an individual production worker were as high as $10,000.[31]

In selecting workers, more emphasis was placed on individuals with basic skills who could be "trained" for jobs when they were hired. The goal was to find the appropriate worker for the job — a concept called "skills on demand."[32] If manufacturing was dominated by "supply chains" of companies providing parts to each other, why couldn't there be a supply chain of humans who could be delivered whenever they were needed by companies? This perspective fit well with the demands of lean manufacturing and just-in-time delivery. Training and education were less important than the ability to access skills when required.

These strategies impacted large manufacturing companies that were traditional centers of organized labor. These were often the companies that had adopted the "high road" worker training strategies of the 1990s. The once-prevalent "high-performance" work organization fell out of favor as companies re-engineered themselves for the entirely new era of globalization. Companies trained relatively few workers and they were less interested in seeing training and education as a means of mobility for those within their companies. They sought to find their skilled workers in the marketplace, and no longer developed or even maintained talent from within. They continuously monitored international competition with the sole focus on whether they could match their prices. If not, plants were moved out of the country with frightening speed and wide-scale dislocation of hundreds of thousands of workers. Between 1998 and 2007, manufacturing employment in the United States declined by 20 percent, with losses increasing substantially in 2008.[33]

The unrelenting pressure from Wall Street for companies to increase their quarterly profits had a significant impact on training and U.S. education policies.

The training market for front-line hourly employees has subsequently shriveled, as the number of these jobs continues to rapidly decline in the United States. Much of the training budget of firms has shifted to white collar and technical training.[34] In the 1990s, many of the largest customized training programs were in industries such as auto, steel and aerospace that were "modernizing" to deal with international competition. Today, many of these firms have closed their U.S. operations or, when they expand their facilities, hire only workers with specific skills and educational credentials. There are few large-scale public training programs left in the United States.[35] Instead, there have been significant increases in training programs for displaced workers. These have been created under the new guidelines in the Workforce Investment Act and Temporary Assistance for Needy Families programs. The new era of worker training is short-term and concentrates on resume writing and techniques for quickly finding a new job. It is aimed at getting workers off of public unemployment insurance benefits as quickly as possible.[36]

The proliferation of IT certification is now a means by which employers can demand validation of new information skills from individuals as a condition of advancement or hiring.[37]

Thus, education and training is shifting from being a responsibility of the employers to being the responsibility of the employees. Moreover, as employers shift the responsibility for training to the individual, they are also increasingly demanding four-year college degrees as opposed to favoring applicants with skills learned on previous jobs. Employers in the manufacturing sector perceive the college degree as a means by which workers demonstrate not only their motivation to complete an important milestone, but also as the basis to effectively receive additional training on the job.[38] By requiring that applicants have a college degree, companies can concentrate on performing employee background checks and drug testing as a means of weeding out candidates who may cause problems. The corporate emphasis on college degrees motivates both state and federal educational policymakers to further reduce their support for vocational and job training programs for the "middle level" skilled manufacturing and construction jobs that require some postsecondary training, but not necessarily a college education.[39]

While many states still support corporate training programs to lure new industry into their communities, there has been a decrease in state economic development programs targeting specific companies and industrial sectors. States like Michigan have eliminated their modernization services and replaced them with diminished general training funds that can be used by the governor to attract new companies. Other states, such as Illinois and California, have eliminated their customized job training programs altogether. Increasingly, states have been dropping general industry training programs in favor of "one-time" training projects targeted at specific companies considering new investments within the state.[40] Not only does this contribute to corporate relocation strategies which play states against one another to achieve the best financial incentive package, but these strategies neglect the need to maintain and nurture the manufacturers within the state.

Even in states where there has been considerable industrial economic growth, workforce development programs are different from the past. The best examples are the southern states such as Alabama and Mississippi that attracted large automobile investments from Japanese and German manufacturers. In these cases, prospective workers are trained at their own expense — or through a major state grant — to qualify a "pool" of workers from which the company can then select. Most state training money is now being spent primarily on training management, engineers and white collar workers.[41]

At the federal level, the Workforce Investment Act (WIA) of 1998 and the Temporary Assistance for Needy Families (TANF) act de-emphasize training in favor of immediate job placement. The result: Many workers find work but are unable to obtain sufficient incomes.[42] In addition, these programs have been significantly downsized. Total WIA adult funding decreased from $945 million in 2002 to $864 million in 2006. Dislocated worker funding decreased 3.6 percent from $1.23 billion in 2002 to $1.12 billion in 2006. The number of individuals trained under WIA decreased from 168,223 in 1998 to 72,322 in 2001.[43]

Most of the training now provided by government programs is short-term and does not promote career pathways or a means to better-paying jobs. In a few states such as Illinois, TANF rules were interpreted to permit attendance at a community college as a means of meeting the training requirements.[44] Yet, on the whole, state programs are now smaller and less directed at the private sector's needs.

What has increased at the state level is an attempt to coordinate both economic development strategies and workforce development strategies through a focus on degree completion. States now believe that granting more college degrees will give their economies a competitive edge in attracting high-tech companies.

States that have taken this approach have assembled coalitions of public universities and community colleges to emphasize policies such as dual enrollment between high schools and colleges, seamless transition from community colleges to four-year colleges and universities, and helping adults with some college credit to return to school and complete their degrees. The primary emphasis is on preparing students for four-year degree programs. The result is diminished emphasis on technical training programs.[45]

As educational requirements became mandatory for workers, new production facilities being built in the United States demanded postsecondary degrees for all front-line employees. When United Motors opened an engine plant in Dundee, Mich., the selection process required all hourly workers to possess a two-year college degree.[46] More formal education was considered a major plus. Sadly for tens of millions of smart, capable American citizens, manufacturing no longer provides an entry-level job for workers without a college degree.

The conventional explanation for this change was that advanced technology was available to workers throughout the world and that motivated workers overseas were undercutting American companies. The defenders of outsourcing argued that this was a natural process and that a small segment of America — manufacturing workers — would have to suffer for the remainder of the society to benefit. To survive, American workers were told to sharpen their skills and find jobs in career areas outside of manufacturing.[47] There was nothing anyone could do about the loss of their good-paying factory job except to retrain for a different economic future — a future in the services sector that, as it turned out, paid lower wages and provided fewer benefits.

The "inevitability" of manufacturing's demise produced a ubiquitous lack of concern for American industry and its workforce, which was (and continues to be) blamed for being part of the problem. If manufacturing was to remain at all, the winning strategy was to aggressively pursue and ask for significant concessions from "overpaid workers," despite significant data clearly indicating that labor was only a very small portion of the total cost of any finished product.

Given these changes in perception, which were being promulgated by thousands of economists supported by corporations and government agencies, training and education in manufacturing began to atrophy. Instead of being viewed as being an important input that could improve productivity and flexibility, training was now considered to be an overhead cost that needed to be eliminated. Attitudes toward work and other "noncognitive" skills such as taking orders, showing up on time and listening to supervisors became more important than possessing technical skills to perform a job. A trained workforce was less important than a "virtual" company that was able to create a process for obtaining "skills on demand."[48]

Federal policies for employment and training began to mirror this view. Instead of looking for ways in which federal skill development programs could be fashioned to protect and preserve American manufacturing, the Department of Labor emphasized the creation of programs that would be "demand driven." This meant training people for jobs that were already available. Companies with low-wage jobs that had high turnover were able to utilize the federal system for entry-level hires.

Even when the workforce system responded to the market demand of manufacturing jobs, it did not build capacity or encourage the skill sets necessary for long-term, highly technical manufacturing endeavors. Instead, the system was designed for short-term fixes for low-wage companies, which helped restore their profitability but did little or nothing to build a competitive long-term and viable economic system. Thus, an area like metallurgy, which required significant foundation skills in mathematics, materials and chemistry, was not found among the training programs supported by the Workforce Investment Act. Yet there was a proliferation of training programs to develop "communications" skills. Some local workforce boards found creative ways to undertake manufacturing training activities, but the general goal of these programs was to achieve employment for individuals at any available job. They did not create the skills necessary for a workforce of the future.[49]

The emphasis on "work first" also contributed to a perverse reordering of training priorities. The system was directed away from a focus on incumbent workers because they already had jobs. It also meant that employer training funds that had traditionally been used in partnership with public funding mechanisms could not be utilized to develop programs for the incumbent workforce. Such programs had existed during the Clinton administration, but were discontinued.

The Workforce Investment Act also provided poor-paying industries with a steady stream of unskilled workers. The program was a subsidy for low-wage industries that could neither attract nor find sufficient workers on their own. Meanwhile, the media hyped up the efforts to lower unemployment and welfare rolls without looking at how public expenditures were being used to channel funding into industries that paid lousy wages.

Finally the new Workforce Investment Act focused only on skills that workers needed to obtain a job and on short-term training. This denied potential workers the ability to develop long-term skills necessary for mastering computer-based equipment in the manufacturing enterprise. In most cases, customized training could not be financed under the act, so skill development of incumbent workers inside manufacturing firms could not be supported.

Within these broad outlines, the Bush administration added its own ideological requirements. First was the overwhelming belief that markets determine the demand for industries. If there is no demand for manufacturing within the United States, then this sector ought to just shrink and disappear. Government efforts such as the Manufacturing Extension Partnership (MEP) program should be abolished because they were trying to "pick winners," an ideological no-no in a capitalistic system. The Bush administration repeatedly tried to kill MEP. While other nations used aggressive policies to improve the health and expand the global influence of their manufacturers, the only major economic policy of the United States government was to pursue a perverse notion of free trade that shifted production offshore and put U.S. industry at a competitive disadvantage.

A second important policy agenda of the Bush administration related to manufacturing was the dismantling of the American vocational educational system. The administration believed that there was no legitimate role for the federal government to play in vocational education, and that if individuals needed to be trained, it should be up to them or their employers to do so. On another level, many in the Bush administration saw vocational education as a barrier to their effort to implement school reform known euphemistically as "No Child Left Behind." While this law has many deficiencies, the idea that the federal government bears some responsibility for preparing young people for work in manufacturing was important in producing programs at the local level to support training needed for entry-level manufacturing jobs. In addition, there were substantial funds from that legislation that went to American secondary and postsecondary educational systems. The Perkins Act remains the largest single federal funding program for American high schools.[50]

But from the outset of the Bush administration, there were attempts to kill the Perkins Act. Part of the impetus came from tight budgets caused by the administration's focus on the war in Iraq; part of it came from the increasingly dominant right-wing ideology that education should focus on teaching the basics of reading, writing and math, and that job preparation should be left to local communities. These arguments were often not expressed directly, but were couched in the widespread view that the goal of the K-12 educational program was to insure that all students were prepared to attend college. The Bush administration de-emphasized any support for training and education of manufacturing skills among the millions of young people who would never go to college either because they weren't good students or because they could not afford it. The misbegotten belief among America's governing elite was that the future would be dominated by high-tech jobs and that mid-level (and essential) jobs like machinist maintenance and repair workers were "low-tech," low-skill, and unworthy of the economic attention of the nation.

In addition, the Bush administration continued to slash expenditures in all federal programs aimed at developing a skilled workforce. According to the Workforce Alliance, funding for federal training and education programs has declined by 29 percent during the past eight years. The United States spent a paltry 0.02 percent of GDP on workforce training and education in 2007, the lowest among all 20 OECD member countries.[51]

The retreat of support for manufacturing skills training and education was not limited to the federal government. In the late 1990s, states started to slash training programs for incumbent workers. They eliminated most efforts at job retention in favor of "big bang projects" — the luring of major investment — mostly from foreign producers into their states. The new paradigm was embodied in the massive subsidies provided by southern states to lure European and Japanese manufacturers.[52]

As a result, interest in training a skilled manufacturing workforce over the past five years has diminished substantially. There are now few state programs left that promote the development of a skilled manufacturing workforce. Instead, states try to target industries such as biotechnology, information technology and health care that offer the promise of "job growth," even though entry-level wages in these industries are considerably lower than in the manufacturing sector. Lacking demand, manufacturing programs at community colleges are now evaporating. Even highly touted community-based initiatives are less involved in training manufacturing workers and are focusing instead on opportunities in areas such as construction and health care.[53]

Most states now promote the idea that the number of workers with a college degree is the best measure of a trained workforce. Mature programs for developing specific manufacturing skills have disappeared, except for those that concentrate on total quality management. Colleges are not focused on programs aimed at increasing the productivity of manufacturing processes or companies.

The situation is far different outside the United States. European countries such as Germany have significant efforts aimed at preventing manufacturing job erosion. An example is in the use of computers in manufacturing processes. Not only could vast reams of data be stored and utilized to adjust and improve production processes, but digital technologies provide new ways in which workers redesign processes to alter products quickly and efficiently for changing market demands. The challenge facing all nations is how quickly new technologies can be implemented within both products and manufacturing processes so that companies can stay competitive by substantially improving quality and efficiency.

In the United States, the National Skill Standard panel on information technology issued one report on this important subject. It then ceased to exist. Individual information technology companies created their own proprietary skill certification programs. Their goal was to create a base of skilled workers and establish a market for their new software platforms and increase their own profitability. These proprietary IT training programs quickly migrated into the public education system as a source of revenue. What resulted was a crazy quilt of certification programs for every imaginable proprietary technology and software program. Most of these certification courses were very expensive for students, shutting out many lower-income workers who could not afford to pay for them.[54]

This is not how things progressed in Germany. In contrast, the Germans integrated these new skill requirements into their training system by creating apprenticeship programs for information technology. Companies, students, labor unions and training institutes — all of the social partners involved in job creation and retention — were brought together to discuss the needs of employers and to work out a solution that benefited the entire society, not just the technology providers.

In addition to apprenticeship training in Germany, unions and corporate management agreed upon specific short-term technology classes that required immediate support in addition to the traditional apprenticeship programs. With government funding and the technical expertise from technology and software providers, German manufacturers began utilizing information technologies to create on-the-job learning systems for workers on the shop floor. In addition, the well-funded and influential German vocational agency, Federal Institute for Vocational Education and Training (known in Germany as the BIB) sought to ensure that the skills they thought important were embedded within European-wide skill standards for information technology. This included a means by which refresher courses could be taught. In addition, Germany tried to develop European-wide standards so that companies operating across borders would benefit from the investment.[55]

The same promising and essential new digital production technologies were unevenly adopted in the United States, especially among many small- and medium-sized manufacturers unable to attract trained workers with the necessary skills in proprietary IT systems. There was widespread misinformation spread to workers and potential workers over the need to take certification tests. No such confusion existed in Germany, where there were concerted attempts to focus the public education system on providing technological training and dissemination beyond the borders of the country.

The payoff for these policies was impressive. Germany has maintained a competitive manufacturing edge; it remains a manufacturing giant generating a large trade surplus; and it has sustained many good-paying jobs that generate large sums of tax revenues. Because of higher training costs borne by the society, German manufacturing remains an essential part of the economy. Unlike the cavalier attitude that is widespread in the United States, no German policymaker would dare argue that the elimination of manufacturing would be good for the future economic success of Germany. Meanwhile, without understanding the importance of an industrial base and the need for tens of millions of well-paid, well-trained workers, the United States is suffering a massive economic collapse.

Restoring Training and Education in the American Manufacturing Sector

As the American economy struggles, the short-term future for new training and education strategies for manufacturing appears bleak. Yet over the long term, the economic crisis should raise important issues about policy changes required to revive American industry, the American economy and America's prospects. This time, the country needs to be ready with a fresh mindset and programs that regard education and training as a significant contributor to economic renewal. It has to be different from the past.

The federal government must understand that education and training policies cannot be stand-alone issues, but need to be embedded in an overall national policy that views manufacturing as essential to America's future. Manufacturing needs policies that will help it generate positive returns to society. If manufacturing is important as an employer of millions of Americans who did not succeed through the formal educational system (especially for those who live in urban centers), then public efforts must be made to strengthen these firms as an important piece of the economic revitalization of major cities. If manufacturing is essential to the development and production of environmentally sustainable products, then there should be governmental regulations and incentives that promote the growth of these firms.[56] Training and education is part of a larger government strategy that also includes technical innovation, new methods of financing expansions, trade laws, labor organizing reform and changes in tax law. It is no longer plausible to argue that education and training alone can be decisive. It should be part of a broad and systematic plan to rescue the American economy.

A second aspect of a renaissance in economic policy is the need to understand that it has to be directed at innovative small- and medium-sized firms that are the heart of industrial communities throughout the United States. Too much of economic and industrial policy has been directed at large manufacturers that have shifted production offshore and show little allegiance to local communities. Big multinational corporations have become less important to most regional economies. Small- and medium-sized firms are often owned by local business people and are funded through local financial institutions. The needs of these manufacturing organizations, and their potential to revitalize America through the introduction of new products, should be a top federal priority. In this regard, the effort of the NIST Manufacturing Extension Partnership — about to celebrate its 20th anniversary — is an important example of the type of program needed to be developed and expanded.

The economic payoffs for MEP interventions with the companies that constitute the backbone of the American economy are vast considering their relatively low cost to taxpayers. The federal government only funds one-third of their operations, with the remainder of funds coming from states and the companies that receive services.[57]

In addition to MEP, there need to be complementary organizations that can train and educate the workforce to help transform these companies. For small- and medium-size firms, front-line workforce education and training is central to their growth and development. Many case studies indicate that firms with greater training and workforce development are more competitive and are achieving higher productivity gains.[58] It is difficult for most of these companies to find the resources necessary to support these activities.

A third part of the strategy is the need to understand the difference between education and training in manufacturing and the role each will play in the renewal of American industry. There is a clear need for formal classes and organized learning, but there is also need for research into the postsecondary education system to generate the manufacturing knowledge that gets converted into training material

237

that can be disseminated through four-year colleges and universities. This knowledge is important for the continued innovation both of educational processes and of the manufacturing enterprise.[59]

On the "training" aspect of manufacturing, many manufacturing workers do not continue pursuing post-secondary education, so there needs to be significant attention paid to making sure they acquire foundation skills in high school. Complex machinery costing hundreds of thousands dollars is being maintained by workers without high school degrees who cannot read, much less comprehend, a technical manual. Too often within the secondary schools, "vocational education" remains a dumping ground for students not headed for college. The programs stress "hands-on skills" without insuring basic competence in the learning skills that are critical once a worker is on the job. Without foundation skills, younger workers entering manufacturing find it difficult to improve their skills. In this regard, some of the recent efforts within Chicago schools to create a new type of high school that stresses strong basic skills in mathematics and English — within a manufacturing context — are a welcome development.[60]

For manufacturers, America's 1,200 community colleges remain the best public option for these activities. Virtually all of these institutions are within 30 minutes of any major manufacturing cluster and they hire a large group of technically trained, experienced instructors familiar with techniques for teaching adults.[61]

In June 2005, the Center for Regional Economic Competitiveness (CREC) surveyed 1,013 community colleges and found that more than 94 percent of them offered noncredit specialized courses. CREC estimated that more than 3.45 million students nationally were enrolled in these programs — or about 20 percent of community college enrollment. More than half of all the community colleges — 55.5 percent — offered specialized training in manufacturing skills, and there were about 871,000 students enrolled in these courses, about 6 percent of all manufacturing workers. The majority of the funding for these programs came from contracts or grants with private companies working in conjunction with the states.[62]

Community colleges can also be important places where underprepared adults working in manufacturing companies can return to school and learn fundamental math and communication skills. This would help them participate in improving the productivity and growth of their firms and is particularly important for immigrants who need adult education skills to advance in their jobs.

A second major role of community colleges will be to develop career paths for individuals to advance into management at manufacturing companies, and for others to move into technical divisions to help improve corporate innovation. Without an upward flow of people into skilled trades and management, manufacturing enterprises become dominated by individuals with college degrees who have little connection to manufacturing and its significance to the future success of the company.[63]

A third role for community colleges comes in aiding the development and diffusion of new learning techniques among manufacturing companies and their workers. The development of interactive computer-based learning systems, which are regularly utilized at most community colleges, can be fashioned into expert company training systems. Larger companies can afford to develop these products on their own, but most small- and medium-size firms find it extremely difficult to develop such systems. Community colleges have the technical capability and are in close proximity to manufacturers to undertake these activities. Most front-line workers under the age of 30 are very familiar with computer-based audio and video products. These instructional systems can be utilized by workers for just-in-time training as they encounter issues on the job. In Germany, public funds are available to companies for the development of these products. Not so in the United States.

There also needs to be more emphasis on the development of formal and informal on-the-job continuous training that becomes embedded within companies. Once this happens, it fosters changes in work rules and processes that, in turn, improve productivity and financial returns. While there is no "one way" to effectively organize manufacturing facilities, most empirical examinations of the highest-performing operations note the direct link between changes in the workplace and increased productivity and profits.[64]

Finally, efforts to restore American manufacturing need to have external allies that promote training and education from outside the firms. Community-based organizations, unions, ethnic organizations, literacy groups and other organizations can serve as important intermediaries to ensure that a well-trained, motivated group of workers is able to step into manufacturing facilities. Their involvement in the process will assure that employment of local citizens is an important factor for the economic viability of their communities. Economic sustainability is a serious local issue. People must be prepared to work in a manufacturing enterprise. These organizations must succeed to maintain manufacturing, wages and opportunities of advancement for millions of Americans.

A rich social network of organizations needs to be developed with an understanding of manufacturers' needs. This will take time and resources, but the payoff in terms of corporate efficiencies and effective recruitment of workers would be enormous. Much of the public workforce system could be built around the activities of these social organizations. In addition, these networks can become potential sources of future innovation and growth of training activities that can restore profitability to the companies and lead to the rebirth of the American economy.

The decline of American manufacturing is not a foreordained conclusion. Education and training will play a vital role in the difficult but essential process of economic renewal. For the past 30 years, manufacturing has shrunk in significance in the American economy. It has lost status among the American people. Even within manufacturing communities, there is widespread belief that it has no future, particularly for young people. Restoring public confidence in American production and innovation is central to changing this defeatist perspective. It will take political leadership and vision, something that — unfortunately — has been in short supply in American life. The future of thousands of American communities rests on whether manufacturing can be restored. This should make us intensify every effort to overcome the challenges ahead.

---

1. Manufacturing Extension Partnership program, "Supporting Economic Development: Community College Support for Specialized Training," July 22, 2008, www.mep.nist.gov/documents/pdf/about-mep/reports-studies/NIST-CC-Survey-121405-v1-MEP-summary.pdf.
2. National Association of Manufacturers, *The Facts About Modern Manufacturing*, 7th Edition, 2006.
3. Jacobs, James, "Community Colleges and the Workforce Investment Act: Promises and Problems of the New Vocationalism," in D. Bragg (Ed.), 2002, *The New Vocationalism In Community Colleges*, San Francisco, Jossey-Bass.
4. Appelbaum, Eileen; Bailey, Thomas; and Berg, Peter, *Manufacturing Advantage: Why High-Performance Work Systems Pay Off*, 2000, Ithaca, Cornell University Press.
5. Babson, Steve, *Building the Union: Skilled Workers and Anglo-Gaelic Immigrants in the Rise of the UAW*, 1991, New Brunswick, Rutgers University Press.
6. Babson, Steve, *Lean Work: Empowerment and Exploitation in the Global Automobile Industry*, 1995, Detroit, Wayne State University Press.
7. Womack, James P.; Jones, Daniel T.; and Roos, Daniel, *The Machine That Changed The World*, 1991, New York, Macmillan.
8. Office of Technology Assessment, *Worker Training: Competing in the New International Economy*, 1990, Washington, D.C., Government Printing Office.
9. Appelbaum, Eileen; Bailey, Thomas; and Berg, Peter, 2000, *Manufacturing Advantage:*

Why High-Performance Work Systems Pay Off, Ithaca, Cornell University Press.

10. Piore, Michael and Sabel, Charles, 1984, *The Second Industrial Divide*, New York, Basic Books.

11. Jacobs, James, "Training the Workforce of the Future," *Technology Review*, Vol. 92, Issue 6, 1989.

12. Appelbaum, Eileen; Bailey, Thomas; and Berg, Peter, *Manufacturing Advantage: Why High-Performance Work Systems Pay Off*, 2000, Ithaca, Cornell University Press.

13. Jacobs, James, 1994, "Skills and Education Requirements" in *Design of Work and Development of Personnel In Advanced Manufacturing*, Gavriel Salvendy and Waldemar Karwowski, New York, John Wiley Sons.

14. Phelps, L. Allen; Brandenburg, Dale; and Jacobs, James, "The UAW Jointly Funds Opportunities and Dilemmas For Postsecondary Vocational Education," National Center for Research in Vocational Education, 1990.

15. Jacobs, James, "Community Colleges and the Workforce Investment Act: Promises and Problems of the New Vocationalism," in D. Bragg (Ed.), 2002, *The New Vocationalism In Community Colleges*, San Francisco, Jossey-Bass.

16. Modernization Forum, Modernization Forum Skills Commission, 1993, Skills for Industrial Modernization, Dearborn.

17. Lafer, Gordon, *The Job Training Charade*, Ithaca, Cornell University Press, 2002.

18. Rothstein, Richard, "A Nation at Risk Twenty-Five Years Later," April 7, 2008, www.cato-unbound.org/2008/04/07/richard-rothstein/a-nation-at-risk-twenty-five-years-later.

19. Commission on Education and the Economy, "America's Choice: High Skills and High Wages," Washington, D.C., 1990.

20. Baugh, Robert, *Changing Work: A Union Guide to Workplace Change*, AFL-CIO Human Resources Development Institute, 1994.

21. Jacobs, James, "Training the Workforce of the Future," *Technology Review*, Vol. 92, Issue 6, 1989.

22. Modernization Forum Skills Commission, "Skills for Industrial Modernization," 1993, Dearborn, Modernization Forum.

23. Osterman, P.; Kochan, T.; Locke, R.; and Piore, M., *Working in America: A Blueprint for a New Labor Market*, Cambridge, Mass., MIT Press, 2001.

24. Luria, Daniel and Rogers, Joel , "Manufacturing, Regional Prosperity and Public Policy," Brookings Institution, 2007.

25. Cappelli, Peter, et al, *Change at Work*, Oxford University Press, N.Y., 1997.

26. Osterman, 1992; Batt, R. & Osterman, 1993, "A National Policy for Workplace Training," Washington, D.C., Economic Policy Institute.

27. Bluestone, Barry and Bluestone, Irving , *Negotiating The Future: A Labor Perspective on American Business*, New York, Basic Books, 1992.

28. Levy, Frank; Tremin, Peter; Aldonas, et al, 2007, "Inequality and Institutions in 20th Century America," working paper, Cambridge, National Bureau of Economic Research. Aldonas, Grant D.; Lawrence., Robert Z., and Slaughter, Matthew J., 2007, "Succeeding In the Global Economy: A New Policy Agenda for the American Worker," New York, Financial Services Forum.

29. Friedman, Thomas, *The World is Flat*, Farrar, Straus & Giroux, 2005.

30. Uchitelle, Louis, *The Disposable American: Layoffs and Their Consequences*, New York, Alfred A. Knopf, 2006; Lafer, Gordon, 2002, *The Job Training Charade*, Ithaca, Cornell University Press.

31. Center for Automotive Research, "Beyond the Big Leave: The Future of U.S. Automotive Human Resources," 2008, Ann Arbor.

32. Cappelli, Peter, *Talent on Demand*, Cambridge, Harvard Business Press, 2008.

33. Luria, Daniel and Rogers, Joel, "Manufacturing, Regional Prosperity and Public Policy," Brookings Institution, 2007.

34. Carnevale, A. and Fry, R., "The Economic and Demographic Roots of Education

and Training," Washington, D.C., National Association of Manufacturers' Center for Workforce Success, 2002.

35. Jacobs, James; Dougherty, Kevin, "The Uncertain Future of the Community College Workforce Development Mission," 2006; Barbara Townsend and Kevin Dougherty "Community College Missions in the 21st Century," San Francisco, Joseey Baas.

36. Shaw, K. and S. Goldrick-Rab, "Market Rhetoric Versus Reality in Policy and Practice: the Workforce Investment Act and Access to Community College Education and Training," *Annals of the American Academy of Political and Social Science*, March 2003, pages 172-193.

37. Bartlett, K., "The Preconceived Influence of Industry-Sponsored Credentials in the Information Technology Industry," Minneapolis, Minn., National Center for Career and Technical Education, 2002.

38. Spence, Robin and Kiel, Brandan, "Skilling The American Workforce On The Cheap," Washington, D.C., The Workforce Alliance, 2003.

39. Holtzer, Harry and Lerman, Robert, for the Workforce Alliance, "America's Forgotten Middle-Skill Jobs: Education and Training Requirements in the Next Decade," http://www.skills2compete.org/atf/cf/%7B8E9806BF-4669-4217-AF74-26F62108 EA68%7D/ForgottenJobsReport%20Final.pdf.

40. National Governors' Association, "Aligning State Workforce Development and Economic Development Initiatives," NGA Center for Best Practices, Washington, D.C., 2005.

41. Rosenfeld, Stuart; Jacobs, James; Liston, Cynthia, "Cluster Based Workforce Development: A Community College Approach," http://www.rtsinc.org/publications /pdf/cluster_wf.pdf.

42. Shaw, K. and Goldrick-Rab, S., "Market Rhetoric Versus Reality in Policy and Practice: the Workforce Investment Act and Access to Community College Education and Training," *Annals of the American Academy of Political and Social Science*, March 2003, pages 172-193.

43. Rubinstein, Gwen and Mayo, Andrea, "Training Policy in Brief: an Overview of Federal Workforce Development Policies," Washington, TWA, 2007.

44. Shaw, K. and Goldrick-Rab, S., "Market Rhetoric Versus Reality in Policy and Practice: the Workforce Investment Act and Access to Community College Education and Training," *Annals of the American Academy of Political and Social Science*, March 2003, pages 172-193

45. Brookings Institution Metropolitan Policy Program, 2006, "The Vital Center: A Federal-State Compact to Renew the Great Lakes Region," Washington, D.C.

46. Center for Automotive Research, "Beyond The Big Leave: The Future of U.S. Automotive Human Resources," Ann Arbor, 2008.

47. Glazer, L. and Grimes, D., "Michigan's Transition to a Knowledge Economy: First Progress Report," 2008, Ann Arbor, Mich., accessible at www.michiganfuture.org.

48. Cappelli, Peter, *Talent on Demand*, Cambridge, Harvard Business Press, 2008.

49. Lafer, 2003.

50. National Assessment of Vocational Education, 2003, Final Report, Washington, D.C., Government Printing Office.

51. Workforce Alliance, 2008.

52. Rosenfeld, 1994.

53. Jacobs and Dougherty, 2006.

54. Jacobs, J. and Grubb, W.N., "Informational Technology and Skills Certification Programs in Community Colleges," in T. Bailey and V.S. Morest (Eds.) *Defending the Community College Equity Agenda*, Baltimore, Md., Johns Hopkins University Press, 2006,

55. Rein, Volker, "Qualifications Frameworks Germany / European Union, The Focus on Competence — Chances for Education and Employability," presentation at the International Association of Community Colleges, New York.

56. Luria, Daniel and Rogers, Joel, 2007, "Manufacturing, Regional Prosperity and Public Policy," Brookings Institution.

57. Luria, Dan; Vidal, Matt; Wial, Howard; Rogers, Joel, "A New Industrial Model for Mature Regions and Labor's Stake In Its Success," Sloan Industry Studies Working Papers, WP-2006-3.

58. Luria, Vidal, Hill, 2006.

59. Jacobs, Dougherty, 2006.

60. Buchele, Mose, "One Year In: A Look at Austin Polytechnical Academy," July 2, 2003, http://www.progressillinois.com/2008/07/02/features/one-year-in-at-austin.

61. Jacobs, 2006.

62. MEP, 2006.

63. Jacobs, Jim and Warford, Laurance, 2006, "Career Pathways as a Systemic Framework," League for Innovation.

64. Luria, Wial, 2006.

7. Erosion of the U.S. Defense Industrial Support Base

Michael Webber
The University of Texas at Austin

"The optimist fell from a 10-story window; as he passed each bar, he shouted to his friends inside, 'I'm alright so far.'"[1]

The United States defense industrial base suffered a massive erosion of capability between 2001 and 2008. By analyzing 16 individual manufacturing sectors that underpin the U.S. defense industrial base, it is possible to determine the true health of the entire defense industry food chain, from small companies up to the major systems integrators.

For 13 of the 16 industries, significant erosion has taken place without any signs of recovery, despite a fairly robust period of economic growth between 2002 and 2007. Only two of the 16 underlying defense manufacturing industries showed growth while one held steady over that period.

The erosion of the defense industrial base identified in this analysis is cause for concern to the overall health of the national innovation system that supports the military enterprise.

Erosion of industrial sectors has occurred many times in history. But the current economic cycle is different. The three main corrective mechanisms — economic growth, research and development investments and improvement of the skill base — either are not working or are not being applied.

Economic growth following the 2001 recession did not pull a majority of these national manufacturing sectors out of their tailspin. There is little investment in basic research and development or in advanced production processes. And there are fewer students enrolled in the science and engineering fields that support these industries. The country is losing a highly skilled workforce that cannot easily be retrained.

Many other secondary corrective mechanisms and potential policy levers exist to turn the situation around, but they are either at risk of being cut or they are being pursued unsatisfactorily. These include the protection of intellectual property, increasing access to capital and establishing flexible currency rates to make American companies more competitive.

Furthermore, the industries showing erosion are still important and relevant to the health of the defense sector — as well as the economy as a whole — as compared to obsolete industries producing goods that are no longer in demand, such as typewriters or buggywhips.

Consequently, the erosion of the defense industrial manufacturing support base is worth the attention of policymakers, who need to determine the root causes of erosion, and the efficacy of different policy levers to reverse the trends.

Over the last few years, the popular press has noted with particular alarm the loss of total manufacturing jobs starting in 2001. The stated cause for such attention has been the concern that cumulative job loss might be a drag on the overall economy, hurting quality of life and the strategic economic and geopolitical position of the United States. The financial collapse of September and October 2008 has borne out such concerns.

Since 1940, total manufacturing employment has varied from a low of 12 million employees shortly after World War II, to a high of nearly 20 million employees at the start of the 1980s, then back down to almost 12 million employees in early 2009.[2]

Figure 1: Total Manufacturing Employment from 1940 To 2009[2,3]

Overlaid on the manufacturing employment chart on page 246 are gray vertical bands that denote periods of economic recession in the United States.[3] The chart reveals that the erosion in the manufacturing base defined by the loss of employment has occurred many times historically, but that the recent downturn starting in 2001 is different from all prior periods. Historically, erosion and the subsequent expansion of the manufacturing base were in sync with the rest of the economy's movements. That is no longer the case.

The erosion of the industrial sector and manufacturing employment that began in 2001 displayed different characteristics in that the loss of jobs was swifter than in previous downturns (though not as severe as the job loss during the early 1980s) and continued well past the end of the recession. More than one million jobs were lost during the eight-month recession ending in November 2001, after which job loss continued for more than another two years, with the loss of an additional two million jobs. Job loss slowed in early 2004, ultimately declining to 13 million manufacturing jobs in late 2008 before a more rapid decline into 2009.

That the erosion would continue in a sustained fashion after the recession ended has been unprecedented since World War II, with other periods of job erosion ending either the same month as when the recession ended (typical), or within two months (unusual).

From an analytical perspective, this extensive erosion invites the question as to whether manufacturing employment is a naturally-occurring and useful adjustment to inefficiencies in the economy, or whether it presents a challenge to the health of the national innovation system. That is, it would be useful to determine whether the manufacturing base eroded in an undesirable way that is detrimental to the country's ability to innovate.

Because of the importance of the manufacturing support base to innovation, and because most discussions about the manufacturing support base use only one top-level indicator such as jobs without digging into individual industries, the attempt here is to provide a more detailed analysis.

The Manufacturing Support Base Is Essential For U.S. Innovation

The manufacturing support base is a key part of the nation's economy. It provides for robust defense capabilities and nourishes the innovation life cycle. In popular culture and the media, commentators and articles that discuss the national manufacturing base are often essentially referring to the aggregate attributes of the sector without paying much attention to the pieces that comprise the whole. Moreover, many confuse the manufacturing base as essentially synonymous with large corporations or prime contractors such as Boeing, Lockheed Martin and Ford. Media reports about profit growth or the number of jobs that have been created or eliminated at these big companies are not indicative of the entire system.

The manufacturing base includes several components that comprise the "innovation food chain." The large integrators are at the top of the chain and include major defense prime contractors and manufacturers whose names are easily recognized. Their products, such as military vehicles, ships and planes, incorporate the innovations and capabilities of the lower-tier suppliers and support industries.

By many modern standards, the major defense systems integrators are no longer considered key innovators. The top tier of defense contractors "have increasingly focused on the complex system-integration function [and] are relying more on supplier expertise to design new subsystem solutions," according to a report by the RAND Corp.[4] The major integrators have shifted their core competencies away from innovation and towards integration, scheduling and management of a vast network of suppliers. They are pushing the burden of innovation lower into the supply chain.[5]

It is no secret that these large companies rely increasingly on smaller companies for their innovation. Instead of making innovation their key responsibility, major integrators now achieve innovation either by purchasing smaller companies that are innovative, or by incorporating those companies into their supply chain.

In turn, the smaller innovative companies are focused on developing new subsystems or specific capabilities. But even many of these companies are integrators, pulling together advanced materials, semiconductors, printed circuit boards and motors to make components or small systems that can be further integrated into larger systems.

This new industrial configuration in which the major defense companies no longer carry primary responsibility for innovation, forces the burden for new ideas and breakthroughs on the middle-tier in the innovation food chain to companies like Cisco, Sony and Goodrich. Furthermore, some companies lie somewhere between the innovators and integrators. For example, jet engines made by GE Power Systems include many complicated and innovative components, but the engines themselves are inserted into larger integrated systems.

The most innovative smaller companies are more directly dependent on the manufacturing support base for their success. They are less likely to have their own in-house machine shop, mold- or printed circuit board-making ability that can be utilized for prototyping. They rely on basic manufacturers to help them with their product and process iterations that are the essential aspects of the innovation process. Their ability to apply innovation depends directly on the existence of a healthy support base that can quickly manufacture advanced mechanical and electronic systems.

This notion of having a robust and innovative manufacturing base is echoed by Michael Porter's concept of the "competitiveness diamond," which includes a prominent role for "related and supporting industries" in competitive sectors of the economy.[6] Studies at Harvard and RAND that use Porter's clusters model find that a business environment that encourages strategic rivalry and competition is the single-most critical driver of innovation and competitiveness.[7,8]

The Harvard study of hundreds of industry clusters worldwide finds that dependence on a healthy local support base allows innovative companies to thrive. In traditional economic terms, this concept is captured in the notion of "transaction costs." If a healthy support base is nearby, then costs are lower. But if the support base has moved offshore, then transaction costs for innovation increase as companies are forced to overcome time zones, language and cultural barriers in order to work with companies that are located far away.

If the manufacturing support base no longer adequately serves the innovative companies, then their ability to be competitive is hindered and innovation does not move up the chain to the top-tier integrators. Consequently, the health of the entire innovation food chain, and thus the entire national innovation system and the defense industrial base, relies on the health of the foundation of the entire system: the manufacturing support base. The manufacturing support base will be analyzed within this context in this chapter

Prior studies of the defense industrial base have looked at the value of small segments of the support base, such as machine tools. This study incorporates other basic industries into its scope. Furthermore, prior analytical studies and policy debates have emphasized a top-down approach to new acquisition strategies needed to keep the major defense prime contractors healthy and prosperous. The current system is designed to ensure innovation and productivity among the top integrators. It embodies a tacit belief that if the major integrators are healthy, then the entire innovation system will also be healthy.

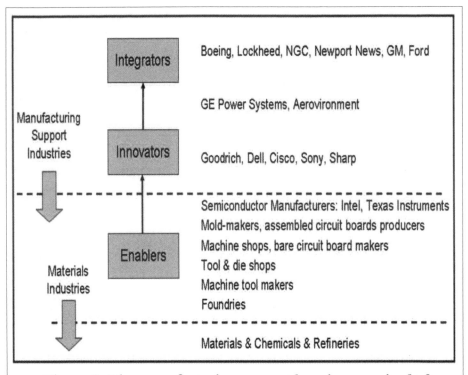

Figure 2: The manufacturing support base is comprised of the sectors that enable innovative companies and prop up the entire national innovation system. An illustrative list of companies and sectors for each category is included in the figure.

This top-down perspective needs to be reconsidered. A perspective from the bottom up is needed.

That is, the health of the big defense prime contractors depends on the innovation capability of the underlying manufacturing support base. If the lowest tier of the manufacturing support base is healthy, then the innovators will be operating effectively, and consequently the top-tier integrators will also succeed.

For semantic purposes, the U.S. defense industrial base is considered to be the end-to-end capability within the United States to design and produce advanced military weapons systems. The manufacturing support base from materials to finished product is comprised of making, bending or shaping materials; producing components; applying treatments; or providing manufacturing-related services such as rapid prototyping.

The materials sector is not included in this analysis, but materials provide the foundation of the manufacturing and defense industrial base. Consequently, a separate study of the materials industries is warranted.

If the overlooked manufacturing support base that props up the entire national innovation system continues to deteriorate in the United States, but grows and thrives overseas, then large numbers of America's most innovative companies might be inclined to move overseas to be closer to production and the necessary support base.

Significant deterioration of companies that design and make discrete components is triggering a fundamental hollowing out of the national innovation system.

Sixteen Industries Comprise the Manufacturing Support Base

The sectors included in this study are those within the manufacturing support base that have a direct bearing on innovation and production of novel mechanical products and systems. The output from these sectors is used directly in the design process of other industries. Their capabilities are considered critical to the ability to apply innovative mechanical designs. Sectors that support the production of chemicals, pharmaceuticals or software are not considered for this study because their connection to mechanical systems is not explicit, though clearly they are an important area for continued innovation of U.S. industry.

The scope of this study also includes the electromechanical, thermomechanical and optomechanical sectors. Each has relevance to the innovation of mechanical systems. If the particular process, function, service or output of the industry is an enabler of innovation, it is included. For example, the machine tool industries are included because the ability to manufacture more complicated forms with better machine tools enables many more design possibilities. The machine tool sector therefore plays an essential function in innovation.

This study does not include automotive, agricultural or aerospace equipment industries because these are integrated systems and therefore do not qualify as components of the underlying manufacturing support base.

The following criteria were used to determine what industries make up the manufacturing support base:

- Their technological advances impact the capabilities of upstream producers or integrators;

• Their output is embedded, integrated or involved in the manufacture of larger systems; and

• Their output must be integrated into more than one type of system. Electronics fit into a range of consumer, military and other integrated products, but jet engines do not qualify because they are dedicated to one type of system.

Using these criteria, the range of manufacturing industries was narrowed from 764 to the 16 considered for this study. Those sixteen industries are shown in Table 1 along with their NAICS codes, and are described in greater detail below.[9,10]

Table 1: Manufacturing Support Base Industries And Their Related NAICS Codes

NAICS Code	Industry Description
3315.........	Foundries
33211.......	Forging and Stamping
33271.......	Machine Shops
332811.....	Metal Heat Treating
332997.....	Industrial Pattern Manufacturing
333295.....	Semiconductor Machinery Manufacturing
333314.....	Optical Instrument and Lens Manufacturing
333511.....	Industrial Mold Manufacturing
333512.....	Machine Tool (Metal Cutting Types) Manufacturing
333513.....	Machine Tool (Metal Forming Types)
333514.....	Special Die and Tool, Die Set, Jig and Fixture Mfg.
334412.....	Bare Printed Circuit Board Manufacturing
334413.....	Semiconductor and Related Device Manufacturing
334418.....	Printed Circuit Assembly (Electronic Assembly)
33451.......	Navigational, Measuring Electromedical and Control Instruments Manufacturing
33591.......	Battery Manufacturing

The 16 industries and groupings are not intended to be the comprehensive list of all industries that are connected to the manufacturing support base for the innovation supply chain.

Some other industries that might be considered include Computer and Peripheral Equipment Manufacturing (3341), Communications Equipment Manufacturing (3342), Electronic Capacitor Manufacturing (334414), and Fiber Optic Cable Manufacturing (335921). A broader analysis could develop a ranking system for the industries and industry groups that hold the most influence in enabling the innovative capacity of broader industry segments.

Methodology for Studying the Manufacturing Support Base

Typical studies and discussion of the manufacturing sector have been limited to aggregate employment statistics by noting job growth or loss with each economic cycle. Though jobs are a useful statistic and provide insight into the overall state of the sector, studying the employment figures alone is not enough to analytically determine whether an unacceptable level of erosion has occurred. For example, in the U.S. agriculture sector, employment has dropped steadily for many decades. However, agricultural output remains high and the United States retains the ability to feed itself and export excess production. Similarly, the number of telephone operators in the United States has dropped dramatically over the last three decades, despite significant growth in the number of phone numbers and daily phone calls. Increased productivity on farms and by the telephone companies more than made up for job losses, thereby yielding growing economic activity for these two industries in the face of declining employment.

Given these two examples and many others like them, it is safe to conclude that studying employment figures alone is not enough to make sound conclusions as to whether a particular sector or industry is deteriorating. Consequently, this report uses three primary indicators to determine whether an industry is eroding: employment, economic activity (contributions to GDP by shipments), and the number of establishments.[2]

If decreases are evident in output, the number of establishments and employment, then the industry is considered to be eroding. If all three indicators are increasing, then the industry is considered to be growing.

For some industries, the picture is mixed, leading to a less conclusive determination of its health. A stoplight chart reflecting all three indicators for each of the 16 industries is compiled at the end of the industry-specific analysis to help compare the various industries and to make a qualitative determination about their erosion status.

Industry-Specific Analysis

Statistics are plotted for each of the 16 industries that comprise the manufacturing support base in order to make a qualitative determination for each as to whether they have eroded, held steady or expanded during the last economic recovery from 2001 to the end of 2007. The three indicators are stacked in the charts, with employment information in the top panel, economic activity in the middle panel and number of establishments in the bottom panel.

The time periods of the last two recessions are also shown as gray bars on the graphs for reference purposes. The data sources are noted in the legends for each plot: 'BLS' refers to data coming from either the Bureau of Labor Statistics' Current Employment Statistics Survey or the Quarterly Census of Employment and Wages; 'ASM' refers to the Annual Survey of Manufacturers by the U.S. Census Bureau; 'Census' refers to the 2002 Economic Census; and 'NBER' refers to the National Bureau of Economic Research. (For an explanation of data sources, see endnote 11.)

Generally, the monthly Current Employment Statistics Survey was used for employment figures wherever possible, and the Quarterly Census of Employment and Wages was used for establishment estimates. Wherever the Current Employment Statistics Survey data were not available, combined employment information from the Quarterly Census of Employment and Wages, and the Annual Survey of Manufacturers were used instead.

For the charts, employment figures include total employees (not seasonally-adjusted) and are plotted in the thousands. The economic activity is labeled "Corrected GDP by Shipments" and presented in millions of 2005 dollars, except for the two industries for which materials costs were not subtracted: metal heat treating and industrial pattern manufacturing. For these two industries, "GDP by Shipments" are plotted in millions of 2005 dollars, but without correcting for materials expenditures. The data on establishments are plotted without any adjustments or corrections.

For some panels that include data from two different sources, the data do not necessarily overlap. These gaps or differences in data are primarily the result of the agencies using slightly differing standards for employment and definitions of what qualifies as an establishment. Because the charts are being used to spot trends rather than quantitative results, these incongruities are not of special concern.

FOUNDRIES (NAICS Code 3315)

Foundries show significant erosion in all three indicators from the levels just before the last recession. Employment dropped from more than 205,000 in March 2001 to less than 150,000 in August 2008, remaining below even the employment levels at the end of the 1991 recession. GDP dropped from just below $20 billion in 2000 to just above $16 billion in 2005, and recovering to almost $18 billion in 2006. The number of establishments appears to be on a steady slide from around 2,800 in 2001 to less than 2,300 in early 2008. Overall, this industry group has experienced significant erosion.

This industry group comprises companies primarily engaged in pouring molten metal into molds or dies to form castings.[3] Ferrous and nonferrous foundries are considered a part of the support base because casting is an initial step for most manufacturing processes. The ability to make castings out of novel materials and to produce more complicated shapes and larger sizes has a direct impact on the entire product innovation process.

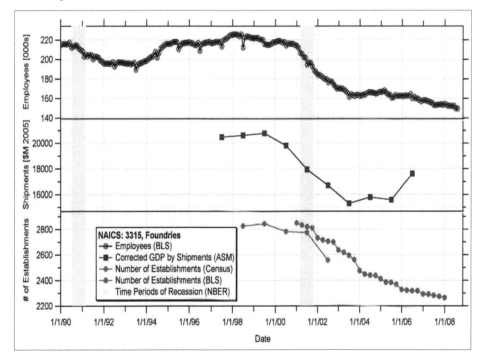

FORGING AND STAMPING (NAICS Code 33211)

The forging and stamping industry shows erosion in all three indicators since the end of the 2001 recession. Employment dropped from more than 130,000 in March 2001 to just over 110,000 in August 2008. GDP dropped from just over $16 billion in 2000 to just over $13 billion in 2006. The number of establishments is on a slow slide from just over 2,700 in 2001 to just over 2,600 in 2008. The increasing GDP despite lower levels of employment and decreasing number of establishments is a good sign and is likely attributable to the widespread productivity gains that took place in the manufacturing sector over that time period.

This industry comprises companies that are primarily engaged in manufacturing forgings from purchased metals, manufacturing metal custom-roll forming products, manufacturing metal stamped and spun products (except automotive, cans and coins), and manufacturing powder metallurgy products.

Six national industries comprise this NAICS group: iron and steel forging, nonferrous forging, custom-roll forming, crown and closure manufacturing, metal stamping and powder metallurgy part manufacturing. Forging and stamping is a part of the manufacturing support

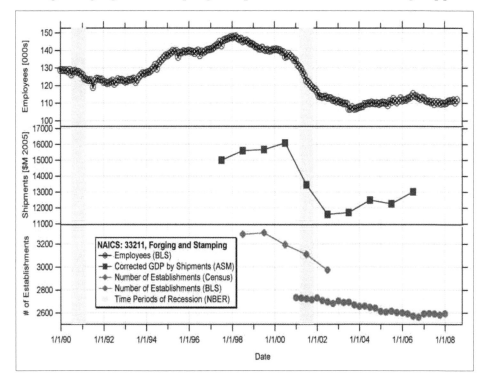

base because its various processes (hammering mill shapes, surface finishing, using rotary motion of rolls with various contours to bend or shape products, stamping, spinning, compacting in a shaped die and sintering) make it possible to manufacture products with different shapes and qualities.

MACHINE SHOPS (NAICS Code 33271)

The machine shops industry shows a typical erosion and expansion as expected with economic cycles. After losing more than 40,000 jobs during the recession of 2001, employment has since grown to exceed pre-recession employment of approximately 260,000 employees by an additional 20,000 employees. GDP dropped from just over $23 billion in 2000 to $19 billion in 2003, then showed a recovery to $22 billion in 2006. The slight decrease in the number of establishments appears to have stabilized at nearly 21,600, indicating a total loss of a few hundred establishments. The slight recovery in GDP and the industry's addition of tens of thousands of jobs suggest that overall this industry has held steady and is poised to expand.

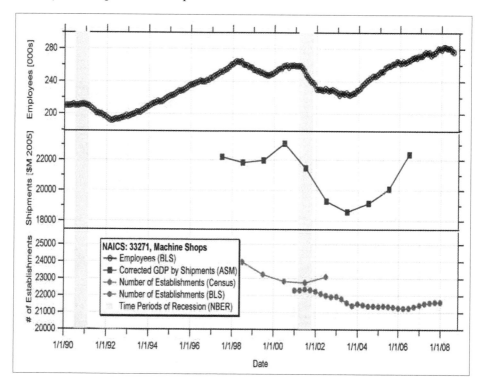

257

The machine shops sector includes companies engaged in machining metal parts on a job or order basis. Generally, machine shop jobs are low-volume, using machine tools such as lathes (including computer numerically controlled), automatic screw machines, and machines for boring, grinding and milling.

Machine shops are a component of the support base because of their ability to provide a service to innovators producing low-volume prototypes and other complicated testbeds. This activity is an important part of the iterative innovation process. The value of machine shops is particularly important for innovative smaller companies that do not have the resources to support those capabilities in-house.

METAL HEAT TREATING (NAICS Code 332811)

The metal heat treating industry shows a mixture of neutral to bad news. After losing a few thousand jobs during and after the 2001 recession, employment has since grown back nearly to prior levels. GDP dropped from approximately $4.5 billion in 2000 to approximately $3.5 billion in 2003, and showed reasonable recovery in 2004. The decrease

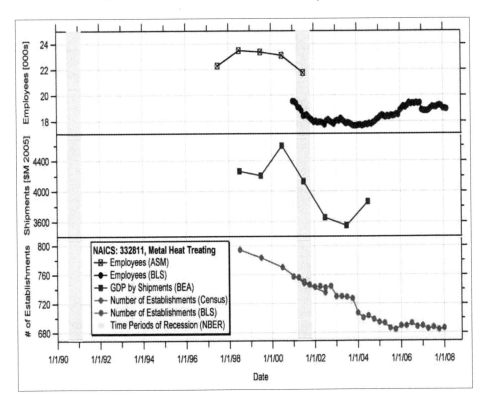

in the number of establishments is continuing. The industry's addition of jobs suggests that it has held steady, but is at the mercy of the late 2008 economic downturn.

The industry comprises establishments primarily engaged in heat-treating of metal using annealing, tempering and brazing. It is a component of the support base because new capabilities, characteristics and outcomes from the treatment and qualities of metals enable new designs of mechanical systems. For example, novel processes that produce materials that have improved characteristics of strength, corrosion-resistance or particular electromagnetic characteristics all have an impact on the innovation and design process

INDUSTRIAL PATTERN MANUFACTURING (NAICS Code 332997)

The industrial pattern manufacturing industry shows erosion in all three indicators from the levels just before the last recession. Employment dropped from more than 7,500 in March 2001 to less than 5,000 in March 2008. GDP dropped from just over $750 million in 2000 to just under $650 million in 2004, after showing a slight increase over the

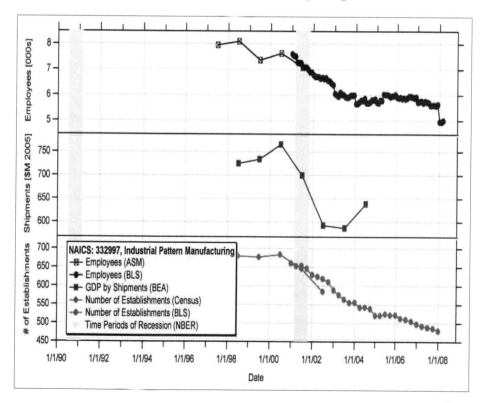

year before. The number of establishments appears to be on a steady slide from around 650 in 2001 to 480 in early 2008. Note that the cost of materials was not subtracted out of the shipments values (because of a lack of data), which makes the GDP information even worse than presented here. This industry has endured significant erosion and does not show signs of recovery.

The industry comprises companies primarily engaged in manufacturing industrial patterns. It is a component of the support base because advances in the production of patterns yields the possibility of a greater range of shapes, casts, molds and tools for the production of complicated parts. The industry is necessary to greater innovation in the manufacture of different designs.

SEMICONDUCTOR MACHINERY MANUFACTURING
(NAICS Code 333295)

The semiconductor machinery manufacturing industry shows a mixture of indicators. According to the BLS data, employment dropped

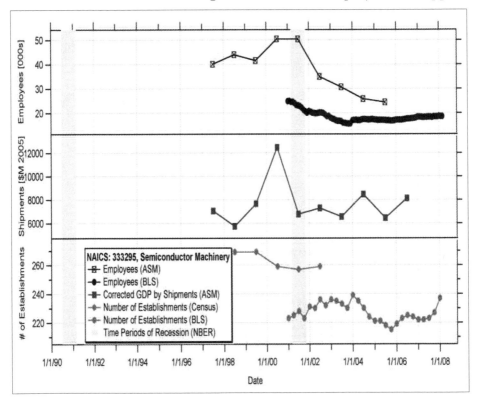

from more than 24,000 in March 2001 to a little over 18,500 in March 2008, while the ASM data show a more severe 50 percent drop in employment, from around 50,000 in 2000 and 2001 to about 25,000 in 2005. The number of establishments has oscillated between 215 and 240. The GDP declined substantially from just over $12 billion in 2000 to between $6 billion to $8 billion in 2003-2005, but it is important to note that market activity for semiconductor machinery in 2000 was abnormally high. Thus, the GDP of this industry remains in 2008 at or above levels from just before the market increase in 2000. That the value of shipments remains high despite drastic decreases in employment is likely attributable to increased productivity.

Overall, this industry appears to be enduring growth and contraction on a cycle that is different from the macroeconomy. Therefore, this industry is holding steady and did not endure significant erosion prior to the market collapse of 2008.

Semiconductor machinery manufacturing includes companies engaged in making wafer processing equipment, semiconductor assembly and packaging equipment and other semiconductor-making machinery. The industry is a critical component of the support base because semiconductor machinery manufacturing creates a host of components that allow a wide range of possible designs. Among all the different industries in the support base, this one is among the most critical. Innovations in semiconductor machinery equipment, such as the integration of novel optics, lasers and control systems, enable greater advances in compactness, transistor density, thermal properties and other characteristics of semiconductor chips.

Because of the ubiquitous nature of embedded electronics and advanced electronic semiconductor components in modern mechanical systems, these improvements have a cascading effect, thereby contributing to a greater level of innovation that expands capabilities, reduces cost and weight, and minimizes the number of components.

OPTICAL INSTRUMENT AND LENS MANUFACTURING
(NAICS Code 333314)

The optical instrument and lens manufacturing industry shows slight to severe erosion in all three indicators. According to the BLS data, employment dropped from approximately 28,500 in March 2001 to 23,200 in March 2008, while the ASM data show a drop in employment from around 21,000 in 2001 to about 16,000 in 2005. The industry's

GDP decreased from just over $2.6 billion in 2000 to just over $2 billion in 2005. The number of establishments has dropped slightly, from nearly 580 to 560. Overall, this industry has experienced significant erosion and, immediately prior to the economic downturn in late 2008, there were no obvious signs of recovery.

The industry comprises establishments engaged in the manufacture of optical instruments and lenses, such as binoculars, microscopes (except electron and proton), telescopes, prisms and lenses (except ophthalmic). It also includes companies that coat, polish and mount lenses (except ophthalmic).

With the increasing integration of optical components in advanced equipment, especially in the telecommunications field, advances in optics and optical instruments allows production of a new generation of products. For example, new designs for miniature lens arrays have led to wavelength multiplexing, which is of great value for optically-based telecommunications equipment. Advances in optical instruments have positive spillover benefits in the design in sensing and control applications in machinery and numerous other industrial applications.

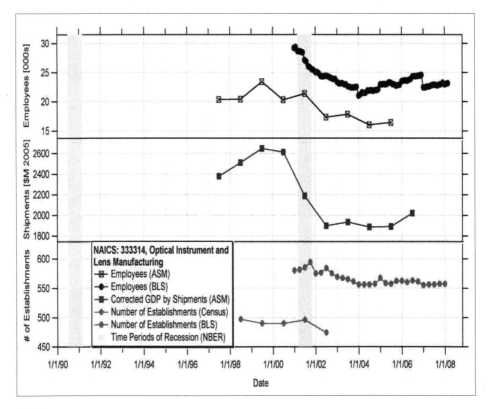

INDUSTRIAL MOLD MANUFACTURING (NAICS Code 333511)

The industrial mold manufacturing industry shows significant erosion in all three indicators from the levels just before the last recession in 2001. Employment dropped from nearly 55,000 in 2001 to less than 38,000 in August 2008, remaining well below even the employment levels at the end of the 1991 recession. GDP dropped from approximately $4.6 billion in 2000 to approximately $3.6 billion in 2006. The number of establishments appears to be on a steady slide from over 3,000 in 2001 to less than 2,300 in early 2008. Overall, this industry has experienced significant erosion during a period of overall economic growth, and shows no signs of recovery.

Firms in this industry engage in manufacturing industrial molds for casting metals or forming other materials, such as plastics, glass or rubber.

It is a component of the defense industrial support base because advances in the production of mold patterns yields the possibility of a greater range of shapes, casts, molds and tools for the production of complicated parts. A healthy mold industry promotes innovation up the sup-

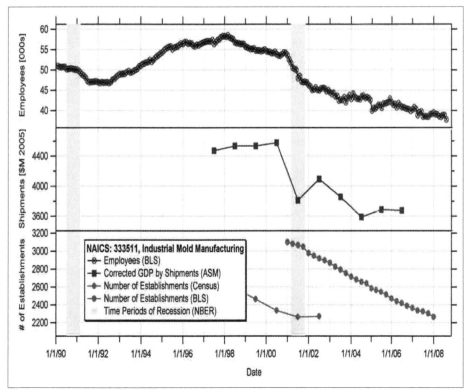

ply chain by allowing companies to develop sophisticated product designs. Because all manufactured items have a shape, industrial molds are considered — along with machine tools and semiconductor machinery — to be one of the most critical industries in the manufacturing support base. In general, mold makers are similar to machine shops, except they produce fewer components at much stricter tolerances, better finish quality and with much higher value per unit. In general, the equipment for mold makers is much more expensive than for machine shops and employees are much more highly skilled.

MACHINE TOOL — METAL CUTTING MANUFACTURING
(NAICS Code 333512)

The machine tool (metal cutting) manufacturing industry shows erosion in all three indicators. Combined employment dropped from nearly 60,000 in 2001 to almost 45,000 in August 2008, remaining well below even the employment levels at the end of the 1991 recession. Employment figures started moving up from a low of just fewer than 40,000 at the beginning of 2004. GDP dropped from approximately $2.5 billion

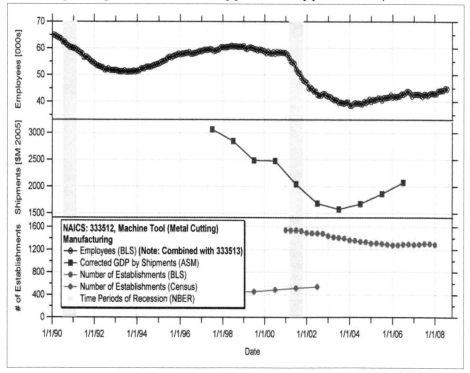

in 2000 to $1.8 billion in 2005, although it has shown slight recovery over the period of 2003 to 2006, due to the impact of tax credits for purchasing machine tools that were in effect during that period. The number of establishments has decreased by about 20 percent, from more than 1,500 in 2001 to less than 1,300 in early 2008. Overall, this industry has endured significant erosion, though it shows some signs of slight recovery in GDP and employment that might continue depending on the severity of the 2008 - 2009 downturn.

These companies primarily manufacture metal cutting machine tools, except for hand tools. It is a component of the defense industrial support base because advances in metal cutting machinery (such as lathes, mills and CNC machines) have a profound impact on the ability to create more sophisticated components out of a wider range of materials. Consequently, it enhances greater innovation up the supply chain because it allows for the manufacture of different designs. Because machine tools provide a fundamental capability in the innovation process (for the creation of prototypes and finished products), they are considered, along with industrial molds and semiconductor machinery, as one of the most critical industries in the support base.

MACHINE TOOL — METAL FORMING — MANUFACTURING
(NAICS Code 333513)

The machine tool (metal forming) manufacturing industry shows erosion in all three indicators. Combined employment dropped from nearly 60,000 in 2001 to almost 45,000 in August 2008, remaining well below even the employment levels at the end of the 1991 recession. Notably, the employment figures have increased from just fewer than 40,000 at the beginning of 2004. GDP dropped more than 45 percent, from approximately $1.4 billion in 2000 to $0.8 billion in 2005, rising slightly for 2006. The number of establishments has decreased from about 700 in 2001 to less than 600 in early 2008. This industry has endured significant erosion, with the growth in combined employment likely the result of growth in the metal cutting component of the industry.

These companies are engaged in manufacturing metal forming machine tools (except hand tools), such as punching, sheering, bending, forming, pressing, forging and die-casting machines. It is an essential component of the support base because advances in metal forming machinery (such as metal presses) have a big impact on the ability to create more sophisticated components over a wider range of sizes and from more diverse materials. Because machine tools provide a fundamental capability in the innovation process for the creation of prototypes and finished products, they are considered to be one of the most critical industries in the manufacturing support base.

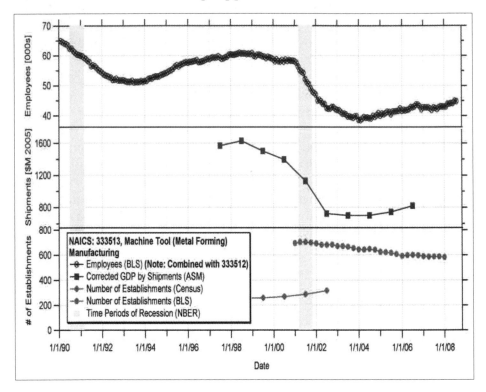

SPECIAL DIE AND TOOL, DIE SET, JIG AND FIXTURE MANUFACTURING (NAICS Code 333514)

The special die and tool, die set, jig and fixture manufacturing industry shows signs of erosion in all three indicators. Employment dropped about 30 percent from nearly 100,000 in 2001 to about 68,000 in August 2008, remaining well below even the employment levels at the end of the 1991 recession. GDP dropped more than 20 percent, from approximately $6.7 billion in 2000 to $5.1 billion in 2006, and has remained at that depressed level for the four years from 2002 to 2006. The number of establishments has decreased steadily from more than 5,500 in 2001 to about 4,200. Overall, this industry has endured significant erosion and does not show any signs of recovering.

This U.S. industry comprises tool and die shops primarily engaged in manufacturing special tools and fixtures, such as cutting dies and jigs. It is similar to industrial mold manufacturing and is a component of the support base because advances in the production of tools, dies and jigs yields the possibility of a greater range of shapes, casts, molds and tools for the production of complicated parts. Consequently, innovation is enabled because of the greater range of possibility in the manufacture of different designs.

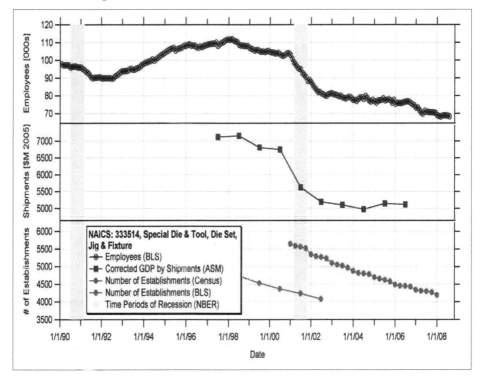

BARE PRINTED CIRCUIT BOARD MANUFACTURING
(NAICS Code 334412)

The bare printed circuit board manufacturing industry shows signs of severe erosion in all three indicators. Employment dropped more than two-thirds from a peak of nearly 150,000 employees in 2001 to less than 50,000 employees in August 2008, remaining well below the employment levels at the end of the 1991 recession. GDP dropped more than 50 percent, from approximately $7.3 billion in 2000 to $3.3 billion in 2006. The number of establishments has decreased steadily, dropping more than 40 percent from about 1,900 in 2001 to about 950 in early 2008. Overall, this industry has endured significant erosion and does not show any signs of recovering.

Establishments in this industry are primarily engaged in manufacturing rigid and flexible printed circuit boards without mounted electronic components. These companies print, perforate, plate, screen, etch or photoprint interconnecting pathways for electric current on laminates.

The industry is a critical component of the defense industry manufacturing support base because of the ubiquitous nature of electromechanical systems that include embedded circuit boards. With innovations in the shapes, densities, compactness, electromagnetic attributes or other characteristics of circuit boards, new designs for systems that include the boards are possible. Boards that are more efficient and have lower noise and electrical losses enable the adoption of ultra-sensitive electronics and low-power equipment. They are in high demand. Because electronics play such an important role in most integrated weapon systems, improvement in this support industry has a cascading

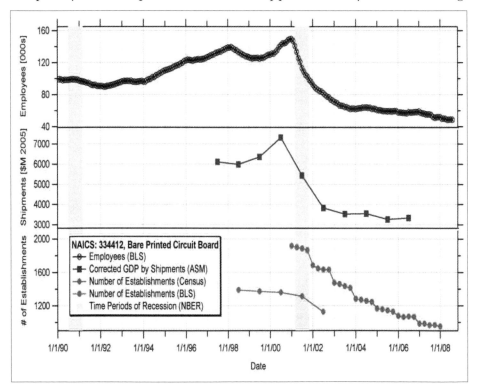

impact, enabling a tremendous level of new innovation to expand capabilities, reduce cost, reduce weight and minimize the number of components. Without a robust printed circuit board industry, the entire U.S. defense supply chain is at risk.

SEMICONDUCTOR AND RELATED DEVICE MANUFACTURING
(NAICS Code 334413)

The semiconductor and related device manufacturing industry shows a mixed picture. Employment dropped more than one-third from 310,000 in 2001 to 200,000 in August 2008, remaining below the employment levels at the end of the 1991 recession. GDP dropped more than 35 percent over the course of a single year, from approximately $76 billion in 2000 to $49 billion in 2001, but has shown some growth since then, eventually reaching nearly $60 billion in 2005. The number of establishments has cycled up from just over 1,600 in 2001 to just over 1,700 in 2006, before dropping back down below 1,600. With erosion in employment, signs of growth in GDP and expansion in establishments, the industry appears to be holding steady.

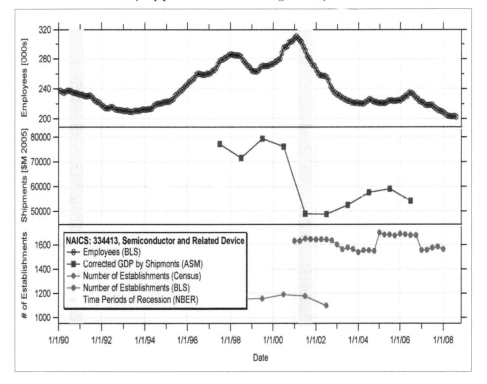

This industry comprises companies engaged in manufacturing semiconductors and related solid-state devices. Examples of products include integrated circuits, memory chips, microprocessors, diodes, transistors, solar cells and other optoelectronic devices.

This industry is a critical component of the support base because of the widespread use of semiconductors and other electronic components in a range of optoelectronic and electromechanical systems. Innovations in the manufacture of semiconductors and electronic devices in terms of compactness, dedicated circuits, transistor density, thermal properties, power consumption and other characteristics have a cascading effect on the systems that incorporate them because of the new features that can be included.

PRINTED CIRCUIT ASSEMBLY — ELECTRONIC ASSEMBLY — MANUFACTURING (NAICS Code 334418)

The printed circuit assembly industry shows a confusing mixture of indicators. Employment dropped more than 20 percent from 67,000 in 2001 to less than 50,000 in 2003, before slightly recovering to just above the employment levels at the end of the 1991 recession near 54,000 in August 2008. GDP dropped approximately 50 percent from $16 billion in 2000 to approximately $7 billion in 2006.

Despite significant losses in GDP and employment, the number of establishments has increased steadily from just fewer than 900 in 2001 to approximately 1,170 in early 2008. The reason for the growth in the number of establishments is not clear. Severe losses in employment and the precipitous drop in GDP have contributed to the industry having undergone substantial erosion.

This industry includes companies that are primarily engaged in loading components onto printed circuit boards. It produces printed circuit assemblies, electronic assemblies and modules. The industry's products are printed circuit boards that have some or all of the semiconductor and electronic components inserted or mounted. They are used in a wide variety of electronic systems and devices.

This industry is a critical component of the defense industrial support base because of the many electromechanical systems that include embedded circuit boards. The industry fosters innovation in the shapes, densities, compactness, electromagnetic attributes and other characteristics of loaded circuit boards. New processes for manufacturing the boards enable tighter design standards, more compact layouts and new designs for a wide range of complex products. New technology for automated loading of surface-mount components onto circuit boards (as compared with through-hole mounting) allow for inclusion of much smaller electronic components. This enables lower-power consumption, lower thermal loads and more compact overall design. Improvements in the production of loaded circuit boards and electronic assemblies have substantial upstream ripple effects on the ability to innovate the design of embedded electronics.

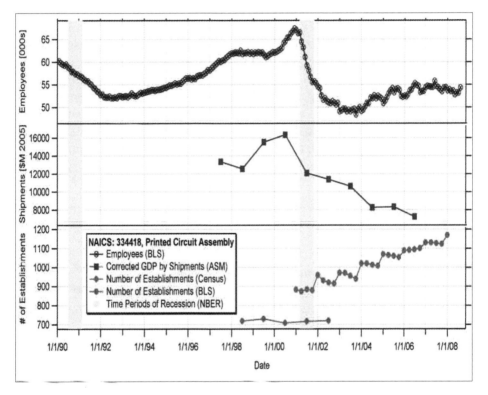

NAVIGATIONAL, MEASUREMENT, ELECTROMEDICAL AND CONTROL INSTRUMENTS MANUFACTURING (NAICS Code 3345)

The navigational, measurement, electromedical and control instruments manufacturing industry group shows neutral to positive indicators. Employment continued a downward, decade-long trend by decreasing from 479,000 in 2001 to 444,000 in August 2008, although more than 20,000 employees were added since the beginning of 2004. GDP for the sector dropped from $68 billion in 2000 to approximately

271

$62 billion in 2002, but has since recovered to exceed pre-recession levels of $75 billion in 2006. The number of establishments has held steady at nearly 7,500. With slight losses in employment, a stable number of establishments and growth in GDP, this industry group overall appears to be expanding and enjoying productivity gains.

These manufacturers produce navigational, measuring, electromedical and control instruments. Their products include aeronautical instruments, appliance regulators and controls, laboratory analytical instruments, navigation and guidance systems and physical properties testing equipment.

These industries are considered a part of the defense industrial support base because improvements in their products change the range of possibility for integrated systems that include them. For example, the new generation of global positioning-based guidance equipment has changed the way vehicles and planes are designed and operated. Improved sensors and control devices have enabled the creation of computer-controlled machine tools that can achieve tighter tolerances, with subsequent impacts on the design of products.

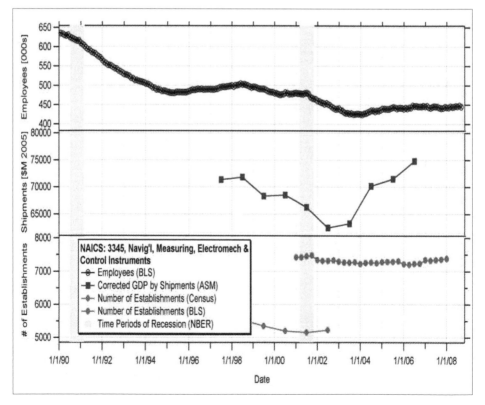

BATTERY MANUFACTURING (NAICS Code 33591)

The battery manufacturing industry has experienced severe erosion in all three indicators. Employment dropped more than 25 percent from a peak of nearly 39,000 in 2001 to 29,000 employees in August 2008, remaining well below the employment levels at the end of the 1991 recession. GDP dropped by nearly one-third, from approximately $4.5 billion in 2000 to just over $3 billion in 2006. The number of establishments has decreased less severely, declining from about 280 in 2001 to about 230 in early 2008. Overall, this industry has eroded significantly and does not show signs of recovery despite massive increases in the number of batteries being consumed worldwide.

The industry is comprised of storage battery and "primary" battery manufacturing, with the former related to rechargeable batteries such as lead acid and nickel cadmium, the latter related to wet or dry primary batteries such as disposables (9V, AAA, AA, C, D, etc.), and watch batteries. These industries are considered to be part of the defense industrial support base because improvements in power density, capacity, cycle life-

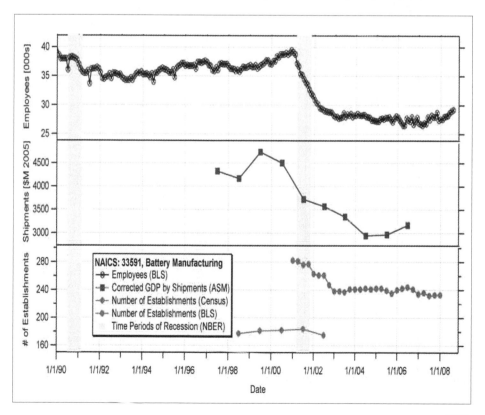

times and weight enable the development of an entirely new range of embedded and portable electronics and power systems. The creation of a new generation of rechargeable and high-power density batteries has revolutionized portable electronics and allows for a range of electronic systems to be built with more powerful and faster processors.

Summary: Which Sectors Are Eroding, Holding Steady or Recovering

For 13 of the 16 industries that comprise the defense industrial manufacturing support base, significant erosion took place in two or more indicators without any signs of recovery. It should be noted that this erosion occurred during a period of solid U.S. economic growth and during a period of robust global expansion of all of the industries analyzed.

An assessment for each of the industries and the three indicators is illustrated below. Black circles denote significant erosion; hatched circles

NAICS	Industry Description	Employment	Economic Activity	Establishments	Overall Status
3315	Foundries	●	◌	●	*Eroded*
33211	Forging and Stamping	●	●	●	*Eroded*
33271	Machine Shops	○	◌	◌	*Healthy*
332811	Metal Heat Treating	◌	●	●	*Eroded*
332997	Industrial Pattern Mfring	●	●	●	*Eroded*
333295	Semiconductor Machinery	◌	◌	◌	*Holding Steady*
333314	Optical Instrument and Lens	◌	●	●	*Eroded*
333511	Industrial Mold Manufacturing	●	●	●	*Eroded*
333512	Machine Tools (Metal Cutting)	●	◌	●	*Eroded*
333513	Machine Tools (Metal Forming)	●	●	●	*Eroded*
333514	Special Die & Tool, Die Set, Jig	●	●	●	*Eroded*
334412	Bare Printed Circuit Boards	●	●	●	*Eroded*
334413	Semiconductor and Related Devices	●	●	◌	*Eroded*
334418	Printed Circuit Assemblies	●	●	○	*Eroded*
3345	Nav, Meas, and Cntrl Instruments	●	○	◌	*Healthy*
33591	Battery Manufacturing	●	●	●	*Eroded*

Figure 3: A stoplight chart summarizing the three indicators for each industry or industry group in the manufacturing support base. Black circles denote that the indicator eroded; hatched circles denote that the indicator held steady or showed significant signs of recovery; and white circles denote that the indicator expanded.

denote indicators that either held steady or showed signs of expansion after initial erosion; and white circles denote expansion.

By looking qualitatively at all three indicators, an overall determination of the industry's status coming out of the recent seven-year recession and recovery period can be made. This is noted in the far right column as one of the three following choices: eroded, holding steady or expanded.

Two industries — machine shops and electronic instruments — both showed signs of health due to expansion in employment or economic activity. One industry — semiconductor machinery — appears to be holding steady. The remaining thirteen industries all showed significant erosion. It should also be noted that many of these indicators were taken up to the time of September 2008, after which demand for products in virtually every consumer and industrial category fell off a cliff.

Sector Relevance

Unlike the fate of many industries that have famously eroded or disappeared due to the complete loss of demand for their products, the 13 industries that have eroded remain important. Their products are still widely used. These industries are far from being obsolete. The worldwide market for the output from these industries continues to grow significantly in size.

Some of the industries have been identified as critical to the national innovation system. For example, the National Academies of Science conducted a study of the printed circuit board industry because of its strategic importance to the development and maintenance of advanced weapons and intelligence systems.[12]

The RAND Corp. conducted a similar study of the erosion of the semiconductor manufacturing technology industry.[13] Furthermore, ongoing concerns about the health and importance of the machine tool industry have generated many other studies that raised concerns.

The U.S. Department of Energy has also noted the importance of batteries for enabling innovation in the energy sector. There are dozens of other industries that are key players in the manufacturing and defense industrial support base that are worthy of more detailed analysis similar to the third-party reports on printed circuit boards, machine tools and the semiconductor industry.

Discussion of Driving Factors of Erosion And Potential Policy Options

As part of this research, several dozen meetings and interviews were conducted with a range of business owners, executives and engineers in the manufacturing support base industries and prime integrators. Also included were individuals from academia and think-tanks who study the economy and the manufacturing base; members of executive branch government agencies, including the National Institute of Standards and Technology, the Departments of Defense and Commerce; trade associations; and staff members for legislative committees and elected officials.

What is clear from these conversations is the widespread concern over the erosion in the aggregate manufacturing sector. Consistent themes emerged about recovery mechanisms and obstacles to implementing them.

The primary corrective mechanisms identified include economic growth, sustained investments in research and development and investments in a skilled workforce. Many other secondary corrective measures were also identified, such as targeted government industrial technology development programs, pressure on international currency valuations, reducing barriers to accessing capital, adjusting tax policies and improving protection of intellectual property.

There is a sense among the those interviewed that the three primary corrective mechanisms either are not working as before, or that they are not being applied by the government. The economic system has fundamentally changed. Furthermore, the sentiment was that the secondary mechanisms, while useful in conjunction with the primary corrective mechanisms or in slowing or preventing erosion, are not suitably robust enough to encourage recovery on their own.

Traditional Corrective Mechanisms

Economic growth was observed to be the most fundamental and effective corrective mechanism to stem industrial erosion. Economic cycles are considered a healthy process for weeding out inefficient enterprises. However, during the most recent 2001 to 2008 cycle, economic growth did not work as it has in all previous economic recoveries. That is, even as the economy expanded, these industries continued to erode.

Widespread concern was also expressed about stagnant national investments in research and development, and the large-scale shift from applied to basic research. Research and development is no longer being deployed to sustain the health of the manufacturing support base of the national innovation system.

All interviewees complained about the skill base of available workers. Small manufacturing companies are concerned that fewer young people are learning skilled trades. Students who do well in math and science are more inclined to attend college than they are in pursuing jobs in manufacturing that depend on their acumen for understanding automation and computers. Modern and productive manufacturers feel that they are not appealing to college-bound students. They are also not satisfied with the much broader base of unskilled workers.

One moldmaker said he had to lay off more than a dozen people during the most recent recession ultimately leaving him with just his sophisticated machinery and one employee. When his business started to recover and he sought to hire a second employee, he could not find anyone with suitable skills. His former employees had already moved on to other positions and were not interested in returning to an industry that exposed them to future layoffs. Thus, in order to expand, he had to train a new employee from scratch, a proposition that takes years in the

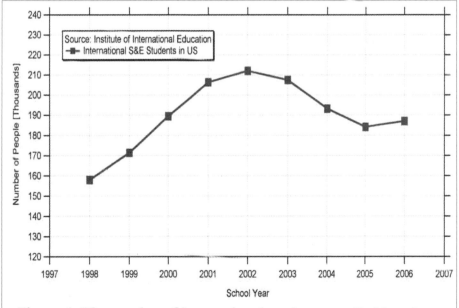

Figure 4: The number of international students enrolled in science and engineering (S&E) fields in the U.S. for the 1998 - 1999 to 2006 - 2007 school years.

mold manufacturing industry because the work is highly skilled and more complex than basic machining.

By contrast, machine shop employment has recovered significantly, partly because the skill required for standard machining can be learned through short courses taught at community colleges. Consequently, there were fewer complaints from this industry and the data show that it has made a significant recovery.

The higher-technology industries in the support base, such as electronic instruments, semiconductors and machine tools, are more sensitive to shortages of college-educated workers in the engineering fields. A recent National Academy of Sciences study noted the relative decrease in the number of American students in those disciplines in contrast with growing enrollment in those disciplines in other countries such as China.[14]

Not only is domestic student enrollment in science and engineering fields considered too low, the number of foreign students enrolling in these fields in American universities has dropped for the first time since statistics were originally tabulated in 1971, according to the Open Doors reports by the Institute for International Education (see Figure 4 on previous page).[15]

Remaining Issues to Study

This initial analysis should be expanded with follow-on studies. It is imperative that United States policymakers understand the true health of the industries that enable innovation throughout the entire society. The concept of the support base should be expanded to include more industries that are worthy of analysis. Industries that are slightly higher up the innovation food chain such as the manufacture of consumer electronics, machinery and engines should be considered a part of the support base for separate analyses.

Of particular value would be a dedicated study on the health of the different materials industries. Advanced materials are a critical enabler for the manufacturing base and, consequently, the entire innovation system.

In addition to studying employment, economic activity and establishments for each industry in the manufacturing support base, more categories that reflect the health of each industry should be considered. Some of these indicators should include total R&D spending, patents filed and the number of products developed. Each industry should be compared to global capabilities, market size and growth.

There also is the need for a rigorous study of policy options and corrective mechanisms aimed at improving the health of the U.S. manufacturing support base that were identified through the course of this research.

Furthermore, there needs to be a much better understanding of the growing demand for skilled workers and the implications for the U.S. manufacturing support base. Different policy mechanisms involved in addressing education, immigration and job retraining must be analyzed.

Another area needing rigorous study is the manufacturing support base's access to capital. There are growing concerns about a shortage of lending institutions with expertise in manufacturing and their willingness to make loans. Determining whether these barriers are the result of a simple risk/benefit scenario, or whether more subtle biases in the system exist would be useful from a policymaking perspective. Furthermore, analyzing the potential effects of government-backed, low-interest loans would be a valuable contribution to this field of study.

Oppressive tax burdens were also frequently cited during interviews as damaging to the U.S. manufacturing support industries. Consequently, analyzing tax policy options that exist and their potential effects (both good and bad) would be useful. In particular, it would be important to determine whether the combination of property taxes and slow depreciation on capital equipment that are built into the tax system introduce an investment bias away from manufacturing industries and toward services or other industries that are not as equipment-intensive.

1. deLeon, Peter, "The Evaluation of Innovation," RAND Corporation, October 1983.
2. "Current Employment Statistics Survey," Bureau of Labor Statistics (BLS), produced with the online tool at http://data.bls.gov/PDQ/outside.jsp?survey=ce, October 2008.
3. National Bureau of Economic Research (NBER) list of "U.S. Business Cycle Expansions and Contractions," http://www.nber.org/cycles.html.
4. Birkler, J.L., et al, "Competition and Innovation in the U.S. Fixed-Wing Military Aircraft Industry," MR-1656-OSD, RAND Corporation, ISBN: 0833033506, 2003.
5. Personal communication, senior executive at prime contractor for the Department of Defense.
6. Porter, Michael, *The Competitive Advantage of Nations*, The Free Press, New York, N.Y., 10022, 1990.
7. Birkler, J.L., 2003.
8. van der Linde, Claas, "The Demography of Clusters-Findings from the Cluster Meta-Study," in Brocker, J., D. Dohse and R. Soltwedel (eds.) *Innovation Clusters and Interregional Competition*, Springer-Verlag, Berlin, Heidelberg, New York, 2002, pages 130-149; also available at http://www.isc.hbs.edu/cp/van_der_Linde_Demography_of_Clusters1.pdf.
9. "North American Industry Classification System, United States, 2002, Expanded Edi-

tion With Added 'Bridges,' " Executive Office of the President, Office of Management and Budget, Copyright 2002, ISBN 1-57980-811-5.

10. "Current Employment Statistics Survey" by the Bureau of Labor Statistics, available via an online tool at: http://data.bls.gov/PDQ/outside.jsp?survey=ce.
- Data from the "Quarterly Census of Employment and Wages" by the Bureau of Labor Statistics, is available via an online tool at http://data.bls.gov/PDQ/outside.jsp?survey =en.
- "The Economic Census of 2002" is available online with interactive tables, reports and search tools at http://www.census.gov/econ/census02/.

11. "The Annual Survey of Manufactures Statistics for Industry Groups and Industries," reports are available at http://www.census.gov/mcd/asm-as1.html.
- "Statistics for Industry Groups and Industries: 2005," Annual Survey of Manufactures, Report M05(AS)-1, U.S. Department of Commerce, Economics and Statistics Administration, Issued November 2006 is available online at http://www.census.gov/prod/2006pubs/am0531gs1.pdf.
- "Statistics for Industry Groups and Industries: 2001," Annual Survey of Manufactures, Report M01(AS)-1, U.S. Department of Commerce, Economics and Statistics Administration, issued January 2003; available online at http://www.census.gov/prod/2003pubs/m01as-1.pdf.
- According to the ASM from 2005 (page 6), "the contribution of nonemployers, relatively small for this sector, may be examined at www.census.gov/nonemployerimpact."
- BEA's Annual Industry Accounts are available at http://www.bea.gov/bea/dn2/gdpbyind_data.htm.
- The CPI conversion factors that were used for 1997-2005 are as follows with the year noted in parentheses: 0.882 (1997), 0.835 (1998), 0.853 (1999), 0.882 (2000), 0.907 (2001), 0.921 (2002), 0.942 (2003), 0.967 (2004), and 1.000 (2005). Conversion to 2005 dollars was achieved by dividing current-dollar information in the year it was reported by that year's conversion factor, e.g. $1,000 in 1997 is equivalent to ($1,000/0.882) = $1,134 in 2005.

12. "Linkages: Manufacturing Trends in Electronics Interconnection Technology," Committee on Manufacturing Trends in Printed Circuit Technology, National Research Council, ISBN: 0-309-65637-0 (2005), available at http://www.nap.edu/catalog/11515.html.

13. Kelley, Charles T., et al, "High-Technology Manufacturing and U.S. Competitiveness," TR-136-OSTP, ISBN: 0-8330-3564-9, RAND Corporation, March 2004.

14. *Rising Above the Gathering Storm: Energizing and Employing America for a Brighter Economic Future*, Committee on Prospering in the Global Economy of the 21st Century: An Agenda for American Science and Technology; Committee on Science, Engineering and Public Policy; National Academy of Sciences, National Academy of Engineering, Institute of Medicine; ISBN: 0-309-65463-7, http://www.nap.edu/catalog/11463.html, 2005.

15. "Open Doors: Report on International Education Exchange" publications are available from the International Institute for Education at http://www.opendoors.iienetwork.org/. Data for Figure 5.1 are from the 2004 and 2006 reports.

8. Supply Chain Globalization: How Surviving SMEs Can Position Themselves for the Future

Irene Petrick
Pennsylvania State University

The worldwide collapse of financial markets demonstrates how hard it will be for small- and medium-sized enterprises to chart a course for the future, while facing stiff international competition and the continued declining stability in U.S.-based supply chains. In October 2008, U.S. manufacturing sector production hit a 26-year low, reaching levels similar to the deep recession of the early 1980s.[1] Business as usual will not be sustainable for many companies. However, despite the current gloomy outlook, many companies will survive and flourish.

Globalization has had both a positive and a negative effect on U.S. manufacturers and their employees. Companies like Procter & Gamble and 3M are headquartered in the American heartland, but make a majority of their sales outside the United States. For P&G, international sales account for 58 percent of its business; for 3M, the number is 63 percent.[2] Conversely, Toyota and Honda, both headquartered outside of the United States, employ more than 73,000 U.S. workers. The reality of the global economy is that large companies have been able to take advantage of an increasingly interconnected world by sourcing to lower-cost global suppliers as well as expanding their sales and operations into international markets.

The luxury of mobility, however, is not shared equally. In the United States, where approximately 97 percent of all firms are classified as small- and medium-sized enterprises (SMEs) with fewer than 500 employees, the grim reality is stiff cost competition, heavy reliance on upper tiers in the supply chain for access to end customers and a shrinking workforce. Unlike larger companies, most American SMEs and their workers are stuck in the United States. Successfully reaching into the global market has become an imperative for survival.

The "China price" has become the standard price point in supplier selection over the last decade.[3] This is true not only in the United States but globally. China has been a dominant force in changing the look of the traditional supply chain. In the U.S. supply chain model, a series of domestically located and linked companies provide components, subassemblies and assemblies to the final producer, typically the original equipment manufacturer (OEM).

The OEM, with its proximity to the consumer or end customer, determines the products to be offered and their features, and often develops the specifications for individual components. Over time, companies in the domestic supply chain were supplanted by lower-cost producers — hence the "China price" syndrome.

As firms within the supply chain have become more specialized in their skill sets, the relative importance of roles of individual firms within these chains has changed. A new approach has transformed the relationship of companies in a supply chain from one based on transactions to one based on value. This has resulted in the emerging notion of a "value chain" rather than a supply chain.

In the value chain model, individual companies leverage their unique capabilities and knowledge — including innovation capacity — to add value to the end product regardless of where in the supply network they are located. As the rest of the world has developed production and, more recently, innovation capabilities, U.S. companies that sit atop the supply chain have looked internationally not only for low-cost suppliers, but also for collaborators and partners.

Large American companies that have been sourcing internationally on the basis of cost arbitrage are now looking internationally for value arbitrage, citing the emerging talent pools in India and China as a draw for their research and development activities. The flow of R&D dollars goes in both directions. Booz & Company reported that in 2007, among the Global Innovation 1,000 companies, U.S. companies performed $80.1 billion in R&D in other countries, and companies headquartered in other countries sponsored R&D projects in the United States at an amount of $42.6 billion.[4]

Here we will trace the evolution of supply chains in the United States from being U.S.-centric, to producing high-end products for the world, to being fierce competitors with emerging world-class suppliers located elsewhere, and finally to where they are today: marginalized and fighting to retain a piece of the worldwide market share.

Yet globalization creates opportunity. Part of missing the opportunities presented by globalization lies in a lack of awareness of how to compete in international markets. SMEs in a supply chain where competition is based on the lowest-priced components and that rely on transaction-based activities are ignoring the importance of innovation and relationship-building to enhance their value within the network.[5]

The growing trend toward "open innovation" where companies such as Procter & Gamble, Toyota and HP look beyond their organizational borders for ideas will provide new opportunities for SMEs with innovative capabilities to enter supply chain networks that previously might have been closed to them.

Moreover, competition based upon providing the lowest-priced products ignores an emerging move toward localization of sourcing, which is being pursued more aggressively with higher energy costs. Fully-landed costs of imported parts and products likely will be more expensive in the future and may favor U.S. SMEs in the U.S. market, thus increasing their competitiveness over seemingly lower-cost international suppliers. Finally, American SMEs could benefit from the potential for the strengthening of other nation's currencies relative to the dollar. Consequently, we will also explore the opportunity side of the equation for small- and medium-sized manufacturing suppliers, discussing the trend toward localization in sourcing with an emphasis on building relationships and focusing on innovation that will be needed for success in the global market.

Globalization's Changing Form: From Aristotle and Columbus to Friedman

Humanity has gone from a point where scientists, engineers, government and business leaders believed that the world was flat (and thus restricted their reach) to Friedman's reconceptualization of *The World is Flat*.[6] Business and other leaders are beginning to talk about the global ecosystem, the global economy and the global market. It is all about interrelationships, influences, speed and breadth of impact. Any company that ignores this risks becoming a marginal player on the global stage. Unfortunately the mechanics of geographically-defined trade are long-standing and pervasive.

The Greek philosopher Aristotle first argued in the 4th century B.C. that the world was round, based on his observations of the circular shadow cast on the moon during a lunar eclipse. Yet it wasn't until 1492, when Ferdinand and Isabella underwrote Christopher Columbus's voyage in hopes of discovering an alternative route to India, that the first true commercial notion of the impact of a round world was established. The voyage was prompted by the economic competition between nation states. For more than five centuries since then, competition between firms has been associated with competition between the nation-states in which those firms were located. Although competition is still gauged between nation-states, the true meaning of global competition at the supply chain- or individual-firm level needs to be reconsidered.

Generally the term "globalization" refers to the interdependence of markets and business activities beyond a single nation-state. But what does it mean to be global in the context of an individual company? In commerce, this can refer to multiple operations in globally distributed locations (global production), to selling to customers in multiple locations (global sales and distribution), to linkages and collaborations with other firms or organizations in multiple geographic locations (global supply chains). For SMEs, the first option — multiple global operations — is often not feasible. The challenges of the latter two often confound small suppliers that frequently lack a strategic long-term commitment to globalization.

The Importance of Niche Markets

Science fiction writer William Gibson noted that the future is here, but that it is unequally distributed.[7] This idea has several important implications for commercial trade. First, it suggests that across the globe there exists every imaginable market niche, each with very diverse sets of characteristics. These niches are defined by different technical expectations, needs and price point requirements, not to mention different market sizes and geographic locations. Reaching out to these multiple markets requires the knowledge that they in fact exist, which further suggests the need for proximity to gain that knowledge.

While large companies have long understood the importance of acquiring direct knowledge through proximity to end markets, there is growing evidence that this practice is being embraced by some SMEs. For example, Quality Float Works, a 93-year-old company that makes ball-like metal floats that can be used in a wide range of applications to control water levels, has been successfully using proximity to gain market insight. This company's leadership visited over 80 countries in a two-year period to try to find unmet needs that might be served by its products. One such need existed in developing countries where potable water is scarce. Quality Float Works addressed this niche market by combining desalinization floats with priming valves and connecting metal rods. As a result, the company's international sales efforts have grown from 3 percent of total revenues in 2003 to more than 20 percent in 2007.[8] Reaching into the global marketplace requires more than just intent: It requires "actionable" understanding of the commercial realities of those market niches. Too often, U.S.-based companies, particularly SMEs, have the intent to pursue globalization of sales, but lack understanding of market niches.

The second implication of scattered niche markets is that success in one market is a good predictor of success in similar and related niche markets. But successfully penetrating overseas niche markets requires a strategic approach to market segmentation that must be done in phases. Studies and anecdotal examples have shown that companies taking a sequential approach to market entry based on similar market niches have proven to be successful. Still, many American SMEs treat global market expansion in a haphazard fashion based on momentary opportunities.[9]

A third implication of a distributed set of market niches is related to the costs of selling into those niches. Very small markets are generally more expensive to reach and serve. Here is where Friedman's global communications principle from *The World is Flat* begins its impact on suppliers. Reaching niche markets as small as one (ultimately suggested by "mass customization")[10] requires the use of the Internet and other highly personalized sales approaches. With ubiquitous and instantaneous global communications brought about by the Internet, it is easier for individual consumers and customers to find individual suppliers.

There are two important caveats to this that are often overlooked. First, the success of a search is only as good as the information that a company provides on its Web site. Company Web sites that do not anticipate potential needs and the interests of niche markets are unlikely to attract notice. As a corollary, company offerings that cannot easily be customized to individual consumers or end customers are neither attractive nor cost competitive. Here again, a company must take a strategic approach to product offerings. This is where SMEs should have an advantage over large suppliers by providing individual customers with specialized service. Unfortunately, few suppliers attain the prerequisite product flexibility and manufacturing agility that is necessary to achieve this type of success.

There is a final implication of globally distributed niche markets. Because many of these markets are so small, the cost of failure to experiment in any one market is relatively modest. True experimentation through a process known as intelligent fast failure almost always yields positive results: Either the experiment is a success and the company provides the marketplace with a feature set at the right price point and growing sales, or the company acquires a deeper understanding of that niche market so that its next offering might be more successful.[11] The former requires insight (and often luck), while the latter requires learning and a long-term commitment to globalization. Too often, SMEs are not actively learning and applying their hard-won knowledge to subsequent endeavors.

The Evolution of U.S. Manufacturing

The current status of U.S. manufacturing is rooted in the historical competition of nation states — in the organizational culture and structure first conceived during the industrial revolution, and in the disintegration over the past three decades of the vertically integrated corporation into firms focusing on core competencies. The new multinational corporations are reaching customers through the coordinated efforts of their supply chains, and they are currently evolving into a value chain. Only those companies that have restructured their activities with respect to the new interdependent relationships that are unfolding are thriving at this point. Many SMEs that continue to take their guidance from larger companies in their supply chain — principally from Tier 1 suppliers and OEMs — are ill-prepared to compete by focusing on features beyond cost. A historical perspective on how the supply chain developed offers insights into the common and current mindset and approach of many SMEs.

The Emergence of Supply Chains

Underlying any production network are the owners of raw materials, the companies that transform them into products, and the companies that sell and distribute those products. Prior to the Industrial Revolution, specialized cottage industries were the dominant form of production, eventually giving way to what might be called the "Titans of Industry" age with the transition to the Industrial Revolution. The factory system[12] was driven by swift, even production flow, where the key competitive advantage was in the rapid movement of materials through the manufacturing process.[13] Because of fixed investments in machinery, throughput and efficiency became critical dimensions of competitive advantage, encouraging firms to focus on volume and on securing access to the raw materials needed to maintain full production.

Firms grew larger and frequently spanned more than one role in the production model. Firms began to concentrate on repeatable processes and interchangeable parts to promote efficiency. Whereas in earlier times uniqueness was valued, now it became the enemy of efficiency. Frederick Taylor's notion of skilled workers performing tasks in a "best way" in the minimum amount of time combined with Henry Ford's relentless pursuit of mechanized production encouraged the modern-day scientific management method and mass production mentality that continues to pervade many manufacturing operations.

The Titans of Industry were the firms that emerged through investment in manufacturing, marketing and management necessary to fully exploit larger volumes of production provided by capital-intensive new technologies. These firms focused on the transformation of raw materials into products or in the assembly of products into more complex offerings, leading to the creation of OEMs that still exist to this day.

Large industrial companies grew via "forward" integration into market distribution and via "backward" integration to control access to raw materials. The result: vertically integrated corporations that spanned all traditional functions including the production of products, procedures for hiring and firing, ordering inventory, research and development, advertising and business strategies aimed at product diver-

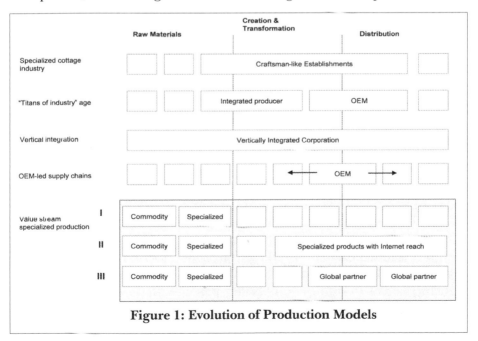

Figure 1: Evolution of Production Models

sification and geographical diversification.[14] Vertical integration birthed even larger firms, many of which began to reach across international boundaries in their quest for raw materials and customers. This gave rise to the multinational firms that currently lead the global economy. Large size remains a primary metric of success.

The OEM-Led Supply Chain

In recent decades, corporations that were once vertically integrated from production of raw materials to product delivery and sales have been outsourcing some or nearly all of the production of goods and services through their supply chains. The trend toward interdependent firms intensified due to several factors, including an emphasis on core competencies, "modularization" of design, the emergence of specialized, complementary companies, and increased global capacity for production of goods and services. The belief that vertically integrated firms should focus their efforts on their core competencies, technologies and skills to achieve competitive advantage encouraged them to begin outsourcing non-core aspects of production.[15] As firms lower in the supply chain began to specialize in technologies, product components or manufacturing processes, a natural distinction could be made between companies that produced a component or subassembly, and those that assembled them into product configurations to meet the demands of the end customer. Manufacturing capabilities began to reside within the supply base.

The automotive industry's OEM and tiered supplier relationship is a good example of this (see Figure 2). Here, in both the retail and after-market supply chain, the customer is served by a series of interconnected firms. The assemblers (OEMs) procure from Tier 1 suppliers who in turn source to lower-tier suppliers. With the exception of raw material owners and suppliers, many of which are still large companies, most of the firms in the lower tiers are small- and medium-sized enterprises. Yet most of the design decisions continue to be made by the OEMs. U.S. automakers — General Motors, Ford and Chrysler — exert tight control over their supply chains, which are dominated by intense cost competition.

An outgrowth of this supply chain approach is an implied set of communication and coordination approaches, primarily aimed at linking adjacent firms within the supply chain. The buyer-supplier relationship began to dominate between pairs of firms, and suppliers in the lower tiers of the chain began to have less interaction with end cus-

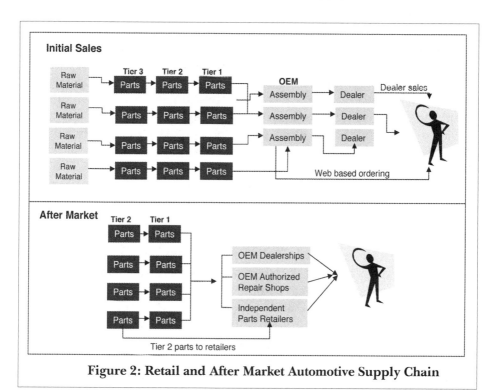

Figure 2: Retail and After Market Automotive Supply Chain

tomers. The disconnect between lower-tier suppliers and the needs of the end customer continues to plague many traditional supply chains and frequently hampers innovation within the lower tiers.

Globalization has further changed the competitive dynamics within the U.S. auto industry as Japanese, Korean and other producers perfected more collaborative supplier and production systems. The Japanese OEMs enhanced communication and coordination among firms throughout their entire supply chains, rather than just among those that work adjacent to each other. The success of the Toyota Production System is well documented yet it is rarely successfully applied, despite repeated efforts.[16] Moreover, the push of Japanese automakers to involve suppliers early in the design and development process has propelled companies like Toyota to achieve the highest levels of quality, customer satisfaction and profitability in the world automotive industry. This is a direct result of its unique approach to supplier management.[17]

Modularization of design increased the ability of OEMs to determine a product's architecture. As a result, companies in the supply chain were only in a position to respond to the OEM's mandated architecture and product feature specifications. OEMs retained responsibility for product design, engineering, assembly and process automation. Modularization enabled suppliers to assume a greater role in developing innovations that supported subassemblies and components.[18]

The OEMs' use of modularized product components and the complexity of the end products have greatly influenced the structure of supply chains. Companies that are producing commodity components that compete on cost are generally located in lower tiers of the supply chain. These companies often exert minimal influence in the direction of product development and have little impact on other supply chain decisions. Relationships between these firms are often transaction-based, with the OEM providing specifications needed for desirable design features.

Suppliers of higher-cost components or assemblies whose features provide for a differentiated final product often have more influence and collaboration in the OEM-led supply chain (see Figure 3).[19] As these companies assume increasingly influential roles in the OEM-led supply chain, the need for collaboration between them rises. Suppliers and their lead OEM share information about the product's performance characteristics, with suppliers providing insight on how they can be best achieved. The OEM still leads the supply chain, but there are meaningful interactions between supplier and OEM that include sharing information, decision-making and planning. This also brings with it a sharing of risk.

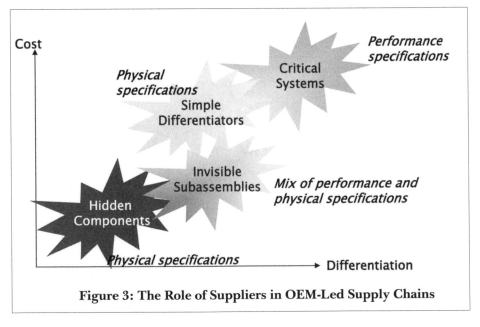

Figure 3: The Role of Suppliers in OEM-Led Supply Chains

A second factor that supported the transition from vertically integrated corporations to OEM-led supply chains was the emergence of firms specializing in management and administration functions that are complementary to the manufacturing enterprise. Companies such as Federal Express and United Parcel Service encouraged corporations to outsource non-core business operations such as logistics, while human resource management, accounting, software maintenance and even design and research and development are routinely done now by service providers located in the United States and offshore in countries like India. Information technology and the adoption of computer-aided design and enterprise resource planning systems further strengthened OEM leadership and influence as suppliers were required to adopt the same financial software and procurement systems.

Individual supply chains differ across industry sectors.[20] The relative importance of declining costs, increasing quality, decreased cycle time and innovation also vary across sectors based on sources of competitive advantage. With suppliers receiving an increasing volume of work that is being outsourced from the OEMs, they have an even greater impact on the quality, cost, technology and delivery of a buying company's products and services.[21] The importance of suppliers' components and subassemblies to the finished product means OEMs have extended the traditional transaction model of supplier sourcing to a much more strategic position of supplier selection and relationship management.[22]

The Shift from Supply Chain to Value Stream

OEMs that lead traditional supply chains are now being challenged by networks of firms competing in a coordinated and collaborative fashion.[23] Companies coordinating their activities in a "value stream" tend to be less linearly organized. Interactions between several firms are orchestrated to achieve a common goal. Thus, communication, collaboration and coordination are not tightly tied to the tiered structure of a supply chain. This is important for SMEs to understand as they seek to remain relevant. It suggests new opportunities for interaction with other companies in the network based on adding value rather than strictly on their position in a tiered arrangement.

Under this emerging structure, the buyer must understand that first-tier suppliers and customers are now involved in design, manufacturing and delivery. Logistics networks are needed to complete the integrated supply chain management cycle.[24] These linkages were most often between Tier 1 and OEM firms, but there is increasing evidence that a growing number of OEMs are forming partnerships with firms deeper in the lower tiers. The OEMs are attracted to companies that possess unique technical knowledge, process and production expertise.[25]

The emerging value-stream model emphasizes participation through distinctive capabilities where collaboration is achieved through common goals. Unlike the traditional top-down OEM supply chain model, in the emerging value-stream specialized production model, a single firm at the top of the structure does not control the activities of the network. Buyers and sellers within the chain exert mutual influence over one another, and decisions about sourcing typically balance the need for innovation with the desire to be cost-competitive. A symbiotic relationship exists between the firms, since collaboration is necessary to bring innovative products to market. Because of the symbiotic relationship, the need for collaboration rises along with the sharing of risk.

The three forms of the value chain presented in Figure 1 on page 287 depict versions of the value chain model that are found in today's production environment. All three versions cover the same territory of raw materials providers, creators and transformers and distributors. But the way that individual firms occupy these roles — their geographic distribution and the way they reach their customers — differs.

In Value Stream I, firms occupy traditional roles within the supply chain across the stages, but with shared influence. As a result, all of the boxes in the creation/transformation and distribution stages are of similar sizes to indicate that relative value can come from many different firms regardless of their position within the chain. Also in this model, the interactions between the firms become a source of competitive advantage as relationships emerge that tightly link the goals of firms within the network.

The medical device industry is a good example of multiple points of influence in the value stream, despite different relative sizes of the individual companies. Intellectual property (IP) is the cornerstone of innovation and a key competitive driver in the industry. Smaller firms with unique IP are often sought after by other larger firms to become key partners. It is not uncommon to find a web of partnerships and co-investors among various participants in the creation and transformation stage of product development. Interestingly, as devices become smaller, the importance of unique manufacturing assets around micro-manufacturing and nanotechnology are driving supplier selection within the value chain. A recent study of manufacturing supply chains in the Pennsylvania plastics industry cluster indicates the importance of supplier-held knowledge in creating successful products in the market. One supplier of plastic components commented on the way that his company leverages its knowledge of resins and manufacturing to help a consumer products OEM develop new products:

> "If a customer brings us a unique product [idea], we can take it and do three designs. We can have a prototype made up in a similar material, and [our customer] can try it out and see if they like it. This gives them a realistic feel of what the product is going to look like. Then we can design the tooling around it. We can build the tooling and do the production of the plastic [resin]."[26]

In Value Stream II, information and communication technologies work to remove some or all of the distribution layers typically found in traditional supply chains. Information and communication technologies enable companies with specialized products to go directly to the end customer or consumer using the Internet. They enable individual companies, regardless of size, to directly reach the consumer or end customer.[27] This "disintermediation" of the traditional roles within the supply chain reduces the overall chain's reliance on traditional paths to the marketplace, and requires firms to increase their understanding of the needs of niche markets. The Internet provides companies with access to a broad pool of potential buyers. It has forever changed the balance of power between producers and distributors.

Amazon.com is perhaps the most famous example of a company whose business model emphasizes the "long tail" of customer segmentation. Amazon's entire business model is about leveraging the Internet to sell products to customer niche markets of one, completely usurping traditional bookstores and retail outlets. Its success requires a different set of internal capabilities involving the intensive upgrade of information technology and the addition of specialists with market knowledge.

In Value Stream III, companies develop partnerships with other, often globally distributed, companies. They do this to leverage both unique capabilities and to acquire access to knowledge and social networks of these dispersed players.[28] Such partnerships take on a new dimension: knowledge flow becomes a critical element in the value that accrues between firms. Partnerships in this type of arrangement are defined by formal legal relationships, government-mandated joint ventures, or by memoranda of understanding.

Boeing's 787 airplane, the Dreamliner, represents a change of Boeing Commercial Aircraft from an OEM-led supply chain to a value-stream approach. In the Dreamliner, Boeing product development engineers collaborated with engineers, designers and manufacturers across multiple suppliers to achieve the innovations embedded into the Dreamliner's design, particularly related to electronic systems and composite airframe structures. Boeing outsourced more than half of the structure of the Dreamliner to suppliers that are also investing heavily in R&D. Not surprisingly, Boeing is treating its more than 130 global building sites as partners and not as suppliers in the strict sense of the word.

The Dreamliner is now delayed by nearly two years, and as of this writing the first flight is not yet scheduled. One of the main causes for this delay can be traced to supplier interaction and management. Though Boeing adopted a value stream model, its supplier management practices did not fully recognize the changing relationships that are required for success in this model.[29]

While there are some similarities with the traditional OEM-led supply chain model, the emerging value stream model exhibits some striking differences:

- The value stream model generally replaces transaction-based interactions between firms in a supply chain with an approach that favors relationships and value-added services;
- Coordination between companies is often greater than in a typical supply-chain model, since firms frequently collaborate on innovation, design and other value-adding activities;
- Within a value stream model, the traditional division of power between the firms — based primarily on size and economies of scale and scope — is replaced by power and influence that resides among companies with unique assets and knowledge; and
- When the value chain is globally distributed and when partnerships and collaboration are emphasized, then access to unique technology and social networks becomes a driving factor in exerting influence and value among all members of the value chain.

In all three versions of the value stream model, the role of raw material providers divide into commodity suppliers and specialized material suppliers. This distinction is important in the global framework in which these value stream networks operate. While there have always been commodity and specialized raw materials suppliers, in the value stream model, materials suppliers that produce commodities that are in high demand or provide unique formulations of materials are valued more highly by other firms in the network than companies supplying readily available commodities.

In value streams, linkages between firms vary based on their degree of formality, depth and duration. Coordination is achieved between individual firms that work harmoniously through a set of common goals. These companies direct their efforts at reducing conflicts by making joint decisions. Within the value stream, companies also pool their resources to undertake mutually valuable activities, such as shared research and development, joint investments in tooling, manufacturing and distribution.

Within a value stream network of companies, close-knit relationships form a barrier to entry to other firms wishing to compete in the same or similar markets, thereby accruing additional value and strength to the firms within the network. This value is often intangible to those outside of the network, and so might be under appraised by potential investors of firms operating in the network. But companies operating within the network of interrelated firms understand that they gain a competitive advantage from the sum of the whole, and therefore assess firms' value to themselves beyond transactions to include leveraged investment dollars.

Innovation as a Driver of Value

Individual technologies rarely define products. Rather, multiple technologies must be considered with respect to one another and with respect to the application into which they are embedded. Because of the complexity of modern products and because of the distributed production that occurs, selecting and refining technologies implies subtle interactions between the technical components and the final product configuration. Integrating these technologies into a final product also influences organizational structures as well. Product-level interactions often require commensurate firm-level interactions, and in a global competitive environment, unique access to technology, expertise and end customer needs are a differentiator in the value stream production model.

Suppliers' Roles in Innovation

At a recent gathering of 30 top executives from noncompeting companies at an innovation summit hosted in Cincinnati, Ohio, by Procter & Gamble and Boeing, discussions centered on how to innovate more effectively.[30] These companies are struggling with how to identify the best talent, fund and manage the innovation process and measure its effectiveness. Without exception, the executives said that leveraging their companies' value stream assets and the talent and technologies that reside within it are a key to their future success. A major barrier, however, was captured by one executive's comment: "Within our company, and even outside of it, information gets shared, [but] insight does not." Without insight, innovation is nearly impossible. Without insight, innovation happens only serendipitously, if at all.

Innovation generally results from market pull or technology push. In the first case, it occurs when there is market demand; in the second case, it is the availability of a new technology that drives innovation. Innovation based on market pull and technology push suggests different roles and responsibilities for different firms within the value stream, based on their proximity to the end customer or their area of expertise. Firms that are distant from the end product market such as raw materials processors or component makers are more likely to innovate around technology product features, while in firms that manufacture the final product or its subassemblies, innovation is often driven by both market demands and technological advances.[31]

Figure 3 on page 290 highlights these roles with respect to the system or product architecture (typically the domain of the OEM or customer-facing firm) and the component and subassembly (typically the responsibility of a supplier within the network). There are basically four combinations of architecture and components, based on the relative novelty of each. The combinations suggest specific sources of competitive advantage for the value stream overall, and opportunities for firms within it.

When existing components are integrated into mature products, the primary competitive drivers are cost and time. Standard commodity components such as batteries and printed circuit boards are desirable so long as the product "delights" the marketplace, the price point is acceptable to buyers and there is not a better alternative product or solution available to the end customer. Activities within the value stream that promote cost reductions, while continuously scanning the environment for possible disruptions to this status quo, promote sustainability of the firms within the value stream network. The supplier's knowledge about process improvements that reduce manufacturing costs is a major contribution to all of the companies within the value stream.

From a supplier innovation standpoint, new components or sub-assemblies that are integrated into an existing product or technology system (lower left quadrant of Figure 4) can result in incremental product improvements. The performance of the product system improves, but not dramatically enough to disrupt the competitive dynamics of the marketplace. Because of modularization, incremental innovation is only possible when the value stream network can leverage suppliers' knowledge of potential substitute materials or alternative configurations that improve the product's performance. Knowledge sharing within and between firms about changes in the market, combined with suppliers' sharing improvements in their components, requires joint planning among companies to achieve incremental product innovation.

Figure 4: Market Pull and Technology Push Innovation In the Context of Supplier Roles and Opportunities

	Existing System	**New System**
Existing Component	**Mature Technology/Product** No new innovation is anticipated; Pricing and timing driven by economies of scale **Opportunity**: Scenario planning for manufacturing and continuous technology searching limits path dependence and obsolescence.	**Architectural Reuse of Technology** Multiple uses for technology as new architectures emerge. **Opportunity:** Likely cost savings through technology reuse across product platforms; requires intensive communication across organizational boundaries.
New Component	**Incremental Product Developments** Component evolution replaces existing solutions. **Opportunity**: Advance knowledge reduces uncertainty, improves product timing and enables joint planning across organizational units.	**Architectural Revolution/Obsolescence** New components, perhaps combined together, enable new system architectures that obsolete existing solutions. **Opportunity**: Close collaboration with technologists and suppliers, and integrated information sharing enables proactive introductions to beat competitors in features and time to market.

The true importance of joint planning, knowledge sharing and collaboration within the value stream network is especially important when existing and new components are being combined to create new systems. With the architectural re-use of technology (upper right), the end-product producer can achieve cost savings and reduce time to market by using existing components to help develop new systems. This is important for several reasons. First, the use of existing components in new systems increases the volume of production for those components, thus benefitting the supplier. Second, increasing volume enables suppliers to more quickly ascend the manufacturing learning curve, thus further reducing costs and improving quality. Integrating existing components in new products reduces the qualification and testing time for those components during the product development process, thus cutting time to market and improving first-yield production for the new products or systems, both of which benefit the final producer and its customers. Rapid and sustained sales, of course, benefit the entire value chain.

Motorola used the strategy of technology re-use in emerging cell phone platforms to reduce its costs and time to market, and even shared sales forecasting data with suppliers to help ensure that components such as batteries were available in the volumes needed to support its product offerings.[32] This resulted in a $600-million savings on a $16-billion product development project, and helped both Motorola and its suppliers plan their activities more effectively. To accomplish these gains, Motorola and its suppliers used online interactions and bidding with its preferred suppliers to improve the way components were sourced. This example of re-use demonstrated the cost and planning advantages of the value stream model. Unfortunately, cost is only one aspect of success, and Motorola has been unable to truly benefit from these advantages in the long run due to an underdeveloped market-sensing capability compared to its rivals.

The most desirable position for a value chain is to create revolutionary systems that render obsolete all other offerings in the marketplace, thus displacing current leaders and creating entirely new markets. This most frequently occurs when new components and subsystems are developed for entirely new products that achieve unanticipated performance capabilities on multiple dimensions and cannot be matched by competitors. This spawns entirely new industries.

An example of this type of revolutionary product introduction is the displacement of computer mainframes with RISC processor-based workstations and, eventually, powerful Intel microprocessor-based personal computers. Another example can be seen with hybrid cars. Though not completely disruptive to the existing auto industry, the growth in hybrid sales now exceeds early hype and the technology is the first legitimate alternative to the internal combustion engine in 100 years. An efficient electric vehicle could completely disrupt the global automobile industry by making obsolete many of the capabilities of the current automotive supply chain. The electric car will not require the volume or diversity of mechanical gears and other linking parts that are so common in the engine-transmission-drive train of the combustion engine. Moreover, the manufacturing and material capabilities of current producers will have little value in electric vehicles that are made of composites or plastics and powered by electric motors that do not require oil as a lubricant.

The Value of Unique Knowledge in the Global Value Stream

Both market pull and technology push innovation models require that at some point in the value stream somebody within a firm recognizes a unique need, a unique opportunity, a unique solution or some combination of these. The essential role of individuals within the value-stream production model must be acknowledged and articulated. Although this might seem obvious, most information technology systems employed in the value chain link firm-to-firm activities and not individuals to other individuals. Innovation is a "contact sport." For it to yield results, individuals must scan their environment and translate what they find into the context of the needs of the firm and the needs of the value-stream network. The more diverse and empowered the individuals are within the network, the better they are at scanning external opportunities and making sense of what they see.

Innovations that result from market pull suggest a very important role for understanding niche markets. India is frequently cited as a very large emerging market, with a burgeoning middle class and pent up demand for a multitude of new products. A closer look at India, however, suggests that niches are far more varied than might be suggested by income alone. The demographics tell an important story. Every one of the country's 28 states and seven territories has its own unique mother tongue. These states and regions have unique cultural backgrounds, often favoring one Hindu god over another (and thus celebrating different festivals). They have different combinations of Hindu, Muslim, Christian and other religions, each of which has its own set of taboo foods or products. And there are distinct differences in climates, which influence what people buy and when they buy it during the course of the year. A company seeking to sell its products to India's 1.12 billion people is, in reality, marketing to many different Indias. A careful understanding of each is essential for success.

Innovation that is derived from market pull requires that the companies most in touch with the end customer have a deep understanding of their customers' needs and wants. If innovation occurs through a process of interaction between companies and their customers, local access to and knowledge of customer niches adds innovation value that cannot be mimicked by firms operating outside the network or from a geographic distance. John Winsor, author of *Spark!*, has observed that "innovation can spring from any part of the company-customer community, but ONLY if the support and encouragement for this environment exists at every level of the business."[33]

The richer the environment for exchange of unique knowledge and the development of collective insight not just in the firm, but within the value chain, then the greater the competitive advantage the value chain will have over competing networks of firms. There is no substitute for on-the-ground observation.

At a summer 2008 workshop with a group of 40 industrial engineers, designers and product developers in Bangalore, the discussion focused on the influences of East-to-West thinking in developing new products.[34] Ideas for new products focused on the different uses of technologies in India as compared to the West. The discussion centered on the challenges of an inconsistent infrastructure and what this might mean for product robustness, and the requirement for reduction in power consumption. Because this group of Indian experts was tied to Western development teams, their insights provided a very different view of market conditions and what was required for success when compared to the hard-wired, continuous process production environments more common in the West. Moreover, because there is such diversity in India, members of the group believed that they could experiment with small product offerings, incrementally introducing or deleting features that have little value within specific Indian niches.

An important feature of the discussion was the different concept of price-performance ratios in India and elsewhere in the developing world. Too often, Western developers view this ratio through their own experience. While "empathetic" design — placing yourself into your user's place — is often very helpful, it can be disastrous when the experience of buyers is radically different from those of designers and product developers.

By contrast, innovation that comes about by technology push favors firms and their value chains that sell into broadly different markets. Scientists, engineers and product designers in these firms have their own professional networks. The broader the collective network, the broader the scanning of potential good ideas. The key to success is enabling them to link what they find into a knowledge-sharing environment where observations from one place can be combined with similar observations to generate a new solution.

The Opportunities for SMEs in a Global Environment

More than 15 years ago, a researcher observed that the traditional product-based strategies of many corporations largely ignored requirements to build underlying skills and knowledge for long-term corporate sustainment. The product-centric "strategy paradigm focuses on only the last 100 yards of what may be a skill-building marathon."[35] Yet today, many companies retain this obsolete product-centric view, and this syndrome is particularly true of SMEs. For SMEs, competing in the global economy often rests on three questions:

1. How can they compete on the basis of cost so as to gain market share?
2. How can they penetrate or create new markets for their current products so as to increase economies of scale?
3. How can they create or penetrate new markets for their current products to improve their margins, without the need for heavy investments in new technology or new market development?

While these are useful questions to ask, they do little to help the SME see over the horizon or to reposition their company within their value-stream network, or assist them in entering a new value stream network.

Head-to-head competition with global suppliers has yielded disastrous results for companies in many industry sectors. There are early indications that large producers around the world are beginning to reevaluate their global sourcing strategies in light of fluctuating currencies, erratic petroleum prices and market turmoil. This could favor

American suppliers selling to U.S. producers, particularly for large parts or components that are expensive or difficult to ship.

Anecdotal evidence from the plastics industry suggests that suppliers with large production presses are faring better against their global competitors than suppliers using smaller presses and molds that are commonly found in Mexico, China and the Asia Pacific region. This trend may continue and expand to other sectors where fully landed costs put the United States more on par with global suppliers. While there is by no means an immediate transition to rosier times, it does means that U.S.-based SMEs should begin rethinking their relationships with American-based producers.

A Skill-Based, Value-Added Strategy Changes the Approach to the Customer

SMEs that focus on the value and skills they bring to their customers must find ways to share their knowledge. The first step is to change the dynamics of their interactions with customers and potential customers. Selling parts and components based on print drawings generated in a routine or even automated fashion and with quotas set by the customer means that schedule and cost become the main deciding factors for selection of suppliers. As more manufacturing knowledge shifts to the supplier base, SMEs can add value by offering insights into how best to produce a part at the lowest price with maximum quality and flexibility for reuse. This expands the decision-making factors in selecting a supplier from schedule and cost to include quality and cost savings over time.

Finally, when SMEs can provide design suggestions based on material and/or manufacturing alternatives, the decision to select a supplier is further expanded to include the value of innovation. The more ways the SME can add value to its customer's product offerings, the tighter the bonds between the companies become. The relationship becomes sustainable beyond simple transactions.

Achieving long-term and sustainable relationships requires a technical sales force with a deep understanding of the purchasing company's product development and forecasting process. They must also know about materials and have the ability to propose alternative solutions. A traditional procurement officer working in a bidding company is unlikely to possess these skills and therefore is unable to facilitate additional business and partnership opportunities.

Instead, the concept of "concurrent" purchasing, whereby purchasing decisions are expanded to include not only the sourcing of components and subassemblies but their design, should be pursued. Concurrent purchasing requires a change in approach for both buyer and supplier. While companies such as Boeing are developing an appreciation for the role that its suppliers have undertaken in production and innovation, most companies have not gone beyond contract negotiations based on schedule, cost and quality issues, thereby limiting their opportunities. SMEs pursuing a strategy based on adding additional value must aggressively pursue deeper relationships with their customers. They must have the professional wherewithal to interact with their customers on multiple levels. This suggests a migration from simply submitting bids to becoming advisers on intangible services and knowledge.

An Innovation-Based, Value-Added Strategy Requires a Partnership Model

The idea of partnership implies a bi-directional relationship on equal footing. This has not been the case in traditional OEM-SME relationships. But SMEs can achieve equality by developing skills, capabilities and solutions that the OEM does not possess. SMEs seeking to compete on innovation are really seeking to differentiate themselves from lower-cost global competitors through enhanced performance, thus justifying a higher price. They can also become suppliers of choice through product offerings that others cannot provide, often rooted in the ownership of unique intellectual property. SMEs deploying this strategy can be the preferred supplier to globally distributed companies.

Some SMEs will find that there is little or no unique differentiation between themselves and their competitors, especially among those that have competed on cost while ignoring R&D and investment into process improvements. Unfortunately this is true of many component suppliers in the U.S. auto industry where cost competition and declining margins have severely strapped their ability to develop or enhance unique skill sets.

For SMEs that have been able to develop unique manufacturing capabilities, acquisition of companies that have expertise in materials or have access to desirable markets might help them better anticipate where and how to add value to their customers. Though it is not an

SME, Corning pursued this approach in its transition from making kitchenware to becoming an engineering services company. Again, although it did this on a much larger scale, Corning's success provides lessons for smaller manufactures. Corning added life scientists and inventors to its payroll. It acquired patents to help secure a differentiated place in the market. While the acquisition of people and intellectual property might be beyond the reach of many SMEs, they can accomplish many of the same goals through partnerships and alliances with other complementary firms.

Open Innovation Offers New Paths To New Customers

SMEs can leverage their unique skills, knowledge and capabilities by pursuing the open innovation initiatives currently underway at a growing number of OEMs and even Tier 1 suppliers. Open innovation as it is currently envisioned by these companies is being pursued through two methods. First, matchmaker companies such as Innocentive, Yet2 and NineSigma offer an end-to-end solution that links "seekers," companies wanting to find solutions to a product development problem, with "solvers," companies or individuals interested in problem-solving and who have a potentially useful solution. The matchmaker company posts the challenges from "seekers" on the Internet and provides secure access to details only for vetted companies or individuals. Frequently, the matchmaker company limits contact between seekers and solvers until a solution looks promising and then the matchmaker provides a secure communication channel between the two.

The second way that open innovation occurs is through company-direct programs. Procter and Gamble's "Connect + Develop" program invites companies and individuals outside the company to submit innovative ideas to P&G through its Web site (https://secure3.verticali.net/pg-connection-portal/ctx/noauth/PortalHome.do). Companies like P&G and Toyota expect that at least 50 percent of their ideas for new or improved products should come from outside of their company. This "not invented here" emphasis offers inventors the chance to link with these large OEMs in a way that is often not possible in the established supply chain.

To successfully participate in open innovation initiatives, SMEs need to develop skills of proposal development, business case presentations and analytics, and technical explanation capabilities that describe an idea's technical details in terms of a solution and value-added potential. In addition, SMEs will have to develop advanced Internet search skills to locate opportunities and identify problem postings.

Global Reach and Global Presence Are Both Needed To Develop International Customers

The holy grail for many American SMEs is to expand their sales to overseas markets. The likelihood of success in a global market for an undifferentiated commodity product is limited due to additional transportation costs and higher relative wage rates in the United States. American SMEs that cannot overcome these barriers are unlikely to prevail in foreign markets. SMEs that invest in research to develop unique capabilities tailored to specific markets achieve a higher level of success. But a change in orientation is difficult even for these companies.

As the number of Internet-savvy buyers grows around the globe — and as end customers and consumers alike flock to the Web as a source of information about products — the likelihood is rising that an SME or even a group of complementary SMEs can be successful. Online sales begin with a Web presence that must anticipate user search needs and interests. Systems that recommend products, such as those developed by Amazon.com, require SMEs to design approaches that are tailored to Internet users who are familiar with such features.

An even less traditional approach involves Web 2.0, an increasingly popular system that creates collaborative opportunities through shared interests and activities.[36] This technology is akin to the business application version of MySpace and other social networking sites. Although the hype often outstrips the performance, it is quickly changing and should be carefully watched by SMEs.

An example of the burgeoning use of Enterprise 2.0 and its role in supply network formation and operations is PM Gear, a startup manufacturing and merchandising company literally organized on the Internet.[37] The company provides high-end ski equipment and apparel. Management of the company's operations is coordinated virtually through the Web, and is the result of social networking interactions that bring customers' needs together with the company's product offerings. The company grew out of an online community referred to as the "Powder Maggots," a group of ski enthusiasts associated with an Internet message board called "powdermag.com."

While the Internet and Web 2.0 can help establish a company's global reach, successfully entering international markets through more traditional paths requires a heavier amount of investment. In order to survive, SMEs must commit to a globalization strategy that includes a series of planned forays into the global environment. Learning by doing, on-the-ground observation, collaboration and a long-term focus will help position them for success.

America's SMEs should reconsider their global aspirations. In order to have survived the grueling period from 2001 to 2008 most SMEs already possess unique capabilities of some type. Determining their value on the global stage requires a broader view. Once again, there is no substitute for being there. Attending conferences, trade shows and participating in other forums where it is possible to learn about needs, opportunities and competing solutions is essential. A depth of knowledge takes time to build and differs from an occasional overseas trip with a trade delegation that is aimed at simply making commercial sales rather than making a long-term focus on innovation, R&D and market development for emerging and future growth. Here is where knowledge is essential, and where discussion, either face-to-face or facilitated by information technology, is essential.

Conclusion

The global economy is undergoing the greatest transition in 80 years. While purchasing power in the United States is shrinking, the middle class is growing in several large countries. Such a trend is fundamentally changing the global patterns of buying and distributing goods and services. The century-old tenets of competition and commerce no longer exist in a world that has been opened up by the Internet. Following strategies that have been successful in the past will present fewer opportunities for successes in the future.

SMEs must change themselves for this new reality. Fierce cost competition will still govern some sectors, but building relationships and capabilities will be the only way to sustain SMEs into the future, where competition will be between networks of firms that add value to a collective whole, and that are flexible enough to meet customer needs in a variety of ways and through a variety of distribution channels.

1. Robb, G., "Factory Sector Weakens Sharply in October," MarketWatch, *Wall Street Journal*, November 3, 2008, http://www.marketwatch.com.
2. Hoovers.com.
3. Engardio, P.; Roberts, D.; and Bremner, B., "Special Report — the China Price," *Business Week*, December 6, 2004.
4. Jaruzelski, B. and Dehoff, K., "Beyond Borders: the Global Innovation 1000," *Strategy & Business*, Issue 53, 2008.
5. Within this chapter and elsewhere in the literature, the terms "chain" and "network" are often interchangeable. The traditional label "supply chain" implies a linear organization of firms. Supply network has a similar meaning of a set of interconnected firms, but it is less linear. Either phrasing refers to a set of firms that cooperates to a greater or lesser extent to achieve the transformation of raw materials into a product that reaches the end customer or consumer. In this sense, the chapter is specifically aimed at manufacturing/production of a product and is not necessarily generalizable to the provision of services.
6. Friedman, T., *The World is Flat*, New York, Farrar, Straus & Giroux, 2005.
7. O'Reilly, T., "Inventing the Future," http://www.oreillynet.com/pub/a/network/2002/04/09/future.html, April 9, 2002.
8. Katz, J., "Small and Medium-Sized Manufacturers: Flexible and Focused," *Industry Week*, http://www.industryweek.com/ReadArticle.aspx?ArticleID=17517, November 1, 2008.
9. Petrick, I.J.; Maitland, C.; Pogrebnyakov, N.; and Ayoub, P., "Pennsylvania Plastics Manufacturing Industry — Profile and Supply Chain Coordination Practices," final report to the Pennsylvania Workforce Development Office, February 2008.
10. Gilmore, J.H. and Pine, B.J., II, *Markets of One: Creating Customer-Unique Value through Mass Customization*, Boston: Harvard Business School Publishing, 2000.
11. Matson, J.V., *The Art of Innovation: Using Intelligent Fast Failure*, 1991.
12. Landes, D.S., *The Wealth and Poverty of Nations*, New York, N.Y.: WW Norton and Company, 1998.
13. Schmenner, R.W., "Looking Ahead by Looking Back: Swift, Even Flow in the History of Manufacturing," *Production and Operations Management*, 10: 87-96, 2001.
14. Nelson R.R. and Winter, S.G., *An Evolutionary Theory of Economic Change*, Boston, Mass., Belknap Press of Harvard University Press, 1982.
15. Prahalad, C.K. and Hamel, G., "The Core Competence of the Corporation," *Harvard Business Review*, 68:79-91, 1990.
16. Womack, J.P.; Jones, D.T.; and Roos, D., *The Machine that Changed the World: The Story of Lean Production*, New York: Rawson Associates.
17. Takeishi, A., "Bridging Inter- and Intra-Firm Boundaries: Management of Supplier Involvement in Automobile Product Development," *Strategic Business Journal*, 22, 2001: 403-433.
18. Veloso, F. and Fixon, S., "Make-Buy Decisions in the Auto Industry: New Perspectives on the Role of the Supplier as an Innovator," *Technological Forecasting and Social Change*, 67:239-257, 2001.
19. For a full discussion of the relative contribution of a component or subassembly to the end product and its impact on supplier relationships, see Laseter, T.M. and K. Ramdas, "Product Types and Supplier Roles in Product Development: an Exploratory Analysis," *IEEE Transactions on Engineering Management*, 4: 104-118, 2002.
20. Petrick, I.J.; Purdam, S.; and Young, R.R., "Impact of Supply Chain Decisions on Small to Mid-Size Manufacturers," final report to the Manufacturing Extension Partnership Program, National Institutes of Standards and Technologies, June 2004.
21. Handfield, R.B.; Ragatz, G.L.; Petersen, K.J.; and R.M. Monczka, "Involving Suppliers in New Product Development," *California Management Review*, 42: 59-82, 1999.
22. Monczka, R.M.; Petersen, K.J.; Handfield, R.B.; and Ragatz, G.L., "Success Factors in Strategic Supplier Alliances: the Buying Company Perspective," *Decision Sciences*, 29 (3): 553-577, 1998; Also see Heriot, K.C. and Kilkarni, S.P., "The Use of Intermediate

Sourcing Strategies," *Journal of Supply Chain Management*, 37 (1):18-26, 2001.

23. See for example, Yusuf, Y.Y.; Gunasekaran, A.; Adeleye, E.O.; and Sivayoganathan, K, "Agile Supply Chain Capabilities: Determinants of Competitive Objectives," *European Journal of Operations Research*, 159:379-392, 2004; Sherer, S.A., "Critical Success Factors for Manufacturing Networks as Perceived by Network Coordinators," *Journal of Small Business Management*, 41:325-345, 2003; Christopher, M., "The Agile Supply Chain — Competing in Volatile Markets," *Industrial Marketing Management*, 29:37-44, 2000.

24. Ansari, A.; Lockwood, D.L.; and B. Modarress, "Supplier Product Integration a New Competitive Approach," *Production and Inventory Management Journal*, 40(3): 47-61, 1999.

25. Petrick, I.J.; Maitland, C.F.; Pogrebnyakov, N.; and Ayoub, P.J., "Effective Supply Network Practices," final report to the Manufacturing Extension Partnership Program, National Institutes of Standards and Technology, December 2007.

26. Petrick et al., 2008 as cited in Note 9.

27. Anderson, C., "The Long Tail," *Wired*, October 2004.

28. Petrick, I.J. and Maitland, C.M., "Economies of Speed: a Conceptual Framework to Describe Network Effectiveness, Small and Medium-Sized Enterprises and the Global Economy," G. Susman, (ed), Edward Elgar Publishing, Chapter 5, pages 61-78, 2007.

29. Lunsford, J.L., "Fastener Woes to Delay Flight of First Boeing 787 Jets," *Wall Street Journal*, November 5, 2008.

30. Petrick, personal communication with executive participations during the Future Forum, Cincinnati, Ohio, sponsored by Boeing and Procter & Gamble, October 2007.

31. Petrick, I.J., "Tipping the Balance of Power: the Case of Large Scale Systems Integrators and Their Supply Chains," *International Journal of Foresight and Innovation Policy*, Special Issue on the Future of Manufacturing, 3(3): 240-255, 2007.

32. Metty, T.; Harlan, R.; Samelson, Q.; Moore, T.; Morris, T.; and Sorensen, R., "Reinventing the Supplier Negotiation Process at Motorola," *Interfaces* 35(1): 7-23, 2005.

33. Winsor, J., *Spark!*, Chicago: Dearborn Trade Publications, 2006, page 270.

34. Petrick, personal communication during Summer 2008 faculty internship in India, sponsored by Computer Sciences Corporation.

35. Hamel, G., "Competition for Competence and Inter-Partner Learning Within International Strategic Alliances," *Strategic Management Journal*, 12(4):83-103, 1991.

36. Petrick, I.J. and Pogrebnyakov, N., "The Challenges in Communities of Creation for Distributed Innovation and Knowledge Sharing," *Supply Chain Management and Knowledge Management - Integrating Critical Perspectives in Theory and Practice*, A. Dwivedi and T. Butcher (eds), Palgrave, 2008.

37. For a full description of this see Winsor (2006) as cited in Note 33.

9. Trends and the Future Of American Manufacturing

David Bourne
Carnegie Mellon University

American manufacturing is at an important crossroads. New technology, long-term increases in energy, materials and overseas production costs and a deep economic downturn provide the United States with an opportunity to take back the initiative of inventing and making products both in new and traditional industries. U.S. manufacturing can reposition the country as a world industrial leader, but it will happen only through the support of a manufacturing infrastructure that skews success to local, American companies. The United States must choose between dependence, mediocrity and economic stagnation on the one hand, and independence, growth and world leadership on the other.

To usher in a new technological era and rebirth of industry the first priority is to set goals for U.S. manufacturing. The United States has operated without a comprehensive industrial strategy since World War II. There are isolated policies that address issues of international trade, research and development, tax incentives and tariffs. But one of the lingering effects of the Cold War is the fear of anything that has even a hint of socialism — state-run industry has been proven not to work. As a result, the United States has forfeited many of the benefits that accompany a clear list of national priorities for manufacturing.

Interestingly, it was Ronald Reagan who initiated a policy of encouraging dual-use research and development and the civilian application of military technology. But these measures were only indirectly related to improving the position of U.S. manufacturing, since the primary rationale was to maintain a strong military. Meanwhile, the country's manufacturing core was left to erode.

The primary goal of a pro-manufacturing policy should be to clearly state that the United States will continue to make what it needs and not lose its national knowledge of how to manufacture both industrial and consumer products. Without such a goal, the country will continue to export its manufacturing know-how and capability to overseas competitors.

One thing is certain: Manufacturing knowledge is held within the private sector and not the federal government. Therefore, the role of the government should be to encourage the development of this knowledge and partner with the private sector to overcome massive global challenges.[1]

There are excellent examples within government that can promote the creation of a new manufacturing paradigm in the United States. The Defense Advanced Research Projects Agency has achieved success by financing national "Grand Challenge" technology competitions. DARPA's autonomous vehicle races generated a huge response from the private sector. These challenges succeeded in demonstrating the ability to create workable autonomous vehicles with state-of-the-art technologies.[2] They were successful at a time when more expensive government initiatives with traditional defense contractors repeatedly failed to generate acceptable results.

The success of the grand challenge competition provides evidence of a strategy that sets goals that are rewarded with guaranteed prizes and contracts. By pursuing a "prize-based" incentive system, the government can vastly broaden the participation in innovation and production to include entrepreneurs, academia, philanthropists and blue-chip corporations. It seeds both small and large business interests alike.

The future of manufacturing in America will be determined by the existence — or lack thereof — of a national policy, the goal of which is a clear statement of national interest, coupled with the creation of modest incentives aimed at encouraging the achievement of the goal, which is to restore and grow the industrial capability of the United States.

Within this context, there are strong business and economic trends that cannot be ignored and can be used to plot a successful course for the manufacturing sector. It is appropriate to analyze these current business and technology trends that can shape an effective strategy.

Learning from the Past

World War II increased the level of manufacturing in the United States, making it the envy of the world.[3,4] That era was followed by Japanese dominance of low-end, low-cost manufacturing in the 1960s. As the decades passed, low-cost production shifted from Japan to China, Korea and Vietnam. The Japanese concentrated on high-quality goods that carried larger profits. Consumer electronics moved from the United States to Japan, then the machine tool industry, and then the automotive industry all moved overseas. Japanese companies like Sony, Panasonic, Fanuc, Honda and Toyota were so successful that they were able to eliminate most of their American competition.

As the United States continued to lose its leadership in manufacturing, there was still comfort in the thought that America remained the world leader in innovation. The research capability of American universities helped generate the computer chip, the resulting digital revolutions, the Internet, software, nanotechnology and pharmaceuticals. Now in virtually every one of these areas — and many others — the leadership position of the United States has eroded to startlingly low levels.[5]

A contemporary example is the focus of research and development of "anthropomorphic" — or human shaped — robots in Japan. These robots are important because the human world is designed by humans for humans. If robots are going to coexist as modern assistants or general-purpose machine tools, then they will assume basic human shapes and functions in order to work not only in industry but within the confines of homes and offices. There have been dramatic shifts in this basic research to Japanese and Korean industries and universities, while only small programs remain at a few elite U.S. research universities.

The United States has already witnessed the near total elimination of its machine tool industry. This is a dangerous development. Having the tools to make things determines what can be made.

It is possible to produce fundamentally different products with five-axis machining centers versus three-axis machines. Laser cutting equipment versus traditional mechanical cutting machines enables production of an entirely new and fundamentally different class of products. It is possible to make a new generation of products with novel deposition processes by making parts by adding materials, versus the traditional means of cutting and removing material. As the United States has been purchasing most of its manufacturing tools from other countries it has ceded its leadership in manufacturing. Foreign machine tool suppliers and the nations that support innovation in manufacturing equipment now determine what can and cannot be made in the United States.

In the case of industrial robotics, the Japanese rapidly augmented their manufacturing systems with simple robotic arms. By 1994, the Japanese led the world in their installed base of advanced robotic systems. Within the next decade, both the European Union and the United States started to catch up in the use of industrial robots, but the most innovative producers of robotics, like Fanuc, remained in Japan. The European Union successfully made the shift and large European robotic companies were able to become competitive, such as ABB. But nothing

Figure 1: Growth of General-Purpose Industrial Robots[6]

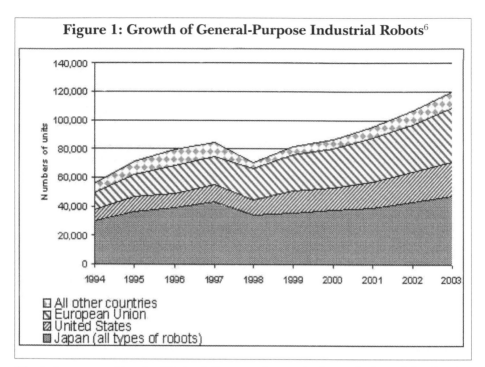

like it happened in the United States, where the large industrial robotics companies (Unimation and Milacron) went out of business.

It is important to reiterate that by controlling the manufacturing tools it is possible to control the type and complexity of products that can be manufactured. There are many features of a robotic arm that determine what it can do effectively. The accuracy, speed and cleanliness of the machine (so that it can be used in clean-room applications), along with its size, power and intelligence determine how and when it can be used in realistic manufacturing applications. If there is a significant improvement in only one of those features, then a robot may become instantly cost-effective for an entire industry. Recently, the increased accuracy of robots has made them become viable in various medical applications. For instance, Intuitive Surgical's Da Vinci System allows medical surgeons to perform very precise inpatient surgeries.

Understanding how the American machine tool and industrial robotic companies lost their competitive stance can help the United States make adjustments for the future. The single most important cause of failure was the industry's inability or unwillingness to design cheaper products. As the market was changing around them, American companies continued to build machine tools that would last forever. U.S. machining centers were built with an emphasis on large, heavy bases that were designed to eliminate vibration and increase precision. Such tools came with a high price. Meanwhile, foreign competitors were designing machines at lower price points by making them lighter and with shorter lifecycles. They used more complex computer controls to compensate for their weaknesses.

With the computer revolution in full swing, the controls, sensors and computer networks built into these machines needed to be updated almost every month. These computer controls were tightly integrated with the machine itself. The result was that the life expectancy of machine tools fell drastically. This in turn created lower price tags. A machine tool could no longer be expected to be a 50-year fixture in a manufacturing company. An expected lifetime closer to 10 to 15 years drastically changed the return on investment calculation. It allowed companies to be more flexible: They could change their equipment to produce new products in a cost-effective manner.

Making matters worse, the U.S. machine tool industry was fixated on developing its own unique controllers and networks to run their machines. At the same time, the computer industry had already built world-class controls and networks. Both Japanese and European competitors initially followed the U.S. practice of using proprietary electronic and software systems, but they wisely switched to commercially available systems based mainly on Intel microprocessors. As a result, U.S. machine tool companies had little flexibility in their controls and networks. They were unable to keep pace with the computer technology of competitors that were building similar equipment.

The marketing departments of major U.S. machine tool companies made one more devastating mistake: They insisted on using proprietary communications networks versus open systems. The results were catastrophic. Corporate America thought that by building proprietary networks and computer interfaces they could control competition by prohibiting a competitor's machine from joining the network. The rapid turnover of machines brought about by new capabilities and lower price points demanded that they be easily plugged into broader manufacturing systems. Manufacturing customers sought out machine tools that could be easily plugged into these open networks and shunned machine tools that could only communicate using proprietary protocols. As a result, the market for machine tools and networks that only supported one company's machines dried up, while the companies that supported open networks flourished.

U.S. manufacturing companies and the machine tool operators and managers working on the factory floor knew and understood these flaws. Their thorough understanding of U.S. suppliers' inability to change and the inevitable failure of the country's major machine tool vendors made the situation even more frustrating to buyers. Engineers could be heard screaming through the halls of manufacturing plants in the 1980s and 1990s: "I just need the machine controls to be the same as the computer on my desk, then they could all be plugged together into a big network."

This industrial failure raises a number of questions. Could any type of U.S. government policy have prevented the loss of the machine tool industry? What can be learned to avoid further losses of essential industrial capability?

In virtually every instance involving the machine tool industry, there was a government program in place with the explicit goal of preventing the outcomes that came to pass.[7] The Part Description Exchange Standard (PDES) program was an attempt to encourage the standardized description of part shapes. The Next Generation Controller (NGC) program attempted to define a standard for a general-purpose, open-architecture machine tool controller that could be easily adapted across companies and industries. Finally, there was the Manufacturing Automation Protocol (MAP) program that attempted to define all aspects of computer and controller networking within the manufacturing environment.

While corporate America and the machine tool sector actively participated in these government-sponsored projects, companies did not act as if they "owned" the results. These projects were burdened by the paralyzing effects of "design by committee." Substantial funding, talent and hopes were put into these projects, but the returns were marginal. A primary goal here is to describe a way to rebuild American manufacturing and avoid the costly mistakes of the past.

Established Business and Technology Trends That Will Shape the Future of Manufacturing

The seeds of the future are present today. There are a few dominant trends that will continue unabated for the foreseeable future and will shape the future of global manufacturing. These trends will be briefly discussed and then used as a springboard for discussing potential technologies on the horizon.

The Rising Cost of Energy

Manufacturing is the process of transforming one kind of element into another. This transformation takes energy — a lot of it. It takes energy to dig minerals out of the ground and transport them to smelting plants and iron works. These industrial facilities use an enormous amount of energy to refine and transform these materials into standardized forms. These materials are then shipped to manufacturing plants, made into consumer goods and delivered to distribution centers and sales outlets. Customers consume energy when they go shopping to buy them. There are many additional energy steps hidden along the path of production.

The final cost of the product is directly tied to the cost of the energy that is required for production and delivery. Over the long term, the price of energy is increasing along with world population growth and increasing global demand for consumer goods. This trend is being exacerbated by an increasing number of extreme weather events, political tensions, environmental concerns and speculative energy markets. Though oil prices have been nearly cut in half after the 2008 financial market crash, other energy costs, such as electricity, have not gone down. It is safe to assume that energy prices will again rise.

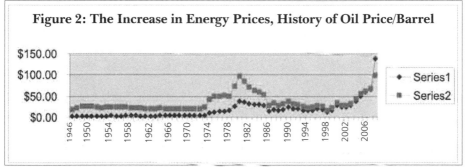

Figure 2: The Increase in Energy Prices, History of Oil Price/Barrel

Strong economic pressures to minimize the amount of energy used in manufacturing will lead to the elimination of intermediate steps and expensive logistics costs. There are large economic incentives to invent new processes that require fewer production steps. If American industry can take the lead in minimizing energy use it may be able to partially recapture losses in manufacturing.

The Exponential Growth Rate of Computing

The continued exponential growth rate of computing capability will have a profound impact on all aspects of manufacturing from the supply chain to production to retail sales. Industrial productivity will continue to rise as computers and embedded microelectronics become more powerful and as their costs continue to decline. Customers can now easily see detailed product specifications, three-dimensional renderings, complex simulations of how products will be used, and attributes such as stress analysis comparisons. Companies that allow customers to comparison-shop from their desktop will be able to increase their potential market size and overall visibility.

Within manufacturing companies, it wasn't long ago that computer controls were the size of a refrigerator for each component in a manufacturing process. Robots, parts loading and unloading systems, gauging and inspection systems and human interface controls all required their own separate computational systems. Manufacturing process components were often linked together with ad hoc networks and controls. The cost savings of eliminating these huge control units are dramatic. Roughly 30 percent to 50 percent of the factory floor was dedicated to machines that have now been miniaturized into the size of a notebook, freeing up factory capacity that was previously unavailable.

Before 2008, virtually all of the control elements had been centralized into a single PC controller. This transition puts the machine controllers on the graph of Moore's Law (Figure 3), which predicts the

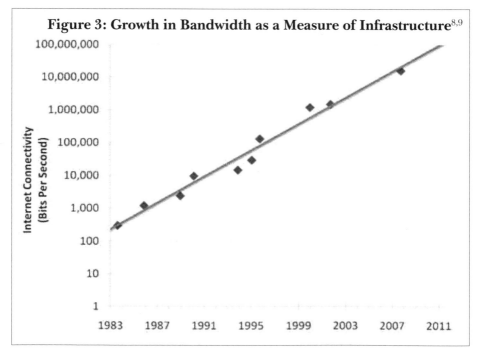

Figure 3: Growth in Bandwidth as a Measure of Infrastructure[8,9]

doubling of capability every 18 months. Over 10 years, computing power has increased by a factor of 100. Internet bandwidth is increasing at an annual rate of 50 percent and over 10 years has increased by a factor of 57. Control and monitoring capability will be built into production machines and networks and will provide operators with data that was never before available.

Manufacturers will be able to analyze sensor logs for the machine's entire existence, maintenance events and complete digital part designs. All of the machine controls will have access to tool databases and virtual self-help instructions on how to operate and maintain every aspect of a machine. At the same time, all of this data can be seen from corporate design departments or even the machine tool supplier's office. This added transparency will make it possible to improve decision-making without making costly trips to the factory floor.

Ubiquitous Communication Over the Internet

High-speed digital communications networks are transforming manufacturing into a radically different business enterprise. Manufacturers are able to take advantage of working 24 hours a day by coordinating with overseas sites and suppliers. Virtual companies composed of single individuals (networked together) are working together over the Internet to produce goods and services from any place on the globe. Yet, the Internet is a relative newcomer to the manufacturing enterprise.

The Reduction in Order or Batch Size

This trend is also known as the number of identical parts made as a group: For the last 30 years, just-in-time manufacturing has been the holy grail of manufacturing. The idea is simple. Make only what is needed when it is needed.

Goods that are held in inventory tie up critical capital until they are sold. But if the time required to manufacture a product is comparable to the delivery time of the product, and the manufacturing site is closer to the customer, then inventory can be reduced to near zero. Such a development, made possible by the continued advancement of computing and communications capability, will have dramatic effects throughout manufacturing supply chains.

This trend is pushing different sectors of the manufacturing industry in two directions. For large producers of commodity and specialty materials such as steel and metals, the trend is toward centralized manufacturing. This allows for greater energy savings through the reduction of unnecessary transportation and capital investment in equipment and pollution controls, and provides for a centralized pool of skilled workers.

Manufacturers of goods sold in large quantities to retail customers are decentralizing their production closer to the point of sale. A decentralized system is relatively protected against natural disasters, political upheaval and terrorist threats. A decentralized system allows companies to avoid intermediate distribution steps between production and final sale of products. Thus, reducing transportation costs to consumers minimizes the carrying costs of unsold inventory and allows manufacturers to tailor their products to local tastes.

Decreasing the Cost of the Workforce

There are several aspects to managing the cost of the workforce. They all depend on keeping the fixed costs of a company low so that it can more effectively compete against foreign competitors. There are times when reducing manpower has backfired because necessary skills have been lost, but the downsizing trend remains prevalent and embedded in the cost-cutting culture. Companies are buying technology and computer programs that replace some of the expertise previously found in the workforce. For example, employee math skills can be augmented by computer programs that perform calculations behind the scenes. Graphical descriptions of production processes provide workers with instructions on how a task can be performed most efficiently, thereby making it necessary for a human operator only to "copy" the work function. As a result, the trend is to lower the educational level of employees, which makes them less expensive as a group.

There are still many areas of manufacturing where advanced manufacturing systems are not being employed, especially in small job shops that cannot afford these systems or do not have the skilled labor necessary to operate them. Unfortunately, this often means that work orders are lost to larger companies (or offshore companies) that have these facilities. Japan and other countries have built effective technology consortiums so that small businesses can borrow, rent equipment or even hire skilled labor on a per-job basis. Facilitating this ability in the United States is an area where government funding can make a significant contribution to American manufacturing.

Increasing Environmental Regulations

Government environmental regulations are growing on a daily basis. Raw material extraction is becoming more difficult due to endangered species laws being enforced and environmentalists becoming more active. In the past, it was not difficult to build huge projects that were challenges to the human mind and spirit. The Hoover Dam was built in five years. President Kennedy's Moon project took nine years. Building the atomic bomb took only six years. Compare that to the commercial nuclear industry, which started its last reactor in 1973 and finished it in 1996 (the Watts Barr Nuclear Generating Station). The last U.S. oil refinery was finished in 1976 in Garyville, La. Virtually every heavy industrial facility faces daunting political and environmental regulations making the United States an undesirable location to consider new projects. Companies operating large-capital and energy-intensive production plants have three options: comply with strict regulations, duck under the radar of the rules or move offshore. The United States has a rare opportunity to reverse these trends because of the strong national call for energy independence.

Technologies on the Horizon for Manufacturing Industrial Products

The demands facing large industrial producers are fundamentally different from the demands that drive manufacturers of consumer products. In general, industrial products require huge infrastructure and enormous amounts of energy to prepare and refine raw materials that have been dug or pumped out of the earth. The world is insisting that these facilities run as cleanly as possible. It is easier to achieve this goal if the facilities are centralized. For example, the production of iron and steel is energy-intensive, accounting for 2 percent of the global emissions of carbon dioxide. The industry must now develop technologies for steel production that reduce emissions and reuse waste products.

New technologies are being developed to effectively lower carbon emissions to near zero. Recently, Klaus Lackner at Columbia University has demonstrated cost-effective carbon capture technology.[10] In his system, a carbon dioxide scrubber can effectively remove one ton of carbon dioxide per day from emissions while using a fraction (10 percent) of the energy required by other systems. Its initial cost in 2008 was high ($200,000 for a prototype system), but costs would drop as economies of scale take hold. The technology developed by Lackner's group involves passing air with heavy concentrations of CO_2 through an ion exchange resin. The CO_2 "sticks" to the resin, which can then be effectively washed with humid air and then disposed of through burial or re-use.

319

This technology has the potential of being used in every industry that produces excessive CO_2.

However, the best approach to eliminating unwanted emissions is to avoid producing them in the first place. Electric arc furnaces show potential, but significant challenges remain since the major process steps of making steel in the furnaces involve undesirable emissions.[11] One production method that is showing potential is called "molten oxide electrolysis," which uses carbon-free anodes that essentially eliminate all carbon gases.[12] Small prototypes of these technologies have already been demonstrated.

A positive way to think about growing environmental regulations is to view them as an incentive for technology innovation that will eventually generate financial benefits. The ideal goal of any manufacturing process is to produce zero waste by effectively using and selling all of the waste products. While 100 percent material re-use might be unattainable, there will be substantial rewards for companies that find even partial solutions. In the production of steel, it is possible to sequester carbon from emissions and use it in byproducts such as road surface material.

Technologies on the Horizon for Manufacturing Consumer Products

New technologies are making it possible to conceive of new products and manufacture them on the spot. Computer-aided product design tools are making it possible to simulate products and their functions in actual use. Analyzing mechanical properties and stress points of products under development is now a part of the design process. Simulations will make it possible to test the intricate and unseen operations of products, such as electronic circuits or mechanical assemblies. While these design features have been available as isolated functions for many years, new systems will see them uniformly employed from concept to production.

As these simulation systems are further developed, they will start to include automated process planning features that can test the feasibility of a given design. They will also allow a designer to visualize complex assembly procedures and how all the parts in an assembly can fit together. In addition, these new features will take on new directions. For example, the inclusion of people in manufacturing simulations is under develop- ment but has never been effectively employed. Human work assignments will be automatically scheduled alongside manufacturing materials and tools.

A key function of automated process planning is that it is becoming feasible to automatically select the best tools to make given parts. These systems not only improve the manufacturing process, but also the design process. For example, it is possible to automatically pick a robot gripper that is best sized and suited to handle a class of parts. It is possible to automatically pick end-mills, drills and other tools for three-axis and five-axis machining. In sheet metal bending, software systems can automatically select appropriate punches and dies.

These new functions are rapidly finding their way into all aspects of manufacturing and will have a profound effect on the so-called "design-manufacturing" wall, since intelligent design decisions can be made based on actual manufacturing capabilities. A designer will immediately know if a product feature can't be manufactured using the available tools. This information can also be used to select a manufacturing shop that already has the appropriate tools. In this way, it becomes unnecessary to purchase extra equipment. Too often, this knowledge is only captured as design heuristics in the head of a designer, which does not allow for easy adaptation to new manufacturing methods and tools.

Manufacturing has evolved to the point where the goal is to produce a product that meets complex specifications that include geometric and "use tolerances" such as mean-time-between failure. Each step in making a part or product will be tested in real time and adjusted to verify that it has been done correctly. This makes it possible to account for any production errors before they create scrap. It is called "closing the loop" — when a process step includes the ability to test the result and, as needed, refine the process. A manufacturing step is executed, the result is measured, a process refinement is calculated and the loop is closed when the specifications are achieved. This is a profoundly important idea that can be utilized in the smallest elements of manufacturing or as a way to view the entire manufacturing process as a single system.[13]

The design process, manufacturing planning and final production are being integrated at an accelerating pace where each level is effectively a closed loop. The total integration of the system makes it possible to plan the manufacturing process that captures the real intent of the designer. This is especially true in the inspection phase, which is used to verify that the goals of the designer have been captured within the manufactured part or product. Final inspection closes the loop at the level of the final product.

It is well known that designers over-specify such things as tight tolerances so that they are assured that parts assemblies have the proper fit. This is an understandable goal, but it means designers do not fully appreciate that production costs escalate with increased requirements for greater precision. Designers do not often appreciate that over-design — by adding unnecessary precision requirements — is not needed to achieve product functions and can radically increase production costs. In this instance, closing the loop allows the true product functions to be achieved without constraining the manufacturing process too much, which can make significant cost savings possible.

New Physical Processes

A revolutionary new paradigm in manufacturing is beginning to unfold. It is based on the concept of three-dimensional printing. Like printing a picture on a page using ink, it is now possible to "print" a material onto a support platform or substrate. The result is a very thin layer of material being deposited in a complex two-dimensional pattern. Another layer of material is "printed" on the original layer and the process continues, building up layer on top of layer. The materials being "printed" are various resins or metallic particles or powders. The patterns can then be cured or hardened depending on the material requirements.

Manufacturing by "layered printing" has spawned many process variants that make it possible to build solid objects layer by layer.[14] To date, three primary processes are in commercial use: stereolithography (a laser selectively cures liquid polymers); selective laser sintering (a laser selectively fuses powdered metals), and fused deposition modeling (extrudes hot plastic through a nozzle in complex patterns). All of these technologies involve making a complex two-dimensional pattern and then adding to it in the third dimension. As can be expected, these systems sometimes involve building "scaffolding" structures as part of the process to support the components of a part during the manufacturing process, which in turn adds a cleanup step at the end of the process.

These developments are leading to surprising results and products. Entirely new classes of parts can be made that were never before imagined. It is now possible to build a ball floating free inside a box with no assembly required. On a more practical level, it is possible to build a strain gauge into a solid piece of steel — again, no assembly required. Therefore, it becomes possible for tank armor to "announce" that it has been hit by a projectile, which can in turn activate various safety functions. Building sensors into the basic fabric of a product can eliminate the need for fastening many parts together and avoids intrinsically weakening the product. The result is all one piece.

Another key application is the rapid creation of tools and dies used to produce plastic parts. In this case, metal powder sintering and heat treatment for hardening make it possible to rapidly produce complex forms that are otherwise very expensive and time-consuming to produce. But metal powder sintering produces tools and dies that are not as hard as their traditional counterparts. Therefore, the tools and dies produced with this new technique are only strong enough to make small batches of parts. The trend, however, is to quickly make tools and dies that cost only hundreds of dollars and produce thousands of parts. Such a system will provide a huge economic benefit over very expensive tools and dies that cost tens of thousands of dollars and that are only economical when they produce hundreds of thousands of parts. The relative cost per part can be similar, but the new technology provides the flexibility to rapidly change parts production as new products are introduced.

Three-dimensional manufacturing has led to predictions that complex products will soon start being "printed." Fritz Prinz of Stanford University describes how an automobile can be produced in such a manner. First four rubber patches — the tires — will be printed, one layer on top of the other, and slowly the material will change to metal — rims and axles. As the layers of the automobile are printed, various materials will come in and out of the "3D" picture. The basic principals of this "crazy idea" already have been demonstrated in the research lab, and while this was far from reality in 2009, the technology makes it well within reach in the 21st century.[15]

Surprisingly, this technology is not particularly expensive. Already, Desktop Factory Inc. has the goal of making 3-D printing systems the same size as a laser printer for less than $5,000.[16] Current systems are limited to the use of just one material, but the technology's evolutionary trajectory will be similar to the first desktop laser printers that started only using black toner before colored inks and toners were introduced.

As these and other technologies based on advanced computing and nano-materials come into use, it will be possible to conceive of virtually unimagined types of products, especially in the medical arena, which demands customized products for different individuals. Other examples are already in the marketplace. Custom blue jeans (http://www.Makeyourownjeans.com), bikinis and golf gloves are being made on the spot for perfect fit and wear. In some cases, these technologies are exhibited as part of marketing campaigns, because there continue to be less expensive manufacturing methods available, but the underlying business fundamentals are rapidly changing.

There is a growing trend of companies taking design orders via e-mail. They manufacture parts and send them that day via express mail to customers. For example, MachineShop.com allows users to create their own designs with free software, get instant pricing and rapid delivery.[17] In the near future, consumers may be able to expect most products (even custom products) to be ordered and delivered to them at home. Amazon.com has proven the feasibility of this business model, but many of these products will be manufactured in quantities of one. In some cases they may even be manufactured within the customer's house, which carries the paradigm to its logical conclusion.

The methods and tools used in production of goods will broaden the imaginations of manufacturers' and product designers' and radically alter what it is possible to produce. It is not hyperbole to hold that the country that develops these manufacturing tools will hold a profound leadership position as a world power.

Case Study on Sheet Metal Bending

The sheet metal industry is an industry that has strong demands for both consumer and industrial products. Every office has dozens of products made from sheet metal: file cabinets, bookcases, fluorescent light fixtures, heat and air-conditioning ducts and internal frames for personal computers.

Sheet metal products begin with coils or sheets of cold-rolled steel. The sheets are sheared into the proper sizes and then loaded onto either punch presses or laser cutters that cut out complex two-dimensional shapes with occasional three-dimensional features such as depressions or complex louvers that act as air vents in a final product.

Automated punching and laser machines marked an important milestone for this industry. These machines produce highly complex two-dimensional geometries by borrowing ideas from computer graphics and printing. The machines are controlled by effectively cutting many connected small-line segments and simple curves to make up the final part shape. The automated production of two-dimensional sheet metal parts burst onto the scene with early computer numerical controlled equipment that paralleled the arrival of the personal computer in the early 1980s. The challenge at that time was how to optimally lay out "nests" of many parts onto a single sheet while minimizing wasted material. Imagine a jigsaw puzzle where the pieces (or individual parts) fit exactly into a rectangular shape. Of course, in practice the individual parts that make up the "nest" are five of one shape, 10 of another, etc. Therefore, the goal is to find the layout for these parts that utilize most of the material in the rectangular raw stock.

This layout or nesting problem was solved manually at first, and then was slowly automated for increasingly complex parts. Even today, producing optimally nesting free-formed parts that are smoothly shaped and fit exactly in a jigsaw-like puzzle is beyond the ability of commercial production systems. However, if the goal is to find a reasonable layout for 100 parts of one kind and 50 parts of another, then automated systems can often outperform their human counterparts. This manufacturing step is necessary in a number of industries that involve cutting complicated two-dimensional shapes of standardized stock, such as in textiles where clothing patterns have to be laid out or "nested" before they can be cut from standard rolls of material.

There are a number of advantages to keeping parts in a two-dimensional configuration. Two-dimensional parts can be conveniently stacked and moved around on the factory floor while using a minimal amount of floor space. The next steps of production involve turning two-dimensional parts into three-dimensional parts by bending and then painting parts and making final assemblies. The transition to 3-D has been a key bottleneck in the sheet metal industry for many years. Figure 4 illustrates

Figure 4: A Part That Has Been Bent Into 3D Shape

a part that was very easy to handle, but after it is bent into the final configuration, it proves to be very difficult to stack and store.

Research groups have developed systems that automate the bending process, which have been successfully commercialized.[18] This process involves balancing manufacturing trade-offs between several critical areas of production: the tools necessary for bending; how to lay out tools to make all of the necessary bends in the proper sequence; how to grasp the part during the bending process; how to move the part from one bend process to another; and how to maintain tolerances in the final 3-D part. What makes this more difficult is the large number of dynamic problems that occur during the manufacturing process.

Many large sheet metal parts elastically bend during handling. This is a relatively easy problem when a human is handling the parts, but is extremely difficult when a robot is handling the same part, because the part is "flopping" around during very precise handling maneuvers. Understanding the effect of drooping is further complicated when parts have narrow "necks" of material, which can permanently deform the part during handling, which effectively scraps the part.

During automated production of parts there is a huge emphasis on making the parts as quickly as possible. When a robot gripper is handling a large flat part and twisting it at high speeds, it is quite easy for the part to slip in the robot gripper. Exacerbating the slippage is the fact that sheet metal is typically coated with a thin layer of graphite lubricant used to keep the sheets from sticking together in a stack. To solve this problem, robot grippers must be equipped with slip-sensors that can detect imminent slippage. One way to avoid slippage is to run the robot and system very slowly. This solution reduces productivity, which is usually unacceptable.

Another common problem occurs after a machine has made an individual bend. When a part is bent, some portion of the bend is elastic (like an elastic band springs back to its original shape after stretching), while another portion of a bend is permanent (or, technically, plastic). In order to produce the correct bend angle in sheet metal, the spring-back component of a bend must be anticipated and purposefully over-bent. Alternatively, the degree of spring-back must be measured and re-bent to produce the correct angle.

A system that combines all of the elements of planning the operation sequence by taking into account complex geometries and dynamic elements is essential to most manufacturing automation tasks. Once there is a system in place that can efficiently plan the manufacturing process for parts — sheet metal bending or any other process — there are many potential uses for this new technology.

Such a system enables companies to predict the cost of production with precision, thus providing them with a competitive advantage because profits are often lost on the production of only a few parts that are difficult to make. Knowing the precise cost of production makes it possible for contract manufacturers to submit competitive bids for work that supports a customer's strategy to reduce costs.

With automated planning and operation sequences, it becomes possible to create complete products such as a filing cabinet with a minimal number of components that can be manufactured.[19] For example, a typical filing cabinet may have as many as 300 component parts, which can easily be reduced by up to 20 percent with changes in the manufacturing process. This has the advantage of further reducing the price of the end product, since manufacturing costs are often linearly related to the number of parts in a product and have only a minimal relationship to the cost of the raw materials.

As the number of parts in a product is reduced, assembly is simplified and less energy is consumed. In addition, only the parts that are in demand need to be made. Excess inventory has a habit of getting in the way of a production process and it must be moved time and time again. As different processes are consolidated in fewer general-purpose machines it is possible to move them closer to customers. Each step of this evolutionary process reduces energy consumption.

It also becomes possible to sell manufacturing machines and tools that have verifiable economic results. Conversely, manufacturing production tools can be purchased with predictable cost savings. In some cases, designers can alter products and parts to avoid expensive retooling, which further reduces the cost of manufacturing.

As the cost of planning manufacturing operations is reduced, the overwhelming balance of work and time in production shifts to setting up machines to make small batches of parts. Therefore, the automation technology must also focus on minimizing setup changes and providing various tools to simplify the setup process. Research of this nature can save a considerable amount of production time by effectively eliminating setups. In turn, this level of automation makes it even more cost-effective to manufacture parts in small batches.

Automated bending is only one example of the potential of the research and development work needed to substantially improve hundreds of different manufacturing processes such as machining, turning, grinding, cutting, punching, etching, painting and welding, among others. Most manufacturing processes continue to be manually planned by human operators and have received little attention from research that has proven to substantially reduce costs.

There is vast potential associated with automated planning and the optimization of manufacturing processes throughout the entire product life cycle. As these benefits are witnessed and verified, companies will pursue these goals covering the full manufacturing spectrum, allowing true system-wide benefits to be achieved.

The planning and control process for total automation will require additional computing power. As computing capability continues to increase, it becomes feasible to automate and plan more processes that have not yet been modernized.

At the same time, the Internet makes expensive machines accessible to the customer base, allowing the cost-effective production of small orders. Making small batches saves money by allowing companies to reduce their cost of work-in-progress and inventory, and to remain flexible enough to handle changes in the business climate.

Automating the entire system increases demand for product designers and planners and reduces the need for skilled machine operators since the skill of craftsmen will be embedded in the software or robot. Finally, with reduced scrap and energy use, the new production paradigm fits with the trend toward more stringent environmental regulations.

Technologies that are compatible with these broad and persistent business trends will shape the future.

Predictions for Manufacturing

Humans are fond of predicting the future. In 1957, Nobel Prize winner Herbert Simon predicted that it would only take 10 years to produce a computer chess program that could regularly beat the human world champion.[20] In fact, the accomplishment had to wait for IBM's DeepBlue program that beat the then world chess champion Gary Kasparov in 1997, 40 years later.[21] So it goes with the prediction of total automation.

In 1952, Kurt Vonnegut satirically predicted the total automation of manufacturing, but there is still a long way to go before that happens.[22] In 2008, 32 faculty members working in the Robotics Institute at Carnegie Mellon University were asked: "How long will it take for robots and automation to effectively replace all of the human functions commonly found in manufacturing?" A small majority said it will be 40 years, with the remainder predicting that it would take even longer. And this group is not known for their conservative judgments.[23]

The idea of total automation or lights-out manufacturing where robots and automation do all of the work in the factory has proven to be unrealistic. There are many reasons why this prediction does not meet common-sense requirements, most of which have nothing to do with automation technology.

Error detection and recovery is still in the infant stages of development. The communication and coordination between a customer request and manufacturing is rarely complete. When a customer provides a design, the manufacturing shop discovers many missing details that need to be solved by craftsmen.

Many other lapses in design require complex discussions with the customer. Furthermore, automatic hardware to set up machines, such as installing particular tools for particular parts, is sometimes not cost-effective. It is possible to automate most functions such as loading tools, but in many cases it turns out to be cheaper and faster for humans to perform many of these functions.

Mass customization remains a dream for the future and is a direct retort to Henry Ford's original sentiment on the subject of mass production when he said: "You can paint it any color so long as it's black." This bit of sarcasm from one of the founders of modern manufacturing was meant to highlight his goal of making products that every man could afford by making them all identical.

But there is a growing list of customizable parts and products that can be instantly manufactured from digital designs. Many medical devices are conducive to this technology since they are often small, have very complex shapes and must uniquely fit to a particular patient. Hearing aid shells and various medical implants are all currently manufactured via "mass customization" tools. In addition, there are self-contained machines that can make small mechanical parts for hydraulic pumps, as well as self-contained machines that can make complete three-dimensional sheet metal parts. These parts tend to be both small and complex, which can be difficult for humans to handle.

In the near future — 20 years — many industrial robots will be shaped like humans with similar sensors and means of dexterity so they can be easily swapped in and out with their human counterparts.

The high cost of energy, transportation and borrowing due to the credit squeeze, coupled with new automation systems that are moving manufacturing closer to the point of purchase, could soon reverse the trend of outsourcing work to China and India. This could be the silver-lining hidden within the recent economic downturn.

By 2050, it is likely that consumers will be able to communicate a design for a new product (or product variant) within a virtual world. After computer simulations instantaneously determine if the product can be made, the consumer will pay for the manufacture of a completely unique product in the real world. For more complex products, a parts list will be automatically prepared and orders sent to factories that will put together kits in the fashion of IKEA furniture. These kits will be suitable for easy transportation (e.g., relatively flat form factor and unassembled). The kit will be automatically packaged and shipped to the consumer's home, where a household assistant robot in human form and function will receive and assemble the product. In turn, this robot may need to secure help from neighboring robotic assistants to build excessively large or complex projects like a new kitchen or a family room.

Most of the formative components for this type of system were feasible in narrow domains in 2009. Although the use of robotic assistants that receive and assemble complex products is currently a pipe dream, the promise of the technology is based on current market forces of expensive energy, ubiquitous computing and the reduction of domestically available skilled labor. These changes represent a paradigm shift no less than the industrial revolution itself.

Areas of Investment and Change

The United States has been a leader in the development of manufacturing technologies, but it has systematically relinquished industries to foreign competitors that have captured the knowledge of how to make things. This industrial erosion started with the machine tool industry and has progressed to flexible automation and robotics.

For this reason, the United States should establish an industrial technology policy with a soft touch that features a series of compelling challenges with the inducement of prizes. The "Grand Challenge" projects run by DARPA to build autonomous vehicles have been a huge success and generated corporate spinoffs to effectively propagate the new technology. Another example is the effort to privatize space in the form of the Google Lunar X Prize, where individual corporations are setting the technical agenda. This new model allows the government to lead without getting in the way.

The goals of these competitions constitute a more successful type of "industrial policy," with the outcomes being driven by the passions of industry and academia. The overwhelming response to these competitions from both corporations and individuals has the potential of carrying research and development results to successful completion and serve as a better model for the development and adoption of future industrial technologies.

There are reasons to focus competitions on novel machine tools, since they have the potential for creating new product areas and because they provide far-reaching benefits to large segments of industry. A challenge to build general-purpose robots that perform very small part assemblies and even nano-assemblies could have widespread impact. So, too, could a challenge to build manufacturing deposition machines that use different materials to make layered, multi-material products.

In addition, there are key product areas that will have huge consequences to the economy once breakthroughs have been made. New challenges are appropriate here as well, such as the development of an engine that gets 100 miles per gallon, or wearable computing products that can be built into clothing.

There is also a great call to reduce pollution in all manufacturing processes, while reducing the energy that is required to achieve these goals. Once again, clear goals could be set to achieve these ends with incentives rather than punishments. A challenge to develop a small desktop steel production process that does not emit pollutants or greenhouse gases would allow for the focus to be on invention rather than financing and managing the construction of large production facilities.

Another challenge could be to develop cost-effective energy sources with fewer pollutants than fossil fuels. For instance, the $30-million Google X Prize is a contest to get privately funded teams to the moon; the first step to mining Helium-3, which can be used in second-generation controlled fusion for power generation.[24]

Government-sponsored contests and prizes are democratic. They can be open to any corporation or citizen. A small group of Americans could conceive of a new engine that can achieve 100 miles per gallon. In the past, this type of innovation may have been met with rancor from the companies that it was meant to help because the idea does not fit with the market strategy of the existing industry. Great pressure has been brought to essentially kill good ideas with the heavy hand of the corporate legal apparatus. But with government prizes in place, negative forces of corporate America can be bypassed until the idea is fully established, potentially with new American companies in position to compete globally.

In short, if we continue to outsource all aspects of manufacturing — manufacturing processes, jobs and expertise — then we will wake up one morning to discover that our corresponding economic and military power has been exported as well.

1, Rodrik, Dani, "Industrial Policy for the Twenty-First Century," report from the John F. Kennedy School of Government (Prepared for the United Nations Development Organization), Cambridge, Mass., September 2004.

2. Urmson, C. et al, "Tartan Racing: A Multi Modal Approach to the DARPA Urban Challenge," April, 2007, http://www.darpa.mil/GRANDCHALLENGE/TechPapers/Tartan_Racing.pdf.

3. "Committee on Defense Manufacturing in 2010 and Beyond," published by The National Academy Press, 1999, http://www.nap.edu/html/defman/app_a.html.

4. U.S. Congress, Office of Technology Assessment, "Making Things Better: Competing in Manufacturing," OTA-ITE-443, Washington, D.C., U.S. Printing Office, February 1990.

5. McMillon, C., "The Economic State of The Union – 2008," *Manufacturing and Technology News*, Vol. 15, No. 2, January 2008.

6. Karlsson, J., "The Boom in Robot Investment Continues – 900,000 Industrial Robots by 2003," from United Nations Economic Commission for Europe, UN/ECE News, October 17, 2000.

7. Bourne, D.A. and Williams, D.T., "Using the Feature Exchange Language in the Next Generation Controller," CMU-RI-TR-90-19, 1990, www.ri.cmu.edu/pubs/pub_231.html.

8. "Charting the Growth of Access to Computing and the Internet," copyright 1998, 2008 by Jakob Nielsen, ISSN 1548-555, http://www.ntia.doc.gov/ntiahome/dn/anationonline2.pdf.

9. Nielson, J., "Charting the Growth of Internet Bandwidth," copyright 1998, 2008 by Jakob Nielsen, ISSN 1548-5552, http://www.useit.com/alertbox/980405.html.

10. Lackner, K., 2008: http://www.goodcleantech.com/2008/06/air_scrubber_can_soak_up_one_t.php.

11. American Iron and Steel Institute, "Steel Industry Technology Roadmap," December 2001, http://www.steel.org/.

12. American Iron and Steel Institute, "Technical Feasibility Study of Steelmaking by Molten Oxide Electrolysis," No. 9956, http://www.steel.org/.

13. Bourne, D.A., and Wright, P.K., *Manufacturing Intelligence*, published by Addison Wesley, Reading Mass., 1988.

14. Wright, P.K., *21st Century Manufacturing*, published by Prentice Hall, Upper Saddle River, N.J., 2001.

15. Amata, I., "Instant Manufacturing," Technical Review, published by MIT Press, Boston, Mass., November 2003, pages 56-62, www.technologyreview.com.

16. Desktop Factory, Inc., http://www.desktopfactory.com/our_product/.

17. An Internet company that makes customized parts: http://www.emachineshop.com/.

18. Bourne, D.A.; Gupta, S.K.; and Krishnan, S.S, "Automated Process Planning for Robotic Sheet Metal Bending Press Brakes," with S.K. Gupta, K. Kim and S.S. Krishnan, *The Journal of Manufacturing Systems*, 1998, Vol. 17, No. 5, pages 338-360.

19. Wang, C., Manufacturability-Driven Decomposition of Sheet Metal Products, doctoral dissertation, Rech. Report CMU-RI-TR-97-35, Robotics Institute, Carnegie Mellon University, September 1997.

20. Simon, H.A., at the 1957 banquet of the Twelfth National Meeting of the Operations Research Society of America.

21. Hsu, Feng-hsiung, *Behind Deep Blue: Building the Computer that Defeated the World Chess Champion*, Princeton University Press, ISBN 0-691-09065-3, 2002.

22. Vonnegut, K., 1952, *Player Piano*, The Dial Press. January 12, 1999.

23. Bourne, D.A., "Technology Assessment of Anthropomorphic Robots — A Survey of the Robotics Institute Faculty," 2008, CMU Technical Report, Pittsburgh, Penn.

24. http://www.googlelunarxprize.org/ — sponsored by Google Inc.

AAM Publications

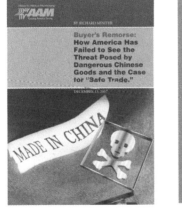

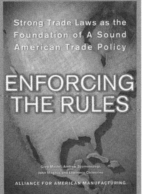

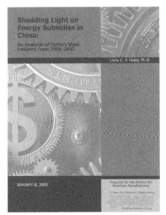

To order please contact info@aamfg.org
or call
(202) 393-3430

www.americanmanufacturing.org